"Our nation's magic is its ability to turn immigrants into Americans. Jessica Lander has written a brilliant and poignant book about how schools can help do this. With her background as a classroom teacher working with young people from around the world, she weaves together history, analysis, and deeply personal stories. This is an important book, and also a beautiful one. Everyone who cares about the future of America should read it."

—WALTER ISAACSON, author of
Benjamin Franklin: An American Life

"*Making Americans* provides just the sort of context too often missing from discussions of immigrant education. But what with its many terrific stories about students and teachers, it is more than informative: fascinating and inspiring, it is also a great read."

—GISH JEN, author of *Thank You, Mr. Nixon*

"*Making Americans* is a beautifully written account of the history and practice of immigrant education in America. With masterful interweaving of legal history, classroom case examples, and powerful student stories, what emerges is a compelling and timely work that informs as much as it inspires."

—SARAH LADIPO MANYIKA, author of
Like a Mule Bringing Ice Cream to the Sun

"Lander deftly portrays varying journeys of newcomer students as they enter US schools and society. Providing well-researched historical perspective along with hopeful current models of promising practice, *Making Americans* will no doubt become a mainstay for all who care to best serve our newest Americans!"

—CAROLA SUÁREZ-OROZCO, director, Immigration Initiative
at Harvard Graduate School of Education

"*Making Americans* is an eye-opening, crucial, and riveting account of how schools and educators have shaped the immigrant experience in the United States. It is an essential history of our nation, interwoven with narratives of students and teachers who are today reimagining what it means to become American. Lander has written a deep and moving book for anyone who cares about the fate of our country, but especially for those of us who are descendants of people who traveled here from afar. Readers of *Making Americans* might even find themselves with a renewed a sense of patriotism, reinvigorated by the stories of people relentlessly working to redefine and make real the American Dream."

—BINA VENKATARAMAN, author of *The Optimist's Telescope* and former editorial page editor of *The Boston Globe*

"*Making Americans* is a powerful affirmation of the importance of belonging and hope in our lives. In this important and groundbreaking work, Jessica Lander outlines what we can do to create conditions in schools and communities that support all students—especially our newest Americans. Along the way, she highlights the stories of people who have made a difference in this great country, as well as those who will have a hand in its future. This is a must-read for all educators. It's a must-read for all Americans."

—DON VU, former teacher and principal, author of *Life, Literacy, and the Pursuit of Happiness*

"The author offers a nice mixture of conversational tone and intriguing research, uncovering important, untold stories in educational history."

—*Kirkus Reviews*

"Jessica Lander's immigrant-origin students—from a kaleidoscope of countries and cultures—come alive in these pages, until we feel we know them. She weaves their stories together with those of previous waves of immigrants who fled war, persecution, and poverty, including her own family. Her message is simple and powerful: New Americans make themselves with help from those of us who are already here. That making starts in school, as should our help. A compelling read."

—ANNE-MARIE SLAUGHTER, CEO, New America

"Weaving together inspiring personal stories, powerful case studies, and a fascinating history of immigrant education in America, Jessica Lander shines a new, hopeful light on a perennial question: How does a young immigrant become an American?"

—PAUL TOUGH, author of *How Children Succeed*

"Lander is an excellent storyteller, and this book is an involving read. A thoughtful, engaging book for any reader interested in immigrant education."

—*Library Journal*

"At a time when more than one in four students in American schools are immigrants or children of immigrants, how schools help 'make Americans' should be a front-and-center topic for the nation. Jessica Lander's compelling book interweaves vivid stories of the past, the present, and the personal—narratives of historic legal decisions, profiles of innovative schools around the country today, and inspiring portraits of her own students in Lowell, Massachusetts. At times moving, instructive, sobering, and encouraging, *Making Americans* will captivate and enlighten all readers. And it will also equip teachers, voters, and policymakers to work together to overcome prejudice and help newcomers build on their talents to strengthen America while pursuing their own dreams."

—MARTHA MINOW, former dean of Harvard Law School
and author of *When Should Law Forgive?*

"*Making Americans* is a powerful affirmation of the importance of belonging and hope in our lives. In this important and groundbreaking work, Jessica Lander outlines what we can do to create conditions in schools and communities that support all students—especially our newest Americans. Along the way, she highlights the stories of people who have made a difference in this great country, as well as those who will have a hand in its future. This is a must-read for all educators. It's a must-read for all Americans."

—DON VU, former teacher and principal, author of
Life, Literacy, and the Pursuit of Happiness

"This is a book only a teacher could write. With compassion and nuance born from her experience in the classroom, Jessica Lander explores what it means to be American for students new to the United States. Too often, in education, students are reduced to numbers. In Lander's hands, we see their full humanity."

—SYDNEY CHAFFEE, 2017 National Teacher of the Year

"*Making Americans* is remarkable. It does an extraordinary job of capturing the experiences and strengths of young immigrants going to school and making new homes. Lander charts a path for how to help welcome newcomers and how communities benefit by doing so. Everyone should read *Making Americans*."

—EVA A. MILLONA, former president and CEO of MIRA (Massachusetts Immigrant and Refugee Advocacy Coalition)

MAKING AMERICANS

STORIES OF HISTORIC STRUGGLES, NEW IDEAS, AND INSPIRATION IN IMMIGRANT EDUCATION

JESSICA LANDER

BEACON PRESS
BOSTON

BEACON PRESS
Boston, Massachusetts
www.beacon.org

Beacon Press books
are published under the auspices of
the Unitarian Universalist Association of Congregations.

26 25 24 23   8 7 6 5 4 3 2 1

This book is printed on acid-free paper that meets the uncoated paper
ANSI/NISO specifications for permanence as revised in 1992.

Some names and identifying details have been changed
to protect the privacy of individuals.

Text design and composition by Kim Arney

Library of Congress Cataloguing in Publication Data is available for this title.
LCCN: 2022023107
Paperback ISBN: 978-08070-1335-9
Ebook ISBN: 978-08070-0666-5

*To my students, who inspire me and
are a light to the nation and to the world.*

CONTENTS

AUTHOR'S NOTE

This is a work of nonfiction. I have tried my best—through historical research, site visits, extensive interviews, and fact-checking—to ensure the stories told are accurate.

In writing this book, I have made certain choices.

The book's title, *Making Americans*, is deliberately ambiguous with respect to *who* is doing the making. It reflects, of course, more than a century of efforts in this country to shape newcomers into Americans—by governments, legislators, communities, educators, and many others, based on their views, their philosophy, and their power. But the key message of this book is that every newcomer is the rightful author of their own American identity: They make themselves into Americans, and the role of educators and others is to support them in this work.

In education, newcomers are often referred to as English learners (ELs) (or English language learners, or English as a second language students, although these latter terms are becoming less popular). However, learning a new language is just one of the many experiences a newcomer faces. Except when specifically discussing language learning, I use the term *immigrant-origin students* to emphasize the full range of experiences of families establishing a new home in a new country; it refers to immigrant children and children of recent immigrants. In the book, I stretch the term to include students from Puerto Rico. These students of course are not immigrants but American-born citizens, although they are often not treated that way. I do so because many of my own students from Puerto Rico have told me they don't feel like Americans, that in moving to the mainland they feel like immigrants to a new country. I mean to reflect that feeling and the fact that, for many, their experiences are similar to those of peers who come from other countries.

I have chosen to use America and the United States interchangeably. It is important to note that America is also appropriately used to refer to Central and South America. The usage in this book is not intended to exclude other important meanings of America.

The book profiles seven school programs across the country, selected after visiting and talking with many exceptional educators. Together, those schools reflect a range of approaches, regions, and sizes. They are intended to be representative of the many powerful programs across the country. Neither I nor the educators there imagine that the schools are without flaws. To the contrary, I was struck by how readily the educators acknowledged many areas for growth.

I have tried my best to capture people accurately in their own words. In writing about history, I note that some of the quotations are disturbing and, sometimes, dehumanizing. By reporting them, I do not mean to endorse those views. However, where the information is important for understanding the past, I felt it was better to confront it.

Because this book focuses on the education of young people whose families came, or who came alone, to this country in the last 150 years, it does not address the history and experiences of Indigenous students, whose ancestors' lands were stolen and communities devastated by European settlers, nor of Black students who trace their ancestry to people who were enslaved and forcibly brought to this country. I urge readers to seek out and read the work of powerful educators and thinkers writing about, advocating for, and working to support these students.

To protect their privacy, I have changed the names of young people who are still minors. For those who are now adults, I have asked them to decide whether they would like me to use a pseudonym for themselves and their family members. For all of the young people whom I have quoted, particularly my former students profiled in the book, I have shared what I wrote and confirmed with them, and in most cases their parents, that they were comfortable with it being published. I am deeply honored that they chose to share their stories, experiences, and wisdom with me, and have given me permission to share their stories with you, so that we all may learn from them.

BELONGING

THE PRESENT: LOWELL HIGH SCHOOL, MASSACHUSETTS

"Can I eat with you?" It was September 2015, and one of my students hovered hesitantly at the classroom's door. Gangly and shy, Wilson was apologetic. He had recently left his home in Puerto Rico, coming to live and study 1,700 miles north in Lowell, Massachusetts. Now, surrounded by nearly 3,400 new peers, he felt lost. Though as a Puerto Rican he was an American citizen by birth, he still often felt as foreign as the many immigrant peers who filled his new classes. Nowhere did he feel he belonged.

I too was new to the community, having recently come to Lowell High School to teach immigrant and refugee teenagers. That first month a routine was born. Each day after my fifth class, as students streamed out, Wilson would shuffle in, carrying pizza, a sandwich, or sometimes a baked potato smothered in sour cream. My desk became our makeshift lunch table. Little by little, I grew to know Wilson. I asked about his favorite classes, his weekend excursions, what he missed most about the island. Then one Friday during our lunch, he had a question for me. Pointing at my hand, he asked, "How did you learn to use those?" Nestled between my fingers were bamboo chopsticks. Wilson, I quickly learned, was mesmerized by all things Japanese. It was a love rooted in anime, which had spurred him to spend late nights reading Japanese history and practicing the *katakana* and *hiragana* alphabets. Over lunch, in a pause between classes, lesson planning, and grading, Wilson and I began speaking about learning languages and cultures.

But our lunches did not remain one-on-one for long. Early in October, Wilson's classmate Nie, a tall, serious Vietnamese girl, asked to join. Nie was quickly followed by Po, an inquisitive Karen refugee from Southeast Asia. More soon followed. By November, lunch in my classroom was bursting with students. Yemeni, Iraqi, and Lebanese girls drew center seats into a circle. A Liberian boy who loved history hung with a freckled Tanzanian boy near the door. In seats along the wall a gaggle of Brazilian girls liked to linger. Two Cambodian girls sat side by side in the front-row desks. Students chatted, ate, hunched over unfinished homework, and peppered me with questions about history we had learned in class.

Lunchtime also offered a master class in cuisines. Po presented classmates with excruciatingly spicy tiny fish. Nie unpacked Vietnamese soups and passed around her spoon. One Lebanese student brought in flaky diamonds of baklava that left everyone licking honey from their fingertips. I watched as students—tentative, curious, enthusiastic—tasted seaweed, egg curries, empanadas for the first time. I watched, too, as Wilson grew less reserved and more talkative, surrounded by his classmates from around the world.

—●—

Almost everyone in the United States traces their origins elsewhere—to ancestors who, whether by force or by choice, built new homes and new lives here. Some arrived four hundred years ago and some four months ago. Some came seeking opportunity for themselves and for their children. Some came fleeing persecution. Many were brutally enslaved and forcibly transported across the Atlantic from the coast of West Africa. Even Indigenous people, whose forebears had lived in America for millennia, were violently displaced from their ancestral homes.

The result is a country of unrivaled diversity. America's plurality has always been a source of strength and for many a point of pride. Our coins proclaim *E Pluribus Unum*, a motto that originally referred to the union of thirteen colonies but now speaks of the union of peoples drawn from a multitude of countries and cultures. The plaque beneath the colossus in New York Harbor has, for more than a century, promised welcome to the globe's tired, poor, and huddled masses.

And yet, that same America has also long fought to turn people away from its shores—especially based on where they come from, what religion they practice, or whom they love. Claiming that new arrivals would take jobs from Americans already here or asserting that newcomers were racially inferior, the United States has excluded them from schools and from jobs. Suspicious of their customs and skeptical of their allegiance, states have passed laws banning them from speaking languages other than English and people have pressured them to abandon their cultural and religious heritage.

Despite the tension between welcome and exclusion, the country has always relied and will continue to rely on new arrivals. They enrich America in hundreds of ways. They bring their talent, determination, and resilience to our shores. They bring tremendous energy and entrepreneurship—contributing to communities, revitalizing cities, founding companies. They generate jobs and economic wealth for the country. They help sustain the country's population: With the birthrate among Americans far below the replacement rate, immigration prevents a shrinking populace. They help the country flourish in a globalized world, through their personal understanding of cultures, peoples, and businesses around the world. They help make America America.

Given the importance of newcomers to this country, a critical question for our future is: How do we ensure that immigrants feel safe, supported, and valued, with the chance to put down roots and build new futures—so that they can become full participants in their new home? In short, *what does it take to make Americans?*

Nowhere is this question more important than in the nation's public schools, because it is in schools that young newcomers often come to understand who they are and who they hope to become. In doing so, they start to author their own American identities.

Today, roughly one in four students under the age of seventeen is an immigrant or the child of immigrants.[1] By 2050, it is estimated that the ratio will be one in three.[2] One hundred years ago, immigrant students studied primarily in city schools. Today, communities across the nation, urban, suburban, and rural, are welcoming immigrant-origin children.

For more than a century, schools have debated, argued, and experimented with the task of making Americans—from the Americanization Movement at the turn of the twentieth century that sought to rapidly assimilate immigrant children, to laws in the 1920s that banned foreign language instruction, to the Supreme Court decisions in the 1970s and

'80s that required schools to accept and support immigrant-origin students. In every decade, immigrant families themselves have played a key role in transforming schools nationwide, courageously standing up for their children's inclusion.

Educating immigrant-origin students is something I think about every day.

I have been a teacher for close to a decade. I taught university students in northern Thailand and in the capital of Cambodia, as well as sixth graders in Boston. And for six years, starting in 2015, I have been a teacher at Lowell High School, a public school in Lowell, Massachusetts, where each year I teach more than a hundred recent immigrants and refugees.

Lowell is an area rich with the stories of immigrants—from the Puritans in the mid-1600s to the Irish immigrants who worked in the textile mills along the Merrimack River in the early 1800s, to the Cambodian refugees who fled genocide in the late 1900s, to the Syrian refugees who began arriving not long ago. Communities from around the world have long found a home in the city. Lowell High School is believed to be the first integrated high school in the United States—open to all since its founding in the 1830s. Today, the school is one of the most diverse in the nation.

In my classroom, students from around the globe study together: Syrians sit next to Salvadorians; Brazilians partner with Burmese. Across an academic year, I watch Zambian, Dominican, Japanese, Nepali, and Spanish teenagers form friendships. In their short lives, my students have traveled far to be here. They came by foot and by bus; they traveled in planes, in trains, in cars; one escaped in a dugout canoe. They have fled war and bloodshed in the Democratic Republic of the Congo and Iraq. They have left islands in Portugal and bustling cities in Mexico in search of economic opportunity. They have grown up in refugee camps in Thailand and Turkey. They have reunited with family members from Cambodia and Colombia. They have fled gang violence and guerrilla militias in Guatemala and Somalia. They come from more than thirty countries in all.

I teach them American history and American civics. But I am also aware that my students are in the process of writing their own American histories and are beginning to contribute to the civic life of their new home. So I strive to provide them with what they might need to become Americans—not facsimiles of past Americans, but vibrant new Americans who will, like those who came before, enrich this country with fresh energy, perspectives, and ideas.

In our classroom I want my students to know that they are valued and that they belong. Like so many teachers, my job is not confined to academics. I mentor and advise, helping students to know themselves, navigate family and friendships, and take their next steps toward college or the workforce. I have developed a teaching practice centered on the belief that my students should have opportunities to share their expertise, develop their voices, and improve their new communities. To reinforce the importance of understanding many perspectives, we interweave the study of US history with the global perspectives of my students. To instill a belief that their voices and ideas matter, I teach my students how to write persuasive op-eds on issues, both local and global, about which they are passionate—and then I arrange for a selection of their pieces to be published in the city's newspaper. To develop their skills as active community members, my classes work for months to bring about systemic change on issues ranging from digital literacy to Islamophobia to food insecurity, and each year they present their work to community leaders at the Massachusetts State House.

Across years, I have watched with pride as my students formed friendships, won academic awards, became community activists, were the first in their families to graduate high school, moved into college dorms, took jobs, planned careers, became United States citizens.

●

The longer I taught, the more I wondered what approaches educators elsewhere were taking to support immigrant students. I knew there must be teachers and principals with innovative ideas and creative programs.

I sought out books on the subject. While there were many books about how to teach immigrant-origin students to speak English, I found surprisingly little that went beyond language to explore the many other ways schools should nurture these students to succeed academically and socially.

I decided to set forth from my classroom to do research. I called former federal officials, university professors, and community leaders in search of innovative educational experiments. While they had some ideas, my most productive conversations came from talking with teachers. They told me of creative educators they knew and exciting practices they had heard of. They generously offered to make connections. Slowly I began to assemble a nationwide map of schools and programs and people.

To understand these experiments, I began to travel—listening to educators and visiting innovative schools and programs. I joined classes at a school for refugee girls in Georgia and at a school for recently arrived immigrants in Texas. I shadowed a principal at an all-immigrant high school in Maryland and a district leader who supports teachers at more than a hundred schools in North Carolina. I listened to teachers, parents, and members of community organizations who collaborate to support immigrant children across five schools in Colorado, and I read books published by the immigrant students of an award-winning teacher in North Dakota.

To understand what we need to do today, I realized I also had to look to the past. I set out to learn from key historical events—federal laws, landmark Supreme Court cases, and national movements—that shaped immigrant education. In addition to reading about the history, I interviewed lawyers, activists, teachers, priests, and members of the families who brought legal challenges. In this way, I assembled the intimate stories of courageous and determined individuals who profoundly shaped the nation—including the first female district superintendent of New York City, who was a pioneer in creating classes specifically for immigrant children; the parochial teacher in rural Nebraska who did not back down after being arrested for teaching an eleven-year-old boy in German; and the four Texas families who risked deportation to advocate for the right for their children to attend school.

I also knew that one other perspective was essential: the voices of immigrant students themselves. I reached out to my own former students—immigrants and refugees from Colombia, Cambodia, Zambia, Iraq, the Dominican Republic, the Democratic Republic of the Congo. Teaching them as freshmen, sophomores, juniors, seniors, I had watched them grow. Now, I asked if they would become my teachers. Would they teach me about their journeys to the United States, their experience in our schools, and their evolving understanding of their place in America? Generously, they agreed.

From these stories—of the past, the present, and the personal—I began to distill lessons about how schools and communities can help make Americans. I concluded that eight elements are essential:

1. opportunities for *new beginnings*
2. supportive *communities*
3. assurance of *security*
4. *chances to dream*
5. committed *advocates*
6. recognition of students' *strengths* and assets
7. *acceptance* for who students are and where they come from
8. opportunities for students to develop their *voice*—and valuing those voices

I have organized *Making Americans* around these eight elements. Each chapter consists of three inspiring stories—one from the history of immigrant education; one describing innovative efforts today by a teacher, school, or school district; and one telling the personal journey of one of my former students—that embody each one of these elements in turn. They show the challenges, creativity, persistence, compassion, skills, and collaboration that have propelled progress so far.

The final chapter includes a section on the work ahead. It asks: What will it take to create schools in which immigrant-origin students thrive—with a sense of belonging and a desire to contribute to their adopted home? The chapter lays out concrete advice to teachers, school leaders, district officials, parents, policy makers, elected representatives, and community members about how they can help achieve this goal.

I want to thank all those who shared their stories, expertise, and wisdom with me. I am particularly grateful to my seven former students profiled in the book, whom I knew from the years they spent in my classroom and who sat for many hours of conversations to share their experiences. They inspire me and give me hope. Their personal stories serve as anchors that ground each chapter. The story of one student, Robert, and his remarkable journey is a thread that runs throughout the book—beginning in this first section, continuing in a middle chapter, and ending in the final section.

Although this book is about educating immigrants, I believe that many of its lessons may also pertain to supporting students whose families have lived here for generations but who are marginalized because of the color of their skin, their ethnicity, their gender, their sexuality, their abilities, their socioeconomic status, or their faith.

As I wrote this book, it became clear to me that the eight elements are all ways to achieve an overarching goal: instilling in newcomers a sense of belonging. Belonging is fundamental. For young people, a sense of belonging provides a foundation for building a life and pursuing one's dreams. And, young people who feel that they belong are moved to invest their talents, their energy, and their heart in enriching their new home.

In the end, then, this book is about the importance of belonging—for those who came before and for those who will come tomorrow—as a foundation for creating vibrant lives here.

—•—

By the winter of 2015, lunches in my classroom were dependably crowded and boisterous. Few seats sat unclaimed. One afternoon, I overheard my student Wilson asking some of his Southeast Asian friends a question: Would they teach him how to eat with chopsticks? For weeks he had been watching. Now he was ready to learn. From my desk, I looked on as his classmates placed, positioned, and repositioned the chopsticks between his fingers, guiding and offering tips as, hesitantly, he began to practice.

A few weeks later, Wilson arrived at lunch flush with excitement. "Look what I found!" Wilson had gone to the local grocery to buy a pair of chopsticks for himself. But the store only sold them in bulk. With a flourish, he pulled from his backpack a bag stuffed with dozens of chopsticks.

Classmates crowded around him as he ripped open the bag and started passing out pairs. The room was suddenly a whir of chopstick-wielding teenagers—Iraqi, Liberian, Colombian, Dominican, Brazilian, Tanzanian, Puerto Rican. Everyone was curious; no one wished to be left out. Vietnamese, Burmese, and Cambodian students were enlisted to instruct their classmates on chopstick technique. Throughout the room students set about snatching up French fries, pizza crusts, pencil stubs. Excitedly, proudly, they held their catches aloft.

THE PERSONAL: ROBERT, PART 1

From a quarter of a mile away, Robert spotted the bushy mane of the lion. Up its head bobbed, and then back down it went beneath a bush. Robert skidded his bicycle to a stop. Bags of onions, beans, and cassava flour strapped to the bike's back swayed precariously. Savannah stretched in all directions: scrub brush, gnarled trees, clumps of tall grass, but not a person or house in sight. It was 2007. Robert was eight, or nine; he can't recall. What he does remember was the realization that went ricocheting through his mind: "Today I will die."

Robert had never seen a lion, but he had often heard them. Once they had attacked his village, coming for the cows his family and neighbors herded. He and other children had hidden on the roof of a hut, while their parents lit bonfires and beat drums. From the darkness the deep guttural roars of the pride reverberated. It was a terrifying sound. Now, here in the quiet of the open plains of the Democratic Republic of the Congo, with a blazing sun high overhead, it was just Robert and a lion.

Silently he berated himself. Why hadn't he waited to bike home with his neighbors? Once a week he and others from his village would wake before the sun to bike three hours to the local market. There he would sell a cow, or sometimes a goat, and purchase staples his mother didn't grow herself. It was a trip he had been making regularly for two years, since the time he was six. That morning the men of his village had lingered in the market sipping beers. Impatient, Robert had angled his bike toward home and pedaled out alone into the savannah.

Now, watching intently the tufts of fur bobbing above the brush, the boy pondered survival. Home was still many miles off. Running would only encourage a chase. Slowly, painfully slowly, Robert turned his bike around. Forcing his gaze to the horizon, he began to pedal. One foot, then the next, his heart thumping against his chest like the village drums. Any minute, he was sure, he would hear the whoosh of the lion leaping onto his back. It never came. Not once did he look back, not until, miraculously, he had returned to the market and to safety. Giddy with relief, he was happy to wait for his elders before biking home once more.

Ten years later, and close to seven thousand miles away, Robert—now a high school sophomore in Massachusetts—would arrive early to our school's library to teach himself how to use a computer. Where was the letter *L*? His finger hovered over the gray keys. There it was! Tap it before it got away. Glancing up, Robert confirmed the correct letter had appeared in Google's search bar. On to *I*. Again his finger floated, then tapped. *O*. Find, tap, confirm. Then *N*. In the frigid morning of a New England winter, the school boilers not yet rumbling, Robert came face-to-face once more with a lion.

———◆———

I first met Robert in 2017, in my US history seminar. He was nineteen and entering his junior year. Our class was the first of the day, and most students stumbled in bleary-eyed, clutching coffees. As caffeine kicked in, my students grew boisterous, calling out, chatting with friends. Robert, though, seemed ages older. He spoke only after careful consideration, a scholar in khaki pants, a dark T-shirt, and a long, worn leather trench coat. Robert was starting his first full school year in the United States, but I didn't know that at the time. With nearly 150 students from more than 30 countries, I was just beginning to learn threads of their stories. Over the next five years, I would learn just how extraordinary Robert was.

In December I challenged Robert's class to become modern-day Progressives. We had spent weeks studying the Progressive Movement, reading excerpts from Upton Sinclair's *The Jungle*, analyzing speeches by W. E. B. Du Bois and Booker T. Washington, and holding mock debates on women's suffrage. As a culminating project, each student would select an issue they cared about and craft an op-ed that advocated for concrete change.

In class, my students quickly filled the whiteboard with ideas: cheating in schools, discrimination, cyber-bullying, opioid abuse, sexual harassment. We moved to the computer labs to research and write. Some, like Robert, had had few opportunities to use a computer before arriving at our school. Many were just learning to harness the internet for basic research. All of this we practiced. While I danced around the room from student to student answering a chorus of questions—Miss! Miss! Miss!—Robert sat quietly in a corner, hunting and pecking with two fingers. After school I sat poring over first drafts of op-eds until my vision blurred, making corrections and suggestions. Out of all the essays, Robert's stood out. His punctuation was haphazard, as was his spelling, but the content was what I cared about. In passionate run-on sentences he demanded better access to education for East African women.

A month later I selected eleven op-eds to be published in the *Lowell Sun*, the city's newspaper. Robert's was one. On chilly January mornings, I worked with him and others to edit and reedit their op-eds, perfecting them for publication. Without fail, Robert arrived early. We sat at student desks discussing global education systems. This is how I first began to know Robert. When his article and photo ran in the newspaper, I clipped a copy and taped it to the wall. "Growing up, I lived in small towns in the Democratic Republic of Congo (DRC) as well as in Uganda. I noticed girls not being treated the same as we boys. I feel that it is inhumane the way they were treated. I saw girls have dreams, potential, and abilities, but they did not have equal rights, respect and opportunities. . . ." His op-ed concluded: "Women are our future, they are the mothers of the next generation. We need to make sure our future is good. We can only do that when we support and value women."

———•———

The first time Robert attended a formal school was in 2010. He was twelve years old and had only recently fled across the muddy Semliki River that snakes a border between Uganda and the DRC. While he was growing up, the closest school was many miles away, and so his mother, Nambi Grace, became his teacher. She bought him grammar books and started him off drawing scribbles, then patterns, then letters, and finally words. He traced and retraced the vowels and consonants of his native Kihema, the language of the Hema people, an ethnic minority numbering roughly 160,000 who live primarily in rural villages along the northeastern jut of the country. In sheer size, the DRC equals all of England, Ireland, France, Spain, Portugal, Belgium, Germany, Italy, Switzerland, Luxembourg, and the Netherlands combined. Spread throughout the country's jungles, plains, and mountains are more than two hundred ethnic groups.

In educational terms, Robert is considered a "student with limited or interrupted formal education," SLIFE for short. In my years of teaching I have had many such students, each with a different story of interrupted schooling. An Iraqi boy who, after losing his sight to shrapnel, had no access to a school for the blind after his family fled to a refugee camp. A young Mexican boy who had been shuffled from house to house, school to school, each move translating into months of misplaced transcripts and months out of class. A Vietnamese boy whose family could not afford school fees. A Syrian student driven from school first by bombs and then, after fleeing across the border, by the need to work to afford food. For some students, our school is one of their first formal educational experiences. For them, we start with the basics of learning how to be a student: how to hold a pencil, how to shape letters, how to sit in desks for long stretches of time. Many of my students entered the United States sprinting to recapture years of lost learning.

Robert grew up herding large-horned cows. The Hema people are historically pastoralists. His family raised a herd of more than a hundred. From the time he was seven, Robert joined others from the surrounding villages to graze gigantic herds, walking along the plains for hours, talking and playing as the cows tore at grass and dusty leaves. From friends Robert picked up Rubira, a local language, and Swahili, spoken up and down the East African coast.

Just above the equator night came consistently at seven, with very little dusk foreshadowing the dark. At home, secure within a fence of thorny brush, Robert helped in the milking, nudging aside stubborn suckling calves. His mom would ignite pillars of dried dung and leaves, a natural mosquito deterrent. On nights with a full moon Nambi Grace would regale her boys with Hema myths: the story of the rabbit trickster or the monster Ekiwezicha who snatched and ate wandering villagers. Robert would grow sleepy listening to her stories, stretched out on cowhide mats, the constellations bright pinpricks overhead.

———◆———

Robert's first lessons on America were delivered by radio waves. It was 2008, Robert was ten, give or take, and Barack Obama was running for president.

Obama was everywhere, cropping up constantly in conversation: in the market where Robert bargained for onions, out on the plains where he herded cows. Families hung Obama's picture in their homes and in their shops. When he won, the people of Robert's tiny village in northern

DRC were jubilant. It was as if he had become their president too. "I was so proud," Robert recalls. America, he reasoned, must be a wonderful place.

In 1998, the year Robert was born, or more precisely the year he believes he was born, his country had erupted in violence. For more than thirty years, the DRC—then Zaire—was ruled by the brutal dictator Mobutu Sese Seko. War broke out in the aftermath of the horrific Rwandan genocide that unfolded in the eye-blink of one hundred days in the spring of 1994. With the world standing mostly silent, neighbors butchered neighbors. Hutu militants galvanized a killing spree of 800,000 Tutsi compatriots, Hutu residents who sympathized with them, and other minority communities. In the months and years following, after opposing forces recaptured the country, more than a million Hutu people fled across the Congolese border. With them came many who had murdered. In the refugee camps and border towns of Zaire, the former militias recruited and regrouped. In 1996, hoping to crush the possibility of a Hutu resurgence, and perhaps, too, wanting to take land, Rwanda invaded eastern Zaire. The country ignited in a two-year war that would ultimately topple the dictator and send him into exile. Peace, though, was short lived. Barely a year later, in August 1998, when Robert was likely just a few months old, militia groups rebelled in the Congolese city of Goma, just 350 miles south of Robert's home. Within weeks the country was at war again.

The Second Congo War, also known as the Great African War, entangled nine countries and dozens of independent militia groups. It dragged across five bloody years, killing more than 3.8 million people, and displacing an additional 2 million. Globally it is considered the deadliest conflict since World War II. The deadliest fighting of the deadliest war in the latter half of the twentieth century took place in the country's northeast corner, in Ituri province, on earth sparkling with ribbons of gold, diamonds, inky oil, and dusty coltan, a compound used in cellphones and laptops. It is land referred to by aid organizations and others as "the bloodiest corner" of the Congo. It was here that Robert was born.

Amid the carnage of the Second Congo War, a simmering decades-long land dispute was rekindled between two groups that lived in the region: Lendu farmers and Hema pastoralists—Robert's people. In an eerie mirroring of the Rwandan genocide only four years earlier, beginning in 1998 Lendu militia marched across the plains and forests, brandishing machetes and brutally burning, raping, and massacring their Hema neighbors. Hema militia retaliated in kind. An eye for an eye. By 2003, more than fifty thousand people, mostly Lendu and Hema, had been murdered in Ituri. As many as half a million more were displaced. Later that year, a fragile peace was declared. Robert was at most five. Sometime right before or immediately following the peace treaty, his father was killed. Robert has no recollection of his father's face.

———◆———

Late one August night in 2010, Robert, now twelve, give or take, visited the home of a friend. Suddenly, piercing the stillness, the boys heard the whistle and thud of bullets in rapid succession. Running outside, they could see flames leaping from thatch roofs. Robert ran.

The other boys ran with him, their breathing heavy. In time they reached the churning Semliki and crowded into canoes that normally held three. In their terror they tumbled six into each. Somewhere along the banks or perhaps under the lapping waves lazed gigantic, pebbled crocodiles. Crocodiles were killers by Robert's reckoning. He had watched as they leapt from the river, dragging his cows under. Even so, up until two years earlier he had cautiously swum in the Semliki, until one afternoon a friend lingered in the water. Robert never saw the crocodile snatch him, but the remains of the boy's body were found downstream a week later. Robert never swam again.

But now, in the darkness, Robert tried not to think of crocodiles. Down into the water they drove their paddles, again and again, until the canoes skidded onto the sandy banks of the opposite shore. Exhausted, they tumbled out into Uganda.

———◆———

Robert speaks little about the weeks and months after he crossed by canoe. I don't ask, not wanting to dredge up memories. Years later, in a refugee camp, he penned his family's names into a tiny notebook. Writing was a way to keep them close. Nambi Grace. Musguzi David. And below: "After one week Hmea [a neighbor] went back to Burasi. Discovered mum and brother were killed by the Lendu. After some time they came and informed us of the attack."

As a high school senior in Massachusetts in 2019, Robert enrolled in my upper-level course, Seminar on American Diversity. As part of the class he and his classmates published a book, each including a personal story. It would be the first time he would choose to publicly share about those months after the attack: "I was desperate and lost. I couldn't accept my mother was gone. I had sleepless nights and days with tears, feeling dead and also wanting to die. I can't find words to describe that time."

Alone and orphaned in Uganda, Robert found a single lifeline, an older woman who had crammed into the canoe with him that terrible night. She had known Robert's mother, and when the refugees landed in the district of Ntoroko, Uganda, she kept watch over Nambi Grace's boy. She found a Hema family who needed help with their cows and took the boy in, raising him alongside their children. Life fell into a rhythm. Robert rose early, as he always had. In slanted morning light he helped milk the cows. In the afternoons he and the other children spent hours throwing water up from deep wells to fill troughs for the herd to drink. In Ntoroko, for the first time, Robert went to school.

In school, everything was new. He sat on a long wooden bench, squashed between other boys and girls, balancing a notebook on one knee. Teachers came in and out, standing at the board and lecturing as their pupils furiously copied: math, science, history, English.

Learning was conducted solely in English. Robert knew none, but he quickly learned out of necessity. Speaking in Kihema, he discovered, would result in a beating. Each morning students—sixty, seventy, sometimes one hundred—scrambled to their feet. "Gooood moooorning teacher, how are you today?" they sang.

At twelve years old, with no formal schooling and no papers, Robert was placed in primary 1, the equivalent of first grade in the United States. Three months later, returning from a school holiday, he found himself moved without explanation to primary 2. Robert did not ask why. He kept studying, skipping classes only on days school fees were collected. He had no money to give. After some months, he switched schools. "Where are your papers?" the teachers asked. "I don't have any, I'm from the Congo," he replied. The new school enrolled him in primary 4. Within months he was moved again, this time into primary 5. One afternoon a young teacher called him to her desk. Out of her fifty pupils, she was struck by his diligence, the speed at which he picked up concepts. "You need to move to a better school," she declared, filling out the paperwork and giving him directions. When he arrived at his third school in two years, a harried man asked him for his grade. Robert paused, ". . . primary 6." The man nodded and pointed in the direction of a classroom.

School was filled with rules, and also consequences. If you spoke out of turn you were caned. If you made a mistake in your workbook or on the board you were caned. Punishments sometimes varied: a slap across the cheek, a pinch and a twist of an ear. Once in math class, his teacher called him forward. Robert can't remember what mathematical mistake he had made, but he remembers the teacher's name, Albert, the only teacher in Ntoroko whose name he still recalls. Robert was made to face the blackboard with his classmates watching. Thwack, thwack, thwack. Forty strokes. Hours later, his backside welted and bruised, Robert asked himself, "How can he cane us like animals? Even to an animal this would not be fair." But the next day he returned to school. The beatings were just a part of learning, although he never liked math again.

Hearing this story many years later I had to ask, "Why did you choose to return?" Alone in the world, in a foreign country, living with strangers, why did he return to a place that caned him for the smallest infraction? Robert seemed perplexed by my question. Not attending seems never to have crossed his mind. But he indulged me. Robert explained, "Once you milk the cows and do housework, there is nothing to do other than listen to the radio and sit . . . or sleep. And I wasn't a fan of sleeping." Education, he mused, was "one of the things that drove me. I always had the passion to learn."

———•———

Robert's favorite school was not a school. An hour's walk from his new home was an office for an international aid organization, and in the squat one-story building was a library. Twice a week Robert made the trek. Sitting on the floor he flipped through books that caught his eye, tracing the outlines of North American coyotes, otters, and alligators. He treasured a hefty textbook on American civics, reading tales of a president named Abraham Lincoln who he learned had freed enslaved Africans. He liked that story in particular. Through used children's books, in an aid office in western Uganda, Robert fell in love with America.

In the library one afternoon he pulled forth a thick volume with a frayed mauve cover, *Best Poems of 1998*. Poems from the year Robert was born. Inside, the words congregated in clumps. It seemed manageable, much more manageable than the long lines of text in so many other books. He asked if he could borrow the volume. The aid worker frowned. "That book is too advanced for you." Robert shook his head. "That's okay, I want to try." Bemused, the man nodded, and a grinning Robert carried the book home. At night with the assistance of a tiny *Oxford English Dictionary*, he set about decoding poetry.

His teachers too would sometimes lend him books. Once he was gifted a chapter book crammed with text, scattered with an occasional black-and-white sketch: a burning house, a wedding. On the cover was a woman's name: *Jane Eyre*. He kept it. One day, he hoped, he would understand her story.

———•———

By 2013 Robert was fifteen, give or take. Refugees kept crossing the churning Semliki. Tensions between the displaced refugees and local Ugandan residents simmered. Dusty government pickups drove through the streets on market day, announcing that refugees would be moved inland to camps. His mother's friend thought he should go, that there would be greater opportunity to study. With no family and no permanent home, Robert agreed.

He had little, so had little to pack. The one thing he did have, was books. Over two years Robert had amassed boxes of used volumes, his prized possessions. Neighbors and friends would puzzle over these boxes. "Why," they asked, "do you keep all of these books?" His response never changed: "This is what I love." On the eve of his departure he picked up one book, put it down, picked up another, put it back. From his library he selected just two books to take with him onward. The next morning, standing by the side of the road, Robert waited, a scrawny orphan in jeans, a black shirt, and sandals woven from worn tires. He clutched a plastic bag, which held his sole possessions in the world: *Jane Eyre* and *Best Poems of 1998*.

When a large truck pulled up, the back open and uncovered, Robert and others scrambled onboard. Men and women, boys and girls stood, swaying slightly as the truck pulled onto the road. From his spot sandwiched between strangers, Robert watched the countryside skim by. They drove through towns and through national parks. Looking out, Robert watched tawny kobs, prized Ugandan antelopes, leaping in herds. He spotted scurrying wild pigs and furry buffalo. For three hours he stared, standing silent, until the truck slowed, and then stopped. They had arrived at the Kyaka II refugee camp, Robert's new home.

CHAPTER 1

NEW BEGINNINGS

To make Americans, we must ensure that immigrant-origin students have the opportunity to create new futures for themselves and for their families. For centuries, many immigrants and refugees have arrived with the hope of new beginnings. They come with the belief that, regardless of the money they have in their pockets, their status in society, their past history, here they can start afresh. The challenge for schools is to nurture this belief and help students realize that possibility.

This chapter tells three stories about new beginnings. The first is the story of how schools across the country at the turn of the twentieth century attempted to assimilate and "Americanize" a new influx of immigrants, and the first woman district superintendent of New York City schools, who launched an experiment to help newcomers that became a model for public schools for the following century. The second is the story of a newcomer center in Houston, Texas, that aims to give students who have been in the country less than a year the academic and emotional support to succeed in American schools. The third is the story of my own Cambodian student Srey Neth, the daughter of survivors of the Khmer Rouge genocide, who grew up dreaming of becoming an American.

THE PAST: THE AMERICANIZATION MOVEMENT

In the first decade of the twentieth century more than eight million newcomers came to America. They disembarked by the thousands, trudging down the gangways of gigantic steamers that crisscrossed the Atlantic at a seven-day clip. They came from the orange groves of Sicily and the countryside outside Naples; they left homes in small shtetls surrounding Kaunas, Krakow, and Kyiv. They set sail from the Grecian coast and from the ports of Izmir and Beirut. Italians, Russians, Romanians, Ukrainians, Slovaks, Serbs, Poles, Greeks, Austro-Hungarians, Armenians, Bohemians. Steamships of Babel.

Those who came from across the Atlantic were different from those who came before. Previous immigrants hailed primarily from northern and western Europe: Britain, Ireland, Germany, Sweden, Norway. But famine, disease, mass unemployment, political upheaval, and bloody pogroms triggered new waves of movement across the continents.

Across the sixty years spanning 1820 to 1880, close to ten million immigrated to the United States. Starting in 1880 and in the decades that followed, nearly double that number arrived, in just half the time. These newest newcomers settled primarily in cities. They fashioned miniature European enclaves—Little Italy, Little Israel, Little Greece—and they enrolled their children in school. City teachers watched aghast as their classrooms ballooned in size. By 1906, roughly one in every six students in New York City came from overseas. Five years later more than half of all students in more than thirty of the country's largest cities were immigrants or the children of immigrants.

In New York, the new arrivals headed en masse to teeming ramshackle streets on the Lower East Side: Houston and Bowery, Essex and Orchard. There they entrusted their future to a school system headed by a recently appointed district superintendent with an unusual vision.

When asked which district she wished to supervise, Julia Richman did not hesitate. To the bafflement of her colleagues, she selected the Lower East Side. According to her sisters, she was drawn by the influx of immigrants and the unique challenges they posed. Richman was accustomed to raising eyebrows. With a square jaw and a piercing gaze, she had often done what was unexpected. Defying her father, she became a teacher at seventeen, a principal at twenty-nine. She refused to marry, though many upper-class women of the time did. When she assumed the role of district superintendent in 1903, she was both the first woman and the first Jew to hold the title. She took charge of 14 schools, 600 teachers, and the educational futures of 23,000 students, many new to the country. "Ours is a nation of immigrants," she declared, two years into her tenure.

"The citizen voter of today was yesterday an immigrant child. Tomorrow he may be a political leader. Between the alien of today and the citizen of tomorrow stands the school."[1]

———•———

I would not wish to have been either a teacher or a student in a New York City school in 1900. Class rosters stretched far beyond teachable. Rooms of fifty pupils were common; classes of one hundred not unheard of. Some months, students were packed so tightly behind shared desks that administrators turned prospective scholars away. There was simply no room to learn.

For many of those who did manage to secure a seat, the schooling they received was ineffective. Newcomers in particular were held back, made to repeat a grade, one year, two years, sometimes three years in succession. In 1911 Congress published a behemoth of a report on US immigration, one of the largest investigations of its ilk ever undertaken. The commission devoted five of forty-one thick volumes to the study of immigrant children in American schools. In these pages, experts reported that, in New York City schools, more than half of Polish Jews and southern Italian children were behind in their education by a year or more.

The findings reflected not student intellect but educational practice. Thirteen-year-old Yiddish speakers, ten-year-old Italian speakers, seven-year-old Russian speakers—all, by and large, were enrolled in first grade. Irrespective of the age or previous education of their newcomer pupils, teachers tended to gear instruction toward their youngest. Partly as a result, dropout rates soared, particularly among frustrated older students; the trend was exacerbated in immigrant enclaves. By law, children had to remain in school until their fourteenth birthday, but tracking down truant students was haphazard, and work papers could easily be forged. A sweeping 1913 report of New York City's school system found that for students who began schooling in first grade, barely half persisted to eighth. For most of those who finished elementary school, few continued on to high school.

Dismayed by the dismal academic success of immigrant children, and only months into her tenure as district superintendent, Julia Richman penned a request to the board of superintendents seeking permission to launch an experiment. Within the schools of the Lower East Side she sought to create designated classes that targeted failing students. Heady with board approval the following September, Richman created, among other experiments, dedicated classes solely for newcomers. Informally they became known as "steamer classes," in a nod to the steamships that brought immigrant children and adults to the United States. They were among the first of their kind in the nation, structured as a six-month primer in English and America.

———•———

Julia Richman's idea for steamer classes, intended to rapidly "Americanize" immigrants, was born from a career built in New York City classrooms and would, in decades to come, help reshape how schools nationwide educated newcomers.

Richman, the child of immigrants from the Austrian Empire, descended from a long line of Prague rabbis. Her family came to the United States as part of an earlier migration of German and Bohemian Jews who arrived in the mid-1800s, preceding their Russian brethren by decades. These Jews began new lives in an American society with minimal overt antisemitism. But by the late 1800s, now-established Gilded Age Jews began to find themselves excluded from elite resorts, restaurants, and high-end hotels, barred from socialite gatherings, and restricted from enrolling their children in private schools and Ivy League universities.

The rise in antisemitism coincided with an uptick in migration from the shtetls. The disembarking masses were strikingly foreign and conspicuously Jewish, a stark contrast to the refined Reform Jewish elite. Their clothes, their language, their strict observance of faith were anything but subtle. Prosperous Jews were appalled and embarrassed. Some historians link the rise in antisemitism to a growing resentment on the part of Anglo-Americans who grew uncomfortable with newly wealthy Jews seeking to join elite society. But some of the prosperous German Jews came to believe that the antisemitism was precipitated by the Ostjuden, as they termed the new arrivals, whom, they believed, jeopardized the status they had worked so hard to achieve.

Jewish philanthropists set about proposing solutions both creative and desperate. Some funded programs to disperse Jews across the country, believing that newcomers would assimilate faster at diluted concentrations. Others financed return tickets to the Old World. But few Ostjuden were eager to leave the cities. Schooling, the elite concluded, was the best solution. And so they set about establishing programs that would swiftly Americanize new arrivals—an attempt to eliminate antisemitism by suppressing their Jewish identity. A mix of self-preservation and *tzedakah*.

A profusion of after-school programs, Sabbath schools, and social ventures were launched in cities up and down the East Coast, with particular concentration in New York. In contrast to Catholic parochial schools, these Jewish associations sought not to compete with but to complement public education, by preparing immigrant children for success in the secular system. Among the most famous was the Educational Alliance, a Jewish settlement house established in the Lower East Side and still in operation today. At its helm, for close to a decade in the 1890s, was Julia Richman.

The Educational Alliance's purpose, as an early brochure stated, "shall be of an Americanizing, Educational, Social and Humanizing character."[2] Housed in a five-story building, the Educational Alliance catered to immigrants young and old. There was a gym, a library, a theater, a rooftop garden, and even baths to foster good hygiene. Tenement residents could partake in English classes, religious classes, vocational classes, art lessons, lectures, and, of prime importance, instruction in how to become an American. Making Americans, Richman and her colleagues agreed, required refashioning the Ostjuden in their own image: prosperous, refined, and discreet in their worship. For children, Yiddish was at times forbidden. Rule breakers had their mouths scrubbed with soap. The tenements, Richman believed, were "full of menace to the entire Jewish community."[3] Americanization would be their salvation.

Julia Richman was not a woman to sit idle. In the 1870s, while still a public-school teacher, each Saturday she had set out to her synagogue to conduct religious classes at the behest of her father. A social progressive at heart, she began to take on leadership roles in a host of Jewish organizations, including her work as a director of the Educational Alliance. By the turn of the century she was devoting extensive time to working for newcomers, Russian Jews and Italian Catholics crammed in the tenements. She assisted in distributing food and clothing. She wrote and published frequently, lectured extensively. She constructed curricula, penned textbooks, co-edited a weekly magazine, and co-authored a children's guide to citizenship. Time and again she found her schedule left no room for meals. She took to signing letters, "In haste and hunger."[4]

Richman was relentless. "Ours is the great opportunity of rendering the rare and holy services of making a true American citizen out of an immigrant child," she wrote in 1905.[5] But her zeal was not always appreciated by the newcomers she sought to serve. In 1908, parents petitioned for her removal as district superintendent. Richman, they wrote, was "entirely out of sympathy with the needs of . . . the community." In seeking to Americanize their children, they said, she sowed division. In the words of the aggrieved, Richman "degraded and lowered parents in the eyes of their children."[6] They likely were concerned too that Richman's strategy would result in their families losing their culture. But leadership believed in her approach and so Richman continued her work.

In the city's superintendent, Richman had an ally. William Henry Maxwell, born in Ireland and educated in Galway, assumed the title of Superintendent of Schools of New York City in 1898. Never before had one man governed all boroughs from the Bronx to Staten Island, from Manhattan to Brooklyn, and up to Queens. New York City schools were suddenly combined into the largest single school district in the nation, a distinction it still claims to this day. When he assumed the role, Maxwell took responsibility for roughly half a million children. Nearly two decades later, on the eve of his retirement, roughly double that number of students studied in his schools.

Bespectacled, balding, and sporting a walrus mustache, Maxwell was a man with a vision and the dominating presence to enact it. Sewing together a patchwork of previously disparate districts tattered by inefficiency and ineffectiveness, Maxwell set about standardizing and innovating: a new comprehensive curriculum, updated vocational training, expansion of the school year, and increases in teacher pay and required qualifications. Local experiments bloomed into citywide initiatives: school nurses, lunch programs, and, at the suggestion of his newest district superintendent, steamer classes for immigrant children.

For the city's schools, the superintendent's goal was clear. "The majority of the people who now come to us have little akin to our language; they have little akin to our mode of thought; they have little akin to our customs; and they have little akin to our traditions. . . It is a great business of the department of education in this city . . . to train the immigrant child . . . to become a good American citizen."[7] To him, Julia Richman's steamer classes were an ideal addition.

In the fall of 1904 Richman opened her steamer classes in the public schools of the Lower East Side, modeled on her work at the Educational Alliance. It was her fervent hope that her experiment would help prepare immigrant children for success in their new country. Within two years, Maxwell expanded the strategy to schools dotted across the city. While in her lifetime Richman's classes would operate only at a relatively small scale, they would become a blueprint for an approach to acculturate newcomers, a model expanded upon over the coming century by school districts across the country.

In 1912, speaking at the dedication of the newly constructed home of the state's department of education in Albany, Maxwell adopted a metaphor born on the stage. The superintendent might have attended Israel Zangwill's new play, *The Melting Pot*, which opened at the Comedy Theater in 1909, a thirty-minute stroll from his office. Elementary schools were, he remarked to his colleagues, "the melting pot which converts the children of the immigrants of all races and languages into sturdy, independent American citizens."[8] In Zangwill's play the protagonist proclaimed, "God is making the American."[9] So too were Maxwell and Richman's schools.

———•———

Each morning in classrooms throughout New York City and across the country at the turn of the twentieth century, flags were unfurled and students scraped back their chairs to stand and promise their allegiance. It was a pledge first penned on a sticky August evening by a harried former Baptist minister and recently anointed advertising executive, coming up fast on a deadline. In 1891, with the four-hundredth anniversary of Christopher Columbus's arrival to America approaching, the highly popular *Youth's Companion* magazine devised a scheme to sell flags. As one, schoolchildren would proclaim their devotion to the nation on the newly conceived Columbus Day by saluting the star-spangled banner. To participate, schools needed flags. *Youth's Companion* just happened to sell them.

Having procrastinated for weeks, Francis Bellamy finally penned a salute. "I pledge allegiance to my Flag and to the Republic for which it stands, one nation, indivisible, with liberty and justice for all." (The text would undergo revisions in later years, including the addition of the words "under God.") According to Bellamy, his twenty-three words took two hours to write. They would, in a revised fashion, be memorized and recited daily by tens of millions of schoolchildren for the next 130 years and counting. Not bad for a night's work.[10]

Bellamy's pledge was also intended as a defense against the new wave of Eastern and Southern Europeans of "inferior race"[11] who were beginning to pour into American ports. America, as he saw it, was under threat from "races which we cannot assimilate without a lowering of our racial standard."[12] The schoolhouse flag and his pledge were a protection, an assurance "that the distinctive principles of true Americanism will not perish as long as free, public education endures."[13]

———◆———

At the turn of the twentieth century, what it meant to be American was on the minds of educators across the nation. Language instruction alone would not suffice. According to reports of the day, disembarking immigrants were accused, falsely, of not knowing how to wash, keep home, or mother effectively. They were believed to be prone to vice, greed, and laziness. Little was seen as salvageable. Language, clothing, customs—all had to go. The new immigrants enrolling in school were "illiterate, docile, lacking in self-reliance and initiative, and not possessing the Anglo-Teutonic conceptions of law, order, and government," remarked Ellwood Cubberley, former San Diego superintendent and future dean of Stanford University's School of Education, in 1909. Laying out a blueprint for public education, Cubberley envisioned a vital role for schools, "to implant in their [immigrant] children, so far as can be done, the Anglo-Saxon conception of righteousness, law and order, and popular government."[14]

By the early 1900s, Americanization was as much a part of the core curriculum as math, science, English, and social studies. All lessons presented an opportunity to instill patriotism. "I hope that every school will be one hundred percent American," the New Jersey Commission of Education enthused in 1919. "Teachers who are teaching foreign-born children to speak and read English are teaching Americanization. The teacher who is teaching children to sing patriotic songs 'by heart' is teaching Americanization, particularly if the children sing them by heart and not mechanically."[15] In all lessons, teachers were encouraged to extoll the virtues of the nation: its military prowess, its upstanding presidents, its far-reaching vistas and plentiful resources. Honesty, obedience, self-reliance, and frequent bathing, too, were considered hallmarks of American identity.

The disdain directed at newcomers was not lost on a little immigrant boy born in the boot of southern Italy and raised in the tenements of New York City. As an adult, Leonard Covello recalled his schooling: "We soon got the idea that 'Italian' meant something inferior. . . . This was the accepted process of Americanization. We were becoming Americans by learning how to be ashamed of our parents."[16] Eugene Lyons, an American journalist born in present-day Belarus and also educated in New York, was similarly scathing about his education: "We were 'Americanized' about as gently as horses are broken in. In the whole crude process, we sensed a disrespect for the alien traditions in our homes and came unconsciously to resent and despise those traditions, good and bad alike, because they seemed insuperable barriers between ourselves and our adopted land."[17] Covello would go on to dedicate nearly half a century to New York schools, as a teacher and then as a founder of an East Harlem school, becoming the city's first Italian principal. He crafted a community-based school that strove to elevate, rather than stamp out, the heritage of his neighborhood's immigrant children. Writing with the insight drawn from both sides of the teacher's desk, Covello bitterly reflected: "The concept of Americanization was based upon the assumption that foreigners . . . were a threat to American political, economic, and social stability, and security. The infiltration of foreign culture, it was feared, would eventually bring about a deterioration of the American 'way of life.'"[18] In schools it boiled down to simple mathematics: Subtract the imported, add the Anglo-Saxon.

Four of my direct ancestors immigrated to America as children, traveling at the turn of the twentieth century to New York City and fashioning new identities in US schools. A nine-month-old, a two-year-old, a six-year-old, and a seven-year-old. The last was my great-grandfather Daniel.

In 1898, Daniel was born in the Pale of Settlement, the region in which the Russian Czar permitted Jews to live; his faith relegated him to a restricted region of a twilight empire. For Jews in Old Russia, his family was well off. His father, Boris, was a merchant and store owner, bestowed by the empire with permission to travel and trade in Riga, St. Petersburg, and Moscow. His mother, Leah, the daughter of brewers and innkeepers, kept home for five rambunctious children, attended to by nursemaids and tutors.

Daniel was born in what is now northern Ukraine, in the tiny town of Borzna, tucked into the elbow of a river, accessible neither by train nor major thoroughfare. In the twenty-first century it has remained just as isolated; horse carts are as common as motor vehicles.

Daniel grew up in Borzna and began school there. But almost from the time he was born, his favorite older sister, Anna, studied many towns away. Borzna had no upper school, and so Anna, from the age of eight, lived primarily with an aunt in the more prosperous town of Romny. Precocious and idealistic, the young girl was soon swept up with revolutionary zeal and dreams of overthrowing the three-hundred-year dynasty of the Romanovs. Sneaking out from school, she attended covert proletariat meetings.

Daniel was six, in January of 1905, when a Russian Orthodox priest led thousands to the gates of the czar's Winter Palace in the heart of St. Petersburg carrying a workers' petition. They were met by ranks of imperial guards, Cossacks, and cavalry, who promptly opened fire. The ensuing bloodbath would give birth to a revolution, the first of two that would ultimately topple the empire. In an attempt at appeasement that October, Russian czar Nicholas II relinquished the absolute authority of the czar, installing in its place a form of constitutional monarchy. Monarchists were furious. As in times past and in those still to come, they turned on their preferred scapegoat, the empire's Jews, whom they believed had actively supported the revolutionists. In the days immediately following the czar's proclamation, more than six hundred pogroms ignited in towns and cities across the Pale of Settlement. Synagogues and schools were burned, storefronts smashed, homes ransacked. Jewish girls and women were raped and Jews of all ages were beaten. In less than a week more than eight hundred lay dead.

On the last day of October and the first of the new government, fourteen-year-old Anna, my great-great-aunt, hid in her own aunt's home in Romny as a pogrom raged outside the windows.[19] Over two days her school was burned, along with two synagogues, two printing presses, and all Jewish-owned shops. Homes were looted, thirty residents beaten, and eight men and women butchered. With the wreckage still smoldering, Boris sent for his eldest. He sold his shop, liquidated his goods, and as frozen roads turned to mud in the spring of 1906, the family fled across Europe—a mad dash to the Atlantic, and then across the ocean by steamer ship, to America.

My family settled in New York and enrolled Daniel in elementary school. Daniel likely partook in Julia Richman's steamer classes for newcomers. But Anna, the spirited anti-monarchist, just shy of her fifteenth birthday, would never experience American schools. The age cutoff at the time was fourteen. Resigned, she attended night school and went to work for her father. "As to my first impressions of the United States, all I remember is that I was as miserable as one could be leaving forever the country where I was born and all of my friends and relatives," Anna shared with her granddaughter nearly seventy years later. "In addition to the drastic change, you must bear in mind that I didn't know the language and really couldn't communicate with anyone. My father got a tutor for us, but it took quite a while before I could read a newspaper. There was no comparison between the home we left and the home here. In Russia, a lot of luxuries, here, a lot of privations."[20]

Thirty years after Boris and Leah had fled with their family they returned to Europe in 1936, a fiftieth wedding anniversary trip financed by their children. By boat and by train they toured France, Jerusalem, Germany, and then traveled east from Berlin to the old country. When Boris and Leah reached the shores of the Black Sea, Boris's siblings were reluctant to greet them. It was no longer safe to associate with Americans. Any record or recollection of whether they returned specifically to Borzna is lost. As elite athletes gathered for the summer Olympics in the shadow of the Third Reich, the couple bought passage back to New York. Five years later, in 1941, as Jews readied themselves for the Day of Atonement, Nazis came to Borzna. By then only three hundred Jews remained, barely a fifth of the community that my family once knew. Within weeks that number was halved. Jews deported. Jews shot. And then, months later, in the depths of winter 1942, the one hundred or so survivors were dragged from their beds. On the outskirts of a nearby village, they were made to stand alongside a ditch—my family's neighbors and friends, their customers and playmates, and possibly too our relatives. Only a few were alive at dawn.

In America, favored by chance and by circumstance, Jews from Borzna survived. My great-grandfather mastered English and forgot Yiddish. He graduated high school and attended Cooper Union, one of only a handful of colleges across the country where tuition was free. One evening, stopping in at a Brooklyn dance social, the boy from Borzna fell in love with a girl from Vienna—my great-grandmother Stell, whose family had fled Austria when she was only nine months old.

Daniel and Stell married quickly, two refugees making a home in a new land. They had a son and a daughter in quick succession. They prospered, choosing to remain forever in New York City. Like so many Jewish immigrants of the age, their faith grew dusty with disuse. They conformed. They assimilated. It was what they were taught to do.

Nearly ninety years after my great-grandfather was born in the Pale of Settlement, I came into the world—wrinkled, wailing, and tinged purple. Borzna to Boston.

THE PRESENT: LAS AMERICAS, TEXAS

Tears coursing down his cheeks, the black-haired Salvadorian boy refused to enter the classroom. He howled and shrieked. Like a vine he twisted his arms and legs around a hallway pole. His teachers could not calm him. The boy had, in 2015, just started at Las Americas Newcomer School, a public school in Houston, Texas.

Before being enrolled at the school, the nine-year-old had endured, together with his mother, a month in captivity—first imprisoned by drug cartels south of the border and then confined by ICE in a detention center. His mother had embarked on the harrowing journey in a desperate attempt to save her son's life from deadly gangs that had targeted him for recruitment. Yet in Houston, while physically safe, the boy was consumed with terror about his baby brother, who had been left behind in El Salvador. Who would care for him? Although he knew that his grandparents remained behind with his brother, he could not be consoled.

While his family was away at work each day, he had watched over his brother. His brother was *his* responsibility.

The school's recently hired social worker, Sarah Howell, discarded strategy after strategy. Then one day the boy's teacher, Stephanie Green, alighted on an idea. Her students were studying the metamorphoses of monarch butterflies, caring for caterpillars and documenting their transformation. Outside she had planted milkweed for the ravenous caterpillars. She asked the boy if he would be the class's caterpillar manager. Each morning it would be his responsibility to feed the caterpillars, sweep up their poop, ensure they were safe. Slowly he began spending a few minutes, then a few hours, then finally whole days in class.

The boy who cared for caterpillars among the blooming milkweed gave Sarah an idea. After school and on weekends, she amassed flora: lavender, mint, basil, chamomile, cilantro, sage, sugarcane. She collected jasmine like that found on mountainsides of Afghanistan and bird-of-paradise flowers like those that bloomed in the valleys of Guatemala. The plants were soft, sturdy, delicate, ribbed, and fuzzy. They smelled bright, woody, peppery, and sweet. She began constructing a sensory garden that would nurture both plants and children.

Other students began accompanying Sarah outside, sitting among herbs or kneeling to weed. Side by side, children planting tomatoes spoke of grandmas back home who grew the same crops. Shriveling bougainvillea sparked conversations about how hard it was to put down roots in a new place.

At Las Americas, all of the students were recently transplanted. The school is a bridge across borders—a newcomer center, designed specifically for recent arrivals. Here, nine-year-olds to fourteen-year-olds, possessing little English and often minimal formal schooling, study for a year, maybe two. In that short span, Las Americas educators hope they can provide their students with the essential tools to succeed in a neighborhood school and in the United States.

Houston is one of the most diverse cities in the nation, and Las Americas lies on the fringe of one of the most densely populated areas of the city, referred to by many as a modern Ellis Island. Las Americas students came from cities in Mexico, Nicaragua, Cuba, India, Vietnam, and the countrysides of Guatemala, Honduras, Afghanistan. They grew up in refugee camps in Uganda, Ethiopia, and Nepal. They speak Turkish and Tigrinya, Urdu and Arabic, Spanish and Somali. Little ones converse in Kunama, spoken in remote regions of Eritrea, and K'iche', a Mayan language spoken in the central highlands of Guatemala. A sign near the school's entrance proclaims: "Welcome to Las Americas, where the world comes to learn English."

———◆———

School registrars working across Houston kept in close communication. That was how, in 1998, Maria Garcia heard of a middle school for new-comers dedicated to immigrant children who were floundering in neigh-borhood schools. The school was taking shape inside the sprawling Las Americas apartment complex, home to families from across the globe. When the founding principal announced he needed a school adminis-trator to assist him in running the school, Maria applied without hesita-tion—the students' stories were her own.

More than two decades earlier, at the age of ten, Maria and her fam-ily had moved from Laredo, Mexico, to rural Nebraska. Speaking only Spanish at the time, she remembers comprehending little and being un-derstood by few. She had always loved school. She arrived early to help her teacher with the computers, communicating through hand signals and smiles. But for years, she and her brothers left the classroom months earlier than their peers to join their family in the sugar beet fields, from sunup to sundown. Perhaps it was her prolonged absences from the classroom that made Maria love learning all the more.

In the spring of 2005, Maria was the first to meet Marie Moreno, a candidate for the role of principal at Las Americas. The initial tour was brief, the school small. At the time, no walls separated classrooms; filing cabinets and bookcases delineated makeshift rooms.

A decade earlier, Marie Moreno had fallen sideways into teaching. She worked as a computer programmer for an oil and gas company. Again and again she was called to the nearby school to collect her niece, who was sent often to the principal's office. Marie became a regular in the school halls, and that was why the principal was comfortable asking for a favor. His students were befuddled in computer science class; he asked if she would observe and advise. Before long, he asked if she would consider teaching. Intrigued, Marie enrolled in education courses, and then took a nine-month leave of absence from her company to become a temporary teacher. Nine months turned into twenty-six years and counting.

When Marie applied to Las Americas, she had, for five years, been an assistant principal working with newcomers. The daughter and granddaughter of immigrants from Mexico, she fell in love with educating immigrants and that was why, eager to lead a school, she applied to Las Americas when the founding principal stepped down.

In the summer of 2005 Marie took charge of Las Americas, with a teaching staff of four and a student body of roughly sixty. Maria Garcia, the veteran administrator, helped to ease the transition. Little, Marie quickly learned, would be straightforward. The school rented space from the surrounding apartment complex. When the apartment building's water or gas was periodically shut off for nonpayment, Marie and her students were cut off too. In a converted space with no real walls, voices layered on top of one another like a collage. "Repeat after me, my name is Imelda," one teacher would instruct. From behind filing cabinets, another teacher could be heard, "Repeat after me, how old are you?"

Marie drew up proposals for purchasing sheetrock and begged her landlord, the apartment complex, for walls. The complex's owners tired of her persistence and evicted Las Americas. The district provided Marie and her students a new home, a collection of trailers, two miles away.

———◆———

At a round table surrounded by middle schoolers in 2019, a confident eleven-year-old led his classmates in reading a picture book. "I see a seal," he read. Around him his peers repeated the line. One girl paused, pointing to a word on her page. How might she pronounce this in English, she asked. Leaning over, he sounded out the word. In the opposite corner five children sprawled on cushions, engrossed in books. Along the wall three little ones practiced writing and listening on the computer. At another table five children worked silently penciling answers on a worksheet. And in the middle of the classroom sat the teacher, speaking quietly with a group of four, discussing a book about butterflies.

The classrooms of Las Americas are carbon copies, each containing small learning stations devoted to reading, writing, speaking, and listening, always in the same position. The reading nook is always along the same wall, the teacher's desk angled at a similar tilt, the circular tables for independent group work in a particular corner. Elsewhere in their lives, newly arrived immigrant students are perpetually guessing, decoding, and deciphering their environment—new language, new forms of instruction, new neighborhoods, new community. Las America's identical classrooms eliminate some uncertainty and anxiety. English class, science class, math class, all organized the same way. Consistency frees the mind to focus on learning.

A decade earlier, in the summer of 2009, Marie had purchased plane tickets for herself and four of her staff to visit other newcomer centers, to learn how they educated recently arrived children. They flew to Fairfax, Virginia; St. Paul, Minneapolis; Brooklyn, New York. Back in Houston they compiled, analyzed, and selected best practices that they could implement at Las Americas. The classroom configuration with distinct stations to study discrete components of language emerged from those early visits.

Marie realized too that she would have to rethink the traditional approach for organizing classes. At Las Americas one fourth grader might be sounding out A, B, C, D and another might be practicing transforming sentences from present tense to past. She and her team chose to group classes by reading level. Teachers tracked students' progress with precision, like marking a child's height on a kitchen wall. Students' gains were celebrated by transitioning them to a new class with more advanced material. In the lower-level reading classes, new arrivals took their place.

Erratic growth was routine at Las Americas. In August the school might be home to seventy students; by the following May, more than three hundred. Marie would intentionally start with class sizes of six, knowing that they would soon expand to thirty. Enrollment at newcomer centers across the nation swell and dip with the currents of global migration and national policy. They stand ready for the child who arrived in the country just last week.

Some people, Marie remembered, were dubious about Las Americas, which looked nothing like a traditional school. Why were thirteen-year-olds learning the alphabet? Some questioned the premise of the school. Did newcomer centers impede children's integration into their new home by separating them, even for a year, from American-born students? Knowing that state assessments of schools depended in part on test performance, some worried that Las Americas students had such low test scores. Marie was stuck: She could raise the school's test scores by choosing to serve students with more English, but that would defeat the purpose of Las Americas.

Clouds hung over the school's future. Teachers grew edgy. Would the school be shut? Would they be able to find new jobs? In 2013, they began resigning. By late spring only one of thirteen teachers remained—the PE instructor. In the front office, Marie turned to Maria Garcia and burst into tears. "I can't do this anymore," she sobbed. Maria shook her head. "We are going to get through this," she promised her boss. "Maria too was an immigrant child," Marie remembers thinking. "She knew we couldn't turn our backs on these kids. If she wasn't there I'm not sure if I wouldn't have walked away."

When word came that summer that Las Americas could remain open, the women began rebuilding. Starting from scratch, they hired and trained new teachers and reestablished the school's culture. They began again.

———•———

One day in the winter of 2017, English teacher Stephanie Green brought into class a terra-cotta pot containing a bulbous barrel cactus, a paddled prickly pear, and a starburst aloe. She had brought the plants so her students could practice writing small descriptive paragraphs. Instead her pupils found toy figurines and began moving them over the cacti and along the rocks. At the base of the pot, in the shallow tray catching runoff water, more toy people waded, some fell face first. Quietly, students narrated, "This part took a long time," "Now we have to cross the river," "That part was scary." Stephanie's newcomers were reenacting their migration north.

Outside, in the sensory garden, social worker Sarah Howell had purposefully excluded cacti and other desert flora, worried that the prickly plants would trigger difficult memories. Now she reconsidered. As Sarah explained, "Just as some students play house, they were playing journey." She understood the value of play therapy. Banishing cacti from the garden wouldn't make her students' memories of the desert evaporate. Perhaps the plants could create opportunities to process the past. In the garden, Sarah, Stephanie, and the children began re-creating a tiny patch of desert.

Students at Las Americas carry with them much more than backpacks. What many of them have witnessed weighs heavy on their shoulders. Pain erupts, triggered by seemingly insignificant actions. For one student, a teacher switching off classroom lights to show slides brought back memories of a month that he was held captive in Mexico. For another, a stuffed elephant called to mind a stampede in his Nepali village. When a child showed up angry in Sarah's office, she knew that at his home food was scarce and could recognize that his classroom outburst might be entirely unrelated to school.

When Sarah had arrived at Las Americas in 2015, almost immediately she began recognizing the signs of invisible scars in the students. Yet there was little research on how to create schools that supported newcomer children who had experienced trauma. So Sarah set about creating her own. She trained teachers on trauma and began constructing a curriculum focused on processing the past and building a future. In circles, students compared holidays—Halloween to Día de los Muertos. They practiced greeting people of different ages; discussed how school expectations were similar to or different from back home; debated what it meant to be a good friend; and reflected on their journeys.

In a back room she helped to expand a school-based pantry—the Closet of Hope. Children who had insufficient food at home or needed warm clothing came there to meet with Lindsey Brook, the school's wraparound resource specialist, and to fill a bag. They carried with them notes from home: "We ask for help with food so we can feed our children, we are grateful for your help." Shelves were overloaded with rice, canned corn, canned pears, canned beans, coconut milk, baby formula, jars of peanut butter. The room also held boxes of shoes, folded khaki pants, and umbrellas; racks with puffy jackets, button-down shirts, and floral dresses; and collections of cleaning supplies, diapers, pads, and first-aid kits.

Sarah shares a tiny office suite with the assistant principal, Jennifer Can. Both trace their ancestry back two hundred years ago to what is today Texas. Sarah's family arrived from Europe and fought in the battles leading to Texas declaring independence from Mexico. Jennifer's family was Mexican until suddenly they were Texan after the dust of war had settled. Jennifer is also the granddaughter of Yucatecan Mayan and Louisianan people. Together they work to nurture students so they can send roots down into the land.

Before coming to the school, Jennifer was a teacher of immigrant-origin students for more than a decade, in education for more than two decades. Her teaching was recognized with awards. She is a proud grandma and self-described "mother hen," and at Las Americas she supports both staff and students. Jennifer sits with parents and prospective students in the main office seeking to understand their journey and the support they will need at Las Americas: the academic help a girl with minimal schooling might need in the classroom; the challenges a boy might be facing when reuniting with his parents. She sits in classrooms, observing and mentoring teachers.

She trains school staff to address discipline issues through a restorative justice approach, by which students take ownership when they act out and solve disagreements with classmates through guided conversations that acknowledge each other's perspectives. Like Sarah, she talks with children when they need her—two friends who got into a fight, a boy who had an argument with a teacher. She sits them down in purple cushioned chairs, "Tell me, *mijo, qué pasó?*"

She seeks to remind students of their potential with praise that is specific and intentional. For the rambunctious child who could barely sit still: "Thank you for sitting down when I asked you to"; for the homesick child: "I'm glad you showed up today." Tiny everyday reminders and affirmations. The school is, Jennifer recognizes, their students' first formative experience in the United States. "I want that experience to be as positive as possible so they have something good to take with them . . . to believe that something great can happen here."

Recently, a ten-year-old Honduran girl showed up in Jennifer's office sobbing yet unwilling to divulge what was wrong. Softly, Jennifer began asking questions. "Do you have a problem with a friend?" Jennifer asked. No. "Do you have a problem with a classmate?" No. "Do you have a problem with your teacher?" No. Question after question. After many minutes, the girl whispered, "I miss my grandma." Like so many of Las Americas's students, the girl had been raised by her *abuela* and *abuelo*. Here in the United States she was learning to live with her parents. Jennifer nodded. "I know your grandma misses you." Rising, she stretched out her arms. "You know," she confided, "I am a grandma, and I give great grandma hugs." She offered the girl a piece of paper to write a letter to home. After some time Jennifer asked, "How are you feeling?" The girl, face dry, looked up. "I think I'm ready to go back to class."

Between Jennifer's and Sarah's offices is a small space filled with couches for children, a space for difficult conversations. Since spring of 2018 it has been home to a white rabbit, which the students named after the Spanish word for snow. Nieve's arrival was prompted by a recently arrived fourteen-year-old boy who refused to attend class. A death in his family had left him with no interest in learning. "I want to go home. I want to farm," he confided in Sarah. Nieve became his reason to return day after day. Like the boy with his caterpillars, he was responsible for Nieve's care and safety.

Nieve soon acquired a gaggle of caregivers. In Sarah's therapy group for boys at risk of gang involvement, she watches children shed surly facades, cuddling Nieve and learning to gently kiss the top of the bunny's head. Nieve, hopping from child to child, creates openings for conversation. They discuss how scary it must be for Nieve to be in a new place. What was it like for Nieve to be separated from his mom? What was it like to be kept in a cage? Conversations children aren't ready to have about themselves, they can have about Nieve.

———◆———

In the fall of 2020—in the midst of the COVID-19 pandemic—the principal of the Jane Long Academy, a middle and high school located just across a parking lot from Las Americas, abruptly resigned. The Houston School District called Marie: Would she consider being joint principal of both schools? For Marie, the answer was obvious: Yes.

For close to two decades Marie had sought to build ties with other schools to help her students succeed beyond Las Americas. For most, she had only a year to teach them language and survival skills. She wanted them to know they continued to have allies, that they had rights, that they could advocate for themselves and their families. But she had no way to support them after they left her classrooms—and no way to know how they fared. Marie had reached out to nearby middle schools and high schools to devise strategies to ease the transition. But when principals retired or moved, she was forced to start from scratch.

By becoming principal of both schools, Marie herself could be the connector, because most of Las Americas' students went on to Jane Long Academy. She could help ensure that successful strategies implemented in one program carried over to the other, that teachers had opportunities to talk and observe each other's classes, and that knowledge about what worked best for a particular newcomer was not lost. In addition, Las Americas, still in temporary structures, suddenly had access to a library, a gym when the weather turned cold, and an auditorium for award ceremonies.

Then, in January 2021, Marie happened upon another way to foster connections between her two schools. The new year had barely begun when she received a text message from Luis, a student who had graduated from Las Americas more than a decade earlier. In 2007, twelve-year-old Luis had traveled by foot and by bus for twenty-four days from his grandparents' home in El Salvador to his parents in Houston. Years later, the screams of desert coyotes still reverberated in his mind. Luis had enrolled in Las Americas soon after the school moved. At dismissal, kids from Long Academy stared at and taunted the newcomers. But within the safety of Las Americas, Luis made friends quickly, and he gobbled up language with a ferocious appetite. He had gone on to become the first in his family to earn a high school diploma, an associate degree, and a bachelor's degree. One afternoon, while collecting his younger brother from soccer, Luis had spotted Marie outside Las Americas. Shyly, he greeted her. He was surprised by how excited she was to hear of his success. "Text me if I can help," she insisted. And so, amid the pandemic, Luis reached out to his first principal in the United States to ask if she would help him become a teacher.

In February, Luis was hired as a teacher's assistant for a special education class at Long Academy, the school whose students had stood on the sidewalk taunting him and his classmates. Just as Luis was set to start, snowstorms gripped Texas. Massive power failures plunged millions of homes and businesses into darkness and cold for days. Burst pipes closed Marie's schools for two weeks. At Las Americas, staff leapt into action, connecting families with resources. They called families: Do you have food? Do you have water? Do you have a way to get warm?

After the power came back on, Luis started as a teaching assistant and students returned to both schools. Outside, in the sensory garden, Sarah had worried that all their plants had frozen and died. Within weeks, though, new buds burst forth from the earth.

In March, another Las Americas alumnus returned to the school. Dante had enrolled at Las Americas in 2014. Until he came to Houston, school had been more than an hour's walk, up and down hills in central Guatemala. Dante still treasured a gift Marie had given him for the first birthday he celebrated in the United States: a picture book written in his native K'iche'. As her student, he had remembered that a Las Americas alumna had visited his class to speak about high school. Now, as a high school senior, Dante came to Marie with a question: Could he be the person who spoke with students that year about the future?

As plants stubbornly broke through the earth of Las Americas's gardens, Dante returned to his old classroom. He soon realized that one visit would not suffice. He began volunteering, helping out around the school, meeting with struggling students. He saw himself in the rambunctious thirteen-year-olds. "I came like you came," he told them. "I came as an immigrant, you came as an immigrant, you don't know English, I didn't know English. Who I am today," he confided, "is because of the teachers here." Dante is looking forward to graduating from high school, going to college. He dreams of one day returning to teach at Las Americas. Dante knows someday Marie, Maria, Sarah, Jennifer, and all the others will retire. He plans to be here when that happens, to carry on their work, doing for others what they did for him.

THE PERSONAL: SREY NETH

Srey Neth just wanted to be a "normal American teenager." And to be normal, she believed, she could not be considered an English learner (EL). Her friends were adamant: To succeed in the United States, she had to graduate from her school's EL program as quickly as possible and begin taking classes with the rest of the student body.

As a freshman at Lowell High School, Srey Neth tended toward shyness. Yet one morning she worked up the courage to ask a teacher to transfer out of EL classes. The woman considered her quizzically. "Oh . . . you might not get out of EL classes in high school." Srey Neth was stunned. "I was like *what*?! . . . I'm going to prove you wrong," she thought. Out loud she said nothing. From an early age she had learned not to openly question an educator. But to be an EL student, Srey Neth had discerned, was to fall behind. It meant you didn't want to succeed, didn't want to go to college. And Srey Neth was going to college. It was a goal that had propelled her halfway around the globe.

Srey Neth was born in the bustling capital of Cambodia, Phnom Penh, nestled in Southeast Asia. From the age of five Srey Neth had been preparing for life as an American, ever since her father moved to Massachusetts and told her someday she would join him. In anticipation, she filled her days with learning: Khmer government school from seven to noon, private Chinese school from one to five, and finally an hour of English at yet another institution. Weekends were devoted to computer classes. Education was expensive, but her father wired funds to help cover the cost. If Srey Neth excelled at Chinese, tuition was waived, and so semester after semester she fought for one of the top two slots. In addition, each day Srey Neth attended a thirty-minute midday session, commonly called a "cram school," a workaround strategy devised by chronically underpaid educators. There, in Srey Neth's words, for the equivalent of ten dollars a month, the public school instructor would teach content that was supposedly, but not actually, covered during official classes. The scheme was obligatory if you wanted good grades. To cover the costs, Srey Neth's mother worked long hours cleaning conference rooms. She promised herself that her children would get the education that had been stolen from her.

Srey Neth's mother was two, give or take, when guerrilla soldiers brazenly marched into Phnom Penh in April 1975. "The Americans are planning to bomb us," the militia bellowed. "Everyone out!" Srey Neth's family, like almost every family in the city of two million, hurriedly packed suitcases and took to the roads. Within days the militants, commonly called the Khmer Rouge, successfully emptied the capital—a ghost city, all too soon to be filled with ghosts.

Pol Pot, the fifty-year-old Marxist and leader of the Khmer Rouge, set out to erase centuries of history. 1975 was no longer 1975. It was Year Zero, the dawning of a new republic. There would be no money, no property, no religion. Your children were not your children—they were children of the Party. Children of Angkar.

Srey Neth's mother and her family, along with most of the country's roughly seven million inhabitants, were assigned to rural work camps. Before leaving, Srey Neth's maternal grandfather, a local police officer, shredded his uniform. Srey Neth's maternal grandmother carefully wrapped a small black photo album in cotton sarongs, tucking it into the depths of her bag. To own a uniform, to wear glasses, to be literate, all were signs of intellectualism, of elitism, of dangerous Western tendencies. Each put you at risk of being shot, or more often bludgeoned to death, since bullets were scarce. Srey Neth's father's father was a politician who favored well-pressed suits. At a checkpoint outside Phnom Penh, soldiers led him away. He was never seen again.

For more than three years, Pol Pot and his army starved, tortured, and worked to death the population of a country largely forgotten by the outside world. A genocide that swallowed more than 1.7 million souls. In the slaughter, Srey Neth would lose her great-grandfather, two grandfathers, fourteen great-uncles and -aunts, and dozens of other family members. Following liberation in 1979, Srey Neth's maternal grandmother, now widowed, returned to the capital, rail thin, gripping the hand of her six-year-old daughter. In her bag was a small battered album containing black-and-white photos of a mostly vanished family.

———•———

Unbeknownst to either Srey Neth or me, in 2013—while she juggled her many schools—I was just across town teaching college women. For many steamy months I taught lessons on leadership, women's rights, and genocide studies. Like Srey Neth, my students were the children of survivors. In a country where one in four had starved or been murdered, everyone had a story of trauma. The genocide remains abrasively palpable. Fields once used as mass graves still bloom, after heavy monsoons, with femurs, molars, the jigsaws of a cranium, frayed shirts, and children's flounced skirts. Beggars—blind, missing arms, missing legs—hobble along city streets. Cambodia has one of the highest rates of amputees in the world, the ramifications of a countryside seeded with landmines. Just over a mile south of Srey Neth's junior high school, and a mile north of where I taught, sat the wreckage of Tuol Sleng High School, for three years the site of the infamous S-21 prison. Roughly twenty thousand people, some barely out of infancy, were tortured and killed in the former school that is now a genocide museum. In English, the school's name means "hill of the poisonous trees." It was a place Srey Neth would only learn about years later in the United States. In her Cambodian schools the genocide was rarely spoken of.

Memories of the era mostly remain locked away in the minds of mothers and fathers, escaping in the form of nightmares or angry outbursts. Among survivors, Srey Neth's family is surprisingly open: Talking about the genocide was not taboo. And so she grew up with stories of starvation. While we lived less than fifteen minutes from each other by motorbike, I would not meet Srey Neth for another two and a half years, more than eight thousand miles away in my second-floor high school classroom in New England.

On the first day of high school in 2015, Srey Neth selected her seat in my class—front and center. She wore her mass of black hair down, so long it tickled the back of her thighs. At the outset, our freshman world history class consisted of eight students from a medley of countries: Iraq, Brazil, Nepal, Yemen, Sierra Leone, El Salvador, Cambodia. By December our class had swelled. By April we were bursting at the seams with twenty-eight students representing seventeen nationalities. Next to Srey Neth sat her best friend, also Khmer. They were my reliable duo, always ready with an answer, hands high. As often as they could, they partnered up, designing a PowerPoint on Mexican influences on US cuisine, writing essays on the internet's impact on global connectivity. When not working, the girls were forever giggling. By the second semester, Srey Neth was a regular at my unofficial lunch period, claiming a desk near mine.

When Srey Neth and her elder brother had left Cambodia, in the spring of 2014, she was just thirteen and she couldn't comprehend why her family was crying. While she understood she was moving to America, as she admitted to me years later, she did not fully grasp the gravity of the move. Naively, she remembered thinking that this was just another trip, like the time her family visited the ancient temples of Angkor Wat, or drove south to the famed Kampot pepper fields. "I'm coming back soon," she remembered thinking, frowning at her family's tears. "Why is everyone sad?" She was simply excited to travel. As the airport escalator carried her away from her mom and her aunts and her cousins, she beamed and waved.

Neither she nor her elder brother had ever traveled by airplane. From the in-flight entertainment system she selected *Frozen*, disregarding the lack of subtitles. Her English was minimal, but nevertheless Srey Neth watched Elsa, the ice queen, on repeat, again and again, and again, until at some point over the Pacific she fell asleep.

At Boston's Logan Airport the siblings were met by their father, who whisked them to nearby Chinatown for crab soup and congee before driving north to Lowell. The following weeks were a jumble of the new and the oddly familiar. Srey Neth tasted sushi, a delicacy her mother had always forbidden, and wandered through nearby forests, marveling at how close the woods were to Lowell. But she was astonished to find Cambodian people everywhere. Khmer grocery stores peddled prahok, the funky fermented fish paste. Khmer beauty parlors and Khmer restaurants lined the streets. There was even a Khmer temple. Perhaps Srey Neth had imagined the flight halfway around the world.

Two weeks after landing, Srey Neth woke early for her first day of seventh grade in the United States, her stomach queasy. She braced herself to be bullied. That was what happened in every American movie she watched. Despite the dread, she was also excited, like in her favorite Disney specials—she would be attending school with white people, or as she described them, "Americans." But when she arrived, a month before summer break, Srey Neth did a double take: her peers at her neighborhood middle school were almost entirely Khmer.

In Lowell, more than one in eight residents is Khmer.[21] Once a center of the industrial revolution that teemed with young immigrants from England and Ireland, the city is now home to the second-largest Cambodian population outside Cambodia. Four decades ago, in the months and years following the genocide, refugees stumbled across the Cambodian countryside, many finding their way to camps along the border of Thailand—tens of thousands, possibly more than a hundred thousand starved and haunted survivors. They joined a stream of displaced people fleeing the aftermath of a region ripped apart by wars—the largest humanitarian refugee crisis since the Holocaust. In response, in 1980 the United States, for the first time in its history, made a yearly commitment to welcome some of the world's displaced. By chance, some of the earliest arrivals were resettled in Lowell. In the former mill town along the Merrimack River, survivors began fashioning a new home. In the following decades more would follow. By the turn of the twenty-first century, the United States had welcomed roughly 150,000 Cambodian refugees.

———•———

Despite living in what was called America's Cambodia Town and going to a school that was predominantly Khmer, Srey Neth felt out of place. Starting school a month before summer break did not help, but she had no choice. Enrollment is linked to arrival, regardless of the month. Everyone already had friends, and no one seemed eager for late additions. She had expected to be bullied; instead she was simply ignored. She kept to herself at lunch, barely touching the flavorless tomato soup, a sad substitute for the symphony of flavors she was accustomed to.

Many of the mainstream students, those not in EL classes, were second-generation Khmer. However, most of them also wanted little to do with newcomers like Srey Neth. Even former EL students kept their distances. They had shed their label and, in the world of middle-school cliques, labels too often defined your social status.

Srey Neth's days were spent in a special class designed just for students new to the country, with an emphasis on language. Her math skills, though, were excellent, far surpassing those of her peers. For math she was placed, in her words, with "the normal kids." The first long-division worksheet she was handed was so easy that Srey Neth couldn't keep from laughing. She loved mathematics and was accustomed to more challenging calculations. But when she turned in her assignment, she recalled that her teacher seemed surprised that she could do the work. "She must expect little of me," Srey Neth realized. She held her tongue, never letting on that the weeks of lessons were, for her, merely review.

Desperately wanting to belong, Srey Neth reasoned that her limited English was her barrier. Like back home in Cambodia, she set about studying with a vengeance. She googled long lists of English words, listening on repeat to monotone recordings to practice pronunciation. Her most successful strategy, however, came from an unlikely source: Japanese anime. Srey Neth loved anime. She began watching dozens, hundreds of shows dubbed in English. With time, she started selecting shows only narrated in Japanese, as they had more exciting plotlines. She switched on English subtitles and learned to speed read.

The following school year, eighth grade, offered a fresh start. Slowly she found friends, other Khmer girls who, like her, had grown up half-way around the world. Lowell was a condensed Cambodia minus the humidity and profusion of fish sauce.

The months marched on. While much was similar, there were notable deviations, particularly in the classroom. Her new peers spoke up more, shot off answers rapid fire, questioned and countered teachers. The last time Srey Neth had attempted to openly challenge a teacher was in second grade, when she pointed out a teacher's miscalculation on a math problem. Her mother was promptly summoned and reprimanded for Srey Neth's gumption. Srey Neth learned to keep quiet. If the teacher relayed wrong information, you smiled and nodded. The first time her eighth-grade teacher in America admitted she didn't know an answer, Srey Neth was baffled. "I had been raised to believe that teachers know everything. I thought that if you don't know everything, then why are you a teacher?" It took time to adjust. "I realized only later that it was a good thing. My brain came to think of it as normal."

On entering Lowell High School, she found it filled with more new normals. Classes were interactive; teachers favored group projects. Peers acted differently, too. When her classmates dressed in low-cut shirts or extra-tight shorts, something that would have appalled her in Cambodia, she realized, startlingly, she was no longer fazed. "I'm too Americanized for my family," Srey Neth confessed. It was a gradual shift that crept up unannounced. When she had first arrived she struggled with homesickness—for her mom, for pepper fish stew and coconut-fried crickets, for family parties in the yard. "I lied to myself to keep from feeling lonely," she explained, refusing to acknowledge that it would be many years before she saw her mother again. Instead, she pretended she was on an extended vacation. But as semester followed semester, "I realized that there was no future for me in Cambodia." Here had become home.

———◆———

As a sophomore, Srey Neth continued joining me most days for lunch, as she had done as a freshman student in my world history class. That year my classroom had rarely been empty at lunchtime, children filling every desk. But now, shifted class schedules meant that few students had the same lunch period I did, and my room was oddly quiet. Srey Neth was one of a handful who came regularly. With so few students vying for attention, Srey Neth grew talkative—direct, spunky, and brimming with ambition. She told me of her growing up, of her favorite school clubs. But mostly she brainstormed ideas. Our school needed a self-defense class for girls, would I look over a draft proposal she had composed? Our city needed additional after-school programs for kids, could I help her compile a list? Idea upon idea. She started bringing me draft proposals to review and edit. October was barely upon us when she started asking me about coding.

One of Srey Neth's favorite anime shows featured a girl who transformed into a computer. Still feeling shy in large groups, Srey Neth dreamed of constructing computer companions. But she knew nothing about coding. One drizzly afternoon she sought me out. How, she asked, could she begin learning computer science? I knew hardly anything about the field, but I went home and started researching. At lunch I began handing over my computer, and Srey Neth began teaching herself the basics of if-statements and loops. At night, she stayed up late watching YouTube tutorials. Barely a few weeks had passed before she showed up excited. She typed in a link and handed my computer back to me. She had a constructed a ping-pong game for me to test.

———•———

One day, over lunch, Srey Neth started asking about college. At home it was a central discussion. Srey Neth's father, who had separated from her mother years earlier, now lived with a Cambodian woman who had come to America as a refugee child, after the genocide, and had attended school in California. For Srey Neth, her dad's partner stepped into the role of "American Mom," teaching her what she herself had learned as an immigrant student. She was adamant—good grades were insufficient. Srey Neth needed to be involved in clubs and community service to be competitive for college. At her urging, Srey Neth signed up for a medley of clubs and volunteer opportunities: chess club, cooking club, environmental club, outdoor adventure club, robotics club, the college-focused GEAR UP program, Khmer club, and, of course, anime club. She studied kung fu and archery and began volunteering at the local Cambodian Mutual Assistance Association, knocking on doors to encourage her compatriots to vote. She curated a tight matrix of extracurriculars that, paradoxically, felt freeing. "Cambodian parents don't want their kids hanging out," she said. "But I had an excuse." As long as she was at a structured activity, she wasn't required to be home, and home had become oddly uncomfortable. Growing up in Cambodia, Srey Neth had lived apart from her father for seven years. Now in America, she struggled to rebuild a relationship. "I'm not that close with him. He tries to be a dad, but it's really hard for me to connect."

Stories of immigration are often intertwined with stories of separation. One parent is typically the first to venture to distant lands. They leave with the plan of returning quickly or of earning enough money to soon send for their children. But "soon" often elongates. One year becomes two, which morphs to five, and sometimes ten. Migration math. Upwards of one in every three immigrant children has spent two or more years separated from a parent.[22] When families finally reunite, reunions are often rocky. After years of FaceTime and Facebook messages, suddenly families are face-to-face. But the toddler is now a teen. Where do you start in rebuilding, or in some cases, constructing a relationship? Parents feel their sacrifice, all the years lost, the missed moments: first steps, first day of school. But children often feel the years of absence. Reuniting with parents is often coupled with leaving behind other family members—grandparents, aunts, and uncles who have for years stepped into the role of surrogate moms and dads. Reunions are messy: There is joy, but also guilt; excitement, but often anger.

In a foreign city, in a faraway land, Srey Neth was relearning how to have a father. She found his strictness confining. She tired of hearing how easy her life was compared to his own growing up in the aftermath of genocide. At the dinner table she drew a blank at what to say. Despite the distance, Srey Neth talked most with her mother. On rambling three-hour video calls Srey Neth detailed her latest dreams, restaged dramas with friends, and regaled her mother with the silly side of school. In Phnom Penh, Srey Neth's mom had been actively a part of her schooling, speaking with teachers and checking up on classes. While she could no longer follow up in person, it was Srey Neth's mother who knew which teachers were frustrating and which were friendly, which classes were challenging and which came easy. It was not that her father wasn't interested. Srey Neth just didn't have the words to tell him. "I didn't want to bother him."

—————•—————

By the middle of sophomore year, Srey Neth had become more fluent in English than either her father or brother, and thus in school she became her own advocate. Her first task: Transition out of the EL program. In Srey Neth's mind EL classes were riddled with "if-statements." If she remained in EL classes, she would be less prepared for the state's standardized tests, required for graduation. If she failed to pass, she could not secure a high school diploma. If she remained an EL student, she wouldn't have access to the challenging content that would make her competitive for college. Srey Neth was not wrong to worry. I have found in years of helping students with their applications that colleges do not always accept EL classes as fulfilling high school requirements. They must be explained and excused.

As with learning English and coding, Srey Neth was dogged. By sophomore spring, she had left behind EL classes, and her schedule brimmed with honors courses. Naturally shy, in those first few months Srey Neth reverted in class to being all but silent. "I didn't have a good vocabulary when I spoke in front of people I didn't know. I didn't use sophisticated language." Her words invariably tangled in her throat. "What came out was very different from what was inside my head. I would think: 'That's not me!' But that's what happened in class."

Srey Neth listened to more Google Translate pronunciations, watched more subtitled anime. As much as she could, she spoke, wrote, and read solely in English. And as her English swelled, her Khmer shrank, as if competing for limited real estate in her brain. "I surround myself with everything English and forget anything else." Despite the crowds of Khmer around her, few at school seemed to value the language. By the start of junior year, Srey Neth was more likely to use Google Translate to look up a word in Khmer: "How did you say nurse again?" "What was the word for government?" She enrolled in advanced Khmer yet found little real-world relevance. "You have an American accent," her mother scolded. When her mom passed the phone to Srey Neth's grandmother the phone was handed right back, "I can't understand your daughter."

Granddaughter and grandmother resorted to texting. But even then, Srey Neth translated every message from English into Khmer before pressing Send. One afternoon, she and three friends made a pact: When together, they would speak solely Khmer. All three felt the pressure not to forget. Srey Neth giggles in her retelling. "We failed after a single day!"

———•———

Thinking ahead while worrying about falling behind, Srey Neth had taken to supplementing her classes with YouTube tutorials. Coding was not the only subject she taught herself. She supplemented most of her math and science classes with her own self-directed, out-of-class study. On Friday afternoons she organized library sessions with friends. The practice paid off: Junior year was a lineup of advanced courses. Although she had never formally been taught coding in school, she was accepted into AP computer programing, the most advanced computer science course on offer at Lowell High. Over lunches, eyes alight, Srey Neth started sketching for me a career as a computer scientist, or maybe an entrepreneur, or maybe a robotics engineer. Each day brought a new plan. By senior year, her schedule was packed tight with STEM, AP, and dual-enrollment courses—high school classes that provided college credit.

More confident and more comfortable with her own progress, Srey Neth began noticing a shift taking place around her. As she moved into increasingly rigorous courses, her classes began to bleach. In EL classes, her peers were every shade, hailing from dozens of countries. But by the time she got to AP, she was struck by the diminishing diversity. In dual-enrollment classes, the contrast was sharper. "Maybe it's because I've been through EL classes with many students of different ethnicities around me, and then gone into classes with none of them around me." For Srey Neth, it was a jarring discovery.

In the spring of her senior year, Srey Neth stood before a panel of judges. All throughout the fall we had stayed late in the school's computer lab working on college applications and exploring possible scholarships. Of those she had applied for, one, if awarded, would fully fund four years of college. She had applied with little expectation of progressing far in the rounds of interviews. But now, in April, she had been selected for the final-round interview. We had brainstormed over lunch:

What questions might they ask? What clubs, accomplishments, passions should she share? Nervously, I wished her good luck.

Alone she stood before the panel. What, they asked, were her ideas for improving Lowell High for future generations of students? Srey Neth paused. She took a breath and began at the beginning, starting with her first days in American schools. She told them about the times that she had felt teachers expected little of her and of her peers, about how that made her feel. She highlighted the shifting composition of her classes as she progressed from EL to honors, honors to AP, AP to dual-enrollment. She wondered aloud whether few had noticed these disparities because few had made the transition, during high school, all the way from EL to dual-enrollment classes. Srey Neth hoped to be a computer scientist but, as she told the judges, she also wanted to work with schools. She wanted all students to feel that much was expected of them. She wanted all students to be able, if they wished, to enroll in the most academically rigorous classes. Four years earlier she would never have dared to speak her mind so bluntly. But now, on the cusp of college, she had cultivated confidence. Fresh from her interview, Srey Neth marched proudly back to my classroom and proceeded breathlessly to describe her interview. She seemed a little taken aback by her own courage.

Less than a week later, Srey Neth raced into my classroom, bouncing up and down on the balls of her feet. Out of more than seven hundred seniors, Srey Neth was one of two to be selected for the scholarship. Giddy, Srey Neth grinned, "I'm going to college!"

CHAPTER 2

COMMUNITY

When it comes to making Americans, the old adage is right: It takes a village. Newly arrived students have left behind their neighborhood communities, faith communities, school communities. These losses often create a vacuum, a sense of loneliness. For many newcomers, schools are their first and most formative community. The more schools help them build connections and friendships, the more children will feel that here can be their new home.

This chapter tells three stories. The first is the story of a powerhouse of a woman who, at the end of the 1800s in one of Chicago's poorest neighborhoods, launched a neighborhood experiment to support the surrounding immigrant community, creating a model for community schools, neighborhood community centers, and the modern field of social work. The second is the story of five schools in Aurora, Colorado, that gained the autonomy to devise ways to support their immigrant-rich community by collaborating with community groups, neighboring businesses, the local hospital, and newcomer families. The third is the story of my own student Julian, who, after leaving his family and friends in the mountains of Medellín, Colombia, found community on a Massachusetts river among a crew team of almost all American-born students.

THE PAST: THE SETTLEMENT HOUSE MOVEMENT

On a summer evening in 1897, a thirty-six-year-old woman with gray eyes and a steady gaze took the stage in front of a hall of educators in downtown Milwaukee. She began her address to the National Education

Association, the nation's first teachers' union, with a caveat. As she readily admitted, she had never herself been a teacher. And yet for nearly a
decade she had worked closely with Chicago's immigrant youth, and, as
she detailed to the assembly arrayed before her, it was her firm belief that
public schools were failing newcomers.

The speaker was accustomed to controversy, and she would only
grow stronger willed in the years to come. Some called her a saint, others an anarchist. She was a pacifist, an activist, an author, and a social
worker before the profession existed. Friends were known to refer to her
as "Miss Kind Heart" and "Beloved Lady." A perturbed former president
Theodore Roosevelt nicknamed her "Bull Mouse,"[1] and the educational
heavyweight John Dewey christened his youngest daughter in her honor.
In a full-page spread, the *New York Times* titled her "The Tireless."[2] When
in a US Senate hearing a New York attorney, Archibald Stevenson, read
off sixty-two names of individuals he believed possessed "dangerous, de-
structive, and anarchistic sentiments," her name topped the list.[3] J. Edgar
Hoover classified her as "the most dangerous woman in America"; the
FBI opened a treason investigation and amassed a more than 160-page
FBI file on her. In its presentation of the Nobel Peace Prize, the first to
be presented to an American woman, the award committee saluted her
as a "mother" to many.[4] "My Dear Spinster" was the playful salutation
muckraking photojournalist Jacob Riis used in their correspondence,[5]
and in the sequel to his explosive *How the Other Half Lives,* he published
a tribute: "They have good sense in Chicago. Jane Addams is there."[6]
Her companion and likely romantic partner of thirty years, Mary Rozet
Smith, referred to her in letters simply as J.A.[7] In short, Jane Addams was
a woman to be reckoned with.

Addams might not have been a schoolteacher, but she was more familiar with the lives of her city's immigrant students than most educators could ever imagine. Living in the heart of one of Chicago's poorest
neighborhoods, Addams was a next-door neighbor to these children.
She befriended mothers and fathers, bounced neighborhood infants on
her knee, and helped wash and shroud the recently deceased. She had assisted in organizing English classes, citizenship classes, cooking classes,
art classes, and music lessons. She had cheered in the midst of crowds
as banners fluttered at a raucous Greek parade, and she had sat with
a family in their home, the table heavy with a Passover feast. On long

afternoons she watched children clamber over a newly installed seesaw, sandlot, and slide, all part of the first playground in the city. The dangers and demands of factory jobs that drew students from their desks were well known to her. She knew by name girls who staggered home exhausted after fourteen-hour stints at the candy factory, the boy who died after being sliced by a machine. There were the thirteen-year-olds employed at laundry houses, the twelve-year-olds who pasted labels, the boys ten and under deployed as messengers. Once Addams had even spotted a five-year-old tying off threads in a cotton mill.

It was this knowledge of the everyday lives and intimacies of immigrants that gave her the conviction to speak. Public schools, in Addams's experience, were not the community centers she believed they should be. But more troubling was that in seeking to fashion little Americans, schools were building walls between children and their parents, between children and their community, between children and their history.

Eight years earlier, in 1889, Addams and college classmate Ellen Gates Starr had opened a social experiment and named it Hull House. They moved into the second floor of a home in Chicago's 19th ward, a brick Victorian mansion fashioned with Corinthian columns that had been built by a millionaire who was recently deceased. In the three decades since Charles Hull had constructed his house in the suburbs, just blocks from the Chicago River, the neighborhood—and indeed the entire city—had become unrecognizable. The sleepy outpost on the swamps off Lake Michigan had been transformed into the hub of the Midwest, a metropolis second only to New York City, with a population that had grown tenfold in thirty years. Factories had sprouted like weeds: train car factories, meatpacking plants, cotton mills, glass factories, garment sweatshops, shipbuilding firms. Trains rumbled in from St. Louis, Cincinnati, Kansas City, Omaha, Detroit. With them came immigrants: Hungarians, Lithuanians, Bohemians, Slovaks, Greeks, Italians, Russians. By 1889, the year Addams and Starr opened Hull House, nearly 80 percent of Chicagoans were immigrants or the children of immigrants. Many newcomers found their way to the tightly packed tenements that now crowded a less than one-square-mile area of one of the Windy City's poorest neighborhoods, the 19th ward. For the next forty-six years, Addams would call it home.

Addams and Starr, both middle-class, college-educated women, modeled their Chicago initiative on the world's first settlement house, Toynbee Hall, opened five years earlier in the Whitechapel slums of London's East End. Dreamed up by a local vicar and a group of university graduates, the gothic hall was to act more like a bridge between cultures and classes. Young upper-class men would for a time "settle" at Toynbee to support local residents.

Addams and Starr drafted a charter in which they declared their intent "to provide a center for a higher civic and social life; to institute and maintain educational and philanthropic enterprises, and to investigate and improve the conditions in the industrial districts of Chicago."[8] Immigrant neighbors were unsurprisingly wary of the well-to-do interlopers, but the ward's children were less so. Thus, the first arrivals to Hull House were the children of newcomers to the country. Hull House opened a kindergarten that soon boasted a waiting list and assembled a boys' club that met weekly. Families soon followed. Addams and Starr started small; they listened, looked, and experimented. Never could they have guessed that their second-floor project would launch a national movement that would leave an indelible mark on the nation's schools.

———◆———

Public schools at the turn of the twentieth century were not to be trusted. That at least was the stance many recently arrived immigrant parents took. Southern Italian families, including many of the thousands that resided around Chicago's Hull House, were particularly skeptical of schooling. Education in the countryside of Sicily, Calabria, and Naples was largely conducted at home, and illiteracy rates trended high. For many, formal schooling carried little relevance or worth for a lifetime to be spent farming under the Mediterranean sun. In the United States, school was looked upon with wariness if not downright suspicion. Italian parents, and many other new arrivals, quickly grew wise to the efforts of US teachers with their pointed curriculum bent on Americanizing their offspring. Schools might claim they taught math and reading, but many immigrant parents believed there was a subtler agenda: lessons in materialism, atheism, immorality, and a wholesale disrespect for family and culture. It was a strategy New York Italian educator Leonard Covello affirmed in his memoir: "We were becoming Americans by learning how to be ashamed of our parents."[9]

Thus many parents came to believe that the less time children spent in US public schools, the better off they would be. Children were often encouraged to drop out early and find work to support the family. At the turn of the century roughly half of all ten- to twelve-year-olds in the city were employed, and immigrant children were five times more likely to be wage earners than their American-born peers.

If they had a choice, many parents preferred parochial schools—small institutions whose classes were held in basements and church halls. Such schools evoked the old country, in language, history, and faith. But even if parents had wanted to send their little ones to the public institutions, in Chicago, like in other major cities, there simply wasn't enough room. An 1896 study conducted by Hull House residents and volunteers reported that the public schools of Ward 19 were woefully unprepared to accommodate the sheer volume of children; the system was short by upwards of three thousand seats.

Such deep-seated parental distrust was not lost on Jane Addams. Speaking once more to the teachers' union, just over a decade after the Milwaukee meeting, Addams was not nearly as self-effacing. In a newly opened Cleveland theater, sandwiched between sessions led by Booker T. Washington and William Maxwell, the New York City superintendent, Addams delivered an indictment: "The public school too often separates the child from his parents and widens that old gulf between fathers and sons which is never so cruel and so wide as it is between the immigrants who come to this country and their children who have gone to the public school and feel that they have there learned it all."[10] Giving voice to the worries of her Italian, Polish, Greek, and Russian neighbors, Addams accused schools of driving a wedge between generations. But it was not just family cohesion that was at risk. Schools' Americanization efforts, Addams explained, were, in actuality, self-defeating. In their hurry to have students shrug off their foreignness, she believed, schools cut them off from role models whose guidance was essential in preventing children from slipping into delinquency and ensuring they were prepared to start a life, raise a family, and contribute productively. By unmooring children from their parents and communities, schools stripped away the discipline, stability, and grounding that families provided young people and sent them, "without a sufficient rudder and power of self-direction, into the perilous business of living."[11] In Jane Addams's estimation, schools were failing to make the Americans that the country needed.

At the time, in 1908, Addams's twentieth anniversary at Hull House was fast approaching, and much had happened in the two decades bookending the turn of the century. In the year Hull House opened, it was one of two settlement houses operating in the country. But the idea sent seeds far afield. By 1895, more than sixty settlement houses had opened in fourteen states, including the Education Alliance that Julia Richman had helped lead in New York. Six years later that number had doubled, the idea taking root as far north as the mill city of Lewiston, Maine, down to the outskirts of the French Quarter in New Orleans, and all the way across the ocean to the annexed islands of Hawaii. By 1910 more than four hundred settlement houses would open their doors in thirty-two states, including six in the country's Capital. Many looked to Chicago's Hull House as the model to emulate.

It was a movement tied to the times—a convergence of simultaneous transformation. Cities were transforming under the weight of industry, demographics were transforming with the influx of steamships, and so too were ambitions transforming for some women, who, having become the first generation to secure a college education, now sought outlets for their intellect. While Toynbee Hall and others of its ilk in England were often overseen by men, the settlement houses of America were, by 1911, run and operated primarily by women. They offered some women a rare opportunity to lead independent lives, to innovate, and to profoundly impact communities.

Hull House was never a one-woman affair, as Addams reiterated frequently. From the outset it was a collaboration of formidable women who came to live and work alongside Chicago's immigrant community. Over twenty years Hull House had grown not just in national influence but also in local impact. What began on the second floor of a Victorian mansion had swelled to consume much of a city block, spilling throughout thirteen buildings. At its height, Hull House boasted a library, a kitchen, a coffeehouse, a dining room, a gymnasium, a theater, a museum, an art studio, a pottery kiln, a playground, schoolrooms, meeting halls, and apartments for residents who came to "settle" for a time in the 19th ward. In the first decade of the twentieth century, the buildings and programs of Hull House saw upwards of ten thousand visitors weekly. They came for the children's nursery and kindergarten, for the myriad of classes and clubs, for lectures by university professors and meetings of labor unionists.

Hull House and similar settlements considered themselves not to be charities, but community institutions that complemented organizations immigrant communities had established for themselves. Rather than prescribe solutions, a common tactic of the time, they continuously adapted their work to support neighborhood needs. What a settlement house must never do, Addams warned, was "lose its flexibility, its power of quick adaptation, its readiness to change its methods as its environment may demand."[12] Like fingerprints, no two settlement houses were alike. But at their core, said Addams, was mutual respect and collaboration. As one Italian woman recalled, the residents of Hull House "treated us on an equal basis."[13]

Perhaps this was why Addams could see in the city's youngest newcomers what many educators missed. "Schools ought to do more to connect these children with the best things of the past," Addams argued. "To make them realize something of the beauty and charm of the language, the history, and the traditions which their parents represent." Teachers, she believed, needed to appreciate children for what they brought and work not to erase but to augment it. "It is easy to cut them loose from their parents," she chided educators. "It requires cultivation to tie them up in sympathy and understanding. The ignorant teacher cuts them off because he himself cannot understand the situation, the cultivated teacher fastens them because his own mind is open to the charm and beauty of that old-country life."[14]

In Chicago, perhaps no initiative better illustrated Jane Addams's respect for immigrants or her approach to educating their children than the Labor Museum she created at the turn of the twentieth century, which showcased industry carried from the old country. At its opening, the museum featured the art and craft of spinning. It featured Italian spindles, Russian spindles, Greek spindles, Syrian spindles. There were spinning wheels, looms, and a growing collection of textiles. In later years the museum expanded to include exhibits in metalwork, woodwork, bookbinding, basketmaking, pottery, and millinery. Every Saturday neighborhood women came not as students but as teachers, showcasing skills passed down through generations. These were skills that some believed public schools, bent on rigid Anglo-Saxon-style Americanization, taught immigrant students to scorn.

As Addams understood, immigration was perhaps hardest on parents. Coming often from distant countrysides to the urban jungles of America, newcomers found that few of their skills or occupations transferred easily or retained their value. Respected artisans now shoveled coal. Skills in dressmaking were deemed obsolete. The language of business and law was foreign, and once close-knit communities were dispersed. But possibly most challenging for parents was to watch their children navigate the new world with more authority and ease than themselves. At the Labor Museum, Hull House attempted to even the scales. Addams would often tell the story of an Italian girl by the name of Angelina, who, so embarrassed by her homely mother, would enter Hull House through a different door. Until, one Saturday, Angelina found her mother presenting the art of spinning to visitors from the University of Chicago. "It was easy to see," Addams described, "that the thought of her mother with any other background than that of the tenement was new to Angelina." As a result, the little girl "allowed her mother to pull out of the big box under the bed the beautiful homespun garments which had been previously hidden away as uncouth; and she openly came into the Labor Museum by the same door as did her mother."[15]

With so many young people employed in nearby factories, Hull House strove to draw a direct connection between the work of children and the skills of parents. It was a subtle shift in power. About the museum, Addams said, "We prize it, because it so often puts the immigrants into the position of teachers, and we imagine that it affords them a pleasant change from the tutelage in which all Americans, including their own children, are so apt to hold them."[16] Although only ever a few rooms in one building in one city, Addams spoke often of the Labor Museum on national tours, and in this way, the museum's distinctive educational approach had an outsized impact.

Hull House recognized that life outside the classroom profoundly affected students' success in the classroom. Thus, in addition to the daily classes and programs, 19th ward residents set about researching and

advocating for policy reform. Hull House became a blueprint for community schools, neighborhood centers, and school wrap-around supports
devised decades later. Residents conducted extensive neighborhood studies in demographics, poverty, education, working conditions, and disease. They documented the cramped conditions of tenement apartments,
where families of five shared two or three rooms and where neighbors
were sometimes separated solely by walls of cardboard. They traipsed after early morning garbage collectors, as part of an ultimately successful
campaign to ensure the city kept streets clean. They interviewed, surveyed, published meticulous reports, and campaigned for legislative reform. Their perseverance paid off. With help from Hull House advocacy,
the city's first public baths were installed in the 19th ward in 1894. Five
years later the world's first juvenile court system opened, directly across
the street from Hull House. Until then, children as young as ten had been
tried in adult courts. An army of Hull House organizers was behind the
creation of the Federal Children's Bureau in 1912, the first government
agency in the world dedicated to the well-being of young people. The bureau's first director was a longtime Hull House resident. Her successor,
Grace Abbott, was as well. Partly as a result of their leadership, national
child labor laws were enacted. Over the decades, Hull House had a hand
in laws reforming workplace safety, workers' compensation, minimum
wage, women's suffrage, and compulsory education.

While addressing much that affected children outside of school, Hull
House also angled to change what went on within the classroom. "When
the little Chicago Italian goes to school on Garibaldi's birthday and is
anxious to tell about the great statesman whom his parents reverence,"
Addams began in an article for the *American Education* magazine, "the
teacher is just as likely to tell him that Garibaldi was not an American,
and instead of letting the boy tell his story he is told of George Washington, and that the boy is an American now."[17] Here was an exchange littered with missed opportunities. The Italian learned that his family and
their history was of little worth. But so too were the boy's peers deprived
of their classmate's expertise. "We send young people to Europe to see
Italy, but we do not utilize Italy when it lies about the schoolhouse," Addams wrote.[18] Hers was an attitude rarely shared at the time, a recognition
that immigrants had much to offer America. If, Addams argued, schools
welcomed newcomers for "the resources which they represent and the

contributions which they bring,"[19] immigrant-rich schools would come to find that the expertise children brought would lead neighboring institutions to regard them not with pity, but with envy. What teachers needed was education in and appreciation for their students' heritage, and what schools needed were curricula that highlighted and honored a more expansive history.

━━●━━

While the Hull House organizers recognized immigrants' strengths, they still favored the eventual assimilation of newcomers. They opposed parochial bilingual programs, arguing that they isolated rather than integrated immigrants. They regarded learning English as necessary for advancement and acceptance. They sought to Americanize their immigrant neighbors. But their aim and approach were different than most. Schools should devote "time and thought" to the "working out of methods that will 'educate' the immigrant children along American lines," wrote former Hull House resident Grace Abbott, "and at the same time will not destroy the traditions round which the family life has been built."[20] For these progressive Chicagoans, valuing diverse histories and contributions was not antithetical to ensuring American patriotism. Rather, America was America precisely because of the contributions of people from across the globe.

It was a belief held by a rapidly dwindling minority at the beginning of a new century, and not even by all settlement house leaders across the country. Notably, the founder of Boston's South End House was himself a member of the notorious Immigration Restriction League (IRL), an organization founded by young Harvard University graduates in 1894. Theirs was a mission diametrically opposed to the beliefs of Addams and others at Hull House. Their attitude toward the recent immigrants flocking to the country's settlement houses was perhaps best encapsulated by Francis Walker, a Civil War veteran, economist, former director of the US Census, and, at the time, president of the Massachusetts Institute of Technology. Writing in the *Atlantic*, Walker described his fellow IRL members' views of new arrivals: "They are beaten men from beaten races."[21]

As if in direct opposition, Grace Abbott opened the Immigrants' Protective League at Hull House in 1908, with the goal of assisting immigrants' transition to Chicago and their new life. But the Great War, ignited in 1914, brought with it a surge in nativism. And the dogged determination and ceaseless campaigning of the IRL soon bore fruit. In 1917, for the first time in the nation's history, the United States imposed sweeping restrictions to general immigration, with Congress overriding President Wilson's veto. The law established a literacy test: Hopeful immigrants over the age of sixteen would be able to enter only if they could read, although illiterate women were allowed if accompanied by literate husbands or adult sons. Erected, too, was a sweeping zone of exclusion, which almost entirely barred those from much of Asia, stretching from the mountains of Afghanistan to the islands of Indonesia to the windy steppes of Mongolia.

Three years later, Addams warned a conference of social workers in the heat of a New Orleans spring: "We are falling back into the old habit of judging men, not by their individual merits or capacities, but that we are thrusting them back into the old categories of race and religion." Immigrants today were like immigrants who came generations before. They were, Addams reminded her audience, "surprisingly like the rest of us. They come with great hopes and work hard to secure a better future for their children." They were drawn to America, she said, for what it represented in the world, "a land of freedom and equality," an ideal the country now seemed bent on eroding. She closed her address with a plea: "re-assure your [immigrant] neighbors as best you may. Tell them that this day will pass, that America will again come to regard them as simple friends and neighbors."[22] But in the early 1920s America's gates were closing, and the day Addams spoke of, when US law would once more open them in welcome, would not come for forty-five years.

THE PRESENT: AURORA ACTION ZONE, COLORADO

Five parents huddled around a collection of laptops in a community center in Aurora, Colorado. All had children enrolled at the same elementary school a few blocks away, and all were recently arrived Bhutanese refugees. All, too, were wearing face masks.

It was spring of 2021, and the Colorado counties that bisected Aurora were among those most severely affected in the state by COVID-19. A year earlier, schools in Colorado, like schools across the country, had shut their doors as a then-novel virus began ravaging neighborhoods.

Living rooms, bedrooms, and kitchens were rapidly transformed into classrooms as learning moved online. Schools scrambled to engage families, particularly of elementary school children, as vital partners to ensure that the virtual classrooms succeeded.

But many Bhutanese parents of the Aurora elementary school faced a special challenge in supporting their children's pandemic education. Before arriving in America, most had lived for years in Nepali refugee camps with minimal access to technology. Few felt confident using computers: How to send an email? How to log into the school's online system to check their children's grades or attendance? How to join a Zoom meeting? Even, how to power up a laptop?

Yet the families belonged to an unusual school community—part of a collaboration among five schools in a single zip code: the Aurora Community-Based Transformation, Innovation and Opportunity Network, or simply the ACTION Zone. Snug within a two-mile area were two elementary schools, one pre-K through eighth grade school, one joint middle and high school, and one high school. Of the ACTION Zone's more than 4,000 students, roughly 75 percent were classified as English learners, and they collectively spoke more than 180 languages. One in seven was a recently arrived refugee. In the hope of raising stalled student achievement, in 2016 the Zone had been granted the opportunity to experiment with school structures, curriculum, and hiring. Key to the plan was the decision to invest deeply in partnering with families and the surrounding community.

Long before the first case of COVID-19 appeared, Asbi Mizer had been meeting monthly with Bhutanese families to discuss their children's educational futures. As a child, Asbi had fled Bhutan for Nepal, eventually resettling in the United States after nearly two decades of displacement. For years, Asbi had helped fellow refugees navigate America's complicated systems: health care, naturalization, food assistance, housing assistance, education. Working with the ACTION Zone, he had begun facilitating meetings of Bhutanese families. He created spaces for them to talk—in Nepali, the language they grew up speaking in southern Bhutan—about their children's education, ideas for school improvements, and ways to implement them. It was in these meetings that, in the midst of the pandemic, the families began to admit to each other they felt ill-equipped to support their children's virtual learning. Discussions begat brainstorming. What if, they asked one another, they created their own community-run digital literacy classes?

That spring, Bhutanese families and students gathered with Asbi, wearing masks and bearing laptops. Those with computer skills paired off with novices. One on one, the experts demonstrated how to accomplish a task. They then shifted the laptop to face their partner. In Nepali, they invited, "Now it is your turn to practice."

———•———

When Kate Garvin approached Aurora Central High School in the fall of 2012 about providing support to refugee students, the best the school could offer her was thirty minutes in the library with students after school. By 4 p.m. everyone had to leave the building—that was when the school closed for the day.

An Aurora native, Kate had recently returned, after thirteen years away, to take a job with Lutheran Family Services, one of the country's largest refugee resettlement organizations. She was put in charge of creating a program, supported by a federal grant, to support the academic success and mental health of refugee teenagers and to foster collaborations with their families. Kate had hoped to design a school-day program at Aurora Central High, but the after-school slot was all she was given. She soon found, though, that many of the school's refugee students couldn't stay after school: Some were responsible for picking up younger siblings, others held jobs. Those who could stay missed the school buses, which left immediately after dismissal, and had to find their own way home. Kate knew that many recent immigrant and refugee families lived two miles to the northwest. She began looking for a tutoring space closer to their home.

The Aurora of Kate's childhood was barely recognizable compared to the Aurora in which she now worked. As a kid, she had chafed at the homogeneity of the predominantly white city. Eager to leave home, Kate joined the Peace Corps after college in 2004, accepting a post in remote Turkmenistan. It was there, living near Afghan refugee families, that Kate first witnessed the impact of forced migration, particularly on education. When she returned to Aurora, Kate was shocked to find it transformed by the repercussions of global wars and national immigration policy. The city had become a home to Bhutanese, Burmese, Somali, Salvadorian, and Honduran immigrants. Roughly one in six residents had been born outside the United States.[23]

It was in this newly global neighborhood that Kate searched for a room to offer academic tutoring. But there were no public gathering spaces or community centers. The dozens of nonprofits that worked with the community's newcomers had offices located miles away, and they struggled with transporting children and families from the community to access services.

Kate realized there was a solution sitting right in the heart of the neighborhood: Crawford Elementary School. It was a public building, paid for by the community, that sat empty every afternoon and evening. "Public schools," Kate firmly believed, "should be public spaces."

Like the city, Crawford Elementary had undergone a metamorphosis: Close to 80 percent of its students were now classified as English learners; one in four was a refugee. Kate approached Crawford's principal. Could the school be opened after-hours, Kate asked, for refugee families in the neighborhood? The principal loved the idea. But, she explained, she lacked the authority to make the decision. So the two women hatched a plan.

Kate set about surveying more than a hundred local organizations: Would they be interested in using the space? And, she conducted neighborhood conversations with immigrant families: What services and support did the community desire? Meanwhile, the principal began seeking the district's permission to start a pilot program.

The district gave the green light to start in March 2013. If five hundred people used the after-hours programs over the next three months, the district would deem the pilot a success. In the afternoons and evenings, Crawford Elementary transformed into a multigenerational community center open to all—immigrant and refugee students, but also Somali aunts, Nepali cousins, Mexican grandfathers. Kate invited tutoring programs for refugee students, legal panels speaking about immigration reform, coordinators helping families with Supplemental Nutritional Assistance Program (SNAP) applications. There was a Bhutanese town hall meeting and a Nepali CPR training course. When Kate typed up her report on June 1, she was beaming: 1,501 community members had made the space theirs.

Over the next three years, the Crawford Community Center grew, averaging 250 in nightly attendance. The school became home to soccer programs, family literacy evenings, faith meetings, art clubs, science clubs, boys' and girls' clubs, Spanish classes, mentoring programs for refugee girls. There were city meetings, Diwali celebrations, citizenship classes, tutoring, Zumba.

Despite the crowds, the community center's existence was precarious, coming close to being shuttered each spring by school budget cuts. The first year, a local pastor galvanized the city council to intervene with the school superintendent. The next year, with the center once more on the chopping block, teachers spoke up. Although the school and the center were separate entities, educators were beginning to notice a difference in their classrooms. When a recently arrived child came to school without a backpack or a winter coat, teachers who had previously sought out friends for donations or dipped into their own funds now could go to Kate, who had amassed a small collection of donations. More immigrant families were attending school events. The center, which had begun running trainings for teachers, helped them better understand their newest pupils. They could no longer imagine the school without the Crawford Community Center.

In the fall of 2015, Jennifer Passchier, who had taken over as principal of Crawford two years earlier, approached Kate with an idea. For years the school had been struggling with academic performance; student test scores limped behind the state average. Instead of implementing small tweaks, Crawford had decided to embark on an ambitious plan of re-imagining the school. She proposed that the community center, which had been distinct from the school—coming to life only from 3 p.m. to 7 p.m.—become a central pillar of the school, from early morning to evening.

———•———

In the state of Colorado, underperforming public schools have four options: close, become a charter school, relinquish control to external educational consultants, or, since a 2008 law went into effect, apply for "innovation status." It was this last alternative that five schools in Aurora opted to try in the spring of 2015. All sat in the same zip code, all served the same families, all were struggling. One of the five was Crawford Elementary. Together they proposed to form an innovation zone—a collaboration linked by common goals, approaches, and families.

To be approved, each of the five would need to present an extensive, school-specific plan—first to their school staff, then to the district, and finally to the state board of education—illustrating how it proposed to reimagine the school and achieve student success. If the plans passed muster, the schools could seek waivers that would allow them greater freedom in allocating their budgets, selecting staff, designing curriculum, and rethinking school structures. In exchange they would agree to more rigorous and more frequent assessment of their progress. While each school's plan would be unique, the five programs were based on four shared pillars, with one being a commitment to partnering with families and communities. In a nod to the global origins of their students, the schools chose as their joint insignia a rainbow globe embraced by five stars, one for each school, and topped with a mortarboard. In the spring of 2016, the ACTION Zone was approved.

That fall Kate faced a daunting but exciting task: The community center would no longer exist as a discrete after-hours program but as an integral part of Crawford Elementary from sunup to sundown. To succeed, Kate believed it would be essential to build community trust. Many schools, she recognized, did not listen to families, particularly immigrant families. In many small ways—staff not trained about the cultures of the children they taught, communications not translated—schools signaled that families were not welcome.

Kate launched a new approach to engage families at Crawford. She wanted to tap into parents' expertise, give them the chance to be leaders in the school, and build networks among families. As part of her plan she organized four groups of families—speakers of Nepali, Spanish, Somali, and several languages spoken in Myanmar. The groups would meet monthly to tackle school and community challenges they cared most about. She christened these ACTION Zone teams Parents in ACTION (PIA).

Among the inaugural PIA groups, it was the school's Somali families who were the most skeptical. Even so, a few agreed to meet. Together the families named a common barrier to their children's success—Islamophobia at the school. From the monthly discussions emerged a proposal: Invite a locally respected imam to speak with each grade, to share cultural knowledge about the Somali community. Over two days that spring, the imam spoke with small assemblies of students. He didn't talk about Islam, but rather about the traditions of his own community and the value of understanding different communities. That afternoon a number of teachers marched into the principal's office. Why, they asked, had she allowed such a person into their school? Worried, the principal consulted Kate. Here, Kate explained, was an example of the Islamophobia the Somali parents had spoken of. As Kate shared with me, "If you are looking at a community leader that way, how are you looking at a child in your classroom?" The school had a choice: Address the issue head-on, or risk further eroding trust with families. Square-shouldered, the principal chose to speak candidly with staff members about the situation. She also began attending PIA meetings to listen and to learn. Within months, members of the Somali PIA were sitting in conversation with teachers, speaking with them about their country, about conflict, about culture.

At the start of the next school year, in 2017, Somali families sought out Kate, eager to schedule their first PIA meeting. That year they joined forces with the Nepali PIA, to successfully advocate for the inclusion of dal and rice.

Trust germinated in the PIA meetings. It grew, too, in an after-school program Kate helped create, where immigrant children and their families interviewed each other about their experiences growing up. From their conversations, families created hand-drawn multilingual picture books that they shared at school assemblies and staff trainings. One teacher recalled reading a story written by a young Bhutanese boy in her classroom, in which she learned that his father, halfway around the world, had been a scholar and a poet. Many of the parents who wrote stories with their children soon after began attending PIA meetings.

Crawford was blooming into a community school. The approach, which was also being adopted in other schools across the country, had its roots in Jane Addams's Settlement House Movement, founded on the belief that everyone in a community had something to learn and to teach, to give and to receive.

As Crawford flourished, other organizations began partnering with it. A university program aimed at providing trauma support for refugee women found it couldn't convince the women to come to its campus, but they felt comfortable at Crawford. An obesity prevention program that relocated to Crawford significantly increased the retention of participants and was able to track outcomes over time. The nearby children's hospital sought out PIA groups for focus group interviews, to more richly understand the health needs of specific immigrant communities.

When budget cuts threatened Crawford yet again, in the spring of 2018, Kate—instead of offering up a plan to downsize—threw out a wild pitch: What if Crawford helped to replicate the community-school approach across the entire ACTION Zone? Each of the Zone's five schools had taken a different approach to engaging families and communities. Most had been only modestly successful. Kate and Crawford's principal approached the Zone's executive director with the proposal. Two months later, Kate was named the Zone's director of family advocacy and community engagement. Her task: work with Paris Elementary, Boston Elementary, Aurora Central High, and Aurora West College Preparatory to nurture four new community schools. Kate set about writing grants, drafting curricula, and devising strategies to scale up.

The following spring, Kate began hiring community school coordinators and family advocates at the five Zone schools, to build partnerships among teachers, families, and local organizations. Heading into the fall semester of the new school year, Kate was exhilarated. She had a team and a goal—she was ebullient about the possibilities. Four months later, halfway around the world in Wuhan, China, patients began filling city hospitals, infected with a new and troubling virus.

———◆———

On March 16, 2020, Aurora students left school for spring break. They did not know it, but it would be months before they would return. In Colorado, COVID-19 was spreading like wildfire. A week later, on the day ACTION Zone students should have returned to the classroom, Colorado's governor ordered schools shut statewide.

Kate's new staff, like many around them, were battered by anxiety and uncertainty; they felt unmoored. "We had lost our community hub," Kate explained. People had been drawn together by the buildings, the public spaces. Now the staff sat at home, forlorn. How could they continue the work of community schools in the absence of meeting places?

Funders and nonprofits—community partners cultivated over years—started calling, emailing, texting: What do families need? How can we help? Kate's team didn't know. But they quickly realized: Even if families could no longer come to community schools, the schools could come, virtually, to families.

The ACTION Zone had many staff who were suddenly without work—teaching assistants, office clerks, campus monitors, academic deans. Could they be redeployed to check in with families, ask how they were doing, assess what support was needed? Kate drafted new job descriptions for school coordinators. Her colleague B Lewis compiled detailed spreadsheets to track families' information. They ran staff trainings, sent out lists of students, and then took to the phones. For many of the staff, it was the first time they had ever spoken with families of students.

In the first month, staff spoke with upwards of 1,800 families, more than half of all families in the Zone. The conversations uncovered individual needs and, together, laid bare systemic challenges and inequalities. Hundreds of families were without internet, leaving children unable to access online learning. Many faced eviction or food shortages. Parents had been laid off or were struggling to access medical care. With data in hand, Kate's team could turn back to the partner organizations that had offered help: We need this many internet hotspots, that many laptops. The community school team had become essential connectors—trusted by nonprofits and businesses, by educators, and by a growing number of families. The ACTION Zone team spent hours updating an ever-changing list of nonprofits, noting those that had been forced to close, others that were now offering rent assistance or distributing food. They worked with the Aurora Children's Hospital to set up a distribution system for fresh food and began handing out more than a thousand heavy boxes each week, stuffed with onions, cucumbers, tomatoes, melons. Kate secured grant funding to hire Asbi and a team of three other family advocates— Ka Paw Htoo, Georgette Kapuku Mabi, and Luis Rico, who collectively spoke Burmese, Karen, Swahili, French, Spanish, and Nepali—to help the schools communicate effectively with immigrant-origin families.

As April turned to May, the staff continued making calls. When they learned that some families couldn't use the hotspots they had received because they lived in dead zones for the internet provider, Kate's team sought out hotspots from a range of providers. Undocumented families were wary of picking up food outside schools because, in the days just before the school closures, ICE had detained a mother waiting to pick up her kids at a nearby school. The staff decided to switch food distribution sites each week, and they hand-delivered food to the doorsteps of some families.

Over two months, Zone staff had more than 3,600 conversations with families, helped more than 200 families apply for rent assistance, and connected nearly 700 families to resources. They made referrals to doctors and mental health providers; they connected families with organizations that could help pay for heating and electricity bills; they distributed donations of gift cards to local retail stores. One evening, staff at one school dialed a nearby pizza shop to order a pie for a family with a father sick with COVID.

The fall semester opened amid continued uncertainty and climbing COVID cases. The Zone schools ping-ponged between remote learning, in-person learning, and a hybrid of the two. As community schools teams pressed on, many people began to notice how their work was slowly changing the community.

Maggie Karr, a family advocate and Karen refugee, watched older, often shy members of her community gain confidence. Ka Paw shared with fellow Burmese families her personal stories of being a teacher in Myanmar, a teacher trainer in Thailand, and a parent in Aurora. She noticed how other parents began engaging more in their children's academics. Kate watched more and more organizations, nonprofits, and community partners join monthly meetings. Michael Abdale, Crawford's principal since 2018, noticed changes in himself. "I used to be a very cut-and-dry principal," he confided to me. As he began reading the books written by the families and children, he learned about the conflicts they had fled and the cultures they carried with them. To help each student, he came to realize, he must understand their story, their history. He began brainstorming with Kate's team about new ways to partner with more families. He made a point of being present in the halls, in the streets, in the community. "This school changed my whole practice," he reflected. "I'm a better listener now, I have more empathy. . . . It's made me a better principal."

Pete Medina, the Zone's newest community school coordinator, saw the transformation over months as families began to trust him. He saw Bhutanese families in his school's Nepali PIA, who, once hesitant to question the school, were now speaking up. In online meetings, they noted that the school's communications were often baffling. They asked him: What did ELD or ALD mean? What about ESS, MTSS, PBIS, BIP, ADD, ADHD, CMAS, GT, GE, GPA, IEP, LRE? Families needed translations not only into Nepali, but out of school lingo. On one call, a parent asked tentatively about how to navigate Google Meet. Before Pete could respond, a tech-savvy mom offered to teach her. When the mom herself admitted she wasn't comfortable with the school's online "Parent Portal," a dad said he could help. The exchanges led to the meeting where families bearing laptops gathered at a local community center.

———◆———

On the morning of August 19, 2021, Kate woke up nervous. The fall semester had started the week before. Now, for the first time in more than seventeen months, the ACTION Zone would be gathering indoors and in person. Families, community members, nonprofit organizers, and educators would be meeting to kick off Parents in Action for the new school year. They'd pay tribute to the efforts of the unprecedented past year and plan the work ahead.

Breakfast burritos were set out. Tables were festooned with pens, nametags, sticky notes. Signs designated tables for speakers of specific languages: Nepali, Spanish, Swahili, French, Karen, Burmese. Sheets of chart paper were posted around the room, waiting to be filled with families' answers to questions: What lessons could be gleaned from a year of education amid a pandemic? What had the schools accomplished with respect to the health and wellness of children, educational opportunities, engagement with families? And where had the schools fallen short?

For weeks Kate's team had been reminding families, calling, texting, and voice messaging. Now, early on that August morning, they began arriving: moms and dads, older siblings, grandfathers, aunts—more than 150 in all.

Principals, too, started arriving. In past years, the PIA launch had rarely been a priority for school leadership. But two days earlier, when Kate had off-handedly mentioned the event at a Zone-wide principals' meeting, the leaders expressed frustration that a training session had been scheduled for the same time. On their own, the principals coordinated and quickly cleared their calendars. At the PIA launch, as families took their seats, principals sat side by side with them.

By 9 a.m. the room was filled. B Lewis, Kate's colleague, stood to speak. Across a year scarred by illness, evictions, food insecurity, isolation, and grief, families had persisted. In the Zone, more than 260 immigrant-origin families had, month after month, logged onto online meetings to collaborate to improve their schools' communities and their children's education.

She opened with a slide show of photographs celebrating a year in action: Burmese parents meeting virtually with college counselors about scholarship opportunities; Nepali families organizing a neighborhood cleanup; Rwandan, Congolese, and Central African Republic parents filming a video about the importance of children attending school daily; Spanish-speaking parents hosting an end-of-year celebration for teachers.

Next, a woman representing Colorado Succeeds, a coalition of businesses across the state, rose to take the microphone. Praising the Zone's commitment to partnering with families and communities, she announced that, out of all the schools and programs in Colorado, the ACTION Zone had been awarded the 2021 Succeeds Prize for Educational Innovation, one of the most prestigious statewide school awards. The room exploded with cheers and applause.

Then the families turned toward one another to begin their work—reflecting on the past year and brainstorming about the future. One of the family liaisons, Georgette, spoke with families at one table, switching fluidly between Swahili, French, and English. Roberto, a Mexican grandfather and community leader, led a discussion with Spanish-speaking parents nearby. At the front of the room, Asbi had dragged together two tables to accommodate more than a dozen Bhutanese family members. Mothers and fathers periodically pushed back their chairs to add sticky notes to poster boards that quickly filled with the community's collective ideas.

Later, in a quiet moment, Asbi reflected: "[The schools] are hearing us, they are seeing us." Word was rippling outward, he said. Parents from other districts were seeking to enroll their children in the five schools. He smiled. "The ACTION Zone is a blessing for my community."

THE PERSONAL: JULIAN

"What does FOB mean?" sixteen-year-old Julian quietly asked a teammate. It was a term he heard often, in the boathouse, in the locker room, on the river, in the school halls. As the boys clambered out of racing shells and hoisted them onto the dock, they ribbed each other. If he mispronounced a word or missed the meaning of a phrase, teammates teased, "You're such an FOB, Julian." The teammate explained: FOB means "fresh off the boat." Irony unintended. Julian chose not to take offense. The high school sophomore had lived in the United States for close to two years, yet the crew team was his first real interaction with, what he termed, "Americans." On the team everyone called each other names, but seemingly with little malice.

Crew, like much that surrounded him, was new to Julian. He had only learned of the sport months earlier, in the fall of 2016. The weeks of practice were excruciating: His fingers burst with blisters, his legs and arms seized in searing cramps. Still, he kept returning to the water.

Julian had grown up not along rivers, but among mountains, at the bottom of sloping neighborhoods in Medellín, Colombia—a city that for decades was terrorized by Pablo Escobar's infamous cartel. He grew up surrounded by family: Fridays with his grandparents eating pillowy *buñuelos*; afternoons with cousins playing video games; family fiestas with steak and chorizo sizzling on the grill. He loved the street sellers peddling bags of tiny potatoes doused in mayo and ketchup and smiling strangers on the street who would strike up conversations. Most of all he loved the mountains. As a kid, his family would drive winding roads, past plantations perfumed with coffee, up and up and up, into the clouds, so high his ears would pop. From such heights he could look down upon forests and valleys and cities. At dusk, from the terrace of their home, he watched the sky blaze orange, red, purple, and then the mountains would come alight with the twinkle of thousands of homes and shops far away.

Here in the United States, he missed his old life and his family. He particularly missed his mother. He remembers the evening he decided to leave his home. He was fourteen, having just finished eighth grade. His father had offered Julian the opportunity to go with him to the United States to further his education. Julian's mother, his parents explained, would stay behind with the rest of his family. It would be a difficult transition, they warned him. Gone would be the privileges, comforts, and community cocooning him. Alone on the terrace he lingered that night, unsure when he would next see his beloved mountains.

In the doorway of a classroom on the second floor of Lowell High, on his first day of school in the spring of 2015, Julian stood rooted, his whole body vibrating. An administrator opened the door and, addressing the teacher inside, announced, "You have a new student." Thirty heads swiveled right, locking eyes on the now-quaking Julian in a borrowed red jacket. As he recalled, "It was one of the scariest moments of my life."

The teacher gestured to an empty seat in the front row, beside a girl with large round glasses: "She is Colombian," the teacher told him. Barely making eye contact, Julian gave a half wave and sank low into the seat. After forty mostly incomprehensible minutes, the bell rang. In the hall a gaggle of new classmates encircled him, "Where are you from?" "When did you come?" Gently they tugged from his hands his printed schedule. Swiftly they assigned students to accompany Julian to each class, to ensure he wouldn't get lost. At lunch Dominican, Peruvian, Puerto Rican, and Colombian peers—including the bespectacled girl from class—beckoned him over to sit with them. Perhaps school was not so scary.

Yet at home, doubt crept in at night. His stomach knotted, his body shook. He dialed home—his real home—more than four thousand miles away. Hearing his mother's voice, he broke down sobbing. Later his father found him huddled on his bed. "Why didn't you come to me?" he asked, perplexed. "I am here with you." His dad quietly asked if Julian wanted to return to Colombia. For long moments, Julian thought. His dad had left everything behind so he could have opportunities unavailable at home. Julian shook his head. He would stay.

Over the following weeks he would remind himself of his decision whenever he grew bothered by small moments: getting turned around in school corridors; struggling to comprehend a cashier; failing repeatedly to slide a wrinkled bill into the till on a city bus. As he explained to me years later, "You didn't want to seem like you didn't know."

At school, though, teachers were patient. Some would quietly translate words into Spanish. Others would urge him to ask questions, answering each in turn. Julian had been in the country less than two months when one teacher invited a local author and survivor of the Khmer Rouge genocide to speak. The class had been reading his memoir. Haltingly, Julian asked the author a question, cringing at his own accent.

But neither the author nor his classmates laughed. Gently the man asked Julian to repeat his question. The author, Julian realized, understood his trepidation, for he too had been an immigrant in American schools.

In Colombia he was accustomed to taunting from classmates. In his English classes, few had been fluent in the language, but that did not stop others from teasing him when he mispronounced words. Julian had attended a rigidly strict Catholic institution. Classes were densely packed. Assignments ran long and demanded quick turnaround. Answers had to be expansive. Julian's mother, a special education teacher of many years, ensured he worked hard. She checked that he had completed his homework each evening. She attended parent conferences, school meetings, and school events. She checked in regularly with teachers. Month after month he brought home awards: best student in the class, best behavior, best story. At the end-of-year ceremonies, time and again, Julian was singled out for honors.

Starting over in Lowell, Julian was prepared for the same routine. Early in his first semester he had stayed up late one night filling two full pages for a homework reflection. The next day, when he added his assignment to the stack, he was shocked to discover he had written a page and a half more than most classmates. "Why did you write so much?" they asked, perplexed. The teacher too seemed taken aback: "Whoa, you don't need to do all this." Julian, embarrassed, wondered why he had worked so hard. Perhaps school here would be more manageable.

At school, Julian also realized that his family's participation was not necessarily wanted. "He has to learn to do things by himself," he recalled a school official explaining to his father. "He has to learn how to be independent." All his life his family had supported, provided, and cared for him. Here, Julian realized, he would have to be responsible for his own success.

◆

Diligent and reserved, Julian, now a sophomore, sat beside the window in my afternoon US history class in the fall of 2016. Still inclined toward shyness, he willed himself to overcome his fear of asking questions and speaking with strangers. Whenever Julian heard a new word he took to Google Translate to sound it out, slip it into a sentence, imprint it on his mind. Despite the stress, he walked about the city and practiced speaking at CVS and McDonald's. He eavesdropped on conversations to grasp slang: cuz, 'sup, dude. To his surprise, others who had been in the country far longer began asking him to translate for them. The more he learned, the easier his EL English classes became. Slowly he realized his language classes, once incomprehensible, were no longer challenging enough.

In December Julian began working on our semester-long op-ed project. He chose to investigate school lunches. He researched rising rates of childhood obesity and explored national and local nutrition programs. Then he did something that no student of mine had done before. He took paper and pencil and headed to the cafeteria to collect data. "On their plates," he reported, "I saw pizzas, hamburgers, chicken nuggets, tater tots, wraps full of meat, and lots of chocolate milk. Just a few students were eating bananas, apples, and oranges, and even though the cafeteria offers salads, no one was eating one." He studied the movement of lunch lines and drew up proposals for how the school could subtly shift what students place on their plates. Then, like Robert, Julian began showing up early and staying late to edit and rewrite. When the top op-eds were printed in the local newspaper, his ideas shone from the centerfold.

Julian's choice of topic had not been accidental. In taking responsibility for his education, he decided also to take ownership of his health. Following his own op-ed's advice, he stopped sipping sodas and munching pizza for lunch. And in March he decided he needed exercise. Despite knowing nothing about the sport, Julian signed up for crew.

Crew quickly consumed his afternoons, three hours a day—on the rowing machine, practicing form; on city paths, running for endurance; on the river, pulling in unison. He fell into bed each night, newly discovered muscles squealing with pain. It was that spring on the dock, that he learned the meaning of FOB.

In Colombia, jocks had always bullied him. When he refused to do their homework or let them copy his assignments, they called him nerd and loser. Their friendship came at the cost of academic integrity, and Julian wasn't willing to budge. For racking up As, they ostracized him. In gym they teased him for being uncoordinated, chubby, and slow. He daydreamed about throwing insults at them, or even punches. But he kept to himself. Crew at Lowell, however, felt surprisingly different. The jokes and slurs seemed a sign you were part of the team. Having joined for the exercise, Julian found community. As he skimmed along the Merrimack River, his worries were swept away by the current. Surrounded by teammates all rowing in unison, he said, "I felt free."

In classes too he found unanticipated communities. That spring I set my students to learning about civics by tackling local challenges. Julian found himself leading a team of students advocating for a citywide gun safety campaign. Increasingly assertive, he directed classmates to collect research and write fundraising letters to city businesses. Then one afternoon he stood nervously in a school hall, trying not to shake as he clutched curled notecards of carefully penned research in sweaty hands before walking into a meeting with the city's police superintendent. Thirty minutes later he stumbled out, stunned. The superintendent had not only listened to the students' proposal, but had agreed to partner with them. It was time to get to work.

Most of my students took on a single task. Not Julian. The author of one op-ed already, he volunteered to write another about our initiative. He spoke with newspaper reporters and appeared on a local radio show. He arrived in my classroom before sunrise to respond to emails and draft press releases.

In May I received an email from a national nonprofit we worked with. It was seeking to convene young people passionate about civics and community change. When Julian came in the next morning, I handed him the application. Two months later Julian found himself riding a train to New York City. From hundreds of students across the country, he had been selected to be one of fourteen people to sit on a national board of youth leaders focused on civics education. Heading to a retreat filled with strangers, Julian fretted. But he soon found that his fellow board members were quirky, chatty, accepting, and passionate about strengthening their communities. Together they practiced public speaking and opinion writing and brainstormed how to engage young people in civics when they returned home. They knitted themselves into a tightly woven group that would meet monthly for the next year to promote civics, plan civics celebrations, and speak on state and national panels.

———•———

In the first week of junior year in 2017, Julian hesitantly approached his honors English teacher. No longer was his schedule filled with EL classes.

He was for the first time enrolled in, as he put it, "regular classes with American students." Bashfully he apologized that he was an immigrant, still mastering English. He worried he might struggle in her class, but he assured her he would work hard. She smiled and reassured him.

In the coming months, to his surprise, he excelled. For group work, Julian partnered with another recent immigrant, a boy from India. They understood each other's difficulties with language. When the class studied literary devices, which was new to both boys, they teamed up to decode the meaning of *allegory*, *illusions*, and *irony*. Class was challenging, but also exhilarating. Upon finishing *The Great Gatsby*, the class threw a Roaring Twenties party. They composed and presented speeches on American identity. By then Julian had come to believe himself to be an American, one who was working actively to better his adopted country. But he wasn't sure others agreed that immigrants could ever be Americans. To his surprise, though, when classmates stood to deliver their speeches, they made clear they believed immigrants could belong.

After classes Julian joined his teammates on the water, this time as a member of the varsity team—stern seat, port side. In the boats he was surrounded by, as he continued to put it, Americans. There he honed his English. His speaking sped up, as did his rowing. Crew felt like family. They trained together, ate carb-loading spaghetti dinners together, laughed together, and supported each other.

One afternoon Julian approached me about writing a new op-ed—not for class, not for credit, but to advocate for an innovative civics education bill under consideration in the Massachusetts legislature. All students, he believed, should have the skills to create change in their communities. He asked for my help. I couldn't say yes fast enough. On an April morning, with permission, he left school early to drive to Boston, where he stood nervously before legislators at the State House to advocate for the bill. Two months later his op-ed was published by a statewide news outlet. I proudly posted it on our classroom wall.

On the first day of his senior year, Julian introduced himself to his new English teacher. Before he could take a seat, she stopped him. "How do *you* pronounce your name," she asked. For three years, he had been introducing himself to teachers as Julian with the English pronunciation of

J. Occasionally teachers would attempt the Spanish pronunciation, but many muddled it. It was easier, he believed, to adopt a name they could say with ease. The teacher, however, held firm, "I want to call you by your name." And she did every day onward.

The semester was barely three weeks old when Julian and I slipped into a large auditorium a few blocks from the headquarters of the Massachusetts Department of Elementary and Secondary Education. The commissioner of education, having heard Julian speak about civics education that summer, had asked him to address the agency's staff. There, before a room of roughly four hundred educators and state employees, Julian stood, trying not to visibly shake. "Three years ago I would have never thought that I'd be capable of learning the skills that I have now," he told his audience. "But it was all with the help of others, especially the teachers that believed I had the ability to do more, and that is how I got to be where I am today, and I would love other students in Massachusetts to feel the same way as I do." The auditorium resounded with applause.

By the start of his senior year, Julian's schedule was crowded with commitments. His grades had earned him a spot in the National Honor Society. His advocacy for civics education had earned him the role of co-chair of the national youth civics board, for which he was regularly being called to Boston to speak. Every afternoon he trooped with friends down to the boathouse. And, for the first time in his life, he was dating— his girlfriend was the quiet, bespectacled Colombian whom he had sat next to in his very first class.

Yet one worry loomed over Julian. In classes, in the halls, on the boats, everyone talked college. Listening to his teammates in the locker room compare near-perfect SAT scores, Julian winced. Despite a 4.08 GPA, membership in the National Honor Society, and national civics recognition, he was still mastering academic English: Words like *aberration, scrutinize, precocious* were unfamiliar to him. Sitting for the SATs had been nightmarish. He had run out of time on the English section, even as the students around him—"Americans" as he called them—sat bored while he madly scribbled. He told few he had scored in the 31st percentile. "I felt stupid," he confided. Knowing that the SATs rarely showcased the strengths of my immigrant students, we focused instead on perfecting essays, researching scholarships, and selecting institutions that looked beyond multiple-choice tests. In free moments he sat in my classroom, working on college essays, often borrowing my computer to do so and claiming a favorite spot near the window.

Then one morning, Julian bounded into my classroom. Eyes wide, he was unable to stand still. He thrust his phone at me, the browser open to an email: "We received an overwhelming number of extraordinary applications, all demonstrating a deep commitment to education, a strong sense of community and the incredible power of youth mentoring relationships," the email began. And then the students around me jumped as I hollered. Julian had been awarded a $20,000 college scholarship.

Senior year cascaded by—classes, civics, crew—and then suddenly it was spring. After the last day of high school, Julian met his teammates to go out once more on the water for practice. As they turned toward home, the team as one shouted the names of the soon-to-be graduates—one stroke, one name, one stroke, one name. Back in the boathouse they formed a circle. Each in turn spoke, recalling silly moments, sharing gratitude, and reflecting how time had slipped by. For Julian, tears rolling down his cheeks, it felt bittersweet. He had found home and community only now to have to leave it behind. But for one more moment he savored this family. A sophomore new to the team turned to Julian. Thank you, he told him, for being so welcoming, for making him feel that he belonged on the team.

CHAPTER 3

SECURITY

To make Americans, we must ensure that immigrant-origin students have an assurance of security. They have left behind family, friends, and familiarity to create new homes here. Many fear that their new community will see them as a threat because of the land they come from, the faith they believe in, the language they speak, or the clothes they wear. Some experience being excluded, bullied, threatened, or physically attacked. Without the ability to feel safe, how can they let down their guard enough to learn? Without security, how can we expect them to believe that America can be their home?

This chapter tells three stories. The first is the story of a parochial teacher in a one-room schoolhouse in rural Nebraska who, after being convicted in 1920 of teaching German to his second-generation immigrant students, refused to back down and took his case to the Supreme Court, ultimately enshrining the rights of students to learn and teachers to teach foreign languages. The second is the story of an award-winning North Dakota teacher, a former National Guard medic, who in 2017 helped her refugee students to testify before the state legislature against a bill that would allow cities to ban refugee resettlement. The third is the story of my own student Choori, an Iraqi refugee who grew up in war-torn Baghdad and slowly learned to feel safe in American classrooms.

THE PAST: *MEYER V. NEBRASKA*

It was a little past one in the afternoon on a Tuesday in late May 1920, during the lunchtime recess, when an eleven-year-old boy began reading, in German, the biblical story of Jacob falling asleep in the wilderness and dreaming of a ladder ascending to heaven.[1] The midday sun sent slanting shadows into the one-room schoolhouse tucked between fields in rural Nebraska.

The boy's teacher, standing nearby, was a small man—so slim in stature that when he rang the church's 100-foot-high bell to call parishioners to worship, he would invariably find himself hoisted ever so slightly skyward.[2] Still, Robert Meyer, the grandchild of German immigrants, had a commanding presence in his classroom. Strict, but not domineering. Rarely, if ever, did he raise his voice, a feat not to be overlooked for a man responsible for teaching every school subject to forty-odd children ranging in age from five to fourteen. In his early forties, he favored round glasses and bowties. He kept his mustache trimmed tight. By that May afternoon in 1920 he was settled in his ways, having taught at the Zion Lutheran Church's parochial school, four miles outside the hamlet of Hampton, for fifteen years.

With barely twenty minutes before regular classes were to resume, the county attorney, Frank Edgerton, stepped across the door's threshold. He had arrived just in time to hear little fourth grader Raymond Parpart read aloud to his classmates as they sat quietly at their desks. He had watched Meyer draw a breath and, willing himself not to flinch, ask the boy in German to read on. Raymond recalled later that a hush settled into the corners of the classroom as Edgerton paced and then paused before him. What was he reading, he asked Raymond. Replying in English, the boy relayed the story of Jacob among the angels. Nodding, the county attorney took the book from the boy's hands and drew Meyer into a corner to confer. You teach German every day? Edgerton asked. Meyer nodded. That was enough. Edgerton left, textbook tucked under his arm, and Meyer turned back to teaching. Two days later Meyer was charged with breaking the law by teaching German. He was arrested and fined $25, roughly the equivalent of $350 today.

Thirty years later, halfway across the country in Cambridge, Massachusetts, the county attorney's son, Harold "Doc" Edgerton, would perfect strobe photography, a method for capturing with stop-action precision the movement and impact of objects through space. A bullet piercing an apple, a tennis player whacking a ball, the liquid coronet and ensuing ripples thrown outward from a single drop of milk. In Nebraska, his father would, in walking into a one-room schoolhouse, unknowingly, like that drop of milk, send out ripples, still in motion a century onward.

———•———

German settlers came early to America. Indeed, many came before the country was a country at all. They arrived in such droves that they drew the ire of one Pennsylvania publisher, who complained in a correspondence that those arriving from Germany were "generally of the most ignorant stupid sort of their own nation."[3] Their growing presence, the writer warned, was a threat to colonial governments. The perturbed businessman was one Benjamin Franklin.

The Founding Father would long be laid to rest before German immigration reached its zenith. At the start of the 1800s German immigrants represented a fraction of all new arrivals. Fifty years later, roughly one in every three foreigners disembarking onto US soil hailed from Deutschland. Alongside Irish immigrants driven westward by famine, German immigrants for a time were the most numerous newcomers. Across a century, from 1820 to 1920, some five and a half million made new homes in America.[4]

Drawn to the country in search of jobs and land, German newcomers were quick to re-create the old country. German churches, German beer halls, German newspapers, German schools. The country's very first bilingual education law was enacted in the 1830s, in Ohio, at the urging of German parents, who were granted the right to request bilingual instruction for their children. In Cincinnati, German immigrants were so numerous that a canal that ran through the city was nicknamed the Rhine, and a north-city enclave became known as Over-the-Rhine, a name that persists today. But the majority did not settle in cities. Enticed by the Homestead Act and similar schemes that offered acres, many staked claims on the Great Plains. They carried with them skills in farming and husbandry and set about tilling the land recently taken from Indigenous peoples, including the Cheyenne, Arapaho, Omaha, and many others. By the late 1800s, roughly a quarter of all German-born residents were engaged in agriculture.

Far from the burgeoning metropolises, it was easier to keep a grasp on tradition and language. As the century drew to a close, German was spoken with such frequency that states set about enacting laws mandating that, in public schools, English must be taught at least part time. In the parochial schools of the Midwest it was common to hear no English uttered at all. On the eve of World War I, after English, German was the most common tongue spoken in the states of the union. But all of that was about to change.

The conflict in Europe triggered a wave of anti-German sentiment across the Atlantic. After the United States entered the war in the spring of 1917, the wave grew to a tsunami. America became feverishly patriotic. On the home front, Americans displayed love of country by zealously renouncing all things German—from the profound to the petty. German newspapers were shuttered, pretzels were stripped from menus, and towns and streets with German names vanished. Germantown, Nebraska, became Garland; Berlin, Iowa, was renamed Lincoln. Bach and Beethoven were silenced in concert halls throughout the States. On returning home from performing at Carnegie Hall, the music director of the renowned Boston Symphony Orchestra was arrested and his Bach sheet music confiscated under suspicion that it contained coded missives among the music notes.

German was scrubbed from the American English lexicon. Sauerkraut after much debate became liberty cabbage; dachshunds were bred as liberty pups. Even illness was not immune. Patriotic Americans were no longer susceptible to German measles, but proudly contracted liberty measles. And in Portland, Oregon, to protect their little ones, concerned parents petitioned the school board to devise a new name for kindergarten.

To be American, many believed, was to be singular in identity. "There is no room in this country for hyphenated Americans," declared former president Theodore Roosevelt just months after the sinking of the *RMS Lusitania*. German-Americans, Italian-Americans, even English-Americans were perilous for the country's preservation. "The only man who is a good American is the man who is an American and nothing else."[5] Echoing Roosevelt, four years later President Woodrow Wilson warned that "any man who carries a hyphen about with him carries a dagger that he is ready to plunge into the vitals of this Republic."[6]

But for many, the gravest threat to America was to be found in the classroom. As educators and others quickly came to believe, the German language was subtly subverting students. Barely a month after the

United States entered the war, East Orange, New Jersey, banned the teaching of German in its schools. Hundreds if not thousands of school boards quickly followed suit. First to go were elementary school language classes; soon to follow were high school courses. Some swapped in Spanish or French, many did away with foreign language instruction altogether. In a few cities where students once studied German conjugations, they now were drilled on the aims of war.

Culling German textbooks, specifically those containing passages lauding the empire, became a top priority for schools. For the president of Maryland's Goucher College, textbooks were the advance guard of the Imperial German Army: "The process of Germanizing America was going on so subtly, but so surely that had the Kaiser stayed his hand for fifteen, twenty, twenty-five years he would not have needed to draw the sword. America would have been his."[7]

From Pittsburgh, Pennsylvania, to Laramie, Wyoming, cities set about burning German texts, often under the supervision of school boards. Bonfires were ignited in the streets of Wisconsin and at the post office northwest of Fargo. Late at night, unknown persons broke into schools across the country in pursuit of German literature, setting alight all they found. The city avenues of Cleveland were lined with metal cans in which eager students dumped German books destined for incineration. In Colorado, at least one school sponsored a book-burning rally, and in South Dakota, high school students marched to the banks of the Missouri triumphantly singing "The Star Spangled Banner" and cheering as their German texts were carried away by the current. On Flag Day in New Jersey, one celebration closed not with fireworks but with a bonfire of schoolbooks. And in North Platte, Nebraska, as the pages of German history curled, blackened, and dropped to ash, crowds joined in the singing of a mock requiem for Kaiser Wilhelm II, Emperor of Germany, King of Prussia.

The idea in America that some written words were too dangerous to survive would soon come to be echoed in Germany. About a decade later, American authors, including Helen Keller and Upton Sinclair, alongside hundreds of others from around the world, would be deemed subversive. Their words would be consigned to the flames, in bonfires lit by the Third Reich.

In the 1920s, the reasons given in the United States for banning the German language ran the gamut. Language classes were ineffective and costly, foreign language instruction hampered English proficiency, German specifically was of dwindling value in the workforce. Some saw banning German as a means of Americanization. As one Iowa native told the *New York Times*, "You are struggling to make Americans out of foreigners, and we are struggling to prevent Americans from being converted into foreigners."[8] Others offered more jingoistic rationales. When the New York City Board of Education unanimously voted to strike German from the curriculum, they argued their decision would shake German morale and would help win the war, even if only slightly. Whatever the reason, the results were the same. Even as the Great War came to a close, the US war against foreign languages and cultures was just heating up.

Cities, counties, and states across the country, as if in a race, scrambled to enact language laws. By the start of the 1920s more than thirty states had passed English-only restrictions for schools. A few went further. In May 1918, the governor of Iowa issued the Babel Proclamation. No longer could one speak foreign tongues of any dialect. Not in schools, not in houses of worship, and not in public addresses. Only English could be heard on trains, on streets, and even on the telephone. Former president Roosevelt was particularly ecstatic about Iowa's efforts: "This is a nation—not a polyglot boarding house."[9]

Less than a year later, across the border in Nebraska, where at the time nearly four in ten residents were immigrants or the children of immigrants, the Siman Act was signed into law. Henceforth, up until eighth grade, students at any school—public, private, or parochial—would be forbidden to learn any language other than English during the school day. Violators should expect fines and arrests. As one state representative asserted, "If these people are Americans, let them speak our language. If they don't know it, let them learn it. If they don't like it, let them move."[10]

It was a little more than a year later that a county attorney walked into a one-room schoolhouse outside Hampton, Nebraska, just in time to hear eleven-year-old Raymond Parpart read aloud in German.

In the 1800s, Raymond's grandparents came from Germany to America and settled on the plains of Nebraska. With others from the old country they set about erecting a church and soon after a school, fashioned first out of logs, then out of sod, and finally, in 1877, out of hewed planks with benches to seat nearly ninety young Americans. Surrounded by open sky, expansive prairie, and fields of wheat and alfalfa, the Zion Lutheran Church became the community's sun around which all life orbited—baptisms, confirmations, weddings, funerals, social gatherings, school. Theirs was a tight-knit congregation, just shy of five hundred baptized souls at the close of World War I.

Raymond grew up bilingual, but much of life in 1920 was conducted in German. When the Siman Act mandating English-only instruction was signed into law, the church, like others in the area, set about finding a workaround. The solution was a simple one: Extend the midday recess by thirty minutes, and in that time conduct lessons in German. And so it came to be that the county attorney found Raymond reading aloud in German on that sunny May afternoon.

Raymond's father immediately posted bail for his son's teacher. But Meyer refused to pay the twenty-five-dollar fine. "It is not a matter of money," he explained. "This is a question of principle . . . I shall not compromise with what I know is right."[11]

It was a courageous stance. World War I was two years gone, but nativism and xenophobia ran thick in the summer heat of 1920. Five years earlier William Simmons, a former Methodist preacher, reignited the Knights of the Ku Klux Klan as a fraternity bent on achieving "100 percent Americanism."[12] America, he believed, was under threat, and Simmons, as a self-declared Imperial Wizard, saw himself as a prime defender of the country. In under a decade the Klan's ranks swelled to four million Americans. Across the country they terrorized, brutalized, and lynched Black Americans. And, in the West and Midwest, some zealous members further turned their hatred on Jews, Catholics, and anyone else they deemed foreign or, more accurately, anyone not Anglo-Saxon and Protestant. Vigilante extremists ransacked churches and whipped priests. They dragged their victims openly through the streets, tarring and feathering them, and enacted elaborate flag-kissing ceremonies. By the mid-1920s, nearly fifty thousand Nebraskans were members of the KKK.[13] Not far outside Hampton, Nebraska, the school attended by Raymond's future wife was peppered with bullets and all the textbooks burned.

When a date was set for Meyer's trial, the local *Aurora Sun* newspaper could barely contain its glee. "Men and women who love the American flag, not only those of Nebraska, but those of all other states, cannot help but feel proud of Judge Fred Jeffers of Hamilton County, and the brand of real, true Americanism that he displayed in upholding the provisions of the Siman law." The paper issued a barely veiled threat to Meyer: "If there are those here who instead of obeying our laws, willingly seek to evade them . . . they should remember that the gates of Castle Garden [America's first immigration center] swing out as well as in."[14]

On a snowy December morning at the close of 1920, eleven-year-old Raymond, wrapped in furs to keep out the cold, traveled by carriage to the local courthouse. Just after 10 a.m. he stood to testify in a grand, wood-paneled chamber, alongside his teacher and his pastor. The following morning the court ruled that Meyer had violated the Siman Act. Supported by the Missouri Synod, one of the country's largest Lutheran denominations, Meyer immediately appealed, and his case was sent up to the state supreme court.

Thirteen hundred miles away in the country's Capital, the US House of Representatives also had immigration on its mind. Two months before Meyer's arrest, Representative Albert Johnson from the state of Washington, chairman of the House Immigration Committee, invited a noted eugenicist to testify. Speaking as a representative of the Eugenics Research Association, Harry Laughlin set forth charts, tables, photos, and other evidence that, he asserted, proved the biological inferiority of incoming immigrants. He warned the committee that the immigrants included many who were "morons," "idiots," and "feeble minded."[15] So taken was Johnson that he named Laughlin the committee's official "expert eugenics agent" and called him to testify again and again.

In December 1920, just days before Meyer was called to the Hamilton County District Court House in Aurora, the State Department presented a report to Johnson's immigration committee. The report read like a warning. A tidal wave of undesirables, it cautioned, was heading toward American shores, and many of these would-be immigrants were "decidedly inferior . . . physically, mentally, and morally."[16] The Red Scare was by then running rampant, and particularly concerning was the mass of displaced Jews from Poland and Russia whom the report derided as "filthy, un-American and often dangerous in their habits."[17]

Two days before Meyer's court appearance, Chairman Johnson took to the floor of the House to declare: "We do not want Japanese, Chinese, Hindu, Turk, Greek, Italian, or any other nationality until we can clean house. . . . The immigration coming now is the most undesirable that ever came to the United States. Look out!"[18] The chairman's solution was simple: Bar immigration almost entirely for a period of two years.

Five months later, newly inaugurated President Warren Harding signed into law the Emergency Quota Act. Johnson's proposed halt on immigration had not survived, but a policy far more insidious was implemented. Total immigration was capped at 355,000 annually, roughly a third of the yearly rate before World War I. For each country a quota was implemented. Yearly immigration allotments were pegged at 3 percent of the population of persons born in that country who were residing in the United States as of 1910. Unspoken was the goal of barring undesirables from Southern and Eastern Europe. In the following year, immigration from some countries was slashed by more than 70 percent.[19]

The next winter, the Nebraska Supreme Court upheld Meyer's conviction. The church's pastor had argued that teaching German during recess helped to knit families together and allowed children access to the faith and traditions of their ancestors. But it was on precisely this logic that the court based its decision. Allowing children to be taught in tongues other than English, the court concluded, "was found to be inimical to our own safety."[20] Foreign language learning led to an inevitable domino effect. To speak German was to think in German, which in turn would lead one to be aligned with Germany. If Meyer had been solely teaching religion, the court might have decided in his favor. But because his purpose was twofold, grounded in fortifying not just faith but also family, Meyer was found in violation of the law. The Siman Act had never been solely about English instruction; rather, the court concluded, it was a means of ensuring that children grew into loyal Americans. For no one, the court assessed, was this more important than for the children and grandchildren of foreigners. Stubbornly, Meyer appealed his case once more, this time to the highest court in the land.

How schools set about making Americans was a key concern for the lawyers on both sides of *Meyer v. State of Nebraska*, which was presented to the US Supreme Court in the fall of 1922. In his argument before the Court, Nebraska's attorney general made the case for preserving the state's English-only education law. Just as the state could compel landlords to install windows to let in light, so too was it "within the police power of the state to compel every resident of Nebraska to so educate his children that the sunshine of American ideals will permeate the life of the future citizens of this republic." If little ones were instructed first in a foreign tongue and not English, he warned, the first language would forever remain the "language of his heart."[21]

Meyer's lawyers countered that the state's strategy for making foreign children into Americans was inconsistent with American ideals. "In our desire for the Americanization of our foreign born population," they wrote, "we should not overlook the fact that the spirit of America is liberty and toleration—the disposition to allow each person to live in his own life in his own way, unhampered by unreasonable and arbitrary restrictions."[22]

By the time Meyer's case made it to the Court it had been consolidated with three similar cases, another from Nebraska and one each from Ohio and Iowa. Together the cases represented a coalition of unusual bedfellows—Lutheran and Roman Catholic, German and Polish. But one more case, which was not yet before the Court, would also prove influential. Just as the briefs were being filed in Washington, DC, across the country in Oregon the legislature passed a law barring students from attending private schools. The ban was the culmination of a vigorous campaign, spearheaded by the KKK, that was blatantly anti-Catholic and anti-immigrant. As one popular slogan proudly proclaimed, "One flag, one school, one language."[23]

In February 1923, four days before the Court heard oral arguments in *Meyer v. Nebraska*, a conservative Columbia law professor, William Guthrie, submitted an amicus brief on the case. Guthrie was chief counsel for a group of Catholic parochial schools in Oregon, which was already challenging that state's new law. While ostensibly supporting neither side in the *Meyer* case, Guthrie drew the Court's attention to the larger implications of state control of children's education. Appealing to the justices' classical educations, Guthrie's brief cited Plato's ideal society in which children would be taken from their parents and raised collectively by the state. It was a plan, he noted, now fervently being implemented in Soviet Russia. As the United States battled Bolshevism abroad, he argued, states on the home front were, perhaps unwittingly, restricting education in ways that bent toward communism. The Oregon law, he wrote, "adopts the favorite device of communistic Russia—the destruction of parental authority, the standardization of education . . . and the monopolization by the state of the training and teaching of the young. . . . Anything more un-American and more in conflict with the fundamental principles of our institutions, it would be difficult to imagine."[24]

At the oral argument before the Court, former Nebraska attorney general Arthur Mullen, a Canadian immigrant, spoke on Meyer's behalf for forty-six minutes. A key question for the justices was whether a state had the power to compel children to attend public school. Pressed by Justice James McReynolds, Mullen held firm. It did not, he argued. "It is a striking down of the principle that a parent has control over the education of his child. This is one of the most important questions that have been presented for a generation, because it deals with the principle of the soviet," referring to school indoctrination in Bolshevik Russia.[25]

Less than four months later, the Supreme Court overturned the lower court's ruling, striking down as unconstitutional the profusion of language laws across the land. The Court grounded its ruling in the logic of *Lochner v. New York*. That case concerned a law that coincided with the birth of the Progressive Movement and Jane Addams' Settlement House Movement. In 1895, New York had passed a law protecting bread bakers from working more than sixty hours per week. A bakery owner in Utica contested the law all the way to the Supreme Court. In a conservative ruling that favored big business, the Court had ruled that the Fourteenth Amendment barred states from protecting workers because doing so interfered with people's economic liberty to enter into whatever contract they wished—even if those contracts forced them to work long hours, to be paid a pittance, and to be treated poorly by their employers. For nearly forty years, until the logic was deemed faulty, business owners exploited workers under the protection of *Lochner*'s precedent. But in 1923, the logic of its conservative decision in *Lochner* would compel the Court to protect the right of a rural teacher to instruct an eleven-year-old boy in German.

Justice McReynolds wrote the majority opinion. For a case overturning anti-immigrant legislation, he was an odd ally. A noted "curmudgeon," McReynolds was bitingly bigoted, racist, misogynistic, xenophobic, and antisemitic. While on the bench, *Time* magazine labeled him, "intolerably rude, antiSemitic, savagely sarcastic, incredibly reactionary, Puritanical, prejudiced."[26] For years he refused to speak to or shake hands with his fellow justice Louis Brandeis because Brandeis was a Jew. But McReynolds's opinion would go on to establish the precedent and sweeping protections for immigrants hoping to educate their children in the language of their ancestors. McReynolds wrote that, in preventing Meyer from practicing his chosen profession of teaching German, Nebraska was trampling on his right to work. But McReynolds did not stop there. Likely moved by the threat of Bolshevism and citing at length Plato's ideas and Sparta's efforts at state-controlled education, his opinion declared that any US law that sought to replicate the Greeks' vision did "violence to both letter and spirit of the Constitution."[27] While commending the states' aim of Americanization, McReynolds declared their method unconstitutional.

Although the case before the Court concerned only the language laws, McReynolds's decision declared that the economic liberty protections in the Fourteenth Amendment applied to many spheres of private life—including the right "to engage in any of the common occupations of life, to acquire useful knowledge, to marry, establish a home and bring up children, to worship God according to the dictates of his own conscience, and generally to enjoy those privileges long recognized at common law as essential to the orderly pursuit of happiness by free men."[28] To support this sweeping assertion, McReynolds cited fourteen previous cases. Curiously, all concerned laws regulating commerce. Not one touched on private life. The sudden discovery that these rights were inherent in the Constitution would later prove highly influential.

A front-page headline in the next day's *New York Times* read, "Ends 21 States' Ban on Foreign Tongues: Supreme Court Decides Pupils Have Constitutional Right to Be Taught Them." The Gray Lady's subtitle: "Justice McReynolds in opinion upholds freedom to acquire knowledge."[29]

Following the Supreme Court's decision in *Meyer v. Nebraska*, language laws were declared unconstitutional. But *Meyer*'s effect was broader. Two years later, the case challenging the Oregon ban on private schools made it to the court. Citing *Meyer*, the Court unanimously struck down that law: States could not compel students to attend public school.

Soon after, in 1927, the Court heard a third case regarding immigrants and education. In the territory of Hawaii the legislature had passed a law severely hampering language schools, small institutions that taught Japanese, Korean, and Chinese, outside public school hours. The law unabashedly targeted immigrants. "These schools are narrow, superstitious shrines for Mikado worship," wrote a College of Hawaii professor, who would go on to become Hawaii's school superintendent. "Buddhism is basically undemocratic and un-American. So long as 95 per cent of the Japanese population of Hawaii remains Buddhist, so long will Americanization be retarded."[30] Again invoking *Meyer*, the Court concluded that parents had the right to teach their children Japanese. In both cases, it was the cantankerous, xenophobic Justice McReynolds who voiced the opinion of the Court.

But just as language books were cracked open once more in schools throughout the country, the gates of America itself were slamming shut. Building on the success of the 1921 Emergency Quota Act, Representative Albert Johnson quickly set about cementing his quota system, and in newly elected Pennsylvania Senator David Reed he found an ally. Together they set about reshaping America. Rather than pegging immigration quotas to the 1910 census, after careful consideration they selected the census of 1890. Undesirable Eastern and Southern Europeans had only come in droves after that date and thus would be most effectively excluded. And instead of 3 percent of the population of foreign-born, they limited the total to 2 percent of foreign-born residing in the United States in their chosen year. Senator Reed brazenly justified the choice in a congressional hearing: "I think the American people want us to discriminate."[31]

The hearings on the new immigration quotas were woven thick with eugenic theories of Nordic superiority. Johnson himself had recently been named president of Harry Laughlin's Eugenics Research Association. On the floor of Congress, elected officials were flagrantly explicit. The quotas were essential, one West Virginia representative claimed, for "keeping pure the blood of America."[32] A South Carolina senator declared, "It is for the perseveration of that splendid [Anglo-Saxon] stock" that the quotas should be signed into law.[33] Not to be outdone, a Maine congressman, thundered to the applause of his colleagues, "It may be even now too late for the white race in America . . . I wish it were possible to close our gates against any quota from southern Europe or from the orientals."[34]

Few spoke in favor of keeping open the nation's gates. Perhaps the most vocal was a young freshman congressman from Brooklyn, New York. It was Emanuel Celler, the grandson of German Jews, who in a letter to the editor just months after being sworn in would highlight history's tendency toward repetition: "What is now being said about the Russians, Poles and Italians was said about the Irish and the Germans when they first came over here."[35] In the winter of 1924, as Congress debated the proposed restrictions in earnest, Celler became one of the quotas' most vocal adversaries. "I can see no logic in accepting in the quota a criminal Scotchman or a degenerate Swede and in excluding a refined and cultured Pole or an industrious and honest Czechoslovak. . . . Not only is the quota law illogical in theory, but it is cruel and heartless in practice."[36] But Celler's was a lonely voice on the floor of Congress.

As cherry blossoms bloomed along the Potomac, Senator Reed penned his argument for the quotas in an article that spilled across an entire page of the New York Times under a headline that said it all: "America of the Melting Pot Comes to End."[37] Just under a month later, President Calvin Coolidge enthusiastically signed the Johnson-Reed Immigration Act into law. On the eve of the passage of the 1921 quota law and just days before being sworn in as vice president, Coolidge had published an article titled "Whose Country Is This?" Open immigration, he asserted, was a threat to America. "The Nordics propagate themselves successfully. With other races, the outcome shows deterioration on both sides." Restricting newcomers now would ensure the country's continuation, as he concluded: "We must remember that we have not only the present but the future to safeguard; our obligations extend even to generations yet unborn. The unassimilated alien child menaces our children."[38] Johnson too was content: "The day of unalloyed welcome to all peoples, the day of indiscriminate acceptance of all races has definitely ended."[39]

The impact of the Johnson-Reed Act is, in the words of historian Daniel Okrent, best captured through the "cold exactitude of numbers."[40] As he detailed, in 1921 nearly 200,000 newcomers crossed the Atlantic from Russia. In 1925, after the quota law was implemented, barely 7,000 Russians were admitted. Over those four years Italian immigration was slashed by roughly 99 percent. In 1914, on the precipice of World War I, nearly 50,000 Greeks had come to America—but a decade later Greek nationals were allotted only 100 spots annually. The entire continent of Africa was eventually granted a mere 1,200 slots. Japan was added to the list of excluded Asian countries. Total yearly immigration was capped at roughly 160,000, with the exception of immigration from Central and South America, which was left open and indeed largely encouraged. And to German nationals—those foreigners so mistrusted four years earlier that a Nebraska teacher was arrested for teaching the Bible in German— America granted the second-largest annual quota, an implicit invitation to immigrate.

In the following year, a failed painter penned and then published a manifesto in southern Germany. In it, he commended the United States for its exclusion of immigrants. The author was Adolf Hitler, the book *Mein Kampf*. A decade later, Johnson and Reed's legislation would be lauded as a model by the Third Reich.

But in America, despite the new preferential immigration status, and despite the striking down of the language laws, German slowly slipped away from school curriculums and church services across the country. America, for a time, had lost its appreciation for other languages. In 1926 the Zion Lutheran Church outside Hampton, Nebraska, held a Communion service for the first time in English, with two in attendance. By the close of World War II, German was no longer spoken from the pulpit.[41]

Although nearly a straight-A student, little Raymond Parpart would, in time, drop out of high school to help his dad. Tearfully he watched friends continue their education. He devoted his life instead to the family farmstead, raising hogs and cattle and tending fields of corn, wheat, and alfalfa. When his two daughters were born, he chose not to teach them the language of his forefathers.

In 1948 Robert Meyer, by then seventy years old, came out of retirement to teach once more. Called to fill a vacancy, he returned to the church community where once he was arrested. On arrival, his former student Raymond welcomed him to stay on his family farm. Raymond's daughters were now roughly the age he was when Meyer instructed him to read about a ladder to heaven on a May afternoon in 1920.

For Raymond's youngest daughter, as she shared with me, it would be the first she had heard of the three-year legal battle and the national court case that had at its center her father. [42] For a year, she too would be taught by Meyer: English and arithmetic, reading and penmanship. But much had shifted over the course of nearly three decades. Two wars against Germany had been fought and won, and immigration to the country had sunk close to its nadir. And, not once throughout that year did Robert Meyer teach her German.

THE PRESENT: FARGO SOUTH HIGH, NORTH DAKOTA

For the umpteenth time that morning, Leah Juelke glanced down at the cell phone on her desk. She was in the midst of the teaching day at Fargo South High School in Fargo, North Dakota. Outside the sky was blue, and the temperature was stubbornly below freezing. Through the class-room door, students were streaming in—recently arrived refugees and immigrants from Nepal, Iraq, the Democratic Republic of the Congo, Myanmar, Mexico, Liberia, China, Vietnam, Zambia, and Eritrea. That morning, though, her mind was a four-hour drive west, in the state capital of Bismarck. There, within the capitol building, three of her students were going to testify before a panel of legislators. Unable to resist, she looked at her phone once more. No update yet.

Two weeks earlier, on Friday, January 20, 2017, Donald J. Trump had been sworn in as the forty-fifth president of the United States. The following Friday, at an afternoon ceremony at the Pentagon, the president had signed an executive order barring, for a time, refugees from seven Muslim-majority countries. And now this Friday, February 3, in a crowded low-ceilinged hearing room, the North Dakota legislature was considering a bill that would grant local governments the authority to ban refugees from resettling in their cities.

In class and at home the bill had swirled through school and city con-versations. Leah's students arrived anxious each morning—would their families, waiting in refugee camps overseas, ever be able to join them? Then one afternoon, Leah opened an email from Lutheran Social Ser-vices, the primary nonprofit resettling refugees in the state. The bill was scheduled for public hearing. Would her students consider testifying?

When Leah asked her class for volunteers, hands rocketed up across the room. She settled on three representatives: Gloria from Tanzania,

Ashti from Iraq, and Aline from the Democratic Republic of the Congo. Between classes and during lunch she helped the girls craft their statements. Together they rehearsed, reviewed pronunciation, and practiced projecting their voices.

But now they were on their own. Leah, nearly six months pregnant and needing to be in the classroom teaching, was unable to accompany them. So Lutheran Social Services arranged to pick up the girls and drive them to the capitol, leaving Leah checking her phone yet again, waiting to hear from her students.

———◆———

Just over four hundred years ago, in the fall of 1620, Leah Juelke's ancestor Edward Doty, a servant, boarded a ship embarking on its maiden voyage from the English port of Plymouth. Sixty-six somewhat storm-tossed days later, he laid eyes on a foreign wooded land. The crew anchored their ship, the Mayflower, and the bedraggled passengers set about constructing a new home for themselves (and forcibly displacing Wampanoag people from their homes).[43] Roughly half of those on the manifest were buried within months. Edward survived, and his descendants traveled inland, away from the ocean.

Much of Leah's family came to the country long ago: from France and England in the 1600s, Prussia in the 1800s, and elsewhere. They settled in Minnesota, near the Red River, which traces a winding boundary with North Dakota. This is where Leah grew up, crossing city and state borders daily to attend Fargo South High School. As a teenager she adored school. Her afternoons were crowded with speech competitions and meetings for a student congress. She was a photographer for the school newspaper and an editor of the yearbook. And she was a member of the school's international club, one of the only American-born students in the group, in her recollection. Of the roughly one thousand students at Fargo South, almost all were white and American-born. The small collection of students from elsewhere were primarily enrolled in exchange programs: visitors from Germany, Sweden, Spain, Argentina, Norway, Japan. Leah had never left the country, but through friends in the club she learned about traditions, religions, and recipes from across the globe.

Four months after Leah graduated high school, two Boeing 767s slammed into the twin towers of New York City's World Trade Center.

Leah watched the second plane hit from a TV in her college dorm. The following morning she learned that her great-uncle, who in 1973 was officially listed as the last combat soldier airlifted out of Saigon, Vietnam, had perished in the coordinated attack on the Pentagon.

Over decades, many in her family had chosen to fight for the United States. Her older brother was an Airborne Army Ranger, and her uncle had been a Green Beret. One grandfather fought in the Korean War, another in World War II. A year after 9/11, Leah enlisted in the Minnesota Army National Guard. It felt like the right thing to do. In the spring of 2003, Leah took a semester leave from university where she had been studying nursing and headed first to South Carolina for basic training and then to Texas for training as a combat medic, where she was promoted to squad leader and for a time temporary platoon leader.

Once back at university, Leah returned to base monthly to drill. There she was one of a handful of women among two hundred men. Despite the grueling drills and the long hours, Leah excelled. On weekends in the fall of 2003, she began training soldiers who were soon to ship out in how to administer CPR, evacuate the wounded on a stretcher, and perform basic first aid. There, Leah fell in love with teaching.

That was how, in June of 2004, Leah found herself in a tiny church classroom instructing recently arrived immigrant middle schoolers how to read and write English. She had taken a teacher's assistant job at a summer school for the Fargo School District. Her students were goofy, sassy, and endlessly energetic. Leah was hooked. She returned the following summer, and the summer after that as well. When the local Girl Scout organization floated the idea of her taking on an immigrant troop, Leah volunteered, becoming scout leader for an all-Liberian troop. After class she and her girls would sit in a circle talking about feelings or would head outside to clean up their neighborhood. She got to know them, and they got to know her. Slowly, in morning classes, Leah began noticing a subtle shift: The girls who were in her troop were markedly more focused during lessons. The relationships fostered in the afternoons carried over into the classroom. In the winter of 2006 Leah graduated, not with a nursing degree, but with an English teaching degree and a certificate in teaching English learners. She set about applying for teaching jobs.

In 2013, a dozen years after graduating from Fargo South, Leah returned to her alma mater to teach. She had spent a number of the intervening years teaching abroad, first in Taiwan and then in Ecuador. Now she was home, working alongside some of her former teachers—a little odd at times, but she had fond memories of the high school.

Between the time she had graduated and the time she returned, an increasing number of refugees had settled in Fargo. Per capita, North Dakota was welcoming more refugees than almost any other state in the nation. When Leah graduated, only a small percentage of the student body were English learners. Now, at Fargo South, the figure is roughly one in ten.[44]

Leah was assigned to teach newcomers and, in her first year, was asked to help design an entirely new class: English 4, the highest level of English language class for immigrant-origin students before they transitioned to studying with native English speakers. With the help of a colleague she mapped a curriculum, crafting lessons on poetic terms, persuasive essays, and complex grammar. For her unit on narrative writing, though, she was stumped. She sought a topic that would be relevant and meaningful. Finally it came to her: All her students were recent arrivals. Between classes and during study hall, they eagerly shared snippets of their stories with her. What if she created an assignment that allowed them to write about their journeys to America?

The assignment would be short: a few pages, due in a week. They'd then move on to another assignment, Leah figured. Within days, though, she realized she had miscalculated. On the one hand, the writing was littered with haphazard punctuation and fractured grammar that would necessitate weeks of instruction. On the other, the stories were so powerful that they demanded attention. In raw, often matter-of-fact prose, her students had laid out their lives: growing up amid war; witnessing family members killed; traveling alone to a foreign land. Leah was stunned. She had not imagined what the families had experienced. She took their pages to other teachers, "Did you know this boy never went to school? Maybe this is why he is failing classes." Like her, colleagues shook their heads. "I had no idea."

When her students read their stories aloud in class, connections among them leapt from the page. Many had left loved ones behind, struggled with English, lived through war, or lived in refugee camps. Students who had rarely talked to each other began speaking. Connections cocooned her class. Sharing was therapeutic. "They already feel like outsiders," Leah reflected. Now they knew they were not alone.

Leah began wondering: Could the stories that connected her children also create connections between her students and the larger Fargo community? In local newspapers she had been reading about hate crimes against newcomers. On Facebook she saw residents demanding that immigrants go back to their countries. On the streets and in grocery stores she witnessed pointed stares and glares directed toward immigrants. Leah began brainstorming: What if together they wrote a book?

The next fall, Leah shared her idea with her new class. "Draw a timeline," she instructed them, "from the time you were born until now." Her twenty students filled the expanse with moments. Students spent weeks drafting and writing. Memories of leaving home and friends, of their first snow in Fargo, of celebrating holidays in America, of making the school soccer team. At night Leah edited, and in class she paired students to review each other's work. And she sent them out into the school to ask other teachers to edit as well. Then, having secured funding, she presented each student with a printed and bound book of the class's stories. Leah lugged boxes of extra copies to the office. In the mailbox of every teacher in the school she placed a copy of their book.

One chilly January evening, two students—a Congolese girl and a Nepali boy—accompanied Leah downtown to speak before the city's school board. Before each elected official lay a copy of their newly published book of narratives. In front of an array of adults, the students stood to share their stories. As they left the lectern, the room filled with applause. The district's superintendent saluted them: "You couldn't make me more proud to be the superintendent of Fargo Public Schools."

Back in her classroom, Leah taped to a wall a photo she had snapped at the school board meeting. Over years that wall became blanketed with Leah's photos: her students at soccer games, wrestling matches, field trips, choir concerts, relay races, debate competitions, graduation. When not in the classroom, Leah can often be found on a sideline, in a bleacher seat, in an auditorium, cheering on her children. For many, she has stepped into the role of surrogate American aunt. Some call her "mum." They linger in her classroom to talk about friends and family. They pepper her with questions about their health, about relationships, about how to apply to college. Knowing that few families can take off work to see their children promenade into prom, Leah arrives, camera in hand, to capture the moment, printing out photos to share with families and posting copies on her wall. Interspersed among the photos is a growing collection of articles: interviews and profiles of her students and their work. "I want my students to see themselves in our classroom," Leah explained, "to feel included."

In the fall of 2015, Leah taped a new photo to the wall: her students standing with a towering John Bul Dau, a former Lost Boy of Sudan. Leah had watched the award-winning 2006 documentary "God Grew Tired of Us," which profiled Mr. Dau's story of walking a thousand miles to escape war before eventually coming to make a new home in the United States. He now traveled the country sharing his story. Would he, she wondered, speak to her students? That summer Leah sent off an invitation and applied for a grant to cover his speaking fee. When, in the fall, she launched the Journey to America project, she took her students to the gymnasium. Alongside the entire school, they listened John Dau talk about his life. After the assembly he joined her students in their tiny classroom. They asked: "Were you nervous to tell your story?" "Were you embarrassed?" He couldn't be embarrassed, he told them. Those experiences, he explained, had made him who he was. Around the room Leah's students nodded. Then, together, they began brainstorming about what stories each student would write.

———•———

On the first day of school in 2016, ten students hesitantly entered Leah's tiny windowless classroom for a new elective class she was piloting: Partnership for New Americans. Half of the students had arrived in the country within the past year and spoke little English. Half had been born in North Dakota or had immigrated to the United States years ago. The course, conceived and started in a school across town, paired newly arrived immigrants with American-born students and others who had lived for years in the country. It was a class that Leah fervently hoped would build bridges across a growing divide.

Leah saw that divide in the cafeteria, where her newest newcomers sat apart from the other students. They kept to each other and to their English language classes. As the 2016 election heated up, her students came to class more and more upset about what might happen to them and their families. Online, she was finding an increasing number of Facebook posts by Fargo residents that were jagged with xenophobic rhetoric. The previous winter a Somali-owned café north of Fargo had been firebombed. Sprayed on the shop's windows days earlier had been the words "Go Home." The Partnership for New Americans, she hoped, would connect the students, fostering empathy and understanding.

At the start, Leah paired new Dakotans with old Dakotans. She crafted lessons that would teach half of her class skills in mentoring and leadership, while the other half would learn the survival skills needed for succeeding in American schools—including how to operate a student locker, what types of clothes to wear in the winter, and what to do in case of a fire drill, tornado drill, or shooter lock-down drill. Many lessons were constructed to cultivate conversations made trickier by the fact that the students spoke little of each other's languages. The student pairs interviewed each other and wrote reflections on what they learned. Sitting in a circle one afternoon, Leah challenged each student to share their partner's childhood memories as if they were their own: A white American-born girl spoke of falling out of a mango tree in the Democratic Republic of the Congo, and her Congolese partner described growing up on a farm in rural North Dakota. Students crafted presentations about Fargo, with mentors helping newcomers locate schools and grocery stores. Months later, newcomers took the lead as pairs researched presentations about their home countries, which they later delivered at a nearby elementary school. Together, Leah's students studied global religions and traditions, taking turns as teachers to talk of Tet, Christmas, Eid, Diwali. Fargo-born students taught lessons on watercolors, Nepali students led sessions on Nepali dance. Come winter, her students hosted a celebration over a table filled with apple crisp and injera, Rice Krispies Treats and fish soup, coffee cake and samosas.

Seeking to nurture friendships, Leah sent students out into the school. One day's assignment: Guide your newcomer partner through the school—this is the library, this is the nurse's office, this is the principal's office. At each stop, their partner introduced themselves. Another day's assignment: Using only words, direct your blindfolded partner from the library to the gym. Then switch.

Time together uncovered connections. Two girls—one born in the United States, one born abroad—realized both were grieving a deceased grandmother. An adopted Fargo-born girl and an Eritrean boy who traveled to the United States alone grew close—both felt like they didn't fit in. Class partners trick-or-treated together, went to movie theaters together. Perceptions shifted. Leah's longtime Dakotan students admitted they had never realized how diverse their school was. If not for the class, would they ever have learned about so many traditions, religions, and customs? In private moments they shared about relatives who made xenophobic comments. How could they say such things about their class partners, they now wondered?

Late in the semester, one of the class's newcomers stopped Leah in a school hallway, elated: "I walked by my partner in the hall. She was with her friends and she waved to me!" In the cafeteria one day, Leah stopped short. Sitting among basketball players was one of her newcomer students. Familiar with cafeteria cliques, Leah cocked her head and then spotted her student's partner sitting across from her. "That was the moment I knew," she told me years later, that something remarkable was happening in the class.

At the same time, though, something very different was happening outside the school. Leah watched with alarm as xenophobic rhetoric and hate crimes spiked. Three days after the semester's end, on Martin Luther King Jr. Day in January 2017, members of the state legislature, four hours west in Bismarck, introduced the bill proposing that cities be granted permission to ban refugee resettlement.

Three weeks later, three of Leah's students stood in that packed hearing room in North Dakota's capitol. So many residents had arrived that morning to speak against the bill that the hearing had been moved to a larger venue. Gloria spoke first. Born in a Tanzanian refugee camp, she and her family had been welcomed into the United States more than a decade earlier. Now a high school senior, she had spent the last semester as a mentor in Leah's partnership class. She was looking forward to graduating and going to college. But, she confessed to the legislators, "I feel scared about my future." Her fear had compelled her to speak. The bill, she declared in a steady voice, was "against what America stands for."

Up next were two students from Leah's English 4 class. In their hands they held their just-published book of narratives. Ashti's family had fled Iraq. She explained to the assembled legislators that her father had been an interpreter for the US Army. Aline spoke next. "I am a published author. I'm in ROTC. Before I say anything I would like to read you my story." Assured and assertive, she read. She described how, on the border of the Democratic Republic of the Congo and Burundi, her family fled the massacre where her father was murdered. When she looked up, a member of the legislature thanked her. But she was not finished and politely said so. "I want to say this. I am not here just to enjoy the life. I am here to pursue my dream. I am here to make my parents proud. I am here to make Americans proud." Please, she added, "I request you to not pass this rule."

That afternoon, after hours of testimony, the state legislature amended the bill so that it simply mandated a study of refugee resettlement. The proposed state ban on accepting refugees has not been reintroduced.

———•———

The screech of a fire alarm brought an abrupt halt to Leah's teaching one afternoon in March of 2017. The alarm, she knew, was a drill. With a sigh, Leah—almost nine months pregnant and, by her description, "huge"—willed herself to stand and shepherd students into the hall. For winter drills the school amassed in the gym. There, Leah took up a spot leaning against a wall. Oddly, the principal did not give the signal to return to class. She watched, perplexed, as he mounted a small stage erected on the basketball court. This wasn't a drill, he explained. Instead he was there to announce the Fargo School District's Teacher of the Year: Leah Juelke.

Of what followed, Leah can recall little. Around her, students burst into applause. From behind the stage, out walked her daughter and husband. The district superintendent appeared and commended her. At some point she was asked to speak. To this day, she has no idea what she said.

That spring semester was busy. Two weeks after the award, Leah's English 4 students spoke before city residents at the downtown bookstore.

After her class had developed their stories in the fall, Leah arranged for entire classes of university students to help them outline and edit. Now her students were invited to speak at the state university. In the weeks following they shared their stories at an elementary school, a middle school, a city library, a nursing home, an art museum, and a church assembly. Audience members approached the students afterward. Thank you for telling your story, they told them. When a Nepali boy shared at a reading that he didn't always feel welcome, a middle schooler raised his hand to say, "We're glad you're here." Once, an older white woman approached one of Leah's Sierra Leonean students: "I've never seen someone who looks like you," she told the girl. "But I like you."

That summer Leah continued scheduling book readings for her students. She didn't have to look far to be reminded why they were so necessary. Early in July, a Somali man was assaulted while moving into his Fargo apartment by attackers yelling racial epithets. At the end of July, in a parking lot three miles from Fargo South, a white woman angrily warned three Somali women to go back to their country. "I'm an American. You're not," she spat. "We're going to kill all of you. We're going to kill every one of you f***ing Muslims."

In talking about that summer, though, Leah chooses to focus on other moments. She recalls one morning in particular when she sat, her infant in her arms, in a pew of a local church surrounded by roughly a hundred Burundian and Congolese refugees. Aline, who had spoken to the state legislators, had invited her to attend a memorial for her father. In her published story for English 4, Aline had written about surviving a massacre, eight years earlier, when her father had been shot and then burned alive in front of her. At the church that morning, there were prayers, songs, sermons, tears, and, later, a feast. Afterward, Leah couldn't help but ask, "Why a memorial now? Hadn't there been one years before?" No, Aline replied. "Before your class, we never talked about my dad in our home. It was too sad." Now, for the first time since his death, she explained, they were speaking about her father.

That fall a new crop of students was about to embark on the Journey to America project when the state's governor came to Fargo South to announce that Leah had been named North Dakota's Teacher of the Year. Two years later, in September 2020, on a Zoom call in the midst of the COVID-19 pandemic, Leah was told she had been named a top-ten finalist for the Global Teacher Prize.[45]

For Leah, the awards mean more opportunities for her students to share their stories—on radio, in newspaper interviews, at public readings. Her students win writing awards and lead professional development trainings. Every year now, Leah heads to the post office to mail hundreds of copies of her classes' narratives of coming to America. She mails the books to members of North Dakota's legislature, as well as to the state's representatives in Washington, DC. She sends them particularly to those who have undermined her students' sense of security, by speaking out or voting against refugees and immigrants. Whether they read the book, she can only guess. But Leah continues to hope and continues to send out her students' stories.

THE PERSONAL: CHOORI

Choori's walk to school was perilous. "Never pick anything up from the street," his mother warned him often. An abandoned cell phone, a pencil, a battery, a piece of string, a paperclip—all might be attached to a detonator and could trigger an explosion.

Choori was born in the Iraqi capital of Baghdad in 1999. He was four when the United States invaded his country. For much of his childhood he lived with his mother, his uncle, and older siblings in a neighborhood along the Tigris River, directly across from the heavily fortified Green Zone—the command center for the US Army.

The walk to school was barely fifteen minutes, but Choori was watchful. "These were life lessons," he would write in my class years later. "It was a mission to finish the day safe and ready for another one." Growing up in war provided many such lessons.

Lesson one: The reverberating wail of sirens from the Green Zone means take shelter. Huddled in their windowless living room, Choori's family listened to the cacophonous blasts of gunfire and thud of rockets.

Lesson two: Fridges are not reliable. Extended power outages were often daily occurrences. Buy only what would last a day or two without spoiling.

Lesson three: Finely ground Arabic coffee stops bleeding. Choori was five when, while he was playing one afternoon, a rocket ripped through the sky. He followed its arc, stepping backward to keep it in view. He tripped, slicing open a gash on his head. Going to the hospital was too dangerous, but his grandmother, ever resourceful, packed mounds of coffee on the wound, holding it tight until it caked to his scalp.

Lesson four: Be mindful of rooftop solar panels. They are a favorite hiding place for snipers.

Lesson five: Expect the army may regularly visit your home. The Iraqi army made a habit of searching the houses of his neighborhood. They pulled the clothes from the closet, scattered plates and bowls on the floor, flipped tables. "Twice a week you have to pick everything up," Choori remembers. "Twice a week you have to fold the clothes, twice a week you have to fix the kitchen. Twice a week you have to buy a new dish, if they broke one."

Anything can become normal with time.

Choori was eleven in 2010 when he overheard his mother and uncle huddled together fretting about the family's finances. As he told me close to a decade later, "That was my last day of childhood." A nearby butcher needed help unloading haunches of meat; Choori took the job. A tobacco store down the road needed someone to sweep; another job. He learned how to trim beards and mix cement. By fourteen his résumé was extensive. Each night he handed his mother the dinars he had cobbled together.

For a time, too, he worked hanging suits in a men's clothing shop in a bustling shopping mall. In 2016, militants parked a refrigerator truck alongside the mall. It was late and the streets and shops were crowded with families celebrating Iftar, the evening feasts during the month of Ramadan. When the suicide bomber detonated the truck, the mall was consumed in a fiery inferno, stealing the lives of more than three hundred souls. In the tight-knit district, everyone knew, Choori included, someone or many someones who had perished. But by then, Choori and his family had been in the United States for just over a year.

I met Choori on his very first day in a US school, a chilly November morning in 2015. Quietly he introduced himself and selected a seat near the door in my freshman world history class. Though I did not know it then, Choori was shivering with nerves. It was not a normal kind of nervousness—"extra nervous," as he later described it. So nervous that if someone had started speaking his native Arabic, he would have been hard put to understand.

Everywhere in his new school—in the halls, in the cafeteria—there was noise and streams of students. Wide-open spaces made him feel safe. Crowds made him claustrophobic. He strained to take in every detail, and in doing so took in nothing. "My brain cannot take loud chaotic places," he explained years later. "When I'm not 100 percent confident, or even 80 percent comfortable, my brain does not have the same strength . . . I can't handle it." Without English how could he understand? Without understanding, how could he be confident? And without confidence how, he asked, "could I stand in the high school and present myself as me?" Who, he wondered too, would want to befriend a boy from Baghdad? To outsiders, he knew, Iraq meant war. It meant bombs, and deserts, and destruction. Five thousand years of civilization distilled into sound bites. He was just another refugee. A statistic. "There's nothing different about you from the hundred who came before," he told himself. "Or from the hundreds that are going to come after."

For Choori, who possessed little English, math and gym offered the only respites of the school day. His mathematics teacher spoke Arabic, and equations were uncluttered by angular foreign letters. Gym he could pass without speaking at all. Other subjects, though, put him on edge—science in particular. He understood little and found the class unpredictable. Within weeks he started skipping.

Choori can sum up his freshman year in the United States in a single word: uncomfortable. The kind of uncomfortable, as he described, where you might be starving but your stomach can only keep down a bite. The kind of uncomfortable that sets your heartbeat racing. So uncomfortable that your brain goes into overdrive, you start overthinking, overreacting.

—————•—————

In Baghdad, many of Choori's school lessons were reinforced through beatings. Each instructor had a preferred method. Some used their shoes, whacking dusty soles against a boy's head. Others pulled hair, slapped with the flat of their hand, spat. A few preferred a long rod, smacking it across the offending pupil's palms. The boys knew better than to pull away. You stood and took it. Anything might invoke a beating: messy hair, untidy clothes, uncut fingernails. "Anything that was one millimeter above what they asked for and you got punished," Choori recalled nonchalantly. "Teachers treated students as punching bags." Choori's science teacher was particularly aggressive. To this day Choori despises the subject.

In 2013, at the age of fourteen, Choori started skipping occasional classes. When a year later he was made to repeat an entire grade after failing English, he began cutting classes regularly. Each morning he walked to school, but with the first bell, he hopped the fence and ventured out into the city. After a time, his principal took to standing on the school steps to head him off. When he spotted Choori he would shake his head, motion with his hand: "Turn around, go away." Choori did not argue.

The city became his classroom. He learned soccer, pool, boxing. He became lovingly familiar with the side streets and back alleys of Baghdad. He knew them by their smell, the perfume of grilled fish, the tendrils of incense, the sizzle of frying falafel. With no phone, no one could check up on him. He made sure to return home in the early evening, as if arriving from a long day of study.

On the weekends, Choori accompanied his mother into the Green Zone. They rode a roundabout route of buses—a precaution to ensure neighbors would not learn they worked for the Americans. For seven hours they cleaned bedrooms and offices—wiping down mirrors, emptying waste bins, running loads of laundry. From a bespectacled electrician, Choori learned to clean air conditioners, a Sisyphean task of removing sand in a desert city. Choori reckons he was one of the youngest people working in the Green Zone.

It was the family's connections to the Americans that helped them escape in 2015, just as the black-clad fighters of ISIS marched toward Baghdad. Around the world that year, extremists carried out brutal attacks: Twelve gunned down at the French Charlie Hebdo newspaper and four more butchered at a nearby kosher market in January; more than two hundred Assyrian Christians kidnapped in Syria in February; twenty-two slaughtered in front of the ancient mosaics of the Bardo Museum in Tunisia in March; more than a hundred Yemenis bombed while in the act of prayer also in March; dozens of Ethiopians beheaded in Libya in April. A calendar of terror.

In the midst of this bloodshed, Choori's family had interviews, filed refugee paperwork, and received immunizations. By May, the Islamic State had captured the western city of Ramadi, barely an hour and a half's drive from Baghdad. Three months later, in September of 2015, Choori's family fled to America.

Escape took a circuitous route. Bagdad to Jordan; Jordan to Ukraine; Ukraine to New York; New York to New Hampshire and finally to Massachusetts. For much of three days, Choori's family lived on planes and in airports. Choori felt filthy. At each airport he pulled off his socks, washing them in the bathroom sink and wearing them still damp. When he finally stepped outside into a crisp New England evening, his teeth started to chatter and refused to still. The representative from the refugee agency who met them laughed. "You think it's cold now; you haven't seen nothing yet."

By early November, Choori was enrolled in school—the start of that long uncomfortable year. With no structured orientation process, students often rely on the generosity of peers. Another boy from Baghdad, also a student of mine, became Choori's guide. Tall, confident, and assertive, the young man had been blinded by shrapnel when he was little. In his mind, over years, he had drawn a detailed map of the school. Day after day, he led Choori through the halls, pointing out classrooms and offices, explaining the layout of floors and buildings.

School rules were learned by trial and error. Three days after Choori started classes, a school dean stopped him in the hall. Frowning, he pointed at Choori's headphones and held out his hand. Choori knew little English, but the message was clear. He handed over the earbuds and never saw them again. He lost a hat in the same way. School seemed to be composed of a litany of rules: no hats, no hoodies, no headphones. Wear your school ID at all times. No going downtown. No phones in class. No eating or drinking in most classrooms. The rules were irksome, many childish. Like so many of my students, Choori had left childhood behind years ago.

As Choori moved each day between classes, surrounded by hundreds of students, his stomach clenched. He longed to pull up his hoodie, plug in his headphones—tune out the chaos eddying around him. But rules were rules. He gritted his teeth and arrived to class after class, tense.

———•———

In 2009, when Choori was in middle school and still in Iraq, he returned home from school one afternoon to find his mother frantic. His uncle had been kidnapped. The family had forty-eight hours to raise an exorbitant ransom. Somehow the fee was collected. Choori still doesn't know how. Two days later, he arrived home to find his uncle sitting in a chair, head down, arms wrapped tight across his body. The following morning the family set out to find a new home. They drove hours to the Syrian border. But Syria wouldn't have them. They returned to Baghdad, parked the car, and boarded a bus bound for Turkey. There they stayed for over a year.

In a foreign city, in a foreign country, Choori enrolled in school, but instruction was all in Turkish, gibberish to his ears. He found it harder and harder to drag himself from the couch where he slept. Soon he stopped attending. Days slipped by. Sleep, eat, shower, watch TV. For three months he shut himself inside. His body shrank in on itself. Then one day he shook himself, walked outside and kept walking. He climbed a mountain that rose above the neighborhood, got lost. Six hours later he found his way home. Choori never returned to the Turkish school, but from then on, almost every day he went to the mountains.

In Turkey, the family applied for refugee resettlement, but they were racing against time. With no legal way to work, they were running out of funds. Thirteen months after arriving, their money ran out. Resigned, the family returned to Iraq. Choori celebrated his eleventh birthday back in Baghdad.

Choori survived his first suicide bomb two years later, when he was thirteen years old. He had just reached for the broom at the barbershop where he worked when an explosion shattered the glass storefront. Ears ringing, blood on his forehead, Choori took off running. To his left, a building was on fire. Down the street he sprinted until he ran smack into his brother, who, having heard the bomb, had sprinted toward the flames in search of Choori.

Just months later, while Choori was riding a city bus, a car exploded directly behind him. The bus miraculously remained intact. Passengers streamed from the sliding door, but Choori remained frozen. "Please keep going," he begged the driver. Nodding, the driver pressed the accelerator. Forty-five minutes later, Choori stumbled from the bus. His sister, upon seeing him, burst into tears. Many of his friends did not survive the onslaught of bombs that savaged the city in 2014. Funeral processions and burial ceremonies became a regular ritual.

But what scared Choori most—more than the soldiers who ransacked his home, the Green Zone sirens, the missiles crisscrossing the sky, or the suicide bombs—were the thin robed figures of Al-Qaeda. He had seen them—long beards, AK-47s slung casually over shoulders—in the back of a truck, driving brazenly through the streets. They were frightening, creating a degree of terror that lodged itself as a physical pain in his stomach. "You look at them and you ask, do you actually exist? You imagine what they have done, the mental brainwash and what they can do to you, it's disgusting."

———◆———

Growing up in Baghdad, Choori dreamed of becoming a soldier. I was shocked the first time he told me. But perhaps it was not so surprising. To Choori, the army was about loyalty. And since that afternoon when eleven-year-old Choori took his first job, unloading meat, he strove to be the person that others could rely on.

When he started school in the United States, Choori was quick to notice the boys and girls who, each Thursday, wore the blue uniform of the Air Force Junior-ROTC program. Freshmen were not allowed to join. But anticipation became the carrot that got him through that long uncomfortable year. As a sophomore he enthusiastically enrolled. In most of his classes Choori was an indifferent student. In AFJROTC, he was committed. There, lessons were about character, discipline, and patience. "Life laws," Choori dubbed them. He committed to a vigorous exercise regime, doing pushups and running laps around the school. He dutifully studied military history. Every Thursday, his face was shaven smooth, his shoes shined, his uniform starched. "They teach you how to build yourself inside," Choori explained. "I got help. I got love. I got people. I got respect."

Choori watched as classmates transformed before his eyes, flippant or arrogant peers morphing into considerate cadets within months.

"They make you give them your best energy," he told me years later. "No matter who you are." The AFJROTC teachers—sergeants and commanders—treated them differently, collaborating on lessons with the older students, often letting seniors lead classes and run drills. They sat and talked with cadets, explained small American mannerisms, checked in on those who struggled. And cadets watched out for each other. Early on Thursday mornings my class was a sea of suited students running lint rollers down each other's pant legs and straightening each other's collars. After school, cadets lingered, helping each other with math homework, science homework, English.

While much of the school felt segregated, with recent immigrants rarely mingling with native English speakers, AFJROTC was a microcosm of the student body, with students from all neighborhoods, all countries—military hierarchies superseding social hierarchies. "ROTC felt like more than class," Choori reflected. "It was more like a living room."

———•———

As sophomore year slipped into junior year, school grew easier for Choori. He learned the cadence of English through rap and hip-hop—The Notorious B.I.G., Meek Mill, 50 Cent. He secured a job. Work became a second school, offering lessons in English and strategies for interacting with others. Week after week, without fail, Choori handed his mother the majority of his paycheck. He found friends from Cambodia, Rwanda, Brazil. Those like him who worked, who juggled family responsibilities, who understood the hustle it took to be an immigrant child, to be relied on to translate Social Security paperwork, electrical bills, and government documents.

He remained, though, an unapologetically indifferent student. "I didn't study that much," he chuckled. "I was out exploring America." Fishing on the weekend, wandering with friends. But as he grew more comfortable, "instead of getting a lot of help," he explained, "I started helping others."

As an eight-year-old in Baghdad, he had learned generosity from a friend, a boy who paid for others' bus fares and bought extra falafel sandwiches for those who needed to eat. Choori too grew to be observant of the needs of others, and he began stepping in to help. When a few years later a friend dropped out of middle school, Choori sought him out at the cyber café where he worked. His friend, he knew, was illiterate.

"Please," he cajoled, "let me teach you." As a fifteen-year-old, he became his friend's teacher.

As Choori became more comfortable with the United States, he did the same here. When a cadet couldn't scrape together money to dry-clean their uniform, he slipped them bills. If a cadet seemed to be struggling, he alerted his sergeants so they could check in. In 2018, nearing the end of his junior year of high school, Choori was invited to become an AFJROTC flight commander, an honor offered to only a handful of cadets. In his senior year he assumed the role of teacher in many of his AFJROTC classes. He led service trips to a regional food bank, spent Saturdays cleaning litter out of city parks.

Over four years, I taught Choori three times—in his freshman, junior, and senior years. Again and again his quiet caring for others struck me. He knew when a friend hadn't eaten at home and would sneak out of school to buy them a fruit smoothie or a sandwich. When one of my students struggled to log on to his school account, Choori devoted twenty minutes to troubleshooting with the boy. After another student of mine failed her driving test, he spent a weekend morning teaching her to parallel park. For months he helped translate for a recently arrived Iraqi peer. On a field trip once, after the end of a long day, with my throat scratchy and dry, I made an offhand comment to myself that I should find some water. Five minutes later I found Choori quietly placing an open water bottle he had purchased on a table near my lesson plans.

But even as school in the United States grew more comfortable, Choori couldn't shake the tightness he felt. "The feeling is always in my gut," he admitted. "My gut is always telling me to be careful, that something's going to happen. So you gotta stay . . ." He inhales deeply. "Ready." The tightness is consuming. It locks his shoulders and clenches the muscles of his back. It knots his belly. It makes him feel on the verge of burping, but that the burp is stuck in his stomach, in his throat, trying to escape.

He constantly looked for escape routes. In every class he located the doors. Who might walk through that door? Will there be a problem? A checklist of what-if scenarios. It's best, he explained, to be prepared. To ease the tension he selected seats facing the door—a student sentinel. In every class for four years he did this. All except one, where the teacher sat him in the back, far from the door. She didn't know to ask. He didn't know to share. His tension simmered. One afternoon the teacher held him back: "You need to turn in your work, you need to be on time." As she went on, his tension boiled over. With a hand he flipped over a student desk. Bang. Then another. Bang. Choori stalked out. He marched to the head of department's office. "Here's what I did," he explained. "I know I need to apologize." And he did, the very next day. They moved on. But the tightness remained.

For many of my students the shadows of past experiences encroach on the present. Without a feeling of safety, it becomes a mammoth task to will the brain to concentrate, to learn. Schools like Las Americas in Houston and others I've visited know this. They hire trained counselors; they build gardens; they create space in the day for students to share about experiences or feelings one-on-one or in small groups. They identify what might trigger unnecessary stress and tension—loud school bells, chaotic class transitions, varied expectations from classes and teachers— and they work to eliminate them. They teach strategies: how to focus, how to process the past, how to build connections. But in many schools, students are left to muddle along on their own, or with the help of individual teachers.

Few places feel safe to Choori: home, his grandma's house in Iraq, on the streets of his Baghdad neighborhood, the AFJROTC classroom. I'm touched when he adds my classroom to the list.

—————

At the start of senior year Choori enrolled in my upper-level seminar, choosing a seat near the window and across from the door. His homework remained sporadic, but during class he was engaged. My students began writing stories about themselves that would form the pages of a book we planned to publish. After some thought, Choori decided to start at the beginning. "I was born in 1999 when Iraq was under an economic embargo by the USA," he wrote. "Nothing was allowed into the country. This led to much hunger and poverty." He had rarely shared his story and he still wondered: Who would care? How was he more than a statistic? But he began to write. For help, Choori sought out his mother and his uncle. He called up his grandmother back in Iraq. "I never spent much time on homework," he admitted. "But I put in hours and hours for that book." Sharing his story required trust. In weekly circle discussions, the class shared bits of their lives, their experiences. "We walked in separate people," Choori reflected. "We left all together."

One morning, Choori came to my classroom with a gray beanbag chair. It became a permanent fixture. From early morning to late afternoon, teenagers sprawled across it, curled up with assignments, dozed off during lunch block. My classroom took on the feel of a living room. I cleared a shelf of books and filled it with Colombian coffee, Chinese green tea, Iraqi cardamom tea, soothing chamomile. Students brought mugs. Our small electric kettle was constantly boiling.

A crew of seniors, Choori included, took to hanging out in my room in the early hours before school started, in between classes, at lunch, after school. Many I had watched grow up over years. They learned to watch out for each other, to support each other. I became their unofficial adviser, reviewing college essays and job applications, keeping tabs on grades. For a handful I began checking in regularly, making sure they were on track to graduate. Choori needed to pass science. When he tried to cut class, showing up at my door, I shook my head and pointed upstairs. Occasionally I walked him there myself, "You want to graduate!" He laughed, resigning himself to forty-five minutes of molecules. I texted daily reminders, "Good morning, time to come to school!"

On wintery afternoons Choori and I talked about post-school plans. The military remained an option, but he was considering college too, or possibly getting a job. It was hard, he admitted, to imagine life in five years or ten. "What did your mom want you to be growing up?" I once asked. He chuckled softly, but not unkindly. "In Iraq you didn't care so much about what your kid was gonna be. His future's not as important, as long as he is alive."

What mattered most to Choori was providing for and protecting his family. Job prospects were measured against the speed with which he could secure his family a permanent home. Outside of school he was a devoted son—he drove his mother to appointments, picked up groceries, translated documents, arranged doctor visits. "This is my responsibility," he explained with no hint of resentment. Only once have I heard him speak of the weight of all that he carries. It was one afternoon when I stopped at the gas station where he worked. In a lull between customers, he sighed. "Sometimes it's just hard. I am a son and a brother," but also, as he detailed, he often assumed the role of the head of the family. His voice trailed off.

I once asked Choori if he sees himself as an American. He hesitated— he was not sure yet. But, he said, the best Americans, like the best Iraqis, strive to help others for no personal gain. For this reason, he believed he could one day be an American.

———◆———

On the evening of graduation, Choori was nowhere to be found. In the parking lot, beside the arena where the ceremony was held, long snaking lines of gray- and red-robed scholars waited for the signal to begin the procession. Hair was curled and sprayed, button-downs pressed straight. Yesterday my students were kids. Now in their robes they looked older, wiser. They stood taller, some helped by three-inch rhinestone heels.

But where was Choori? I set a group of his friends to calling him. I conferred with my head of department, who had also shepherded him through semesters. Where could he be?

A teacher gave a cue, and the lines grew solemn. In rows of two, students began entering the arena. And then I felt a tap on my shoulder. I whirled around. There was Choori—mortarboard slightly askew, robe unzipped, but here. "Sorry, miss!" He had driven his family, he explained, and gotten stuck in the line for parking. He grinned apologetically. I laughed, shaking my head and letting out a secret sigh of relief.

Forty-five minutes later, after the speeches and the songs, Choori strode across the stage. He was the first in his family to earn a high school diploma. Most of the hundreds of families arrayed in the bleachers heard only another name in a long procession of names. But my hands grew red from clapping.

CHAPTER 4

OPPORTUNITIES TO DREAM

At the center of American identity is the concept of the "American dream"—the promise that this is a country where anyone, from anywhere, can achieve a brighter future for themselves and for their family. It is a powerful magnet that draws newcomers from around the world. In reality, many have been denied that promise, due to laws, prejudice, lack of resources, and other barriers. Making the American dream possible for all people to achieve is an aspiration that the country must strive for. To make new Americans, we must start by ensuring that students have the opportunity to dream—and then that they have a fair chance to transform imagination into reality. The best schools champion and invest in their students' dreams, providing young people with the skills and knowledge they need to fulfill them.

This chapter tells three stories. The first is the story of a Mexican American and Puerto Rican family who, in 1943—after their children were denied access to the "white" school in Westminster, California—organized families to fight for their children's futures by suing four school districts in a case that would ultimately desegregate California schools and lay the legal groundwork for *Brown v. Board of Education.* The second is the story of a program that partners with the families of newcomers at a large high school in Lawrence, Massachusetts, whose students, in the wake of citywide gas explosions in 2018, began dreaming of ways to protect their new city. The third is the story of my own student Safiya, who, after terrorists attacked her school and threatened her family, fled

Iraq and, in her Massachusetts school, became a young civics leader who dreamed of helping her new community.

THE PAST: *MENDEZ V. WESTMINSTER*

In the heat of late summer in 1943, Soledad Vidaurri set off from her brother's newly leased asparagus farm to the nearby 17th Street Westminster School, in Orange County, California. With her were five little ones: her two daughters, Alice and Virginia, and her niece and nephews, seven-year-old Sylvia and her younger brothers, Gonzalo Jr. and Geronimo. Likely the sun was already high, a slight breeze playing in the palm fronds at the school's entrance. The school year was set to begin, and Vidaurri had arrived that September morning to enroll the family. Yet, when she handed in the enrollment papers, the school administrator looked up and scrutinized the children.

Despite being cousins, the kids looked little alike. Vidaurri's daughters were light-skinned and hazelnut-haired. They carried with them, too, the French surname of their Mexican father. Their cousins, in contrast, had skin the color of rich sienna, glossy black hair, and the last name Mendez. Peering at the children, the school administrator calmly told Vidaurri that her daughters could stay, but that the other three were not welcome. Sylvia and her brothers, the administrator explained, would have to attend the Mexican school a mile away. Livid, Vidaurri turned on her heel, refusing that morning to enroll any of the children in school.

Mexican schools, as they were termed, were relatively new to California. In 1913—the same year Sylvia's father, Gonzalo Mendez Sr., was born across the border in Chihuahua—Anglo parents (as those of European descent were called at the time) in Pasadena, California, petitioned the school board to open a separate school for Mexican children. Forty miles south in the district of Santa Ana, where just over two decades later Sylvia herself would come into the world, an elementary school for the first time in its history designated classrooms solely for "Spanish" students. These were some of the first, but like the profusion of orange groves in the citrus belt of Southern California, they were quickly cultivated with similar intentionality.

Up and down the West Coast and in nearby Arizona, New Mexico, and Texas, once-integrated classrooms and schools were quickly segregated. By the start of the Roaring Twenties, segregation was standard practice, and not just in education. Following the model of the Jim Crow South, local and state governments in the American Southwest set about drawing divisions throughout public life. Residents of Mexican ancestry were barred from lunch counters, prevented from living in certain neighborhoods by restrictive covenants, relegated to the balconies of movie theaters, and allowed access to public swimming pools one day a week, after which the water would be drained and the pool scrubbed.

School segregation was long established for others. In the 1860s, partly at the urging of the state superintendent of schools, California adopted a law authorizing cities to establish segregated schools for "Negroes, Mongolians, and Indians."[1] Ongoing integration with these "inferior races," the superintendent argued, would "result in the ruin of the schools."[2] For a time, districts were only required to educate students of color if ten or more parents petitioned the local school board. If there were too few, school officials had the choice whether or not to grant them access to the "white school," and thereby any formal education at all. By the close of the nineteenth century, Black parents had successfully, at least by law, integrated California schools, although segregation of Asian and Indigenous children remained on the books. In all these laws and policies, however, Mexican children were never mentioned.

Legally, former Mexican citizens were granted protection under the final terms of the Treaty of Guadalupe Hidalgo, which ended the war between Mexico and the United States in 1848. Although Mexico lost nearly half a million square miles of land, equivalent to all of Western Europe and then some, the treaty ensured that their former citizens could remain and would be granted full citizenship and privileges in their new nation. This concession on the part of the United States was significant. At the war's end, the country was still seventeen years out from abolishing slavery, twenty years out from granting citizenship to Black Americans, fifty years out from recognizing that right for all US-born children of immigrants. It would take seventy-six years for that same right to be extended to Indigenous peoples, and a full one hundred and four years until the ending of racial restrictions on who could, and who could not, become a citizen of the United States.

How the United States has viewed individuals of Mexican ancestry provides a striking illustration of how race is a social construct that reflects shifting views and prejudices. In the mid-1800s, the government broadly considered them "white." In 1930, the US Census added "Mexican" as a distinct box for the first time. A decade later the category was dropped, and individuals of Mexican ancestry became officially identified as "white" once more. The view would change yet again in the 1970s.

It was the movement of people across land early in the twentieth century that prompted Anglo parents and school boards to begin aggressively segregating children of Mexican ancestry. The Mexican Revolution, beginning in 1910, dr···e many refugees to El Norte. With them came immigrants—often actively recruited by US agricultural, mining, and railroad companies—to fill the gap in cheap labor once dominated by Chinese and Japanese workers, who were now almost entirely banned from immigrating to the United States following the Chinese Exclusion Act of 1882 and the Gentlemen's Agreement with Japan in 1907, under which Japan voluntarily agreed to restrict emigration. And while the 1924 Johnson-Reed Act all but shut US gates, the doors to Mexico remained largely open. Consequently, in the twenty-year span between 1910 and 1930, the Mexican population across the United States tripled. In California, the community grew a staggering sevenfold. Of course, seen another way, less than a century before, the land had belonged to Mexico and not the United States. Thus perhaps more accurately, southern immigrants of the time should be understood not as newcomers but simply as people returning to the land of their grandparents.

In classrooms across the Southwest, new arrivals forever altered the school-age population. By the close of the 1920s roughly one in ten students of the Golden State was of Mexican ancestry. Just south of Los Angeles, in the schools of Orange County, where Sylvia Mendez would spend her childhood, the ratio was closer to one in six. Feeling threatened, Anglo parents actively sought to segregate schoolchildren. The reasons given were multitudinous: Mexican students were said to be unclean, disease ridden, slower learners, and overall lacking in moral fiber. Some argued that separation from white students was advantageous for Mexican students, as it helped them learn English, disregarding the fact that many children of Mexican heritage were already bilingual. Others insisted that the academic achievement of Anglos would be stunted if they studied alongside their Mexican peers. Many more stood by the claim that segregation was essential to the effort of Americanizing newcomers. While elsewhere in the country parochial schools, like that of

Robert Meyer in rural Nebraska, were under attack precisely because they created separate schools based on ethnicity and thereby stymied Americanization efforts, in the Southwest the opposite logic was employed. Only in separate schools, educators claimed, could Mexican children be successfully taught how to become American. The fact that many of those same students were American-born seemed to be, for these educators, immaterial.

The justifications, rooted in prejudice and xenophobia, succeeded in instituting widespread segregation. Districts were deliberately gerrymandered, and non-Mexican families were allowed to transfer to out-of-district schools. One 1931 survey of California school districts containing large Latino populations found that more than 80 percent of those districts had established segregated elementary schools. The remaining school districts maintained segregated classrooms.

These newly branded schools were a study in contrasts, differing from their counterparts in design, curriculum, staffing, and expectations for pupils. Like many segregated Black schools in the Deep South, the Southwest's Mexican schools often had fewer resources and tended toward the dilapidated. A shack was an accurate description for many Mexican schools of the era. Buildings were overcrowded, run-down, and ill furnished. As one Southern California principal recalled, battered and discarded furniture from the Anglo schools would be shipped across town to the Mexican schools. "Mexican teachers," so named not because of heritage but because of place of employment, were largely underqualified and underpaid.

But perhaps most divergent was the course content itself. While Anglo students across the Southwest were instructed in advanced arithmetic, classical literature, and the natural sciences, their Mexican peers were groomed for a very different future. For Mexican boys of the 1920s and '30s, school hours were often devoted to carpentry, blacksmithing, and agriculture, while girls were instructed in the arts of pottery, basketry, rug weaving, home care, and cooking. A 1920 Pasadena principal proudly reported that as early as possible Mexican girls were taught to use a sewing machine, and over a decade later, just south in the district of Garden Grove, a first-grade teacher devoted class time to teaching students how to use a washboard.[3] In the eyes of educators, this is what it meant for Mexican students to become American. These were courses that, in the words of a district superintendent in El Monte, outside Los Angeles, would "help these children take their place in society."[4]

It was assumed that Mexican students would drop out early. Skipping school to work was not only acceptable, but some schools encouraged it. As one student recalled their principal advising them: "If you have to go and pick cotton, you get out and pick cotton and just quit school."[5] Indeed, too much education was dangerous, as one Texas superintendent reminded educators: "If a man has very much sense or education either, he is not going to stick to this kind of work." It was thus the duty of "the white population to keep the Mexican on his knees in an onion patch."[6]

Gonzalo Mendez's family was one of the many who fled Mexico's revolutionary violence, having come to the United States at the close of World War I. His family settled in the district of Westminster in Southern California and enrolled their small son in school. Up until fifth grade, Gonzalo and his sister, Soledad, attended and excelled at the Westminster School, studying alongside Anglo peers. While they were students the institution began the process of dividing classes and separating children. At fourteen years old, needing to provide for his family, Mendez dropped out and went to work in the orange groves. There he met his future wife, Felícitas Gómez Martinez, a woman with a round face and a vibrant smile. Like Mendez, Martinez had moved early in life. Born on the island of Puerto Rico, she and her family had been drawn first to the economic opportunity of the cotton fields in Arizona and then on to California. She too had been forced to leave school early to help her family. The couple fell in love under the oranges, married at the height of the Great Depression, and opened a small cantina in nearby Santa Ana. Soon after, Gonzalo Mendez proudly became a US citizen. He and Felícitas had three children in quick succession, Sylvia, Gonzalo Jr., and Geronimo. Together they made a vow to provide their children with the education they both had been denied. And so, in 1943, having recently moved back to Westminster, it was only fitting that Mendez would seek to send his children to his alma mater.

———•———

Gonzalo Mendez dreamed of owning his own farm. It was a dream he spoke of with his family friend and local banker Frank Monroe, the grandson of German immigrants. In the fall of 1942, as Monroe scrambled to help a family to lease their asparagus farm, Mendez came to mind.

Seima and Masako Munemitsu were raised in the Kochi prefecture on the southern island of Shikoku in Japan. They arrived in the United States as teenagers, married young, and set about raising a family of four, two boys and twin girls. When their first son was born they named him Seiko and gave him the middle name Lincoln, in honor of the sixteenth president of the United States.[7] At the age of twelve, Seiko became the owner of a forty-acre asparagus farm in northern Westminster. His parents, barred by law from obtaining US citizenship, were also ineligible to own land, but their American-born son could. As a young property owner, Seiko also became the family's financial translator and in doing so endeared himself to the friendly local banker, Frank Monroe.[8]

The Munemitsus' twin daughters, Akiko and Kazuko, were six when on the morning of December 7, 1941, a naval base more than two thousand miles away erupted in flames. The following afternoon, with the carnage of Pearl Harbor seared into the nation's mind, the United States declared war on Imperial Japan, entering at last the Second World War. Two and a half months later, President Franklin D. Roosevelt signed Executive Order 9066, greenlighting the incarceration of thousands of Japanese Americans—whom the government deemed "dangerous."[9]

For the audacity of sitting on the board of a Japanese language school and being involved in a Japanese social club, the US government classified Seima Munemitsu a threat. In May of 1942, just as the final stalks of asparagus were being harvested, Seima was arrested and subsequently forced from his home and imprisoned in a New Mexico prisoner-of-war camp. Three days later Masako and the children were given one-way train tickets to Arizona. They arrived at a desolate windswept stretch of desert wrapped in barbed wire. The Poston War Relocation Center, built on land taken, despite objections, from the Colorado River Indian Tribes, would grow to be the largest of ten incarceration camps built across the country. Together the camps imprisoned roughly 120,000 people of Japanese heritage, two out of every three of whom were American citizens. At its zenith, Poston would incarcerate more than 17,000 individuals, including the Munemitsu family, giving the prison the dubious distinction during the war of becoming the third-largest "city" in all of Arizona.

But their faithful friend Frank Monroe would refuse to desert the Munemitsus even after they were incarcerated. Soon he found a family willing to lease their land, and in late spring of 1943, the Mendez family moved to the sprawling asparagus farm in Westminster.

The following fall, when Gonzalo Mendez's sister returned with the children from Westminster School fuming about the school's decision, he thought there must be some misunderstanding. He returned to the school the following day to clear up the confusion, but he too was informed his children would not be admitted. They were directed instead to Hoover Elementary School, a dilapidated squat building sitting forlornly in a dusty stretch of earth in the heart of the neighborhood's *colonia*, a small segregated Mexican neighborhood. Where the main Westminster school had manicured lawns and a rambling playground, Hoover had stretches of dirt, separated from a cow pasture by electric fencing where children were known to get shocked. With no cafeteria, or even benches, students took their lunch sitting cross-legged on the dirt.

Mendez, whose neighbors were Belgian immigrants and Oklahoma migrants who had been pushed westward by the dust bowl, and who all sent their children to the main Westminster School, was indignant. He and his wife stopped sending his children to Hoover, only relenting when many weeks later the district superintendent himself ventured out to the asparagus farm to see why Sylvia and her brothers were absent.

On the farm, after the fields had been tended, Gonzalo and Felícitas Mendez began to talk, then to plan, and then finally to organize parents to challenge the school district. As Felícitas would later testify in court, "We always tell our children they are Americans, and I feel I am American myself, and so is my husband, and we thought that they shouldn't be segregated like that, they shouldn't be treated the way they are."[10]

The following September, joined now by thirty-five fellow Latino parents, the Mendezes presented a petition to the Westminster School District. In straightforward prose the parents laid out their logic: "We believe that this situation is not conducive to the best interests of the children nor friendliness either among the children or their parents involved nor the eventual thorough Americanization of our children. It would appear that there is racial discrimination." They closed with a reminder of the times. Just that summer Allied troops had charged through the waves off Normandy. Paris was recently liberated, and, as the parents penned their letter, American soldiers were fighting their way through the fields and forests of Belgium toward the heart of the Third Reich. "Some of our children are soldiers in the war," the parents reminded the district. "All are American born and it does not appear fair nor just that our children should be segregated."[11] The Mendezes with others appealed first to the county superintendent and then to the district superintendent. Both times they were flatly told there was nothing to be done.

Organizing Southern Californian Mexican parents in the early 1940s was not something to be undertaken lightly. Over a decade earlier, one afternoon in February 1931, plainclothes police officers surrounded a popular park in Los Angeles. Hundreds of park visitors, many of whom were Mexican-American, were interrogated, some detained, a few deported across the southern border. The raid was one of the first of its kind in the country, but more soon followed in the coming months and years.

The raids and resulting mass deportations were carried out by the administration of the thirty-first president of the United States, a businessman who had never before commanded elected office. Herbert Hoover was barely eight months into his presidency when the New York stock market plummeted, pitching the country into what would become a decade-long depression. Desperate to stem the burgeoning crisis, President Hoover in his second State of the Union, following Black Tuesday, sought a scapegoat. "I urge the strengthening of our deportation laws so as to more fully rid ourselves of criminal aliens."[12] Two months later, in early February, he called again on Congress to fund a "vigorous alien deportation drive." The raid in La Placita would take place less than three weeks later. The end goal, later adopted as a slogan of the era, and then again as a sentiment shared nearly ninety years later by the forty-fifth president, was to preserve "American jobs for real Americans."[13]

Across the country, a mostly unofficial but still government-directed so-called Mexican repatriation policy was put in place. It was a plan concocted by Secretary of Labor William Doak, who spuriously claimed that the country was inundated with waves of unlawful immigrants. His key tactic, fear; his main target, Mexican immigrants. With restrictive immigration laws, he explained, "we can make America stronger in every way, hastening the day when our population shall be more homogenous."[14] An article published in the *Nation* that spring ran with the title "Doak the Deportation Chief."[15]

In the coming months, raids rounded up and deported many. But many more were coerced by the threat of raids, and even more perniciously by social workers, relief aid workers, and other local officials who intimidated residents, going door-to-door and sometimes bed-to-bed in hospital wards, to falsely threaten that Depression-era assistance would be cut off and urge residents to "repatriate" to Mexico, despite the fact that many were American-born.[16] Government officials were indiscriminate in their intimidation and deportation, rarely distinguishing among those who were undocumented, legal residents, or US citizens. Many were handed train tickets and given little time to pack. Across a decade, as many as 1.8 million people were deported or coerced to leave the country. Of those, 60 percent were US citizens; many were children born in the United States. Few were ever allowed to return. The message was clear: for those of Mexican heritage, it mattered not how many generations they had lived on the land, and it mattered not whether they were a citizen. In the 1930s, the government refused to consider them "real Americans." At the epicenter of the mass forced exodus were the communities around Los Angeles.

Thus, in the early 1940s, to be of Mexican ancestry and to choose to organize and advocate, even if one was a US citizen, meant taking a significant risk. But for the sake of their children, it was a risk Felícitas and Gonzalo Mendez were willing to take. In January of 1945 they appeared before the local school board. When they were denied yet again, they used money they earned from the Munemitsu farm's bounty to hire a lawyer.

David Marcus, with a receding hairline and a pencil-thin mustache, was a trim man with an olive blush to his skin. The son of Jewish immigrants from what are now Poland and the Republic of Georgia, Marcus was an accomplished civil rights lawyer practicing a thirty-minute drive away in Los Angeles. When he was introduced to the Mendez family, he was heady with a recent victory, a sweeping case desegregating pools and other city facilities in nearby San Bernardino. In the Mendezes' story, Marcus saw the chance to go further.

In the opening days of March 1945, Marcus filed a class-action lawsuit against four neighboring school districts, Westminster, Garden Grove, El Modena, and Santa Ana, on behalf of five fathers—Gonzalo Mendez, William Guzman, Frank Palomino, Thomas Estrada, and Lorenzo Ramirez—and their fifteen children, as well as five thousand additional students of Mexican heritage. The children, Marcus asserted, were "forbidden, barred and excluded" from attending the school of their choice, "solely for the reason that said children or child are of Mexican or Latin descent."[17] In doing so, the districts violated the children's rights to equal protection under the Fifth and Fourteenth Amendments of the United States Constitution. Less than a month later and nearly six thousand miles away, American troops charged across the German Rhine, nearly 350 miles from Berlin. Soon after, the local Westminster school board called Gonzalo Mendez at the asparagus farm. They offered to grant his children admission to his alma mater if Mendez agreed to drop the case. But the Mendezes refused. For them much more was at stake.

———— • ————

As spring settled into the valleys of Southern California in 1945, David Marcus and Gonzalo Mendez set out in search of families who would agree to testify. They drove into the fields—avocado, sugar beet, and lima bean—to speak to farmhands. They knocked on doors in the crowded *colonias*. On the asparagus farm, Felícitas Mendez took over daily operations, thereby allowing her husband to fully devote his time to the case. She spearheaded organizing local parents while her husband and Marcus drove farther afield.

As they collected evidence outlining systemic discrimination by the state, across the Atlantic world powers were dismantling a regime rooted in racial hierarchy. Two months before the Mendez trial was set to start, deep in a bunker beneath the streets of Berlin, as Russian artillery rumbled throughout the city, Adolf Hitler raised a gun to his temple and pulled the trigger. Seven days later Germany surrendered unconditionally to the Allied powers. But the war in the Pacific Theater raged on. Following the fireworks of July 4th, Marcus stood before federal Judge Paul John McCormick, the son of Irish and English immigrants, ready to do battle against the school districts of Orange County.

With no explicit law to justify their segregation, the four school districts grounded their defense in language. The districts did not discriminate, or so they argued; they simply separated and supported students who needed additional assistance learning English. It just so happened that all such students had Mexican ancestry. It was a pretext Marcus would, in court, doggedly dismantle.

On the first day of trial, one after another, Marcus called moms and dads to take the stand. His questioning ran as if on a loop: Did your children speak English before they started school? Yes. Do you speak English with your children in your home? Yes. Did school officials ever give your children a language test to determine school placement? No. Where were your children born? The United States of America. Again and again he asked parents to relate what happened when they sought admission to their school of choice. As if one, they described being told that Mexican children were not allowed.

Marcus, it happened, had some personal understanding of what it felt like to be told, as a child of immigrants, that he didn't belong. As Marcus shared with his family and as his eldest daughter shared with me decades later, as a boy he had played the violin at a recital. Because he was Jewish, he was told to play behind a curtain, hidden from view. Another boy stood before the crowd miming the motions.

But it would be the afternoon testimony on that first day of trial, of Garden Grove's school superintendent James Kent, that would begin to unravel in earnest the schools' claim. With little effort, Marcus got Kent to concede that the students attending Mexican schools were American and that many spoke English. Why then, if the schools were set up to support Spanish speakers, Marcus inquired, were those who spoke English still segregated? Kent's answer appeared assured: "Mexican children have to be Americanized much more highly than our so-called American children. . . . They must be taught manners. They must be taught cleanliness." Kent confidently considered himself an expert in such matters. Indeed, as a student at the University of Oregon he had composed his thesis on the very topic of segregating Mexican students in Southern California schools. As he went on to explain, there was much that Mexican students must be taught so as to succeed in America, specifically "cleanliness of mind, mannerisms, dress, [and the] ability to get along with other people." For the benefit of the court, Marcus encouraged Kent to elaborate on the particulars of the hygiene Mexican students lacked. Kent's answer again did not falter: "In the care of their heads, lice, impetigo, tuberculosis, generally dirty hands, face, neck, ears." "Do you keep a record of dirty hands and face?" Marcus challenged.[18] No, Kent was forced to concede, the schools did not.

But, when peeled back, Kent's primary justification for segregation came down to degrees of intelligence. Mexican children, he believed, were just not as smart as their Anglo peers. When Marcus asked Kent to estimate to what extent Hoover school students, including all three Mendez children, were inferior, his answer was swift: 75 percent. From where he drew that calculation, he did not say.

At the turn of the twentieth century French psychologists, at the behest of the Ministry of Education, developed a test to measure natural intelligence. The goal was to distinguish between learning disabilities and laziness. An intelligence quotient (IQ) test followed and was quickly and enthusiastically adopted by US eugenicists and educators.

In 1924, the same year the United States instituted its immigration quota system, a University of Texas instructor set out to determine the difference in IQs between Mexican and "white" children, ignoring that Mexican children were officially "white." He concluded that Mexican children had 85 percent of the intelligence of so-termed white students. Mexican students, he asserted, were outsmarted by English, Jewish, Chinese, and "American" students, again disregarding the fact that most of the Mexican students he tested were likely American-born. He claimed too that while "white" children got smarter with time, Mexican children plateaued at around age nine. "Obviously, as the children grow older," he concluded, "the superiority of the whites becomes greater."[19] Four years later a University of Denver psychologist tested over one thousand Mexican students and claimed that they had a dismal median IQ of 78.1, squarely classifying them as "feeble-minded."[20] Studies like these, which gave the appearance of applying cutting-edge scientific research to the classroom, provided educators with license to discriminate. Curriculums were quickly altered to be commensurate with students' supposed maximum intelligence.

In a California courtroom, on the first day of trial, James Kent testified that Mexican children were academically inferior to Anglos and to educate them together would be a disservice to both, impeding progress for one while hampering support for the other. It was an argument his colleagues would reiterate in the following days, and it was an argument that rankled Marcus. When, during the pretrial hearing Judge McCormick asked if segregation might be linked to intelligence, Marcus's denial was so vehement that the judge was taken aback. "Don't get angry about it," he chided. "I just asked you the question." To which Marcus curtly replied, "It strikes home, your honor."[21] What the judge did not know, nor would likely any of the school officials arrayed in the courtroom, was that for all of David Marcus's European Jewish heritage, this case was profoundly personal. Marcus's wife was a Mexican political refugee, and together they were raising their three daughters to be bilingual.

Over the following days Marcus pummeled, seemingly with relish, the logic of the schools. Throughout two weeks of trial, the court heard from two dozen witnesses: parents and children, school superintendents, teachers, principals, and one university professor. A fourteen-year-old girl charmed the judge with her eloquence, and a mother of two pointedly asked how the government could have considered her son Joe qualified to fight overseas for the US Navy, if they did not consider her eight-year-old Bobbie qualified to be educated in an integrated classroom. For their part, the school officials were nothing if not inventive in their attempts to justify segregation, seamlessly weaving in new rationales when old ones frayed.

Illustrating the districts' idiosyncratic application of policy, Marcus elicited that other non-Anglos, including Japanese and Filipino students, were not segregated. Indeed, paradoxically, while California law permitted the segregation of Asian students, the Munemitsus' children had attended the main Westminster school, while the Mendezes', not barred by law, were denied. But Marcus did not stop there. What of those students who no longer had a "language handicap," he asked. Such students, the superintendent of El Modeno explained, should remain segregated, as they were leaders who would inspire their less intelligent peers. Kent argued it would be entirely unfair to put a "lone Mexican child in a group of forty white children." Segregation protected students from the taunts of Anglos. Here, Judge McCormick could not help but interject: Isn't it "the duty of the school authorities to endeavor to inculcate into the disrespectful Anglo-Saxon child some respect of the other child?" Alas, Kent explained, there was simply not enough time in the school year. When Marcus had the audacity to ask if perhaps bilingualism might be educationally advantageous, Kent was dismissive: "In the schools, we are not teaching languages. In the schools we are trying to arrive at an educational cultivation of our American ideals." When Kent explained that schools taught American history, Marcus mused that given California's historical ties with Mexico, Mexican children might be at an advantage. Kent held firm. Anglo children, he purported, inherently had a better understanding of the state. The Westminster superintendent, Richard Harris, elaborated: "In an English speaking home . . . there are certain cultural backgrounds which undoubtedly were formed, many of them, and came in earlier days from England. Out of those come Mother Goose rhymes."[22] It was apparently due to this critical deficit that Mexican children could not yet be considered true Americans.

In the courtroom, in the very first row of seats, every single day of the trial, sat the entire Mendez family. Still quite young, it would be years before Sylvia, Gonzalo Jr., and Geronimo would grasp the magnitude of their parents' actions. As Sylvia would share with me more than seventy years later, "I never realized back then that my parents were fighting for equality, freedom, and justice . . . I just thought they wanted us to be able to go to a beautiful school with a nice playground . . . and not the horrible school in the barrio."[23]

In the final hours of the multiday trial, Marcus called two unusual experts to the stand—a former school principal and a university professor of anthropology and sociology. It would be one of the first times in an American civil rights case that a lawyer would draw on social science research. The pair were straightforward in their testimony. Countering the districts' argument that segregating students in its "Mexican" schools aided them in learning English, they testified that it actually hindered them. Yet that was not all. "There is no question," Professor Ralph Beals explained, that "segregation slows up such a program of Americanization."[24] Both agreed that segregation was still more insidious. It would be the conviction of educator Marie Hughes that would reverberate after the close of trial: "Segregation, by its very nature, is a reminder constantly of inferiority, of not being wanted, of not being a part of the community. Such an experience cannot possibly build the best personality or the sort of person who is most at home in the world, and able to contribute and live well. . . . In order to have the people of the United States understand one another, it is necessary for them to live together, as it were, and the public school is the one mechanism where all the children of all the people go."[25] It would be a full six months before Judge McCormick would hand down his decision.

———•———

By August of 1945, the Munemitsu family had survived more than three years of incarceration in Arizona. It was three years of blistering summers and frigid winters, three years of windstorms and endless dust. Few were allowed to pass beyond the barbed wire, but the Mendez family would sometimes drive the 250 miles to the camp to pay in person the rent for the Munemitsus' farm. The remainder of the farm profits, which were plentiful, the Mendezes funneled into their court case.

While Sylvia's parents fought for integrated schools in California, the twins, Akiko and Kazuko, attended school in Arizona in a long adobe building hastily erected by the incarcerated Japanese Americans. They were instructed in a curriculum authored by the federal War Relocation Authority, with lessons stressing loyalty and nationalism. Each morning the young American-born citizens stood and pledged their allegiance to a country that granted them neither "liberty" nor "justice."

The little girls were likely home on the day in early August when their country dropped an oblong-shaped bomb, code-named "Little Boy," on the city of Hiroshima in the country of their ancestors. It was a bomb of such ferocious energy that as many as 80,000 men, women, and children died almost instantly, some seeming to vanish from the earth, leaving behind shadowed outlines on walls and stone steps. Three days later the United States dropped a second bomb on the coastal city of Nagasaki. The deaths of close to 200,000 souls in the following moments, days, and weeks, would be attributed to America's atomic bombs.

Less than a month later Imperial Japan surrendered, and in the deserts of Arizona the US government, with no attempt at apology, told the Munemitsu family they could go home. The Munemitsus were welcomed back to the asparagus farm by the Mendezes. In the aftermath of a world war, together the families farmed the land while the little ones played in the barn and among the crops.

The Munemitsus and Mendezes had lived together for five months when, in the winter of 1946, Judge McCormick handed down his decision. In a blistering twenty-page ruling, the judge eviscerated the school boards' arguments. McCormick grounded his authority in *Meyer v. Nebraska* and the right of students to "acquire knowledge." The schools' actions, he concluded, demonstrated "a clear purpose to arbitrarily discriminate against the pupils of Mexican ancestry." It was a policy, he found, that would "foster antagonism in the children and suggest inferiority among them where none exists." Separate schools, even if identical, would not suffice. "A paramount requisite in the American system of public education is equality," McCormick reasoned. "It must be open to all children . . . regardless of lineage."[26]

The school districts promptly appealed, and the following December the case was taken up by the US Court of Appeals for the Ninth Circuit. This time, Marcus was joined by a powerful coalition of allies who each submitted an amicus brief to the court: the American Civil Liberties Union, the American Jewish Congress, the Japanese American Citizens League, the attorney general of California, and the National Association for the Advancement of Colored People (NAACP). The last brief was penned by two young lawyers, Robert Carter and Thurgood Marshall, who had been watching the *Mendez* case unfold from afar. As Carter would reflect years later, they saw *Mendez* as "a dry run for the future."[27]

The specter of Hitler hung over the federal courtroom on the day of appeal. In argument, David Marcus was explicit: "If we accept the premise . . . that a school board can do anything it desires and not be in violation of the Federal Constitution, a board can start segregation with children of Mexican descent, go on with Germans and other national origins . . . and we'll have the same situation we had in Germany."[28] Four months later the court of appeals upheld McCormick's ruling, striking down as unconstitutional the segregation of Mexican students in California schools. Reporting on the outcome for the *Nation*, a clairvoyant Carey McWilliams mused that the *Mendez* decision might "sound the death knell of Jim Crow in education."[29] Two months later, the governor of California—son of immigrants from Sweden and Norway—one Earl Warren, signed legislation ending in the state all legal school segregation of students, regardless of race or ethnicity.

Six years later, Governor Warren would be tapped by President Eisenhower to become chief justice of the United States Supreme Court. One of the very first cases that would come before his Court would be one argued by an author of an amicus brief in the *Mendez* case, the NAACP's Thurgood Marshall. The case, *Brown v. Board of Education of Topeka*, had at its center a nine-year-old Black girl from Kansas. Like Marcus, Marshall would draw on social science research to buttress his argument and he would have in his files the briefs and notes from the *Mendez* case, which Marcus had generously shared. A year later Warren, writing for the Court, echoed Judge McCormick: "To separate [African American students] from others of similar age and qualifications solely because of their race generates a feeling of inferiority as to their status in the community that may affect their hearts and minds in a way unlikely ever to be undone. . . . We conclude that, in the field of public education, the doctrine of 'separate but equal' has no place."[30] Schools throughout the country were ordered to desegregate. It was an order that would transform education by ending legal segregation, although in the decades to come it would not be sufficient to truly integrate the country's schools.

In Southern California, Sylvia, Gonzalo Jr., and Geronimo enrolled for a time at the Westminster school, studying alongside the Munemitsu daughters. When their lease on the asparagus farm ran out, the Mendez family returned once more to Santa Ana. Nearly a decade later, Seima and Masako Munemitsu took their twins, soon after they turned twenty-one, to visit Japan, the one and only trip the girls would make to their parents' first home. Together they toured the islands, as Akiko shared with me, wandering through ancient temples and bustling cities. But mostly they spent time in Kochi, staying with their grandmother and filling their days with family. In the eyes of their cousins, the twins were quintessential Americans. They wore jeans, lived near movie stars, and walked down streets the cousins thought were littered with dollar bills. Throughout the trip the girls were peppered with questions. But of the war or the family's incarceration, much was left unsaid.[31]

For decades the story that started on the asparagus farm would go largely untold. Half a century and more would slip by before Sylvia and Akiko reconnected, coming together to publicly share their history. Sixty-four years after Felícitas and Gonzalo Mendez testified on behalf of their children, a high school in Los Angeles was named in their honor. And then in 2011, their daughter, Sylvia Mendez, now retired from a career in nursing, was invited to the White House. There, in recognition of her family's commitment to desegregate schools, President Barack Obama placed around her neck the nation's highest civilian honor, the Presidential Medal of Freedom.

THE PRESENT: ENLACE, MASSACHUSETTS

"I always worry that no families will come." Allison Balter was pacing in front of the fourth-floor stairwell. With closely cropped copper hair, Allison exudes warmth. She is quick to smile, but often has her sleeves scrunched to the elbow: She means business. In 2015 she launched an experiment, which she now heads: ENLACE Academy. (The name is an acronym for Engaging Newcomers in Language and Content Education, and is given the Spanish pronunciation, en-LA-say.) Her school of two hundred is embedded within Lawrence High School in Lawrence, Massachusetts. Allison was driven by a question: What would a teenager who had been in the country less than two years need not just to survive but to thrive? She and colleagues envisioned a program for ninth graders, designed specifically for those students who might struggle most—children with so little English that they could understand neither their teachers nor their textbooks. But it was not just language Allison worried about. As she knew from years of teaching, almost everything was unfamiliar for a newcomer: Classes might involve group work instead of individual assignments, expectations for written essays might be markedly different, history would be unfamiliar. Students would be struggling to make friends, find jobs, battle homesickness. Allison wanted a program small enough and supportive enough that, after a year, when the newcomers entered tenth grade with peers in the larger high school, they would have the confidence to know they belonged.

Without fail, Allison stations herself each morning at the top of the stairs to ENLACE, laughing, joking, and fist-bumping students. I joined her one day. "Here come the three musketeers!" she called out, greeting a gaggle of young women, hair pulled high into buns, who giggled as they walked by. "Good morning Alejandro, I hear you're leading class today!" She high-fived a gangly boy, a mop of curls tickling his eyebrows, and gently reminded another to stow his headphones. Her greetings slipped from Spanish to English, English to Spanish. "*Buenos días*, how are you doing this morning?" A boy paused to think. "I am well." For each student she had a question, "*Cómo te va en historia?*" "Did you apply for school government yet?" Or a compliment, "Beautiful nails," which sparked a shy smile from a girl with polka-dotted polish. But today was different. Today Allison was waiting not just for students, but for their families.

Even when ENLACE was only an idea, Allison decided that if her program was to succeed, she would need to partner with parents. Ten years earlier, in 2010, about to embark on her first year of teaching, Allison had volunteered to help run a kind of community garage sale to raise funds for her new elementary school. As the morning wore on, she assisted one family who carefully selected a tower of toys. Eyeing the stack, she offered to help carry the collection to the family's apartment in the housing projects across the street. The parents welcomed Allison into their home, chatting with her in Spanish while the children played. When colleagues learned of her visit they were shocked. "You went into the projects?! Are you okay?" The reactions stayed with her. As she began her first year of teaching, she would hear assumptions made again and again about her students' homes and families. "Parents don't care about their kids' education," "Parents should just let us do our job," "Parents are why children don't succeed." Allison vehemently disagreed with such beliefs. From her own experiences, she knew that families were children's most important teachers. And that was why, when she would later map out ENLACE, family engagement was a central pillar.

A young mother climbed the stairs, "*Cómo estás?*" Smiling broadly, Allison invited her down the hall to a classroom with a circle of chairs and a side table piled high with muffins. A second mother appeared, then a third. Allison and her team were hosting what they have come to call Café con ENLACE.

Lawrence neighbors Lowell, where I teach. A twenty-minute drive separates the two high schools. Both cities are dense with the hulking carcasses of abandoned textile mills, slowly being repatterned into offices and luxury condos. They are cities made prosperous, for more than a century, by immigrants. Today, Lawrence and Lowell remain cities powered by newcomers, though Lawrence is also one of the poorest communities in Massachusetts. Despite the proximity, though, our communities look little alike. In Lowell my students come from more than thirty different countries, but in Lawrence, a majority of newcomer students hail from the Dominican Republic.

ENLACE is tucked into two floors of a protruding wing of an enormous high school, a sprawling campus that houses upwards of three thousand students. Its out-of-the-way location affords the school within a school a modicum of calm. The two floors are home to just the roughly two hundred students enrolled in the program. Over much of the last decade, the surrounding school has undergone almost constant metamorphosis. Having stumbled through years of chronically low student test scores and abysmal graduation rates, the district fell into receivership in 2011; the state came in to remake the schools. Students, classes, and grades were shuffled and reshuffled in an attempt to raise scores and graduation rates. In the most recent iteration, most of the school's programs were merged into a lower school and an upper school. ENLACE is one of the few that stands separate.

On the fourth floor, a bell rang and the last students slipped into classes. A mother balancing a chubby-cheeked infant climbed the stairs. A shy toddler in fuzzy brown boots trailed after her. Allison could not contain her cooing. Parents kept coming, fathers, mothers, siblings. In the classroom, the circle of chairs slowly filled with families. Though they traveled only a few miles to reach the school that winter morning, theirs was the continuation of a journey that had crossed an ocean and traversed 1,600 miles. They were families who had left homes, and jobs, and relatives, driven by dreams for their children. They had arrived at ENLACE that morning to help ensure those dreams became reality.

———◆———

In 2010, as a new teacher in Lawrence, Allison was assigned to teach immigrants and the children of immigrants, all still mastering English. She was new to the city. Having grown up in Connecticut, Allison came from a family long established in America: English and Irish immigrants who came in the 1600s, Russian Jews who arrived in the 1900s. In her new classroom she saw her pupils for less than an hour a day, and she was responsible in that time for providing language practice that would help students in their primary classes. Night after night she stayed up fretting. She felt ill equipped to support her students. Few resources were readily available. Allison called friends, sat in on colleagues' classes, cobbled together lessons, improvised. And then, only two months into the semester, her elementary school bloomed with mold, forcing them to temporarily relocate. Classes were dispersed throughout neighborhoods. For the next six months Allison taught her second, third, and fourth graders in the attic of a repurposed church. "It was a good introduction,"

Allison chuckles. "Education is about being flexible, even when all of the forces are against you."

Mold, attics, and limited support notwithstanding, Allison fell in love with the community. Her second year, in a real classroom once more, she approached her principal: She wanted to design a class specifically for newly arrived immigrant students who would stay with her most of the school day. Approval granted, Allison set to work designing a curriculum, and for the following year, she began teaching her school's newest newcomers.

Five years later, in the winter of 2015, Allison heard rumblings of a plan to redesign the city's behemoth high school. The superintendent and district leadership team were considering a program for newcomers entering ninth grade and were looking for a leadership team. Allison did not hesitate. She applied and was soon named principal. At a local coffee shop, she and her new leadership team began sketching a plan on brown butcher paper. Allison had roped in a former colleague, Lindsey Mayer, who within months became ENLACE's founding dean of curriculum, and Jeannette Jimenez, a Dominican immigrant and Lawrence social worker, as director of student support. Plans took form over plates of nachos and *tostones*. In August of 2015, ENLACE opened its doors. As one of her first acts as head of school, Allison and the newly formed leadership team began reaching out to their families.

Strong family engagement in school is a powerful predictor of success. Studies show that when teachers and families collaborate, student test scores shoot up. So too do attendance and graduation rates. Students are less likely to act out in class or drop out of school. Rates of college enrollment tick up. The effect is not just noticeable in students. With teachers too the impact is discernable. Educators who collaborate with families report that their teaching is more fulfilling. They say they are less overwhelmed and tend to remain longer in the profession.[32]

But few schools and few teachers know how to begin building such relationships. Dr. Karen Mapp, a Harvard professor and former Boston public school deputy superintendent, has devoted a career to rethinking family engagement, from national policy down to the neighborhood school. She believes that the work begins with what teachers think about their students' families. Too often what comes to mind is parents' deficits. Families don't have enough money or time. They don't speak enough

English, or have enough education. Well intentioned or not, focusing on what parents lack discourages educators from trying to collaborate with families. Any school serious about engaging families, Dr. Mapp believes, must start with recognizing the array of assets those families possess. Mindset matters.

Allison and the ENLACE team understood this. If they wanted families to be at the center of their new school, they would need to intimately understand and respect families. They planned all-staff trainings. But they also decided that, as much as possible, ENLACE teachers should come from the community. Zach Marshall-Carter, a biology teacher, graduated from Lawrence High in 2014. Much of the school's math department, too, are proud alumni. One-third of ENLACE's staff had been students at the school.

Over lunch the teachers swapped stories from school days not so long ago, quick to laugh at how much they had forgotten. They talked about much-loved teachers, favorite clubs. But they also remembered the disparities. As Daniela Ayala, a math teacher, explained to me, "If you were one of the good kids, you were prioritized. And other kids were just . . . there." Back in 2012, *Boston Magazine* printed a scathing portrait of the city. "With 76,000 people squeezed into 6.93 square miles, violent crime on the rise, and a public school system that's the worst in the state, the once-proud 'Immigrant City' has become an object lesson in how to screw things up." The title declared: "Lawrence, MA: City of the Damned."[33]

Zach, a sophomore at Lawrence High when that article ran, was incensed. So too were many of his peers. "We were so outraged that someone would call this place that we loved damned. The article suggested that everyone here wouldn't amount to much." Students took to the streets. They marched and published articles. A friend of Zach's started a newsletter, "What's Good in the Hood," that highlighted the city's strengths, with Zach serving as layout editor. Their experiences made many of the young teachers fiercely loyal to their school and to their city. For Daniela as a student, Lawrence High was a haven. Elementary school had been rough: "I felt very alone and othered in this country." Like most of her students, Daniela is from the Dominican Republic. She came to America when she was only five. During high school, home, she shared, was at times challenging. But, she added, "teachers stepped up and provided what felt like home." Lawrence High was for her a place of stability, of love. For her students now, she hopes to offer the same.

Many teachers intimately understand the journey these families have taken. The parents who arrived on that chilly winter morning for the school's Café con ENLACE were like their own parents. ENLACE staff know from experience that schools are often unwelcoming to immigrant families. Parents must learn to navigate unfamiliar school systems and new expectations. School bureaucracy, challenging even to American-born parents, can prove impenetrable for newcomers. For those still mastering English, translators can be scarce. Students step in to help. At one school I visited elsewhere in the country, staff had to resort to phoning a Chinese restaurant down the road to patch together a three-way conversation with parents. And there are other barriers built through biases and unquestioned assumptions. As a teacher, I've heard educators give a range of reasons why immigrant families don't show up in school when asked: "In their culture they don't believe in educating girls"; "*they* just don't believe education is as important." Based on my experience, I know these assumptions are wrong. Indeed, my students' parents have often given up everything familiar to give their children a brighter future.

In the ENLACE classroom, families filled the circle of chairs. Laminated photographs were splayed out in concentric circles on the floor. A mosaic of pictures depicting professions: *Artista, Carrera de Psicología, Maestro, Dentista.* "What career do you hope your child will have?" Allison asked in Spanish. Moms and dads bent down, crouching to examine options. Some were quick in their determination. A man scooped up the photo of a pilot. A woman selected the image of a teacher. The mother with the baby considered her options for many minutes before slowly bending to choose a doctor. Futures selected, the parents introduced themselves. One father started the conversation: "It was my dream to be a pilot and I didn't get to. I hope, if he wants to, my son will be able to be one." Around the room everyone nodded; the feeling was familiar. Here, they hoped, their children's futures would be different.

———•———

At ENLACE, the school year kicks off not in the classroom but in students' homes. In the weeks leading up to Labor Day, ENLACE staff fan

out in pairs into the community. Their goal is twofold: introduce themselves to their soon-to-be students and learn directly from their pupils'
parents. "What are your hopes for your son this year?" "What do you
dream your daughter will become?" The visits are often accompanied
by ever-refilled cups of coffee. Tables are laid with plates of pupusas and
arroz con habichuelas. Teachers meet moms and dads, but also chubby
baby sisters, shy younger brothers. They shake hands with cousins, aunts,
uncles, *abuelas, abuelos*. Allison and ENLACE's art teacher, Shaddai Vargas, once found themselves in a living room seated among a family's
church friends, carried away in a sing-along.

"Teachers generally are accustomed to only seeing families in school,"
reflected Jennifer Suriel, ENLACE's dean of student and family engagement. But for many families, she noted, school is neither a comfortable
nor a welcoming place. "Traditionally you were called to school only
when something was wrong." Home visits are often similarly a sign of
trouble, reserved for check-ins on truant or unruly students.

Even if teachers believe that their students' parents possess assets,
most schools create few opportunities for teachers to learn from families. Parents, as Dr. Karen Mapp explains, are typically invited to participate in very limited ways—attending student plays, contributing to
bake sales, helping with homework, following school rules. These are
one-sided relationships, like a conversation where only one participant
speaks. And they are relationships that are largely confined to school
buildings, where teachers, not families, feel most comfortable.

In 2017, I coauthored a book with Dr. Mapp and veteran teacher Ilene
Carver. We called teachers across the country to learn about best practices for partnering with families. From them we heard of school structures that, whether they meant to or not, made families feel small, like a
hindrance rather than a strength. There was the front office staff who ignored or spoke curtly to families when they arrived; the back-to-school
nights where educators presented a litany of rules and regulations; the
special education meetings jumbled with so much jargon it was hard
for parents to comprehend; the family-teacher conferences scheduled
in hours that conflicted with parents' work. Teachers who wanted to
create strong relationships with families would need to take a different
approach. We asked them how they began building trust. Many told us
they began with home visits.

At ENLACE, families don't come to teachers, teachers come to families. They come when invited: early morning, midafternoon, at the cusp of dusk. When they arrive they don't speak of rules. They are here to listen to dreams. Teachers see their students and their families through a different lens. Foundations are laid in living rooms and built on trust and mutual respect. In Allison's third year as a teacher, and her first at a new school, she had participated in such home visits. She knew firsthand how they shaped her relationship with both her students and their families. So, when ENLACE opened in 2015, Allison called in experts to train the staff.

With students, like with families, Allison and her leadership team strive to create a program where everyone has a chance to be heard. Mornings at ENLACE start with a check-in, a chance for advisory classes to take the pulse of the student body. One winter morning, thirteen students pulled chairs into a circle in the back of a classroom. The lights were switched off, a gentler transition for teenagers still rubbing sleep from their eyes. Projected on the board was an assembly of emojis, each labeled with their corresponding emotion: cheerful, ecstatic, lonely, calm, furious. One girl, pink jacket draped like a blanket across her knees, started off, "I feel joy today because tomorrow . . ." She glanced at the teacher, *"mañana?"* Getting confirmation, she proceeded. "Tomorrow is Friday!" A boy with thick glasses followed excitedly, "I feel . . . all the feelings!" Grinning, a girl with long wavy hair pulled high into a ponytail proclaimed, "Today I feel happy because today I have one year here."

Too often new arrivals are the quietest children in school. They might sit silent for months, their ears and minds struggling to decipher new sounds. Early on, words have a tendency to lodge in the crevices of the brain, or get caught somewhere in the throat. Unable to speak confidently in English, often unable to be understood, and sometimes actively discouraged from speaking in their primary language, children might not speak at all in class. Vividly, Daniela, the math teacher, told me about her own second-grade experience. Once, she and her classmates were asked to read at home and have their parents sign a form to confirm they had done so. Still mastering English at the time, Daniela did not comprehend the instructions. Another student obligingly translated them as, "You need your parent's name on the sheet." The next day Daniela proudly produced her reading log, on which she had dutifully written her mother's name. The teacher was livid: "You forged your parent's signature!" Daniela was sent to detention. Tears rolling down her cheeks, she wondered what she had done wrong.

Across the country, teachers of immigrant-origin students are faced with dueling responsibilities: ensure students master a new language and simultaneously keep pace academically. For students and teachers it is a grueling task. Unspoken compromises are common. Language often takes priority. Children can fall behind academically.

At ENLACE, Allison is in luck. In most years, all or nearly all of her pupils speak Spanish. Many of the staff can slip between languages. Instruction is lubricated by ample use of Spanish. Discussions about cell replication and World War II are brisk. It is a strategy well suited for Lawrence, yet not for neighboring Lowell, where my students collectively speak more than thirty tongues. At ENLACE, Allison can ensure that every student can voice opinions, engage in academic arguments, ask questions, and be understood. I slipped into Daniela's math class one afternoon. In the back I watched as a girl, gold earrings dangling, completed a graph and shivered with excitement. The class moved on to writing and graphing equations. Forty minutes sped by. Suddenly the bell rang. A boy looked up, shocked. "Miss, *por qué es que cuando yo pongo atención y entiendo la clase, la clase se va más rápido!*" (Why is it, when I pay attention and understand the class, class goes faster?) He was still shaking his head as he stowed his binder.

Between classes and lesson planning, Daniela texts families. Almost daily, she checks in with the mom of a gangly young man who can be a handful. She sends one-liners, sometimes longer missives. One afternoon, I watched Daniela send a photo of the boy hunched over, immersed in his graph. "I wanted her to see how hard he's working," she explained. Families have come to expect her texts, and also her calls. On the phone she shares about Yulissa's success on a test, Pedro's struggle with a math concept. But conversations are often wide-ranging. With trust established, parents themselves begin to share. They speak of factories that have unexpectedly cut their hours, of sleepless nights, of loneliness, of the isolation of raising children in a foreign land. Their worries are the worries Daniela's mom had during her own growing up. When these parents speak, it is hard for Daniela not to hear her own mother's voice. "When a student is being frustrating, I think back to that conversation with their parent. They are doing it all for their kid. You hear the concerns and the way parents pour themselves out to you. It's not just my student, it is their child, it is their baby. I have to do my part.'"

———◆———

In 2018, fifteen days into Daniela's first year of teaching at ENLACE in Lawrence, her community exploded.

It was a Thursday. The last school bell had rung, but young thespians were still practicing their lines, members of the Junior ROTC program were marching in the halls, and sports teams were running drills across the back fields. Just before 5 p.m., houses across Lawrence, Andover, and North Andover erupted into flames.

Daniela was in the parking lot, where she spotted her younger cousin, and current student, crying. "Dad says Lawrence is on fire, that we have to get out!" Allison, still in her office, remembers the urgent command over the loudspeaker: "Everyone evacuate!" Students and teachers pounded down stairs. On the football fields, they crowded together and watched smoke billowing upwards over the city. Allison's wife texted within minutes, "Are you okay?" "We don't know what's going on," she texted back.

Calls began jamming the Lawrence Fire Department phone line. Firefighters doused one house, only to have another erupt. A fiery whack-a-mole. A ten-alarm blaze. A little past 5 nearly twenty houses caught fire almost simultaneously. More followed suit. Over the radio, the dispatcher's disbelief was audible: "This is crazy!"[34] Driving toward the smoke, the Andover fire chief couldn't believe his eyes; it was "Armageddon. . . . an absolute war zone."[35] Three blocks from the school, a student from the city's alternative high school pulled into his friend's driveway just before the house exploded. The entire chimney shot skyward and down. The car and the boy, who just that morning had received his driver's license, were crushed. He would die hours later.

At Lawrence High there was a scramble to get kids home. But many had nowhere to go. Upwards of one hundred houses had caught on fire, hundreds more had to be evacuated. Firefighters and officers from across the region poured into the streets to do battle against the blaze and to run house to house shutting off gas meters. Preliminary reports indicated that the explosions were caused by built-up pressure in pipes long slated for an overhaul. Day became night. Power was cut off to large swaths of the city.

No school bell rang the next morning. Some 50,000 residents had not slept in their beds. ENLACE's staff scrambled to find families. Days were devoted to calling moms, dads, grandparents, aunts. Where are you living? What do you need? Families were in shelters, in motels, sleeping on relatives' couches. Allison and her team amassed grocery gift cards, bags of clothes, donations of cash. One family had arrived in the country only the week before. Now they were displaced. No one knew when they might return to their new home.

Close to a week later, on the afternoon students returned to the classroom, ENLACE's art teacher, Shaddai, gathered pupils in a STEM club he ran. Lessons set aside, they sat in a circle and talked. One girl could not contain her tears. They rolled in silent streams down her cheeks. If they slept in their homes, would they explode around them? Was it safe to stay in America? Question after question.

As the kids trudged out, Shaddai was struck by an idea. A week earlier he had happened upon an announcement: *Samsung: Solve for Tomorrow!* The company was inviting students nationwide to submit project ideas about how to use STEM to solve local problems. There would be state winners, national finalists, and three classrooms—selected from across the country—that would receive a grand prize of $100,000 each. Sitting alone at his desk, Shaddai wondered if the disaster could become an opportunity. The following week he shared the competition with his students. They did not hesitate. Together they set about converting fear into community action.

Across the Commonwealth of Massachusetts, state officials, gas companies, and lawyers all scrambled to understand the explosions, to secure months of emergency housing for displaced residents, to find safe ways of powering the city. In a classroom on the fourth floor of Lawrence High, newcomers to the country stayed late, researching the chemical properties of natural gas, the history of the region's aging gas lines, the effects of gas leaks. They began investigating how devices in houses could detect leaks, and how to safely divert a buildup of pressure in the pipes. With LEGOS, PVC piping, and rubber bands they began devising prototypes for a new type of safety valve that could safely release high-pressure gas.

The newcomers called up state officials and the region's gas company to ask for meetings. They also talked with their families.

The fires forged strong bonds between ENLACE staff and families that year. The semester had only just started, relationships barely begun in living rooms during home visits and over ice cream at a summer orientation. Even so, by the time Lawrence exploded, the seeds of trust between home and school were already taking root. When, in the wake of the fires, ENLACE staff reached out by phone and by text to ask how they could help, families responded. As the temperature began to drop and with many families, and also teachers, still displaced or without power, ENLACE invited families to a Café con ENLACE family gathering. Staff pulled chairs into a circle—a circle that quickly filled with families. They came because they knew that the staff cared. "Everyone has a voice here," Allison explained to the circle of families. "We want everyone to participate and contribute." For much of the next hour, she listened as families spoke, as they shared their hopes, their fears, their questions.

———•———

In the first days of January 2019, a classroom in Lawrence filled with shrieks and screams. For their work in trying to address the region's devastating gas explosions, ENLACE's newcomer students, all in the country less than two years, had been named state winners of the Samsung Solve for Tomorrow STEM competition. Their reward: $20,000 to purchase technology for the school. Within a day, reporters and TV crews descended upon ENLACE from local news, state news, and Univision, one of the nation's leading Spanish-language networks. The teenagers swung from shy to giddy and back again. "I learned I can help the community . . . [that] we can be the change," one girl shared with a reporter.[36] *"Yo tengo muchos amigos que perdieron su casa en [las explosiones]"* one boy explained. With this project, he confidently told the reporter, they were helping to make sure such explosions never happened again.[37] On camera another student hesitantly added: "The project inspired me to study engineering in university. In the future I want to create technology to prevent violence."[38] Never had they imagined people outside their small community would care about a project led by children new to the country. They couldn't have been more wrong. Following the news crews came local and state officials, and within weeks, the students were sitting down with representatives of the gas company, whose system had led to the explosions. Just two months later, the ENLACE team was selected as one of ten national finalists. Across Lawrence and beyond, people couldn't stop marveling. On social media, support flooded in—from peers, parents, the city's mayor, even the gas company. The children had become the city's rallying cry.

In the first week of April, in a huge New York City auditorium, Allison and the art teacher Shaddai watched, beaming, as two ENLACE students took the stage in front of hundreds. Neither had lived in the country for more than a year. Both were still mastering English. Yet, proudly they presented to judges, students, and teachers, describing their plan to help keep their community safe. Through a livestream of the event, their city watched and cheered them on, "That's my boy on stage!" "Go ENLACE!" The following evening, after a day of sightseeing, the two students were invited aboard the *USS Intrepid*, berthed on the city's west side, for their final task: to present their work to hundreds of New York students. Allison and Shaddai struggled to contain their nervousness. But, much to their amazement, the ENLACE students were soon surrounded by an enormous crowd of Spanish-speaking students who seemed astounded to see the newcomers honored. For hours the ENLACE students held forth, sharing their story, fielding questions. They switched rapidly between tongues, English to Spanish, Spanish to English. From the sidelines, Allison snapped photos for moms and dads, brothers and sisters back home.

The children returned to Lawrence as celebrities. They had not secured the grand prize, but as celebrated national finalists, they were awarded $50,000. Together they used the funds to buy 3D printers for the school and laptops for students in the program. Back in their classroom they celebrated and continued tinkering with their prototype gas valve. But they were also, increasingly, thinking of the coming year. In mere months they would be leaving ENLACE, graduating and transitioning into the larger high school. There would be new teachers, new schedules, new expectations. They were excited, but also nervous.

Allison shared their worries. Her pupils might only be moving downstairs, but the distance felt far greater. When they left the calm and support offered at ENLACE, how many, she worried, would feel lost? For Allison, her hope rests in the families, and in the connections she and her staff build with them.

ENLACE looks and feels like few schools I've seen. Relationships are built in the home and nurtured in the classroom. Communication is constant and so too is collaboration. When families asked to be connected to their new city, the dean of student and family engagement, Jennifer, helped to arrange a community fair with representatives from local nonprofits and organizations. When moms and dads ask curiously about what class instruction looks like, they are welcomed into teachers' classes. "What do you notice?" teachers ask in return. "What feedback and advice can you give us?"

Back in 2015, when the ENLACE leadership team was still mapping out the program on paper, together they settled on the name ENLACE. In Spanish it means connection. For Daniela, the name is fitting. She had been a newly minted teacher when her city exploded, and it had become abundantly clear to her that her effectiveness in the classroom would be measured by the strength of the connections she made—to her students, and also to their families.

When I joined families at Café con ENLACE, I was welcomed into a passionate debate about what skills children will need to secure the futures their families envisioned. Around the circle they shared ideas. Students will need to be versed in technology, and to develop a fluency in writing and problem solving. Schools should help them develop their ability to think critically and creatively, to communicate ideas clearly. "What does your child need to succeed?" Allison asked the circle. Answers came in a cascade. As one mother explained, she might not know yet what her son will choose for a career, but there was one thing she was sure of: "I'll be there to support him."

Two months after I attended Café con ENLACE, schools nationwide, including those in Lawrence, shut down amid the burgeoning COVID-19 pandemic. Teachers scrambled to figure out online teaching platforms, and districts strove to get students access to the internet and to food. What became immediately apparent was that, if schools were going to succeed in educating students in the midst of a shutdown, they would need to collaborate with parents. Now, as Dr. Karen Mapp recently reflected about the situation, "The only way to do education was in partnership with families." Schools began reaching out, trying to make connections. Some were successful, many were not. Most schools simply did not know where to begin. While ENLACE's teachers and students also struggled to adapt, what staff did know was that in their students' homes were powerful teachers. The trusting relationships ENLACE had built helped the transition to online school. In the weeks to come, just as in the years before, those moms and dads, those *abuelas* and *abuelos*, would be ENLACE's essential partners.

THE PERSONAL: SAFIYA

"When I was nine years old I attended a girls' school in Samarra, Iraq. One afternoon a group of men came to our school with guns."

Seventeen-year-old Safiya, jet-black hair curled for the occasion, took a deep breath and glanced up at a sea of faces. She stood before hundreds of students within a high-ceilinged hall of the Massachusetts State House. "Focus on me," I had advised. "Pretend no one else is here." For many muggy hours the previous afternoon the two of us had practiced. Safiya had paced the confines of my classroom, reciting her speech over and over. All the scribbles and underlined words on her crinkled paper resembled modern art.

When she and her classmates headed into the State House the following morning, her anxiety was everywhere, in her toes, churning in her stomach, fuzzy in her head. "I was scared . . . I didn't have perfect English." In our classroom Safiya was rarely shy. For months she had orchestrated our class's civics efforts, resolutely advocating for commonsense gun reform. It was for her outspoken leadership that, out of thousands of students statewide, she was being honored that morning, singled out by a national civics organization for her tenacity in working to effect lasting change in her community. The senate president spoke to the assembled students. Then, suddenly it seemed, Safiya's name was announced. "We would like to present this year's Massachusetts Student Civics Change Maker award."

Safiya stood up so fast her head spun. As she later shared with me, she worried that her audience would be unable to comprehend her English and would doubt that she was deserving of such an honor. "My speech was about who I am. I wanted them to understand where I came from and what I did." I watched her step up to the podium, take a breath, look up. Our eyes met. She nodded and began to speak.

Safiya made only passing reference to her life in Iraq that morning, quickly pivoting to the all-consuming civics work of her peers over the past many months. Of the attack on her school, much was left unsaid. She spoke only briefly of the cacophony of yells that sliced through morning Quran recitations. She did not describe how her teacher hurtled out of the classroom. She did not speak of the nearby school bombed by terrorists a few years earlier. Only in passing did she mention the kindly security guard with a salt-and-pepper beard who successfully fended off the attackers that day, but who would, a day later in the neighborhood, be gunned down in retaliation. Would the school suffer a second attack? No one knew. "Come directly home after school," her mother instructed sternly.

Safiya grew up in the city of Samarra on the banks of the Tigris, a two-hour drive from Baghdad. In the ninth century, the city's ruling caliph commissioned a mosque that, for four hundred years, would be the largest in the world, splendent with a staggeringly large snail-shell minaret wrapped in a wide, sweeping ramp that spiraled to a tiny room from which the muezzin would proclaim the call to prayer. In 2003, early in the American War—as the conflict is often called in Iraq—when Safiya was just two years old, US soldiers replaced the muezzins atop the minaret, which was an ideal lookout. In retaliation two years later, terrorists bombed the chamber at the minaret's crown, ancient bricks raining down. For years after, few ventured up the exposed winding stairs, which were too easy a target for snipers.

Safiya has few personal memories of the violence. As a child of war, the distant echo of bombs was ever present, but unremarkable. She was only four when the Al-Askari shrine, barely a mile from her house and one of the world's holiest Shi'i sites, was loaded with explosives and blown skyward, setting off a bloodbath of sectarian violence. What she does remember is her mother's watchwords. If her brother went to the coffee shop: "Be careful." If she walked to her sister's house: "Be careful."

Safiya's family are carpenters and teachers. For generations, the men have sculpted dressers, tables, intricately carved lattice screens. At school, many of Safiya's instructors were also her aunts. The family has deep ties to the city and the land. If asked, they can trace their lineage back and back and back, all the way to 'Alī ibn Abī Ṭālib, the cousin and son-in-law of Islam's founder, the prophet Muhammad.

Safiya was seven when her middle brother's car exploded. Her brother was a soldier in the Iraqi Army, but unbeknownst to many, he had been collaborating with the US Army. One afternoon he set off to meet friends to fish. He had just turned the ignition of his car when a neighbor called out with a question. The question saved his life. As he stepped out to answer, behind him the car burst into flames. The blast's force threw him across the street. Where the driver's seat had been, only a crater remained. Many hours later, Safiya's brother limped through the family's front door, head bandaged, arm in a sling. Safiya remembers the silence. "Everyone was in shock."

Safiya was eleven when she was awoken early one morning by a deafening explosion followed by a cacophony of shattering windows. Most of all, she remembers the screaming—her sister's screams, her brothers' screams, her parents' screams, her own screams. Outside their home, the wreckage of another car smoldered. Miraculously, no one was injured in the attack. Soon relatives descended on Safiya's family to soothe and sweep glass.

But it was clear that home was no longer safe. Collaboration with the Americans had placed a bull's-eye on the entire family. Within a month, Safiya's father sent his sons across the Turkish border, promising his boys the rest of the family would follow.

Safiya had never crossed an international border. She remembers only excitement. Not once did she imagine she would not return. She packed clothes, a box of family photos, and her favorite stuffed toy, a colorful clown with a goofy grin. Her father packed carpentry tools. Her mother brought thick blankets patterned with flowers and, carefully wrapped, a glass lemon squeezer, a wedding present from her mother-in-law. They left behind almost everything her father had lovingly carved for their sprawling home. The sturdy beds, closets, nightstands, sculpted coffee tables, and swirling lattice scriptures.

After a multiday journey on crowded buses, her brothers met Safiya and their parents at a Turkish bus stop and escorted them to a second-floor apartment. Her mother unpacked the blankets, Safiya pulled out her clown. Together they tried to reassemble a life. A month later her sisters and their husbands and children arrived. Only then did Safiya begin to realize they were likely not returning to Iraq. "But I didn't feel sad," Safiya remembers. "We were all together." Family meant home.

But Turkey was not home. Home was where you felt welcomed. And it was quickly made clear her family was unwanted. "As a refugee you were looked at differently, you were treated differently, you didn't have the same freedom." Her parents and siblings were not permitted to work. When Safiya went to enroll in seventh grade, she was turned away. She knew not a single word of Turkish, and without the language, the school refused her entry.

Roughly half of all school-age refugees worldwide are not in school.[39] The reasons are varied: Parents might have safety concerns or lack the right documents; classrooms can be overcrowded; students might need to work or be unable to comprehend the language of instruction; schools might simply choose to turn students away.

Safiya's first Turkish teachers were two teenage girls, neighbors who lived upstairs. They didn't speak a common language, but the three became inseparable. They played volleyball in the street, cooked endless bowls of macaroni, hid on the balcony and lobbed water balloons at their brothers. One morning Safiya awoke to her first snow. *Kar,* the sisters pronounced slowly, teeth chattering, gesturing at the swirling flakes. Safiya nodded. *Kar.* Snow became one of her first Turkish words.

Under her neighbors' tutelage Safiya mastered the outlines of the language. The sisters were patient, Safiya a quick study. Within a year, she had passed a test allowing her access to formal education. Safiya had always loved school, but she soon realized that, despite her rapidly expanding language skills, she remained unwelcome. If she showed up late, or was sick and missed days, no one noticed. If other students forgot their homework, they were publicly reprimanded. For her and the one other refugee in class, teachers were studiously indifferent. Not once that year did Safiya turn in an assignment.

———•———

As Safiya studied, her parents persistently prepared paperwork for refugee resettlement. She knew never to touch her father's cell phone. At any moment the UN might call with an offer of asylum. A year would pass before the anticipated call came. Exhilarated, the family flew to the Turkish capital for interviews. They returned to the second-floor apartment with the hope that they would soon leave it forever. But refugee resettlement requires prodigious patience. Years slipped by, punctuated by follow-up interviews and additional paperwork. Safiya was fourteen when her family was informed that a decision was in the offing. Her mother took to sitting at the computer morning, noon, and night, refreshing the page that would someday tell them if they had a new home. One afternoon, the page reloaded with a decision. Safiya's mom let out a scream that brought the family running. They were going to America.

By the summer of 2015, after more interviews, more paperwork, and a series of medical tests, Safiya and her parents were green-lighted to travel. Her oldest brothers were as well. Her sisters, who had applied later, were still waiting. But twenty-six-year-old Amir, the family's youngest son, was not called for his final medical test. Neither were his wife and sons. He began to panic. Safiya's parents tried to reason with him. Have patience, they counseled. But he was terrified he would be left behind. He caught whispers of refugees trying their luck on the seas. In 2015 alone, one million people fled to Europe, braving turbulent waters in overcrowded and dilapidated dinghies.[40] Reluctantly, Safiya's father arranged to sell the family home in Iraq. With his portion of the sale, Amir bought passage for himself, his wife, and their sons, then two-and-a-half years old and five months old. In Turkey the remaining family waited with bated breath. And then a call came, not from the UN, but from Amir. They had reached Greece safely.

Five weeks later, the tiny lifeless body of Alan Kurdi washed up on the beaches below the Turkish city of Bodrum, only fifteen miles from the Greek island of Kos. The photo of the crumpled body of the three-year-old in his bright red shirt and blue shorts horrified the world. Along with Alan, his five-year-old brother, and his mother, close to four thousand drowned in sea crossings that year alone. Alan was only months older than one of Safiya's nephews.

———◆———

A month after Amir climbed out of a dinghy on a Greek beach, Safiya and her parents were handed plane tickets. The rest of the family, they were assured, would follow. Safiya and her parents repacked the photos, the stuffed clown, the glass lemon squeezer. Misreading their tickets, they arrived twelve hours early for their flight. With little to do,

Safiya spent hours mapping the maze of terminals at Atatürk Airport. Exhausted and disoriented by the time they boarded, she slept eleven hours, waking only as they began to descend. Heavy-eyed she watched the sinking sun catch in the skyscrapers. To her, New York looked gilded in light. A day later, the family stepped out into New Hampshire. Rain misted the tree-lined roads. As the family drove south toward Lowell, Massachusetts, her mother shook her head in wonder. "Is this a road or is it a painting?"

Safiya was enrolled in ninth grade. She knew only a smattering of English: yes, no, thank you, red, yellow, blue. But unlike in Turkey, lack of language would not bar her. She had barely crossed the threshold of her first class when two girls, one in a tightly wrapped hijab, bounded over to introduce themselves in Arabic. At lunch she squeezed into a table crammed with Iraqi, Syrian, Lebanese, Yemeni teenagers. The girls became her guides. They directed her to classes, explained the concept of a GPA, reminded her she could sit while answering a teacher's question.

Within days she had mastered the art of "active listening." Watch the teacher, nod, dutifully copy. "If I did this, the teacher wouldn't call on me." In class she resembled a bobble-head doll. The trick worked—most of the time. In English, her teacher seemed forever to be asking incomprehensible questions. "I would get confused and nervous. Everyone's looking at me and she's expecting me to answer her and I don't know the answer. I don't understand her!" To end the humiliation, Safiya offered up everything she knew, "Yes. No. Yes. Thank you." Only after the teacher walked away would she wonder, "What did I say yes for?"

Day after day Safiya staggered home exhausted. Her goals shrank. Don't stand out. Survive. "I didn't have big dreams. Just get through this year. Hopefully next year will be better." In the evening, at the kitchen table, she painstakingly translated homework word by word. Articles about the Roman Empire, questions about photosynthesis, all incomprehensible in class, revealed themselves. Unlike in Turkey, she never once missed an assignment. Her parents remained stalwart cheerleaders. "Remember Turkey. You can do this too."

And unlike in Turkey, teachers refused to let her slip by unnoticed. They corrected grammar, reviewed punctuation. They told her they understood language learning was frustrating, exhausting work. With time

Safiya realized she wasn't alone. Her peers were also mastering a new language, a new culture, a new way of being. More than vocabulary or grammar, for Safiya, that first year, she learned to be patient. A mantra of reminders: "It will be okay. You will get through this." Deep breath.

Come June, she could string together phrases. "Why not?" or even, "Yes I would like that." Practicing her language skills, Safiya tentatively started making new friends: a girl from Colombia, another from the Ivory Coast. On weekends her family fired up a tiny charcoal grill and roasted carp spritzed with lemon. They seared eggplants and mashed them into baba ganoush. It almost felt like home.

Turkey had always been transitional. "We always knew we were leaving." The pointed stares, the under-the-breath slurs, the teachers who ignored her. There was no belonging there. Safiya had sought solace in believing home was with her family. But now her family was scattered. Two brothers lived with her and her parents in the United States, but Amir, recently granted asylum, was now in Germany. Her sisters remained stuck in Turkey, their applications inexplicably stalled.

In their US apartment, lined with curling ivy vines, they followed news out of Baghdad, grim faced. Night after night Safiya and her father debated politics—10 p.m., 11 p.m., midnight. As a young man in the 1980s, her father had championed Iraqi democracy. Then Saddam Hussein had seized power. Safiya's grandmother, and namesake, was terrified her son would be targeted. She hurried home and built a roaring blaze in their brick bread oven. One after another she fed to the flames her son's library on nation building, reducing the ideas to ash. Her son could not fault her; he understood the danger. But he carried his ideas and his passion, teaching them years later to his youngest daughter. When asked what her family expects of her, Safiya answers quickly: "They want me to be active in my community, to give back." Community activism would begin to knit her to her new land.

———————◆———————

I met Safiya at the start of her third year in America—one of nearly thirty students in my cramped early-morning US history class. She gravitated toward a back corner seat. Safiya was calm, quiet, and rarely ruffled by the antics of her classmates. It would take until midwinter before she would begin to make her voice heard.

As a key part of my history class, I orchestrate a semester-long civics project. My students learn how democracy works not just by reading about it, but by trying to make change. Each year my classes decide on one local issue—student hunger, mental health, online bullying—and over a semester they try to help implement programs or laws to address it. When I introduced the project to Safiya's class, I assigned them the task of finding an issue. A week later, current events supplied our answer.

In Parkland, Florida, a nineteen-year-old had stormed his former school, gunning down fourteen classmates and three educators in a gruesome six minutes. The next morning our class gathered, shaken, scared, angry. There was hardly any need for debate. Gun violence was the class's unanimous, solemn decision.

For Safiya, the shooting unearthed long-buried memories. News photos of children evacuating the Florida school merged with her recollections of the morning attack in Samarra. It seemed to her inconceivable that American schools were unsafe. She poured herself into reading reams of articles about gun violence, cataloging school shootings, organizing lists of state gun policies. At home her family watched Iraqi news, talked about Iraqi politics. Safiya had thought America was devoid of challenges, but in our class, she began to wonder if she could have an impact.

She realized she'd need help. Her class's plan was ambitious: They decided to push for the passage of a state gun reform bill and simultaneously to create a citywide gun safety initiative, engaging local law enforcement and more than forty businesses and houses of faith. Teamwork would be critical. For two years Safiya had surrounded herself primarily with Arabic speakers. But state- and city-level change needed wider networks, new friends. With gravitational force, Safiya drew her classmates around her: students from Japan, Brazil, Zambia, Spain, Puerto Rico. They began showing up early and lingering after class. Their desks filled with spreadsheets, drafts of memos, lists of state representatives. Safiya shocked herself when she realized she no longer struggled to make new friends or make herself understood.

That spring, everywhere I looked Safiya was there. At lunch in the cafeteria she carried around clipboards with petition signatures, striding up to students to urge them to push state representatives to pass gun reform legislation. Pages and pages of signatures amassed in her backpack. In class I might find her consulting a huge map of Massachusetts that she and her peers had created to help identify which representatives from which communities needed to be convinced. She gently explained to her peers how to write personal letters to a legislator to share reasons why new gun laws should be passed. Within weeks more than a hundred handwritten letters were mailed. In the computer lab I watched as Safiya toggled among spreadsheets, emailing and re-emailing houses of faith, urging them to participate in our city initiative.

She worked throughout the day, and often into the evening. I know because I began receiving text-message updates from her mom. At the beginning of the year I had asked my students to sign up their families for a texting phone app that translated conversations into more than eighty languages. That first afternoon, a message from Safiya's mother popped up on my phone. "Hello dear, thank you for teaching Safiya. I hope that she will be at a level befitting her . . . I look forward to everything." Starting in September, we began texting weekly. She was not only Safiya's champion, but she quickly became mine as well. "Thank you for your kind effort," "A thousand well wishes." Text antidotes following exhausting days. At a family night in October, she enveloped me in a hug. "You must come to our house so I can cook for you," she insisted. Someday, I promised. As our civics work expanded, Safiya's mom would send updates, and sometimes photos of her daughter in pajamas poring over draft memos and spreadsheets on their couch.

Often I would find Safiya sitting on the floor outside my door a little before 7 a.m., when I came in to unlock my classroom. "Ms. Lander, what needs doing today?" One afternoon, in a break between editing proposals, Safiya quietly told me of the attack on her school. Her voice was soft. "I don't want what happened in Samarra to happen to anyone."

One afternoon in April, Safiya, her classmates, and I met after school to deliver our proposal to a state representative. Trundling up a narrow, dimly lit staircase and down a crooked hall, Safiya was perplexed: "Where were the armed security guards? Where was the fancy mansion?" In Iraq, politicians were seemingly unreachable. But here a representative extended his hand, welcomed her into a tiny office. "He's talking like a normal person." She couldn't get over the ordinariness of it all. A little shyly, she handed him a stack of more than four hundred signatures the students had amassed. Back on the street after the meeting, the kids laughed and traded high-fives, all tension evaporated. But the meeting stayed with Safiya hours, days, weeks later. She hadn't believed that anyone would listen if she spoke. They wouldn't understand her. But her representative had listened. And if he would, maybe others would. In Iraq young people were taking to the streets. "I realized I have the opportunity here to help make something better," Safiya mused. "Why would I be silent and not do anything?"

Two weeks later, Safiya barreled into my room. Their bill—the one the class was fighting for, had written letters and collected signatures in support of—had just been voted out of committee, a key step in the measure becoming law. She could barely contain her excitement.

Safiya would find herself, in May, at the State House receiving an award for her activism. In the audience her parents beamed, her mom holding a cell phone high, livestreaming the speech for her daughters in Turkey, her son in Germany, her extended family in Iraq. As Safiya continued to speak from the podium, her voice grew stronger. "I am only a student, but if I see an issue that needs fixing, I can work on it, indeed it is my responsibility to help fix it. . . . When I have an idea or care deeply about an issue, I can speak up. And when I speak up there are people here who will listen to me and my friends."

———•———

I met Safiya and her peers early the next day, a Saturday, in the parking lot of a neighborhood church. Working with the city police and the county sheriff's department, we spent the morning running the gun safety program we had spent a semester preparing for. With their newfound confidence the kids spent hours laughing, joking, even dancing with the officers in the moments between sharing information about gun safety with city residents.

Hours later after we packed up our tables and signs, tired and a little sunburned, I drove a mile down the street, to keep the promise I had made to Safiya's mother many months before. I was ushered inside to a kitchen table groaning with golden biryani, bowls of okra soup, platters of hummus, plates of chartreuse pickles, and a bubbling casserole of *tepsi*, an Iraqi specialty of fried and layered tomatoes, potatoes, and eggplant. I stood, overwhelmed by their generosity. "Sit, sit!" Safiya's mom beckoned. We feasted. Safiya acted as translator, but language became immaterial. We laughed, we talked, we joked. Food is its own language. As midday became midafternoon, I FaceTimed with Safiya's sisters in Turkey. Hours slipped by. We sipped sweet cardamom tea and thick Arabic coffee in tiny porcelain cups. It was long past dark by the time I left, apologizing profusely that I really must head home. "You must return soon," Safiya's mom made me promise.

———•———

As she settled into her senior year, Safiya stepped into the role of class mom. She watched out for her friends, checked in on her classmates, reminded me to eat. She set about creating order in the hubbub of my classroom. I would turn around and she would be there, before school, at advisory, during lunch, after school. We talked often, about academic work, family, college, the future. Often our conversations centered on her civics work. The summer after her award, she had been appointed to a national civics student leadership board and had flown to San Francisco to collaborate with student activists from across the country. Now, outside of school, she was contributing to programs that would allow more students nationwide to learn the skills to engage in their communities. At home family conversations had shifted to debates on US politics, US challenges.

As her confidence blossomed, she noticed other changes. Like many of my students, Safiya was forgetting her first language. She looked up Arabic words with increasing frequency. Her brothers, her mom, her sisters overseas all teased her incessantly. During her senior year Safiya took classes with "white people," her term for students born in the United States. School had led her to believe that such students "worked harder" than her and her immigrant peers. "I was just learning basic English and they were learning things like physics." But as a senior, in class everyday with students who were second-, third-, fourth-generation Americans, Safiya was surprised. She had thought that native-born students were "just Americans." But the girl sitting across from her turned out to have an Egyptian grandmother; the boy a desk away had parents born in Cambodia. Perhaps they were more similar than she had realized. "I learned that we all struggle with the same things."

———•———

Since our history class, Safiya has spoken often at statewide civics celebrations, canvassed for local officials, trained roomfuls of teachers from
across the state on civics education. Young people, she says, must speak
up. "This is where we live, we need to share opinions, we need to vote. . . .
Maybe we don't have that much experience in life, but we can have ideas.
Our voice is important and we can create change." It was in junior year,
she later told me, through our civics work, that she began to feel like she
belonged. "I think I began to understand the community I was living in.
And, how to say this . . . I felt like I could help."

Recently I asked Safiya what home meant to her now. Hers is a global
family, rent by war and dispassionate bureaucracies. One sister still waits
in Turkey. One sister, tired of living in limbo, packed up her paused life
and crossed the border back into Iraq to take her chances. One brother
still lives in Germany. Of his three sons, one was born in Iraq, one in Turkey, one in Germany—the modern refugee crisis told through brothers.
In the United States, Safiya has taken on the family role her elder sisters
might have played. She translates bills and paperwork, acts as interpreter
at doctor visits. She does this lovingly for her parents, "This is my responsibility. They had to leave just for us. This is the smallest thing that
I can do for them."

As a child, home was Iraq, family, friends, history. As a displaced
teenager, home was family. But now? "Here," she sighs, "is home. Here
is where I'm growing up and where my kids will grow up." And it is here
where Safiya aims to fulfill her dreams for her future. She hopes that one
day America will see her as belonging here. She is not sure yet if it does.
Likely, she says, she will remain "American and." She believes the same
would be true if ever she visited Iraq; no longer would Iraq claim her as
solely Iraqi. "I'm half and half." Safiya seems at peace with the duality.
Home, Safiya tells me, "is in the heart."

CHAPTER 5

ADVOCATES

To make Americans, we must ensure that students have committed advocates in their new country. National, state, and local policy—who is welcomed into the country, how schools are funded, how teachers are trained, and what curriculum is taught—deeply shapes the lives of young newcomers and influences their success in school and beyond. We need advocates, from community members to policy makers, who believe in and who fight for programs and policies that give newcomer students the best chance of success in their new home.

This chapter tells three stories. The first is the story of President Lyndon B. Johnson, who began his career teaching at a segregated "Mexican" school along the southern Texas border and who advocated for landmark legislation that reopened America to immigrants and transformed American education. The second is the story of the district director for English learners in Guilford County, North Carolina, who in 2017 changed how teachers at more than one hundred schools taught immigrant-origin students. The third is the continuation of the story of my student Robert, who, after years living as an orphan, reunited with family in a Ugandan refugee camp, advocated for his own education, and was eventually admitted as a refugee, landing in the United States on the day Donald J. Trump was elected president.

THE PAST: LBJ AND EDUCATION

In the blistering summer heat of 1928, a lanky twenty-year-old arrived in Cotulla, Texas, sixty miles shy of the Mexican border, to take up a post as an elementary school teacher. Unable to continue paying for college, he had opted to teach for a year to finance his own education. He arrived in a sharply segregated town, the railroad drawing a steely divide between residents of Mexican and Anglo ancestry. The tall young man was to be employed on the wrong side of the tracks, teaching at the newly constructed Mexican school. At the time, the United States was still nineteen years away from the *Mendez v. Westminster* decision desegregating California schools, and twenty-six years away from the *Brown v. Board of Education* decision desegregating schools nationwide.

Never before had the young man commanded a classroom, but that did not stop the local superintendent from appointing him, the only male teacher, as principal, on the spot. His confidence belied his inexperience. He was strict and academically demanding. Like many of his colleagues, he showed little interest in the traditions and cultures of his immigrant-origin students and was known to spank his students for speaking Spanish while on school grounds.

But what set the young principal apart from many fellow educators of the time, his pupils would later recall, was that he was not contemptuous of Mexican students. According to former students, he was compassionate and seemed to care.[1]

Within weeks of arriving he had cajoled the local school board to help fund sports equipment and had written to his mother asking her to send two hundred tubes of toothpaste for his students.[2] He arrived at school early and often stayed after classes, organizing baseball, volleyball, softball, spelling bees, speech competitions, and debate contests, all of which were a novelty at the small, segregated, ill-funded school. While many of his peers in the region were prone to believe their Mexican students were inherently inferior, he instead faulted dire poverty, low expectations, and blatant discrimination as the reasons his students struggled to succeed. He believed they could have a future beyond the cotton and sugar beet fields and worked to instill that confidence in his students.[3] Almost weekly, as a former student would later recall, he would remind them "that any man, born and raised in the United States who would educate himself, regardless of what race, or how poor, or how rich he was, he could very easily wind up being the President."[4]

But the young principal would not stay long in the classroom. The next year he would return to complete his degree in education, but it would see little formal use. Soon he moved east to the nation's Capital. Seven years later he successfully ran for the US House of Representatives, eleven years more and he became a US senator, and in 1960, thirty-one years after teaching the children of immigrants in a segregated school at the country's edge, Lyndon B. Johnson would take on the mantle of vice president of the United States of America.

Three years later, on the afternoon of November 22, 1963, LBJ was sworn in as the thirty-sixth president on a Dallas tarmac, in the cramped cabin of Air Force One. To his right stood his wife, Lady Bird; to his left, the just-widowed Jackie Kennedy, her husband's blood splattered across her pink suit. Only feet away rested the casket containing the late President John F. Kennedy.

Late on his fourth evening as president, LBJ picked up a phone and called Reverend Dr. Martin Luther King Jr. The call was short and cordial. Dr. King was direct. "I think one of the great tributes that we can pay in memory of President Kennedy," Dr. King told LBJ, "is to try to enact some of the great, progressive policies that he sought to initiate." LBJ did not disappoint. On the phone, in his tumbling Texan twang, he promised to "support them all."[5]

Two days later the new president carried Dr. King's words to Congress. "No memorial oration or eulogy could more eloquently honor President Kennedy's memory than the earliest possible passage of the civil rights bill for which he fought so long. . . . It is time now to write the next chapter, and to write it in the books of law."[6]

The agenda might not have been of his making, but over the coming months President Johnson took up the cause of civil rights with a vengeance. In his first State of the Union, he committed himself to the legacy and proposed policies of the late JFK, "not because of our sorrow or sympathy, but because they are right." Racism, intertwined with poverty, the president declared, relegated too many Americans to "live on the outskirts of hope." Throwing down a gauntlet, the president declared an all-out "war on poverty."[7] Among his most powerful weapons: education.

That spring, the nation approached the ten-year anniversary of the landmark *Brown v. Board of Education* decision, but for far too many children, it was as if the case had never been won. In southern schools, less than one percent of Black students studied alongside white peers.[8] White mobs threatened and brutally attacked Black students across the country. Police, local elected officials, governors, and members of Congress were often active accomplices. Stalwart segregationists closed schools rather than face integration and funneled taxpayer dollars to seg-regated private institutions. Desegregation had become, in many states, a student-by-student battle, fought in the classrooms and in the courts.

In 1957, one thousand members of the 101st US Airborne Division had been sent to Little Rock, Arkansas, to protect nine Black teenagers attending Central High. In 1960, US Marshals had formed a human shield around six-year-old Ruby Bridges as she integrated a New Orle-ans elementary school. In 1963, Alabama governor George Wallace had promised not to integrate schools in the state. "I say segregation now, seg-regation tomorrow, segregation forever."[9] He stood, stiff-necked, blocking an auditorium doorway at the University of Alabama in an attempt to bar two Black students, Vivian Malone and James Hood, from entering and attending. On that evening, then-President Kennedy had proposed a civil rights bill. Months later—after Dr. King spoke from the steps of the Lincoln Memorial to a quarter of a million activists, after the bombing of a Birmingham church killed four little girls, after Kennedy's assassina-tion—LBJ would receive the call from Dr. King and would promise he'd ensure the bill would become law.

Shepherding the civil rights bill through the House was a now white-haired Emanuel Celler, the fiery Brooklynite who as a freshman repre-sentative forty years earlier had fiercely opposed the immigration quo-tas. Now chairman of the House Judiciary Committee, Celler doggedly fought to get the bill through the House and over to the Senate.

On June 19, 1964—or Juneteenth, a day celebrated for ninety-nine years to mark the end of slavery—and marking too the one-year anni-versary of President Kennedy's having proposed the bill to Congress, the US Senate voted in favor of the Civil Rights Act. Of the twenty-two senators from the original secessionist states, only one, Texas Democrat Ralph Yarborough, voted yea. Two days later, and nearly nine hundred miles to the south, three young civil rights workers, Michael Schwerner, Andrew Goodman, and James Chaney, went missing outside Meridian, Mississippi. It would be more than a month before their remains were unearthed. On the very same day their bodies were discovered, Presi-dent Johnson ordered airstrikes on a country half a world away, and in the following days he would ask Congress for authority to attack North

Vietnam—which would, in years to come, lead to the president's political undoing.

But back in July, just before Independence Day celebrations, President Johnson triumphantly signed the Civil Rights Act into law, thereby banning discrimination on the basis of race, color, sex, and also national origin. Notably, schools were barred from receiving federal funds if they remained segregated, and the attorney general was invested with the power to compel schools to comply. *Brown v. Board of Education* now had teeth.

———◆———

When President Lyndon B. Johnson strode into the House Chambers in January of 1965, a broad grin stretched from ear to ear. He came to Congress with a resounding mandate from the nation, having just won a landslide electoral victory, bolstered by Democratic control of both the House and the Senate. That evening, heady with confidence, LBJ sketched an ambitious blueprint for the "great society" America could become. It was an idea he had first floated seven months earlier, but now wielding presidential powers due not to an assassination but to an election, it was time to implement the vision. His plan touched on almost all aspects of life: voting, civil rights, employment, crime, healthcare, consumer protection, city planning, the environment, the arts, and immigration. But topping his list was a commitment to transform education, from the time babies left the cradle to the time they graduated college. He vowed that "every child must have the best education that this nation can provide."[10]

And so, on Dr. King's birthday, the president called up the reverend to ask a favor. His prized education bill was soon scheduled for hearings, and he needed civil rights leaders to lend a hand in convincing members of congress to ensure its swift passage "before the vicious forces concentrate."[11] Less than two weeks later, the bill's architect, US Commissioner of Education Francis Keppel, appeared before Congress to speak on behalf of America's children.

Keppel was, in the words of *Time* magazine, an "intense bolt of activity," a bespectacled man who regularly clocked eleven-hour days and who had through sheer force of will transformed the federal Office of Education from the "custodian of highly forgettable statistics to the nation's most energetic nerve center of academic ferment."[12] At the age of thirty-two, he had been named dean of the Harvard Graduate School of Education. It was only fourteen years later, at the invitation of President Kennedy, that he had come south to the Capital. His wife thought he was crazy to take, by his own admission, "a scut job with low standing and low reputation,"[13] but Keppel ardently believed in integration and equal access to education: "The war against segregation," he unequivocally claimed was "education's war."[14] Like LBJ, Keppel favored coalitions. "Education," he believed, "is too important to be left solely to the educators," and in civil rights leaders he saw natural allies. With the promise of a Great Society on the horizon, Keppel took up the challenge of reimagining schools, conceiving a blueprint for how government could assist in the transformation, which he soon shared with Congress.

Not long thereafter, on the first Sunday of March 1965, civil rights activists, having just crossed the Edmund Pettus Bridge in Selma, Alabama, were confronted by a wall of state troopers brandishing nightsticks. With no provocation, the police, many mounted on horseback, charged the activists—trampling, brutally beating, and tear-gassing all they could reach. On the surrounding sidewalks, white bystanders sent up a raucous cheer. Mere hours later, halfway around the world, the first US combat troops landed on the beaches of central Vietnam.

A week after national television captured the brutality of Bloody Sunday in Selma, President Johnson came once more to Congress to resoundingly declare that "to deny a man his hopes because of his color or race, his religion or the place of his birth—is not only to do injustice, it is to deny America." He swore to send a voting rights bill to Congress that week and left no room for delay or compromise. Thirty-six years earlier in a schoolroom in southern Texas, he told his colleagues, he had wielded limited power to tackle discrimination. In his mind's eye he saw his Mexican students who "knew even in their youth the pain of prejudice." As LBJ recounted, "They never seemed to know why people disliked them. But they knew it was so, because I saw it in their eyes. . . . Somehow you never forget what poverty and hatred can do when you see its scars on the hopeful face of a young child." Now with the power to help his former students, and with them millions of others, the president unapologetically vowed to "use it."[15]

Not a month had gone by when, on Palm Sunday, on the front lawn outside a one-room schoolhouse in Johnson City, Texas, LBJ signed into law the Elementary and Secondary Education Act (ESEA). It was a law, the president promised, that would "bridge the gap between helplessness and hope for more than five million educationally deprived children." Beside him sat an elderly woman in a blue dress and pearls—Johnson's very first teacher, on whose lap, at the age of four, he began learning his letters. In the audience were school friends, college chums, politicians, and also his former students from Cotulla's once-segregated Mexican school. "As a son of a tenant farmer, I know that education is the only valid passport from poverty," Johnson reflected. "As a former teacher— and, I hope, a future one—I have great expectations of what this law will mean for all of our young people. As President of the United States, I believe deeply no law I have signed or will ever sign means more to the future of America."[16]

ESEA, which would be reauthorized and renamed repeatedly over the following decades—notably as the No Child Left Behind (NCLB) Act of 2001 and later as the Every Student Succeeds Act (ESSA) in 2015— marked a turning point for federal involvement in education. With a signature, federal funding for K–12 schools doubled. Money was allocated to build libraries and buy books, as well as to fund innovation, research, and education centers. But the lion's share of funding was directed into ESEA's Title I, earmarked for schools with large numbers of low-income students, and it was this provision that would immediately begin reshaping classrooms.

While the 1964 Civil Rights Act enabled the government to withhold money from segregated schools, limited federal funding meant minimal compliance. But now, suddenly, real money was on the table. In the words of Harvard professor Gary Orfield, where the Civil Rights Act was the "stick," ESEA became the "carrot."[17] Almost immediately Commissioner Keppel issued guidelines requiring districts to submit plans to fully desegregate within two years. Those who refused, he promised, would see no federal dollars. The following school year, roughly one in every seventeen Black children in the South studied alongside white peers. Five years later, one in three attended integrated schools.

———◆———

In 1965, in the weeks and months after the passage of the Elementary and Secondary Education Act, Congress would churn out legislation at a

dizzying clip. As spring slipped into summer, LBJ signed into law his promised Voting Rights Act, barring voter discrimination; established Medic-
aid and Medicare, aimed at ensuring the poor and the elderly access to
healthcare; created the Department of Housing and Urban Development
(HUD) to expand federal housing assistance; and launched a program to
give low-income preschoolers a "Head Start" on their education. Before
revelers rang in the new year, the president would also sign laws aimed at
curbing pollution; strengthen·ng veterans' benefits; and expanding access
to college, through financial assistance, for low-income students.

In Congress, one of President Johnson's key allies and legislative
generals was Chairman Emanuel Celler. Expertly, he strove to build the
president's Great Society. But perhaps no battle was more deeply personal than the one he waged that year on behalf of aspiring newcomers.
Celler had arrived in Congress as America's gates had swung all but shut,
and for four decades he had relentlessly worked to drag them open once
more. For years he had been largely thwarted, but then a great-grandchild
of Irish immigrants ran for the country's highest office, campaigning on
the promise of immigration reform. In the summer of 1963 JFK sent
an immigration proposal to Congress. Immigration policy, he wrote,
"should be generous; it should be fair; it should be flexible," allowing the
country to face the world "with clean hands and a clear conscience."[18]
Just months later, the president was shot dead in Dallas.

The immorality and inflexibility of US immigration law had been
brought into sharp relief in the late 1930s as European Jews rushed to acquire US visas, only to find their countries' quotas already filled. In 1939
representatives considered a bill that would admit, above what was allocated by quota, 20,000 German, predominantly Jewish, refugee children.
But the bill was never voted out of committee: "20,000 charming children," remarked the wife of the US Commissioner of Immigration and
also, incidentally, President Roosevelt's cousin, "would all too soon grow
up into 20,000 ugly adults."[19] That spring, when the SS St. Louis steamed
into Miami waters carrying in its berths more than nine hundred Jewish
men, women, and children, the ship's huddled masses were turned back.
Germany's yearly quota was full. Close to a quarter of the ship's refugees
would be murdered in Nazi Europe.

In the wake of Hitler's Holocaust, it became suddenly unpalatable to
speak in defense of Anglo-Saxon racial superiority, but that did little to

restructure US immigration policy. When, in 1952, the new McCarran-Walter Immigration Act was passed under President Truman, the discriminatory quota system was kept largely intact. And, while Congress had repealed the Chinese Exclusion Act a decade earlier, Asia as a whole was given a paltry number of yearly slots. More perniciously, hopeful Asian immigrants were assessed not by nationality, but by ethnicity. A British-, French-, or Canadian-born citizen of Chinese ancestry hoping to immigrate to the United States was forced to compete for one of China's 105 yearly spots.

Senator Patrick McCarran, himself the son of Irish immigrants, had no compunction in recycling the rhetoric once used to malign his parents and other Irish newcomers, bullishly defending the act that carried his name: "If this oasis of the world shall be overrun, perverted, contaminated or destroyed, then the last flickering light of humanity will be extinguished," he contended. Times were dire, McCarran believed, and "untold millions are storming our gates for admission and those gates are cracking under the strain."[20]

By the 1960s, the momentum of the Civil Rights Movement, led by Black activists across the country, was shining a spotlight on inequality and discrimination that was hard for many to ignore. And that spotlight shone also on the treatment of immigrants. The country must "remove all elements in our immigration law which suggest there are second-class people," Vice President Hubert Humphrey argued.[21] In taking up the torch of his fallen predecessor, LBJ included in his first State of the Union address a promise. "A nation that was built by the immigrants of all lands can ask those who now seek admission: 'What can you do for our country?' But we should not be asking: 'In what country were you born?'"[22]

The arguments of those opposed to immigration reform often focused on the economy: Strict quotas protected American jobs. But the justification was a thin veneer for more deeply rooted beliefs. Just like their predecessors from Eastern and Southern Europe, prospective immigrants from countries as far-flung as China, Cameroon, and Trinidad were decried as spies, subversives, and individuals who were wholly unassimilable. America was under threat, testified one agitated congressman from Georgia, from "hordes of Red Chinese, Indians, [and] Congolese cannibals."[23] Representatives from Arkansas and Kentucky warned that welcoming people from the nations of Africa or even nearby Jamaica would only add to "racial tensions and violence."[24] And John Trevor Jr., the son of one of the architects of the 1924 quotas, echoing the words of his father, warned that the "new seed" would pollute American stock.[25]

Others, in an acrobatic contortion of logic, argued that ending discrimination against people from Asia and Africa would discriminate against those of Anglo-Saxon origin. The proposed bill was biased, North Carolina Senator Sam Ervin argued, because it denied preferential status to countries like England, which had given the United States its laws, language, and literature. He warned that the bill would allow Ethiopians and others from Africa "the same right to come to the United States . . . as the people from England, the people of France, the people of Germany, the people of Holland, and I don't think—with all due respect to Ethiopia—I don't know of any contributions that Ethiopia has made to the making of America."[26] Senator Ervin would later extend this to imply that Africa as a whole had made few contributions, ignoring the major role that millions of enslaved African people and their descendants had played, for more than 350 years, in building the nation.

Over four decades, Celler had heard every line of argument. Of the 435 men and women in the US House of Representatives, the seventy-seven-year-old dean of the House was the only member who had been present for the original passage of the 1924 Immigration Act that established the quotas. And his name would be attached to the final bill that would, as summer turned to fall, be sent at last to the White House.

The Hart-Celler Immigration and Nationality Act put an end to a quota system based on national origins, favoring Northern and Western Europe. Preference in immigration would be given to reunifying families and to the highly skilled, and broad caps would be placed on immigration from the Eastern and Western Hemispheres. (Limiting immigration from the Western Hemisphere was a new policy, which would come to have important consequences.) America's gates were open once more, though discrimination remained. Immigrants who openly identified as LGBTQ+ were barred from admittance, an act of prejudice that would take another twenty-five years to reverse.

On a brilliantly blue afternoon in early October 1965, at the feet of Lady Liberty and within sight of the shuttered halls of Ellis Island, President Johnson signed the Hart-Celler Immigration Act into law. In doing so, LBJ declared that the country was correcting "a cruel and enduring wrong in the conduct of the American Nation," repairing an immigration policy that had been "twisted" and "distorted" and that had become "un-American in the highest sense." A playful breeze wove through the crowd of several hundred who stood as witnesses. To the president's left stood the late JFK's brothers, Senators Robert and Ted Kennedy. To his right stood New York's own Emanuel Celler. Likely he was smiling as the president closed his remarks. "America was built by a nation of strangers . . . the land flourished . . . because it was nourished by so many cultures and traditions and peoples . . . the lamp of this grand old lady is brighter today—and the golden door that she guards gleams more brilliantly in the light of an increased liberty for the people from all the countries of the globe."[27]

In celebration of American Education Week in late 1966, President Johnson flew home to Texas. He drove south toward the border, stopping to pick up his former student Daniel Garcia, who had once visited the White House, and now rode with him as he returned once more to Cotulla. Outside the formerly segregated school, the one-time principal spoke to a boisterous crowd that included alumni and current students. Though he may have been a teacher, it was here, as he shared, that "I had my first lessons in the high price we pay for poverty and prejudice." On the lawn, he extolled the progress that had been accomplished: the laws passed, the schools funded, the programs created. Where some educators questioned whether the children of immigrants were truly American, LBJ was unequivocal in speaking to his former students: "All the energy, the efforts, and the investment that goes into education is meant for one person—you, the American student."[28]

But there was more work to do. A staggering number of students of Mexican heritage were struggling in school, many failing to graduate elementary school, few venturing further. Within the five Southwestern states, Johnson noted, more than half of all Mexican-American children had less than eight years of formal education. "America has slept long enough while the children of Mexican-Americans have been taught that the end of life is a beet row, a spinach field, or a cotton patch."[29] Until the students of Cotulla and their peers nationwide had the opportunity and a fighting chance to graduate high school, graduate college, maybe even secure a PhD, the president refused to be satisfied. America, he explained, would be better and stronger for the academic achievements of these students.

It would be the president's erstwhile colleague, Texas senator Ralph Yarborough, who would take up the call to action. While the senator and the president had a tempestuous relationship, they shared a commitment to civil rights and short careers in education. Like Johnson, Yarborough had been both an elementary school teacher and a principal, and likely for this reason, he was a fierce proponent, and frequent author or cosponsor of education bills during his thirteen-year tenure in Washington.

Elected in 1957, Yarborough had worked within the halls of the Senate for only five months when, nearly a thousand miles away, behind the Iron Curtain, the Soviet Union thrust a satellite the size of a beach ball into outer space. Sputnik was the world's first artificial satellite successfully launched into orbit above the Earth. Far below, in the United States, its launch triggered a national reckoning. How was it that the Soviet Union had bested the United States? The country's schools were quickly indicted as a prime culprit. In the spring of 1958, *Life* magazine ran a scathing five-part series captioned "Crisis in Education," which compared the academic prowess of a Soviet boy with the middling accomplishments of his Chicago peer.[30] For years Congress had struggled to pass meaningful federal education legislation, stymied in part by its members' refusal to tackle segregation head-on. But not a year after Sputnik had orbited the globe, a National Defense Education Act was successfully rammed through Congress and quickly signed into law. Public schools were now a battlefield in the Cold War, and the new law financed powerful weapons in the fight against Soviet Russia: Federal funding was directed at vocational training, counseling for gifted students, loans to support college access, and development of education technologies. Allocated, too, was seventy million dollars a year to strengthen instruction in science, math, and foreign languages.

In the four decades since state legislatures had waged a war against foreign language instruction, the incentive to learn tongues, German or others, had shriveled. The National Defense Education Act transformed the field. In the five years following, enrollment in language classes exploded; one study reported such classes more than doubled. As quickly as schools had rushed to remove language courses from their curriculum at the close of World War I, now they scrambled to reinstate them as the Cold War heated up.

Yarborough, called by some the "Patron Saint of Texas Liberals,"[31] was a proud Texan son. When President Kennedy came to visit in the fall of 1963, Yarborough had ridden in the doomed motorcade, sitting beside the then vice president. With his colleague assuming the presidency, Yarborough became a reliable advocate for the Great Society agenda, and in doing so angered many in the Lone Star State.

In October 1966, as the deserts of Arizona cooled, the National Education Association held a conference in Tucson and invited Senator Yarborough to attend. A key objective for the organizers was to unveil the results of a yearlong survey of Spanish-speaking students in the country's five Southwestern states. Boldly titled *The Invisible Minority,* the report was a damning analysis of US schools' failure to teach, nurture, or invest in Spanish-speaking students, all of which, as the report accused, "keeps the Mexican-American an 'outsider' in his own land." Rather than celebrate and elevate students' language and also notably their cultural heritage, students were told time and again that "if you want to be American, speak American." The irony was not lost on the report's authors. As they cited explicitly, the National Defense Education Act was furiously funding language classes for "Anglo-Americans," and thus, "while [schools] strive to make the monolingual student bilingual, they are making—or trying to make—the bilingual student monolingual." What schools needed was dedicated funding, trained teachers, innovative curriculum, and successful approaches for honoring and engaging immigrant-origin children. In short, the nation needed programs that recognized language and culture as an asset and strove "to build on it rather than to root it out."[32] Galvanized, Yarborough hurried back to the Capitol, gathered together his aides, and began drafting new education legislation. Only a week after the Tucson conference had concluded, President Johnson drove to Cotulla to call out schools for failing Mexican students.

Two months later Yarborough introduced a bilingual education bill aimed at addressing the disparities unearthed in the NEA survey—a concrete answer to LBJ's aspiration. Whereas a decade earlier such a bill would have garnered lackluster support, in the heat of the Civil Rights Movement and with the threat of Soviet Russia, the proposal became wildly popular. In the coming months more than thirty related bills were introduced. The final legislation targeted low-income English-learner students, providing grants for schools hoping to develop innovative programs—bilingual and others, train teachers, create educational re- sources, and engage parents. In under a year, at the dawn of 1968 the Bi- lingual Education Act was signed into law, inserted as Title VII of ESEA. It became the first federal legislation directed specifically at supporting the educational futures of newcomers and their children.

Yarborough was elated, but also unsatisfied. Despite his advocacy, only a quarter of the funding he had asked for had been allocated. It would be an entire year before any funds were appropriated for his programs, and another five before the Supreme Court would weigh in on what responsi- bilities schools nationwide had toward their immigrant-origin children.

But in 1968, funding for the Great Society was being diverted into a proxy war with the Soviet Union that was playing out in the jungles of Vietnam. With no end in sight, President Johnson announced he would not seek reelection, curtailing his advocacy for his dream of a Great So- ciety. Four days later, as evening fell in Memphis, Reverend Dr. Martin Luther King Jr., having just stepped out onto a motel balcony, was, with the firing of a single bullet, assassinated. Across the country, communi- ties erupted in flames and lamentations.

THE PRESENT: GUILFORD COUNTY SCHOOL DISTRICT, NORTH CAROLINA

In the fall of 2019, eleven fifth graders huddled in the corner of a class- room. Intently they pondered a strip of calculator paper, six feet long, bearing a sentence in thick black lettering: "When corals are under stress, they expel their algae, lose their color and will eventually die." Their teacher, a gregarious Jamaican woman in a blue pencil skirt, had posed a challenge: Could they rearrange the sentence and retain its meaning?

Excitedly, students at Allen Jay Elementary School, in Guilford County, North Carolina, took scissors to the paper. Five sets of hands now clutched five sentence fragments. A Pakistani boy directed a class- mate holding a snippet of the sentence to stand to the left, another to stand in the middle. A tall Mexican girl assumed command, "Fiza, switch with Wilmer." Their new sentence: "Corals are under stress When they expel their algae, and will eventually die, lose their color." "That doesn't make sense!" exclaimed a tawny-haired student. Classmates giggled, others groaned, then one gasped: "Hold up!" Surging forward, a girl orchestrated students to swap. Satisfied, she stepped back to read: "When they expel their algae, corals are under stress, lose their color and will eventually die." Around her, classmates broke into applause.

The day's lesson was part of a districtwide experiment for Guilford's nearly 7,000 English learners, who make up about one in ten of the roughly 70,000 students enrolled in the county's public schools. They are dispersed across classrooms in 126 schools, which are scattered across 650 square miles of North Carolina, an area double that of New York City. At its center sits the city of Greensboro.

Greensboro is a city with a legacy of igniting transformation. More than sixty years ago, on the first of February in 1960, four teenage boys walked downtown, entered the local F.W. Woolworth Five and Dime, took a seat, and requested cups of coffee. The waitress refused, saying, "We don't serve Negroes here."[33] Courageously, the four remained until closing. The following morning they returned, accompanied by more than twenty others. That spring Black college and high school students and white allies, following the lead of the Greensboro Four, sat down at segregated lunch counters across the South and requested food. They sat down in Nashville, Miami, Dallas, Charleston, Atlanta, Baton Rouge, and Richmond. They sat down in Jackson, Mississippi, Tuskegee, Alabama, and Lexington, Kentucky. Despite being targeted with threats, violence, and arrests, they sat down in fifty-five cities in all. Not six months passed before the Woolworth's manager in Greensboro quietly conceded. Four Black employees were the first to order from the desegregated lunch counter. One ate an egg salad sandwich, another chose the meatloaf.

It would take another decade for Greensboro public schools, as well as those across the county, to integrate Black students, seventeen years after *Brown v. Board of Education*. Today's schools would be unrecognizable to residents half a century ago. The schools are home to students from more than fifty countries, and they speak more than one hundred languages. Most speak Spanish, Arabic, or Urdu. Some speak Laotian, Korean, Albanian, Russian, Twi. Others are fluent in Jarai, spoken in the central highlands of Vietnam; Hindko, heard on the plateaus of Pakistan; and Dinka, common along the Nile in Sudan. A handful each speak Somali, Swedish, Serbian. Five students converse in Polish. Another five in Pohnpeian, spoken on an island in Micronesia.

But by 2017, Mayra Hayes, after nearly fifteen years as Guilford County's director for English learners, was still unsatisfied with the district's progress in serving EL students. Over her time in Guilford, Mayra had implemented new curricula, adopted education programs, recruited tutors, and crafted professional development. Many students succeeded, but not nearly enough. Yearly test scores crept up in math or reading one year, only to sink back the following spring. Of district students who started in kindergarten or first grade, roughly one in seven remained classified as English learners eleven years later. "We needed to do something," Mayra recalled. "The status quo wasn't working."

Then, while attending an education conference in Los Angeles in the spring of 2017, Mayra wandered into a presentation. EL classes often prioritize basic vocabulary, repetition, and dumbed-down texts, the presenting professor explained: language first, content later. Too often students never caught up. Instead, the professor argued, teaching academically rigorous content should never be paused. Her idea was not hypothetical. The approach had succeeded in some New York City schools. Snatching her notebook, Mayra started furiously scribbling. "It was the first time I felt excited in a long time," she described. As applause filled the hall, she made a beeline for the professor. That afternoon she texted Guilford County leadership: *I have an idea.*

Mayra's task was daunting. Some of Guilford's EL students attended sprawling urban programs, with 2,000 pupils; others studied amid dairy farms, in schools with barely 200 enrollees. Some studied with an EL teacher for only thirty minutes a day, while others spent their entire day in newcomer classes. At an elementary school just outside downtown Greensboro, roughly one in every four students was an EL student. Six minutes away, at another elementary school, the number was just 8 out of 660. In the fall of 2017, she set out to implement a districtwide experiment. For Mayra's idea to succeed, she would need to convince 140 teachers, nearly all in different schools, to work together to reimagine instruction.

———◆———

At the age of ten, Mayra Hayes first dreamed of becoming a teacher. Four years earlier, in 1974, Mayra and her mother had boarded a plane in El Salvador bound for New York. The small family settled on Long Island

Sound. Home was not always stable. Yet at school, in the classroom of her elementary EL teacher, Ms. Toner, Mayra felt welcome. Ms. Toner, hair in a bun, glasses hanging from her neck, was unfailingly patient, explaining perplexing math problems over and over again until they clicked. She never raised her voice and always smiled. "When I first came here," Mayra mused, "she was my safety net."

When Mayra moved on to middle school, life began to unravel. Wanting to avoid home, she took to slipping out of the house with her skateboard, coasting along the hills of the North Shore. In her new school, too, she felt out of place. "I straddled two worlds," she recalled. "I wasn't white enough for the white kids and I wasn't Spanish enough for my own people." She started skipping class, leaving to pick up her baby sister from daycare. Once again a teacher stepped in. Ms. Chasnow quickly caught on. It was she who, coordinating with the school counselor, found a full-day preschool for her sister; who, upon learning that Mayra loved home economics and woodworking, ensured she enrolled in both; and who asked Mayra to report on her classes every afternoon to prevent her from skipping—bribing her with Jolly Ranchers, Mayra's favorite candy. When, in seventh grade, Mayra was suspended, Ms. Chasnow arrived on her doorstep, arms filled with assignments, to ensure she wouldn't fall behind.

In 1991, twenty-three-year-old Mayra's dream came true. She was assigned to teach middle school math and science in Queens. But to her horror, Mayra realized her sixth graders, not she, controlled the classroom. They cussed, called out, flung balls of paper, laughed when she turned to the blackboard. Day after day, she ended up sobbing in the principal's office. Patiently, he coached her. He found her a mentor, encouraged her to shadow veteran teachers, regularly popped into class to lend a hand. Still, Mayra struggled. After yet another frustrating Friday, Mayra trudged into his office. Crestfallen, she confessed she was handing in her resignation. For forty-five minutes the principal listened and passed across tissues. Then he nodded and told her he would see her back on Monday. Three days later, surprising herself, Mayra returned. She kept coming back. Her confidence grew. But her dreams shifted. She set her sights on school leadership.

A decade later, in 2001, Mayra became a middle school principal outside Charlotte, North Carolina. Years earlier she had followed a boyfriend south. The relationship hadn't lasted, but Mayra stayed. She taught Spanish, and then EL. She fell in love with a fellow math teacher. She was hired as an assistant principal and then a principal. One afternoon in 2003, her supervisor arrived at her office clutching a newspaper clipping. Guilford County, about a hundred miles away, was in need of an EL director. Her supervisor urged Mayra to apply.

———•———

By 2003, Alicia Serrano had been teaching in Guilford County Schools for a decade. Growing up, Alicia had lived in Argentina, Indonesia, and the United States. She had grown confident in the classroom. But when, in 2001, she started to teach EL classes, she was flummoxed. How could she support kindergarten newcomers one hour and fifth-grade newcomers the next? There were no books, no curricula, no professional development, no support. Indeed there was no dedicated EL department. Everything to do with immigrants was assigned to the district office responsible for students with disabilities. Alicia scrounged materials and peppered other educators with questions: What are you teaching? What support do your EL students need?

Then, a year later, in 2002, federal policy forced districts, including Guilford, to rethink the education of newcomers. President George W. Bush had signed the reauthorization of the Elementary and Secondary Education Act. The law was renamed the No Child Left Behind Act (NCLB), and it was reimagined. States would need to implement annual standardized tests, schools receiving federal funding would need to ensure students were making increasing progress toward proficiency, and, for the first time, the progress of particular categories of children would be monitored—among them English learners. In 2003, Guilford welcomed its first districtwide EL director: Mayra Hayes.

Alicia vividly recalls Mayra's arrival in the district. Mayra was striking. She was effusive. She spoke of their students as "our babies." One afternoon Mayra arrived at Alicia's school, her car brimming with instruction books, curricula guides, and CDs. "My door is always open," Mayra promised. Alicia was skeptical. With teachers sprinkled throughout more than a hundred schools Mayra would surely be too busy. But when Alicia was confused about a concept or concerned about a student, she called and Mayra would come to her classroom that very afternoon to brainstorm.

As she settled into the district, Mayra set about assembling a team. She wanted master teachers who could mentor and coach the county's teachers. Her first such hire was Bob Egan. Early in the 1990s, Bob overheard a fellow teacher scoff when asked to adapt their instruction for newcomers, "I'm not changing what I do for anyone." Many colleagues, he sensed, considered his EL students a problem. Then Mayra showed up and started asking questions: "How can we make sure EL students are being identified for the academically gifted program? How can we help their families have a voice in education and in our community? How are our ELs impacted by particular district initiatives?" Bob joined Mayra as an EL coordinator in 2006.

Two years later, Mayra approached Alicia. She couldn't possibly coach others, Alicia protested. Mayra disagreed: She would grow into the role. Nervously Alicia accepted. Next to join was Soledad Lardies-Dunst. Soledad had started as a Spanish teacher a few months before Mayra was hired. She had moved from Argentina to teach, but at the end of her first year, her position was eliminated. Mayra, still new to the district, had already garnered a reputation. Hesitantly, Soledad reached out. Within weeks Mayra hired her as an EL teacher. Soon she was having her present to district teachers on ideas for incorporating vocabulary and methods for testing writing skills. In 2008, Mayra called Soledad: Would she join her districtwide team as a coordinator? Soledad didn't hesitate.

Last came Randall Saenz. Randall vividly recalled when Mayra came to Guilford: "With Mayra we were no longer teachers scattered across the district." Mayra glued disparate teachers together to form a family. Born and raised in Costa Rica, Randall had been teaching EL for two years already. In Mayra, he found a fellow advocate for ensuring his students had educational resources and their parents had translators. In 2017, he joined Mayra's team.

In addition to the four came men and women who sifted through data and managed testing, and interpreters who spoke Spanish, Vietnamese, French, Swahili, and Arabic—thirty-five people in all. Mayra sought out individuals who would challenge her and who would empathize with their students. As she explained, "It's all about getting the right people on the bus."

Daily, the team gathered for bowls of pho, spicy tamales, and thick pupusas cooked by a Honduran mother in the district. They swapped stories, spoke of their childhoods, shared struggles. When Alicia wished to pursue a master's degree, Mayra arranged her schedule to ensure she could. For Soledad she did the same. When a Vietnamese interpreter, and alumna of district schools, spoke of opening a hair salon, Mayra found a training program for her. "Her expectations are high," Alicia reflected. "But Mayra looks at her staff as people first." Colleagues become friends and, over time, an extended family. As the team coalesced, around them district demographics shifted. When Mayra arrived in 2003 one in fifty students was classified as an English learner. By 2017 the count approached one in ten.

◆

A girl from Guatemala, warm in a fuzzy pink pullover, mulled over words under her breath, "not fair, unfair, unjust." In a third-grade classroom at Doris Henderson Newcomers School in 2019, a dozen newcomers practiced substituting synonyms in a paragraph about the Greensboro sit-ins. A brown-haired boy contemplated "pick" and "select," altering their tense so either could nestle in a sentence before him: "They _____ Woolworth's department store . . ." Across the table a boy muttered, "*comprar,* shop, *comprar,* shop." A fifteen-minute drive separated the children from the lunch counter they were learning about.

Today, Guilford's newest arrivals have the opportunity of starting at Newcomers, a six-to-nine-month buffer to help them become acquainted with US classrooms, culture, and academics before transitioning to a neighborhood school. Everyone at Newcomers is from elsewhere. A mural of the earth fills the front door. Encircling the globe are greetings: *Bienvenido, Willkommen, Karibu, Aloha,* خوش آمدید, *Soo Dhawoow,* स्वागत, 欢迎, *Fáilte,* Welcome. The school is a testament to the vision and persistence of Mayra and her team.

◆

Mayra had been EL director less than a year when, in 2003, she flew first to New York City and then to the California coast to visit long-established newcomer centers. Upon her return she promptly presented to Guilford's school board her findings and a proposal for a newcomer center. They said no. A year later she tried again. Again no. Every few weeks a child, recently arrived from the steppes of Nepal or a Ugandan refugee camp, would be placed in a neighborhood school alongside American-born students. Some classrooms had resources and support; many did not. Mayra's team approached the school board again. For a third time they denied the request. Stubbornly, in 2006, the team petitioned once more. Guilford County had a new superintendent and the district was seeing a sharp spike in new arrivals. Their Newcomers School opened the following fall.

Over the course of a year, roughly four hundred children will move through the classrooms of Newcomers, nine-year-olds to nineteen-year-olds. Expectations are high. "If our students have one year of growth in reading," the school's curriculum facilitator, Maria Valeria Rivas de Kouba, explained, "we are not doing our job." Newcomers would never catch up. "We would only be maintaining the gap." With small classes, highly trained teachers, volunteer tutors, reading specialists, carefully crafted curricula, concentrated resources, and dedicated counselors and social workers, students learn in two months what in other schools might take seven.

Yet year after year, the North Carolina Department of Public Instruction has assigned the school an F rating. School scores are based on the percentage of students attaining proficiency on annual tests and the percentage of students who demonstrate growth. Few newcomers in the country less than a year can demonstrate proficiency on academic tests in English. Growth is measured by comparing students' progress across years, but the school's students take the state test only once during their time at Newcomers and thus can't demonstrate improvement. Fortunately, district leadership knows that the rating tells only a small part of the story. They see the results in their students and they have come to believe in Mayra and her team.

Trust took time. Again and again Mayra's team showed up. When a summer literacy program needed an attendance database, the EL department offered its templates and support. When the magnet schools' fair needed extra hands, Mayra's team set up tables, handed out packets of information, and directed families. When a national program offering free dental care offered to treat district students, Mayra's team launched a partnership. When books for a summer reading program for Indigenous students arrived late, the EL department drove door to door dropping them off with families.

By 2009 the department had developed a reputation. So when Mayra and her EL coordinator Bob rang the assistant director of transportation, he was amused but not surprised. More and more newcomers were arriving in Guilford, and many struggled with schoolwork. Could a bus be converted, they asked, into a mobile tutoring program that drove directly to the homes of immigrant families? "They have bookmobiles, they have blood-drive buses, they have all kinds of buses," Mayra reasoned. "If you can give an x-ray on a bus, you can tutor kids on a bus." District officials were skeptical. The EL team was undeterred. A few months later a "Homework on Wheels" bus pulled up to an apartment building. On-board sat teachers and many from Mayra's team. For two years, until funding ran dry, twice a week the bus parked alongside apartments and more than thirty kids came running. Parents came too. Interpreters took to riding the bus, translating for parents their children's homework and answering questions about school.

In the fall of 2017, the new superintendent approached Mayra. Could the district, the superintendent asked, create a dual-language program? Mayra hurried to the principal of Allen Jay Elementary to propose a Spanish program. The principal shook her head "no." Mayra was taken aback. "It would not be fair," the principal explained. "My students are one-third English speakers, one-third Spanish speakers, and one-third Urdu speakers." Mayra nodded. A year later Allen Jay Elementary opened a Spanish program and one of the first dual-language Urdu programs in the country.

One morning in 2019 I visited Allen Jay and I watched as five first graders sounded out Urdu words: خاندان: family, پھول: flower. On a rug three more traced the swooping grace of letters. Most of the children were from Pakistan, brought here or born here, except one blond-haired girl who, until a year ago, spoke only English. Many of the teaching assistants were mothers in the community. At pickup, the principal greets parents. One older Pakistani gentleman without fail greets her with a stately *hola*; she returns *assalam-o-alaikum*.

Just months after the Urdu program launched back in 2017, Mayra returned from the LA conference with a plan not for a program or a school, but for an entire overhaul of the district's approach to teaching immigrant-origin children.

In a second-floor classroom at Ragsdale High in 2019, three boys—from Mexico, Colombia, and Puerto Rico—debated possible meanings of "in pursuit." Before them lay a sentence lifted from their reading: "On an autumn night in 1607, a furtive group of men, women and children set off in a relay of small boats from the English village of Scrooby, in pursuit of the immigrant's oldest dream, a fresh start in another country." *"Como buscando, sí?"* one boy asked his peers. The others nodded tentatively. Across the room Nigerian, Nepali, and Eritrean students rolled "furtive" across their tongues. "Maybe it means stealing," one proposed. "Looking for a way out?" another added. "Sneaky," offered the third. Eavesdropping, their teacher suggested substituting each into the sentence. "If you visited three years ago," confided Randall Saenz, one of the EL coordinators on Mayra's team, "you would have seen kids reading: 'Chimpanzees are eating bananas. Bananas are yellow.'"

In the sweltering southern summer of 2017, Guilford's EL teachers, drawn from more than one hundred schools, gathered in a district training room to learn about Guilford's new districtwide experiment. Excitement, curiosity, and apprehension thickened the air that morning. Mayra was blunt: Many of their babies, their students, had been stalling, remaining in the EL program for seven, ten, even eleven years. Across the nation, school systems faced similar challenges, but new national policy demanded that the district innovate. No Child Left Behind, formerly the Elementary and Secondary Education Act (ESEA), had been reauthorized, renamed, and once again reimagined, now as the Every Student Succeeds Act (ESSA). ESSA established expectations for how long newcomers should take to adequately master English. In an attempt to ensure that children were making progress in language acquisition, districts would be required to report every English learner who, after five years in the district, still remained in EL programs. In response, Mayra was asking her teachers to restructure their lessons and rethink their materials. Together they would implement an approach born of a bicoastal partnership between a professor and a practitioner.

More than a decade earlier, in the heart of New York City, a woman responsible for supporting many of the city's EL students had been stumped. Maryann Cucchiara's students, scattered across five boroughs, could converse in basic spoken English, yet after years in the school system, many failed to grasp grade-level classwork. Maryann knew the problem intimately. For more than two decades she had taught EL students in city schools. But recently she had learned of a scholar across the country who, she hoped, might have an answer. Berkeley linguist Dr. Lily Wong Fillmore had devoted a lifetime to understanding how children acquire language. She was intimately familiar with the challenge: Her own parents had left China for California in the 1930s, and she had learned English in American schools. Students stalled in mastering English, she realized, because few were exposed to, as she put it, "juicy" texts. Who could master a language if they were stuck reading *See Spot Run?* Nervously, Maryann emailed Dr. Fillmore: Would she be interested in implementing her ideas in New York City classrooms? To her amazement, Dr. Fillmore wrote back: She was all in. Maryann was ecstatic. "I struck gold. I got the superstar of all superstars!"

Dr. Fillmore flew east and together the two women set to work, crafting not a single curriculum, but an approach to training teachers. EL classes favored simple texts and isolated grammar rules. In classrooms, the duo demonstrated to teachers how they could use rich, grammatically demanding language—sentences stuffed with dependent clauses, adjective phrases, and compounds. Students would need to slice open sentences, like frogs in a biology class—identifying the parts and making inferences about their functions. They turned some of the city's schools into mini-laboratories to refine their approach, they trained school leaders and teachers, they lugged angular tripods and bulky video cameras on the A train to film classes across the city.

Three years later, in 2010, the Council of the Great City Schools, a coalition supporting more than seventy of the largest urban public schools across the nation, reached out to the bicoastal team. Collaborating with the council, Maryann, now retired from her district role, and Dr. Fillmore began working with Boston schools, Fresno schools, Chicago schools. They ran more trainings, created online courses, and spoke before crowds. In the spring of 2017, Dr. Fillmore spoke at a council conference in Los Angeles. In that audience Mayra reached for her notebook.

In Guilford, as elsewhere, many considered the EL program remedial—a class to practice pronunciation, trace letters, sound out phonics, review grammar. At times, classes were devoted to parsing homework assignments assigned by other teachers. No more, Mayra was adamant. Rather than teach vocabulary and grammar in isolation, language learning would be teased out of studying animal adaptations, immigration histories, and ancient civilizations. Rather than read simplified books, students would analyze articles drawn from *Smithsonian* and *National Geographic* and would decode newspapers as well as grade-level books.

———◆———

In Guilford, on the first day of professional development in 2017, the room buzzed. Skeptics argued the approach was doomed, the texts were too complex, finding new material was too time consuming, students weren't ready. One high school teacher marched up to Mayra. "Doing grade-level content won't work," she declared. "My students can't do it." Mayra listened, but held firm. "They can and they will." Pausing, she asked, "May I give you a hug?" Taken aback, the teacher nodded. "I believe you can do this," Mayra whispered. She added she believed their children could as well.

In the coming weeks, as students returned to schools, Soledad, Alicia, Bob, and Randall fanned out across the district. They sat in the back of classrooms, conferred with teachers, sometimes even, at a teacher's urging, stepped in to teach. They tracked down complex texts and helped craft lessons that teased meaning from the sentences. Once a month teachers regrouped, swapping notes and trading lessons. To shrink the miles between classrooms the EL team launched a newsletter: See how students in this class are working collaboratively to deconstruct and reconstruct complex sentences; take a look at how this teacher has made a wall of synonyms using colorful paint sample chips to help students visualize subtle difference between words—*hungry, starving, famished.* Soon the newsletter was brimming with photos snapped in classrooms, videos of students debating passages, lesson plans constructed by teachers. Slowly, in classrooms, teachers began noticing a shift: Their students, some for the first time, were speaking in complex English sentences, incorporating new vocabulary, asking insightful questions about class texts.

Not everyone bought in. Bob still found some teachers using pictures books with high school students. Soledad patiently listened as an elementary teacher slung questions: How will my students ever understand such material? Principals too stonewalled: Focus on basic grammar, they urged. Mayra drove zigzags across the district, sitting with each naysayer in turn. What support did they need? Could she invite them to observe a class in another school? Could a coordinator co-teach a lesson? Teacher by teacher, principal by principal.

One morning, many months after the rollout, Mayra watched an elementary teacher lead an entire lesson using a book filled with simple, staccato sentences. Next she drove to a high school where for ninety minutes a teacher plowed through grammar rules. By the time Mayra made it back to her car she slumped in the driver's seat, despairing. "What have I done? Am I doing the right thing?" Engine off, Mayra sat silently—but not for long. She had visited classrooms in New York, she had read about schools in Boston, Baltimore, and Oakland, and she had seen results in Guilford County. Turning the key in the ignition, Mayra wound her way back to the office, planning during the entire drive. The next day she returned to both schools to meet with the teachers and with the principals. The coordinators offered additional coaching and came in to co-plan. Success, they knew, would require Mayra's whole team.

———————◆———————

By the summer of 2017, Cassie Ott was rounding the corner on two decades of teaching EL students. But she had had enough. The material she taught was dull, the books drab. She had been trained to focus on the basics: "remediation versus acceleration," as she put it. That August she attended Mayra's training. What she heard was confounding. Surely her students weren't ready for grade-level work, particularly not her newest newcomers. Skeptically she began rewriting lessons, ready to watch the approach fail. When one morning a newly arrived Colombian fourth grader complained, "Miss, this is too hard," Cassie fretted. Yet she persisted, giving him the skeleton of sentences and worksheets to organize his thoughts. By the class's end, beaming, he presented a paragraph of ideas. Cassie was stunned. She and her students began debating droughts in sub-Saharan Africa, adaptations of geckos, civil rights change-makers. Something odd was happening, Cassie realized. For the first time in years she was excited to teach.

Elementary school teacher Susan Wiles, like Cassie, found herself questioning years of training: Why *was* she teaching grammar out of context? Why *were* her students reading books so many grade levels below their English-speaking peers? Mayra's new approach was, she recalled, "mindboggling . . . an enormous paradigm shift." In monthly meetings, she and colleagues sifted through texts. "We were shocked," Susan remembered. "The books we'd been using year after year were truly boring!" Hurriedly, they began amassing new libraries. A thirty-minute drive away, Deborah Taylor's high schoolers were unrecognizable. She would announce the day's task, dissecting juicy sentences, and three students would race for the scissors. Sue Buchholtz's fourth graders, who had shown little language progress in years and who dragged their feet to EL classes, now ran into the room. "Miss, Miss, today the teacher used 'overjoyed,' and we read that word yesterday in your class!"

Many of the educators were the sole EL teacher in their school; but Mayra's team knew that rethinking instruction needed time and teammates. One Monday each month, they brought in platters of cookies and arranged for childcare. Drawn like magnets, EL teachers descended on the district office to draft lessons and troubleshoot. When one elementary teacher broke her arm, she nonetheless showed up, arm in a cast, ready to share ideas, refusing to miss even a single meeting.

For Alicia, the transformation she saw in classes was staggering: First graders mastered words like *refreshed* and *ventured out*; they wrote sentences contrasting African and European folktales. It was work that three years earlier she would have expected of fifth-grade newcomers. Sitting in the back of a classroom one day, Randall nearly fell out of his chair when a fourth-grade boy spontaneously shouted, "I love reading in this class!"

By the fall of 2018, non-EL teachers took to stopping their EL colleagues in the halls. Students once shy and silent were raising their hands, asking questions, and explaining concepts in math, in science, in social studies. What, they marveled, had triggered the transformation? Principals too had taken note. They goggled as newcomers debated the meaning of vocabulary when they observed classes; they began inviting

EL teachers to train colleagues. The principal at Allen Jay Elementary called Mayra. Could the EL department coach her entire staff? Without hesitation Mayra said yes.

Ask Mayra to explain their success, and she overflows with stories about the remarkable people she works with: the teacher starting an after-school mentoring program for newcomers, the teacher who steps in to train colleagues, the staff members who stay late to meet with students for no extra compensation, the interpreters who run support programs for families, the district superintendent and chief academic officer who have championed the new approach to teaching. To her teachers she repeats over and over: "This success is not my success. It is because of you," she insists. "It is because of your hard work."

Ask teachers and district staff and they often share other stories. The time a teacher needed textbooks and stared flabbergasted when Mayra strode across the school's parking lot carrying a stack. The summer day after a teacher was reassigned to a new classroom when Mayra turned up with cleaning supplies to scrub desks. The evening a principal texted, unsure how to support a dual-language student, and Mayra arrived the following morning to talk with the boy and his teachers. The student who needed a wheelchair, and how Mayra secured one. The mother who needed an advocate in court, and how Mayra helped find someone. How Mayra and her colleagues had, after a devastating fire engulfed an apartment, arrived within hours at the hospital bedside of a grieving family. How, when a tornado savaged a swath of schools, the EL department had gone door to door delivering food to families whose homes were damaged. One afternoon, Deborah Taylor, new to her middle school and also a new mother, had dialed Mayra, distraught. Overwhelmed and isolated, she declared she was ready to quit. "I'm coming right over," Mayra soothed. She did, and together they talked. And then Mayra made connections to teachers and administrators. "She talked me down," Deborah confided. Years later Deborah was still teaching at the same school.

In the summer of 2019 the district's yearly test scores were released. In their office Mayra's team stared, stunned. Compared to two years earlier, nearly 50 percent more EL students were deemed proficient in reading. The number of students proficient in writing had roughly doubled. State test scores in science, reading, and math had shot up. And while two years earlier, less than two hundred students had been able to graduate from the EL program, that year more than four hundred exited.

Weeks later, when they revealed the results to their teachers, the room bubbled over in whoops, shouts, and applause. Then it was time to get back to work—teachers welcoming new students, interpreters meeting with parents, district staff coordinating testing and analyzing data, Randall typing up the next newsletter, Bob modeling a lesson, Alicia searching the public library for exciting books, Soledad training a new hire. And Mayra driving from school to school to school, doing whatever was needed.

Once a week, after her team heads home for the evening, Mayra locks the office and heads downtown to a nearby university to teach a graduate education course on supporting immigrant-origin students. In her class, soon-to-be teachers draft lessons, discuss how to foster class culture, learn how to incorporate complex texts. With her students, Mayra speaks of growing up as a newcomer. Nine of Guilford's newest hires have come from Mayra's courses.

On the evening of the last class of the semester in 2019, Mayra locked eyes with each graduate student and soon-to-be teacher. "Remember," she concluded, for their soon-to-be students, "you are their safe haven. You are the place where they will be able to talk, where they will feel safe to come in and try. And not be afraid of their accents, and not be afraid of making a mistake. You are their advocate." The responsibility, she acknowledged, was daunting. But, she reminded them, they were not alone. Wherever they chose to teach, there were teachers and administers to help. Find the person in charge of EL students, she advised. Learn who could support them and their students. "And," she added with a smile, "If you want to stay in Guilford County, hand me your résumé."

THE PERSONAL: ROBERT, PART 2

After climbing down from the truck, Robert stretched. The fifteen-year-old was stiff and very much alone. It was 2013 and Robert had just arrived at Kyaka II refugee camp in southern Uganda, carrying nothing more than a few bills in his pocket and his two books, *Jane Eyre* and *Best Poems of 1998*.

United Nations aid workers ushered the refugees into lines. "Who speaks Kiswahili? Kinyarwanda? Kihema? Luganda?" Robert could now read simple English and speak Swahili and Rubira fluently, but he was most confident in his native Kihema. One by one the displaced were led into a tent. When his turn came he found two women inside, one holding a questionnaire and one ready to translate. Quietly Robert took a seat. "Where are you from? Why did you come here? What happened in your home?" Robert answered each carefully, pausing as the young woman next to him translated. "Who are your parents? Where were you born?" But this time when Robert answered, the woman did not translate. Instead she turned sharply, seeing him for the first time. She repeated the questions, and a confused Robert repeated his answers. The woman stared, momentarily speechless. "*Ruhanga wange!* You are my nephew!"

Robert, a Congolese orphan who had for nearly three years lived on the Ugandan border believing he was alone in the world, had found his family.

What happened next Robert remembers only in pieces. Hugs, tears, laughter, whoops. The aid worker was giddy with excitement. What Robert does remember was the feeling that settled like a blanket across his shoulders: He was safe.

Over rice and seared beef Robert learned of his lost family. The young woman—who just by luck was Robert's translator that day—was Enid, his father's younger sister. Also in the camp were four of Robert's uncles, all close to his age. Enid, the eldest and the head of the family, was just twenty-two. When they reached his new home, a tent amid a sea of tents, the reunited family celebrated long into the night.

From above, Kyaka II Refugee Settlement resembles an uppercase *E*, encompassing an area of more than thirty square miles. In 2013 Robert lived there alongside 22,000 refugees and asylum seekers, mostly from the DRC. Today Kyaka II has roughly five times that number of residents; it is one of thirteen refugee "cities" spread across Uganda.

Unlike many countries in the world, Uganda has opened its doors to the displaced, creating policies that not only welcome refugees but give them the right to work, farm land, access health care, and attend primary school—rights and opportunities rarely granted refugees in the countries to which they first flee. The United Nations has described Uganda's model as one of the most generous in the world. Almost every day the displaced cross its borders. They come fleeing civil war, roving militia, ethnic violence, extended droughts, Ebola outbreaks. Close to one and a half million refugees currently live in Uganda. After Turkey and Colombia, Uganda today has the third-largest refugee population of any country and hosts one of the largest refugee camps in the world.

Suddenly with a family to call his own, Robert could create a home. He fell into an easy friendship with his uncles, farmed maize and beans, and after only a few months helped his newfound family construct a two-room house of mud and reeds that dried hard in the sun. And once more Robert enrolled in school. When he had left the border town, Robert had been enrolled in primary 6, the equivalent of sixth grade in the United States. But when his aunt brought him to school, he was placed in secondary 1 (eighth grade in the US). Robert nodded and said nothing. In his experience school levels seemed arbitrary. If he could keep up with the work—and he could—why not keep progressing in grade level?

At school, Robert became his own advocate. Over the next two years he plowed through four grades, and for his diligence he won a scholarship that paid for much of his education. He slept at school during the week, often waking long before the sun came up to study before a full day of classes that stretched into the early evening.

In school and out, Robert read voraciously. Within a year of living in the camp he could finally understand *Jane Eyre*. He fell in love with the long-suffering British heroine who lost the one she loved most. The first time he read it cover to cover, he cried. He tore through British classics, cultivating a passion for Shakespeare. In a three-inch-tall notebook he carefully copied Shakespearean quotes that struck him. When he could find them, he read books by African authors—*Houseboy* by Ferdinand Oyono, *Blossoms of the Savannah* by Henry R. Ole Kulet. Perhaps not surprisingly, he was captivated by *The River Between* by Kenyan Ngũgĩ wa Thiong'o—the story of two communities at odds, the shadow of colonialism, the search for education.

———•———

When Robert first came to the camp he could converse in four languages. But here everyone seemed to speak a different tongue. In Uganda alone there are more than forty living languages, not including those spoken by the mosaic of refugees drawn from ten different countries living in Kyaka II. Soccer games in the scrub brush, card games late at night, long walks through camp, they all became classrooms. Robert listened and contorted his mouth. Friends corrected him, encouraged him. Within two years he was conversing in Luganda, Runyankole, Rutooro, Rukonjo, Rwamba, Rukiga, Rubira, Swahili, English, and Kihema. By seventeen he was a master of ten tongues.

I learned Robert was a polyglot at the start of his senior year of high school in 2018. On a wall of my classroom I had taped a poster listing simple English salutations and questions. Gathering my twelve freshmen advisees early one Friday, I tasked them with filling in translations in their home languages. Spanish, Portuguese, Arabic, Khmer, Vietnamese, Luganda. My sole Ugandan advisee was gnawing off the end of his pencil, his face scrunched, attempting to work out the spelling of words, when Robert came over offering help. "You know Luganda?" I asked. "Yeah," he replied nonchalantly. "I learned it in the camp."

Later I would ask him just how many languages he knew, and it was on that autumn afternoon that I began to hear a little of Robert's story for the first time. For decades, US immigrant education programs were designated as "English as a second language" programs, ESL for short. For Robert, "English as a tenth language" would be accurate.

———◆———

At school in the Ugandan refugee camp, Robert became America's stalwart advocate. He fell into heated debates about which country was the world's greatest superpower. In Robert's mind there was no dispute: It was America, because it stood up for others. He had never met an American. Yet he was confident that they were the type of people you could sit next to, share a meal with. America, Robert explained to his peers, "is the only country where you can be free." When others shook their heads, Robert stood firm.

In 2013 Enid had begun the process of applying for resettlement for her family, including Robert. By then she and Robert's uncles had lived in Kyaka II for a decade. It was a long shot, as fewer than one out of every one hundred refugees across the globe is ever resettled. But in the camps, survival was fed by a diet of hope. Everyone knew someone who had been resettled. By the time Robert was seventeen in early 2015, he had friends who had left the camp for Sweden, Canada, Norway, Australia, and America.

Then in April of 2015, Enid's name was called. Their case was under review. That summer it seemed that so many of Robert's friends were handed plane tickets. Again and again he went to see them off. On Facebook he hungrily followed their new lives. But as the months dragged on without news about his family's application, he gave up hoping. It would take more than a year before they were called to the camp's offices. They were indeed on track for resettlement. In the summer of 2016 the family underwent a flurry of immunizations and tests. No one took the time to explain what shots were what, but dutifully he submitted to the needles. His arms bruised and sore, Robert returned to school. He soon began studying in senior 6, equivalent to twelfth grade.

A month later the family was called again, this time for lessons in American culture. Their teacher, a young woman, had the dubious task of summarizing for a room of one hundred how to survive in the United States. She talked about laws and expectations, customs and considerations—US Living 101. This is how you find a job, apply for food stamps, flush a toilet. Remember not to beat your kids. Don't use drugs. What caught Robert's attention most, though, was when the woman turned to the room's teenagers. In the US, she told them, they could go to school. Robert was ecstatic. "I get to study with white people. This is amazing!"

———•———

Robert left the refugee camp on a Thursday at the beginning of November 2016. In the preceding days, he and his family had emptied the contents of their two-room home—mostly clothes and cooking pots. Over the years, Robert had amassed a new library, and once again he parted with almost all of his collection. Everything was gifted, carrying on a tradition of passing on essentials to families who were still waiting. Passing on hope, as if to say, may you too pass along these pots someday.

Friends came to see them off. How many times had Robert come to hug families goodbye? Now it was his turn. It didn't feel real. It couldn't be real. Borrowing a friend's phone, he snapped picture after picture as if to prove to himself, and the world, that he and his family were moving.

In the Ugandan capital of Kampala, Robert waited, alongside other refugees, at a hotel for their flight. He quelled any bubbles of excitement. It was safer not to hope too much. And then, on the eve of Robert's new life, his past reached out once more.

An aid worker had asked an offhand question about a woman she knew who lived in Kampala. "She speaks Kihema. Maybe you know her?" So few people spoke Kihema that Robert's family was curious. When they dialed the woman's number, on the other end of the line was Robert's great-aunt, Kabatuku Grace, the older sister of his mother's mom.

Kabatuku Grace arrived at the hotel Monday morning. She wore a beautiful dress patterned with diamonds and a vibrant orange cloth wrapped across her shoulders. For a long time she held Robert's face in her hands. They sat in the hotel garden and talked and talked and talked. They spoke of his mother, her niece. She had heard of the attack that had occurred six years earlier, but she had not known he had survived.

There was not enough time, not nearly enough time. Robert was blissfully happy and terribly sad. Holding her wrinkled hands, he promised to return one day. She smiled, nodding. "I'm so proud of you. You've grown into a man and even with all that has happened . . . you have a very good life ahead of you. You're heading to a good place. Be a great person who I will be proud of."

———◆———

The next morning Robert packed a small suitcase. As before, he had little to bring: four pairs of jeans, a couple of shirts, a few pairs of shoes, his medical and immigration papers, and two books, *Jane Eyre* and the *Best Poems of 1998*. The bus to Entebbe International Airport departed the hotel at 3 p.m. on Tuesday, November 8, 2016. Seven thousand miles away, it was morning in America. Up and down the Eastern Seaboard people were heading to the polls.

For months, Robert had been following the US presidential election. He tracked the polls closely. Two weeks before he left the camp, Robert crowded into the house of a friend and together they watched Donald Trump and Hillary Clinton spar on a Las Vegas stage. "She wants open borders," the businessman blustered. "People are going to pour into our country . . . they have no idea where they are coming from." What would happen to his family, Robert worried, if Trump won?

It was dark by the time Robert ascended the airplane's stairs. He held his breath; at any moment he was sure someone would tell him he couldn't go, that there had been a mistake. But no one came. As the plane sped down the runway, Robert kept watch from the window, tracking the twinkling lights of the city and the dark stretches of jungle until they grew indistinguishable.

Somewhere over North Africa, Robert tasted sandwiches for the first time. He wasn't sure what to make of them. A flight attendant wheeled by offering a selection of sodas. Hesitantly he selected a ginger ale; hours later he sampled a root beer. At some point while stretching, Robert caught a glimpse of a couple kissing in the row behind him. He spun back around, astonished. Kissing in public only happened in movies, he had thought. While Robert and his family nodded off, across the Atlantic election polls started to close along the East Coast.

When the plane touched down in Belgium, the bleary family stepped out of the jetway into a sea of white. Never before had Robert seen so many white people. As they navigated through the airport, Robert kept looking around him in wonder. Thousands of miles away, Donald Trump had just won Ohio.

Sometime later, while waiting in the terminal for the flight to Newark, Robert was startled to hear a wail. A woman was sobbing uncontrollably into a phone. "Trump is winning! I won't be able to go back." Her cries echoed through the hall. But there was no time to confirm the report, as Robert's flight to America was boarding. Although they did not know it yet, while Robert and his family waited to board a plane bound for America, Donald Trump was mounting a stage to deliver his acceptance speech as the forty-fifth president of the United States. As Robert skimmed westward over the clouds, his soon-to-be country was hurtling toward turbulence.

———•———

Stepping off the plane into Newark International Airport, Robert stopped abruptly. His eyes zipped back and forth. Why was everyone so tall? Why was everyone walking so fast? He turned to his uncles: "This is crazy! People are walking as if they are running. What are they chasing?"

Hours later they boarded the final plane, to New Hampshire. There they were met by a representative from a local resettlement agency who deposited them at a motel. To Robert and his uncles, everything was fascinating. They tried out all the beds and twirled the knobs of the stove. Enid shook her head. "What have I done? I came with all these boys, I came with trouble." The boys laughed; they were already putting on a pot of water to boil macaroni. The room had a TV and, never having had their own, they tried switching it on. It was then that Robert learned that Donald Trump would be his president. He was shocked, but not yet worried. This was America, he assured himself. He had read about its system of government, and he knew that there were safeguards. It was not like other countries. He would wait and see.

Robert and his uncles spent the following days exploring. They woke early and ran in the biting November chill. They walked for hours. Everywhere they saw people in cars; no one seemed to travel on foot as they did. "What about those who don't have cars?" they wondered. Everything appeared different—as if, Robert described, he had been reborn. He knew nothing about anything.

A week or two later the family moved to a small apartment in Lowell, Massachusetts, and the boys enrolled at Lowell High. At eighteen, with six years of formal schooling, Robert was placed in tenth grade. School officials knew it was the only way to give the boy any chance, however slim, at a high school diploma. In three years he would age out of the system.

———◆———

On his first day of school in the United States, standing in the middle of a cavernous cafeteria, Robert felt very much alone. He had arrived excited, confident. He had seen American movies, listened to American music, read American histories, followed American politics. He was prepared. But now, standing on the edge of the crowd with his Afro and wearing his shirt and jeans from the refugee camp, he felt glaringly conspicuous. Everyone knew he was different—that he didn't belong.

Then with the first bell, he was swept up into a torrent of students, carried along through branching tunnels and hallways. As the flow ebbed, with students streaming into classes, he found himself alone in an unmarked corridor. Many minutes later, breathless, he finally located his first class. When he slipped inside everyone was already seated.

Overcome by shyness, he muttered his name before sinking silently into a seat. That afternoon he rode the bus home, exhausted and deflated.

The next day was not much better, nor the day after that. In the halls he edged past classmates who danced and spoke at top volume. They draped casual arms over each others' shoulders as they walked. Some he caught kissing in the corners of stairwells. In classes they chatted away in Spanish, Portuguese, Khmer. Robert had been raised to be reserved, precise in his words and actions. How, he wondered, could he ever fit in?

At lunch he gravitated to other refugees from East Africa. He sat mute as they talked of video games, basketball, football. All of this was new, and Robert could think of little to add. Perhaps it was wise to say nothing at all. Classes, at least, came easy. Robert was a natural scholar. Despite having attended school for only a handful of semesters from first to twelfth grade, he found his new schoolwork surprisingly easy. On his first history paper he dutifully wrote two cramped pages on slavery. When he handed it in, the teacher seemed shocked. "You only needed to write one." In other classes he was assigned short stories and small essays. Where, he wondered, were the novels he treasured?

There were new rules and new expectations to learn. But he was used to that, having attended more than half a dozen schools. There was less copying and more group work. In Uganda, if a teacher droned on, you remained sitting; but here, when a searing bell scissored the air, class would end whether the teacher was finished or not.

As in Uganda, each instructor had their quirks and personal preferences. There was the teacher who snatched away your phone without warning, the teacher who refused bathroom requests. There were the teachers who smiled and those who seemed forever serious. And, there was the teacher who called him Richard. He tried to correct her, but the name stuck and in time Robert relented. It seemed easier to answer to the new name. The most pleasant surprise was how kind his math teacher was. Forty strokes in Ntoroko had left welts and a dislike of numbers. Here, his math teacher was strict, but also warm. When students struggled, she worked with each individually until they understood.

Perhaps most challenging was the sheer quantity of typed assignments. Rarely in his Ugandan schools had he had access to a computer.

His first typed assignment in the United States, he later recalled with a chuckle, might best be described as a collection of letters scattered across a page. His teacher seemed on the brink of laughter herself: "You should really take computer classes." Not knowing who to ask for lessons, Robert, like he had so many times before, began to teach himself. As in Uganda, he became his own advocate.

He started showing up before the first bell to practice hunting and pecking on a computer in the school library. His uncles' teasing was merciless: "Robert must be going to school early to flirt with girls!" Robert just shook his head. Alone in the library, in the dead of a New England winter, Robert surrounded himself with the past. He searched for images of lions and savannahs, national parks and the snaking Semliki River. In the camp it had seemed so easy to forge friendships, to make connections. Languages, ethnicities, nationalities had mattered little. Here, everyone seemed divided. "There was no group that I could fit into," he told me many years later. He hated to admit it, but after all his years of built-up excitement, school in America was a disappointment. Robert shrank into himself. For a young man who could converse in ten languages, in his first months in America, Robert became all but mute.

Eight years before, when he had climbed out of a canoe on the muddy banks of Uganda, Robert had learned how to keep going. "Even though I felt sad, I still needed to live my life and accept whatever was happening." A survivor's strategy. "If I felt like I didn't fit in, then I wouldn't want to come to school, or maybe I would hate my classes and I wouldn't do the work."

Like in Ntokoro, Robert took charge of his future: He willed himself to not think of the past, or even the present. As before, he began, slowly, to make connections—first with teachers, later with peers. "Those conversations gave me a little confidence," to keep going, he told me years later. "Even though I felt different, I still felt like at least some people knew me."

CHAPTER 6

SEEING STRENGTHS

To make Americans, we must recognize that students bring many strengths, and we must be willing to listen and learn from them. When schools and communities focus on what young people lack—mastery of English, sufficient academic preparation—it becomes easy to lose sight of the remarkable assets students possess. And if schools do not recognize, draw on, and celebrate these strengths, students will too often fail to see in themselves all they have to offer.

This chapter tells three stories about efforts to recognize and unlock the strengths of immigrant-origin students. The first is the story of a Chinese immigrant mother, a young lawyer, and a Chinese immigrant activist who, in 1969, brought a lawsuit against the San Francisco school district, for letting newcomers who spoke little English flounder in class. The case led to a Supreme Court decision that schools nationwide must provide academic and linguistic support to immigrant children. The second is the story of a principal who in 2015 opened a school for newly arrived students, in Bladensburg, Maryland, which uses sports, counseling, and a creative approach to grading to fashion a new way to educate immigrant-origin students. The third is the story of my own student Carla, a Dominican immigrant who, after struggling in school, returned to my classroom after graduation to mentor her immigrant peers.

THE PAST: *LAU V. NICHOLS*

In a first grade classroom at Jean Parker Elementary, in the heart of San Francisco's Chinatown, twenty-two-year-old Lucinda Lee prepared for parent-teacher conferences. In the fall of 1968 she had embarked on her first year in the classroom. Lee had come to the profession as an early member of the National Teacher Corps, an aspirational training program created in the flurry of LBJ's Great Society legislation, and she was placed at a school just blocks from her childhood home. Of the parents she met that week, one stuck in her mind: an outspoken mother recently arrived from Hong Kong.

Kam Wai Lau was, Lucinda Lee recalls, direct, confident, and unafraid to advocate for her shy six-year-old son Kinmon, who often went by Kinney. In her son's teacher she saw a potential ally. The classes of Jean Parker Elementary at the time were filled almost exclusively with recent immigrants and the children of immigrants from China, many of whom were still mastering English. But, of the school's staff, Lee was, in her recollection, one of just two teachers of Chinese heritage. "Miss Lee, do you speak Chinese?" Lau asked at their meeting. Lee, whose immigrant father had ensured she spent twelve years attending daily Cantonese classes, nodded. "Then, can't you teach my son math in Chinese? At least one subject in Chinese, wouldn't that make sense, so he doesn't fall behind?"[1]

To Lee, it was a simple and logical solution, a way to ensure her twenty-odd, mostly Chinese-speaking youngsters kept pace academically. Vividly Lee recalled her own white kindergarten teacher, Ms. Thompson, who seemed to forever be admonishing her entirely Chinese-speaking class, "No Chinese here. No Chinese here." Even as a five-year-old, she found the reprimand grating, but only as an adult would she put words to the feeling: "Basically she was telling us to be silent." It was a reproach that weighed on Lee throughout elementary school, high school, and college. Only with distance did she wonder, "What if Ms. Thompson had taught us differently?" And now Kinney's mother was asking her to do just that. Excited, Lee approached her principal. But she was promptly informed that only English should be spoken in the classroom. Lee, as she would share with me, was upset, but not surprised.[2]

For years the city's Chinese community had advocated on behalf of its youngest. During the 1960s, spurred in part by the passage of the 1965 Immigration Act, San Francisco's Chinese population had almost doubled. By 1970, roughly one in every thirteen city residents and one in every six students in the public schools traced their origins to China.[3] But the school system seemed largely unmoved by the slew of meetings, detailed studies, proposals, and protests brought by many families living in Chinatown. In an attempt to appease them, the district offered a forty-minute English language class once a day to one in four of the students in need of such support. It also piloted a small bilingual program. In the neighborhood's largely segregated schools, dropout rates ran high. Like in many parts of the country at the time, if you were an EL student, you either swam or you sank.

Helping to organize and protest was a graduate student in his early thirties who was a classical pianist and a scholar of ancient Semitic languages. Ling-chi Wang had grown up on the Chinese island of Xiamen before fleeing with his family to Hong Kong just before the communist takeover in 1949. For college, Wang came to the United States, carrying with him a passion for ancient civilizations. He settled into graduate school on Chicago's South Side. But in the summer of 1966, in the heat of the Civil Rights Movement, Wang flew to the Bay Area to visit his then girlfriend, and future wife, and her family. At college in Michigan he had avidly read the words of Reverend Dr. Martin Luther King Jr. and Malcolm X, and in Chicago he watched from a distance as Black Americans protested and organized. But, Wang told me, it was only after he arrived in the crowded streets of San Francisco's Chinatown that the lessons became personal. Deplorable working and housing conditions, segregated employment practices, police racial profiling, high student dropout rates—he saw it all. At the summer's end, Wang transferred to the University of California, Berkeley, where he began studying by night and organizing by day.

While Wang began to hold meetings, contact city officials, and write articles to draw attention to wholesale discrimination against the country's Chinese residents, some commentators were claiming Chinese immigrants were so successful that they didn't need help. That December, *U.S. News & World Report* published a multipage article on Chinese Americans. "At a time when Americans are awash in worry over the plight of racial minorities—one such minority, the nation's 300,000 Chinese-Americans, is winning wealth and respect by dint of its own hard work." Chinese Americans, unlike African Americans, the article asserted, did not resort to violence and did not rely on government support. For a century, Chinese immigrants had been both unwanted and considered inassimilable. In an abrupt about-face that belied reality, they were now being positioned as the American Dream personified, "a model of self-respect and achievement . . . moving ahead on their own—with no help from anyone else." Their communities, the article declared, had little crime, high employment, and sweeping student success.[4] Americans of Chinese ancestry were, many would soon begin to say, a model minority.

Wang saw this idea as a dangerous myth, and he set about dispelling it. He saw firsthand the effects of indifferent schools that passed Chinese children on from grade to grade regardless of whether they could understand English. A polyglot who spoke four languages himself, Wang began advocating for bilingual education. In the midst of Lunar New Year celebrations in the winter of 1969, Wang helped convene school officials—almost all the descendants of Irish, Italian, and English immigrants—and furious Chinese parents, teachers, and students. Outside, students marched in a downpour, brandishing hand-lettered signs, "Don't teach us to be white."[5] They met, and clashed, in the auditorium of the Commodore Stockton Elementary School, once known as the segregated Oriental School, and before that the Chinese School. The school officials conceded little. After cofounding the Concerned Chinese for Action and Change the previous year, Wang kept on organizing. In spring 1969, drawing on the tactics of the Civil Rights Movement, he cofounded with other activists an organization called Chinese for Affirmative Action, which aimed to tackle systemic discrimination.

One block away from Wang's office, a newly minted, self-described brash twenty-five-year-old lawyer, Edward Steinman, set up shop. A Chicago native and son of Russian immigrants, Steinman sported a large beard and tied his long locks in a ponytail. He had come to the city on a fellowship funding lawyers to work for legal aid organizations that offered their services to low-income communities. It was at that legal aid office, in the fall of 1969, that Steinman met Wang. They quickly fell into conversation and then collaboration.

Volunteering at the legal aid office was a law student who also happened to be the roommate of teacher Lucinda Lee's then boyfriend and future husband. When the boyfriend's roommate shared with Lee that Wang and Steinman were preparing to go up against the city's schools in support of the community's non-English-speaking students, Lee knew who she had to tell: the mother of one of her students, Kam Wai Lau.[6]

Kam Wai Lau was not the first Chinese mother to stand up to the San Francisco schools. She was following in the footsteps of another determined woman who had confronted the schools more than eighty years earlier.

Mary McGladery was eleven when she traveled alone from the outskirts of Shanghai to San Francisco in 1868. She was not Irish, as her name might suggest. Rather, soon after arriving in America she took, or was given, the name of a matron at a home established to take in women and children seeking shelter. At the home she alone was from China, and it was here, as she would describe years later, "that I first learned to speak the English language and acquire American manners."[7] Mary was just eighteen when she met and soon married another young immigrant, Jeu Dip, who anglicized his name to Joseph Tape, and who had arrived in the US just years before laborers, including many Chinese immigrants, hammered in the final spikes of a railroad connecting the country from coast to coast.

Many of China's first immigrants to America were drawn by the promise of gold. Indeed, a common Cantonese nickname for San Francisco, and sometimes more broadly the West Coast, was *Gam Saan*, Gold Mountain. Sought after for their diligence and their willingness to work for little, often by necessity, men of the Qing Empire were enticed to cross the Pacific by American recruiters. They became mainstays in the mines, and also on the railroads. They were employed in the fields and in the factories; they cobbled shoes and cleaned clothes. Most lived in California, and within the state they were most numerous in the port hub of San Francisco. On disembarking, many newly arrived Chinese immigrants made their way to Stockton Street, Sacramento Street, and other places in a neighborhood that quickly grew into the country's first Chinatown. But by 1870, when Mary was just thirteen, the United States was already turning against immigrants from the East.

A flurry of city ordinances swept through San Francisco, many with such blatant racist intent that they bordered on the absurd. Laundries too small to afford horse-drawn delivery carts, most often operated by Chinese proprietors, were taxed seven times more than large, wealthy laundries.[8] Rooming houses were required to be spacious, an ordinance enacted with an eye toward shuttering crowded Chinatown accommodations. Peddlers were barred from hoisting poles heavy with vegetables

across their shoulders, and to protect residents' ears, the ringing of cere-
monial gongs was banned throughout the city. The state of California also
passed laws specifically taxing Chinese fisherman and miners. The state
passed laws, too, preventing Chinese residents from becoming natural-
ized citizens, owning property, and testifying in court against their white
neighbors. Many such ordinances and laws were struck down, but more
sprouted in their place. They were actively cultivated by a growing mob of
anti-Chinese activists whose ranks were bolstered by labor unionists and
recent European immigrants. When the economy did a nosedive in the
early 1870s, the country's Chinese residents became easy scapegoats. In
1875, the year of the Tapes' marriage, President Ulysses S. Grant signed a
law banning the immigration of Chinese convicts, contract laborers, and
prostitutes. In practice the law excluded most Chinese women altogether.

Just five months before the Tapes' first child, Mamie, was born, upwards of 25,000 people gathered in downtown San Francisco to debate
the fate of prospective Chinese newcomers. Addressing a raucous crowd,
California's governor, William Irwin, declared that Chinese immigration
threatened Anglo-Saxons and endangered "everything that goes to make
up American civilization."[9] In a statement that would be cited in a US
Senate hearing, the meeting's organizers would go on to declare that
Chinese immigration constituted "an evil of great present magnitude."[10]

In Congress and on city streets the accusations slung at the Chinese
immigrants mimicked those that had been flung at earlier arrivals, and
they would be recycled in future decades to attack successive waves of
newcomers—that Chinese people spoke a different language, worshiped
different gods, kept different customs, wore different clothes, ate different
food—as a result, they were considered unassimilable. Their immigration
was portrayed as a flood set to inundate the United States. They were accused of being riddled with disease and lacking all morals. And, though
in 1870 Chinese residents—both immigrants and American-born—accounted for less than one in every six hundred people across the country,
many argued that American jobs, everywhere, were at risk.[11]

But the anti-Chinese rhetoric and regulations did not stop the Tapes
from seeing themselves as proud Americans. The middle-class couple
prospered. Mary Tape was an accomplished artist; Joseph Tape was a
respected broker and interpreter. After Mamie's birth they moved to
a house many blocks outside the city's crowded Chinatown. As Mary

would recount, "We have always lived as Americans, and our children have been brought up to consider themselves as such."[12] Perhaps that was why, when their eldest turned eight in 1884, Mary marched Mamie down to the Spring Valley Elementary School, mere blocks from their home.

Just four years earlier, state law would have barred Mamie's enrollment. But California school segregation, which had been established in the 1860s and barred "Negroes, Mongolians, and Indians," had been recently rewritten, scrubbing all mentions of race or region. Regardless, when the Tapes arrived at school, Principal Jennie Hurley stubbornly refused to admit little Mamie. Steadfast in their conviction of what was just and confident in their position as middle-class Americans, Mary and Joseph Tape promptly sued the school board of San Francisco.

Given national sentiment, it was a courageous step. Less than two years earlier, in the spring of 1882, representatives had convened in the Capital—many likely having traveled on tracks laid by Chinese laborers—to pass the Chinese Exclusion Act, which prohibited most migration from the Qing Empire. The ban was the first in the nation's history targeting an entire ethnicity and nationality. Initially imposed for a decade, it would be renewed and remain in place for the next sixty years. In 1882 nearly 40,000 Chinese immigrants arrived in America; three years later the number admitted was just twenty-two.[13]

In San Francisco, the school board stood against the Tapes. As one board member declared, "I would rather go to jail than allow a Chinese child to be admitted to the schools."[14] But at the dawn of 1885, the city's superior court handed down a ruling requiring the elementary school to enroll Mamie. Furious, the school board appealed to the state's supreme court. Leading the charge was the city's new school superintendent, Andrew Jackson Moulder. He was the same official who, as state superintendent of schools more than two decades earlier, had staunchly petitioned the legislature for school segregation, arguing that such "inferior races" would precipitate "the ruin of the schools."[15]

Now in his later years and holding power in San Francisco, he had softened little with age. When, in the first days of March, the California Supreme Court ruled in favor of the Tapes, Moulder was ready. The next morning he shot off a telegram to a friend in the state assembly: "I fear the decision of the Supreme Court admitting Chinese will demoralize our schools." He proposed a simple solution. The legislature must promptly pass a new segregation law. "Without such action," he warned, "our classes will be inundated by Mongolians. Trouble will follow."[16] Moulder must have been elated that evening when his friend telegrammed back to confirm that the desired bill had within hours been overwhelmingly approved by the assembly and would be taken up by the state senate the following morning. Barely a week later the bill became law. School segregation of Asian and Indigenous children would remain on the books for more than sixty years, until the advocacy of the Mendezes and other Latino families in Westminster, California, would topple it in 1947.

Not a month passed before Mary Tape once again tried to enroll her daughter at the neighborhood school. When she was once again turned away, she wrote to the school board: "Dear sirs, Will you please to tell me! Is it a disgrace to be Born a Chinese? Didn't God make us all!!!" Her daughter, she detailed, dressed like white children and played with white children. Why then could she not study with her peers? "May you Mr. Moulder, never be persecuted like the way you have persecuted little Mamie." She closed with a warning. "I will let the world see sir What justice there is When it is govern by the Race prejudice men!" As Mary asserted, Mamie "is more of a American then a good many of you that is going to prewent her being Educated [sic]."[17]

But their daughter needed an education. Resigned, the Tapes enrolled Mamie in the only institution that would take her—the Chinese School, hurriedly opened by the city government. A century later it would be the same school where Ling-chi Wang would convene a gathering of school officials, parents, and students to demand the city not forget its Chinese children. But in the 1880s, to be of Chinese ancestry in America was to live under constant threat. A month earlier and three hundred miles north in the city of Eureka, an angry mob had torn through the local Chinatown, smashing property and threatening inhabitants. The city's three hundred Chinese residents were given twenty-four hours to leave, or else face the gallows. In the following months and years, pogroms ignited in cities and towns up and down the West Coast. From Seattle to Pasadena, Chinese families were violently driven from their homes. Shops were vandalized, homes burned, residents beaten. In September of 1885, in Rock Spring, Wyoming, white miners—many immigrants themselves—savagely turned against their Chinese colleagues, torching homes and murdering twenty-eight men. Two months later in Tacoma, Washington, a vigilante mob dragged Chinese residents from their homes and marched them at gunpoint to the trains. A gleeful resident reported to the territory's governor that Tacoma was now "sans Chinese, sans pigtails, sans moon-eye, sans wash-house, sans joss house, sans everything Mongolian."[18] In the months to come, Tacoma would be one of many to expel Chinese residents from city limits.

On a blustery October afternoon less than a year later, with thousands in attendance, President Grover Cleveland presided over the dedication of a colossal green lady standing proudly in New York City's harbor. "We will not forget," the president declared, "that Liberty has made here her home."[19]

In the winter of 1970, in the heart of San Francisco's Chinatown, Ling-chi Wang and Edward Steinman began gathering parents willing to sue San Francisco's public schools. It was "the last resort," Wang would explain, "after all known channels for seeking equal educational opportunity had been exhausted."[20] Wang called on moms and dads who had stood by his side at protests. Steinman, whose legal cases revolved around defending residents in landlord–tenant disputes and sweatshop wage violations, began asking clients if they had children enrolled in the public schools. Together they compiled a list of nine families of Chinese heritage who were ready to go up against the city on behalf of their thirteen children and nearly three thousand Chinese students who did not yet speak English. Of the children named in the case, seven were American-born; and of the three thousand represented, more than half received from the schools no language support whatsoever. Lucinda Lee's first grade pupil Kinney Lau was named as the lead plaintiff.

Steinman—young, self-assured, and optimistic—predicted the case would be an easy win and opted to take his chances in federal court, concluding that he had a higher likelihood of being assigned a liberal, and therefore sympathetic, judge. But luck was not on his side when the case was assigned to Judge Lloyd Burke. As Steinman would relate to me, "I realized immediately I was going to lose." Burke, in Steinman's description, was a "notoriously conservative" man with a tendency to stroll into work at eleven and leave by two.[21] But Steinman spent the following months doggedly conducting depositions and amassing an extensive paper trail documenting the district's knowing negligence. The district's own reports were obligingly explicit. In 1969 one report concluded that for Chinese-speaking students, "the lack of English means poor performance in school. The secondary student is almost inevitably doomed to be a dropout and become another unemployable in the ghetto." The long-term consequences on economic success were stark: "They are trapped as surely as if there were barbed wire around Chinatown."[22]

As Steinman documented educational neglect, halfway around the globe, in an effort to disrupt North Vietnamese supply paths, the United States secretly began carpet-bombing the Kingdom of Cambodia. It was a military decision that would in time destabilize a dynasty and trigger a genocide. When news of the bombing broke in April of 1970, infuriated US students massed in protest on campuses nationwide. On a May Monday afternoon at Kent State University in Ohio, members of the state National Guard opened fire on hundreds of college students. In less than a minute, four undergraduates were shot dead. Nine more were injured. Less than a week later, tens of thousands of protesters descended on Washington, DC, and a similar number on City Hall in San Francisco.

As the protests passed mere blocks from Steinman's office, the young lawyer was holed up concocting a brazen strategy on behalf of the city's newcomers. In state court at the time it was not unheard of for a judge to allow the winning side of a case to draft a proposed decision for the judge's review. And while the practice did not carry over to the federal courts, Steinman had chutzpah. Shamelessly he approached Judge Burke: "I know, your honor, I'm not going to win this. To avoid wasting your time . . . let me take a stab at writing the decision you would write against me."[23] The judge promptly agreed. And so, Steinman set about crafting a decision against himself, in such a way as to open the door for appeal.

But as the protesters continued to march, Steinman deliberately dragged his feet before submitting the draft decision. He was buying time. By chance he had heard of a government document soon to be released, and it was for that document that he waited.

In the wake of the 1964 Civil Rights Act, Congress had created the Office for Civil Rights (OCR), within the Department of Health, Education, and Welfare (HEW), primarily to oversee the desegregation of schools. Just that March, the office had appointed a new director: J. Stanley Pottinger, a thirty-year-old Bay Area lawyer whose grandparents decades earlier had traveled here from Germany, Ireland, Wales, and the remote reaches of the Orkney Islands. For six weeks during the previous summer, Pottinger, his wife, and their one-year-old had driven a bright-green station wagon through the fertile valleys of Salinas, Sacramento, and elsewhere, at the direction of the local HEW office. His goal was to determine whether ESEA Title I funding was reaching schools responsible for teaching children in the state's many migrant labor communities. In the forlorn and dusty shell of a former Japanese incarceration camp, Pottinger watched scrawny boys play, using a rusty exhaust pipe and a roll of adhesive tape as a bat and ball. "I didn't know where the money was going in the school system," he would tell me years later. "But I could tell you where it was not going."[24] The summer trip stuck like a burr in his mind.

When Pottinger stepped in months later as OCR director, his staff came to him, concerned. In Texas and Arizona schools, Latino children were being abandoned in the backs of classrooms, left with crayons and colored paper. OCR appeared to have little authority to compel schools to teach their students. Pottinger was baffled about what to do. But examining the 1964 Civil Rights Act, he hit upon an idea.

The Civil Rights Act banned discrimination based on national origin, among other things. But in practice, what did it mean for schools to discriminate against immigrant-origin children? The exclusion of the Mendez family in Westminster had been obvious discrimination, but for Pottinger and his staff the practices of the Texas and Arizona schools, as well as those in the California migrant camps, exemplified other, subtler forms of discrimination. Rarely did schools, Pottinger found, "take affirmative steps" to ensure their students could speak and understand English. Common too was the practice of funneling immigrant-origin children into a series of classes that amounted to educational "dead-end[s]" or misclassifying students' language gaps as signs of learning disabilities. And with students' families, schools as a whole made little effort to communicate in their home languages. All these practices, Pottinger believed, amounted to discrimination based on national origin.[25]

On May 25, 1970, Pottinger released an official memorandum issuing strong guidance for all schools where at least one in every twenty students was an English learner.[26] As he would later go on to testify before the Senate, in an echo of Chicago's Jane Addams, he believed the burden fell on schools "to adapt [their] educational approach so that the culture, language, and learning style of all children . . . (not just those of Anglo, middle-class backgrounds) are accepted and valued." Children, he asserted, should not be forced to abandon their heritage at the schoolhouse door.[27]

The very next day, on the other edge of the country, Steinman entered the memorandum into the record of his case and submitted his proposed draft decision to Judge Burke.[28] And that same day, Burke issued his decision in support of San Francisco schools. In the proposed draft, Steinman recalled, the judge changed only a single errant adverb. Satisfied, the young lawyer promptly appealed against the decision he had himself written.

———•———

It would take more than two years from when Kinney Lau's case was appealed to the Ninth Circuit Court of Appeals to when the court reached its decision. They were not quiet years for the city's schools. While Wang worked with the Chinese community and Steinman to bring their case, the NAACP was simultaneously suing San Francisco for stalling on racial desegregation of schools citywide. Segregation was, they argued, not confined to the former Confederacy. In the summer of 1971, San Francisco became the first major city outside the South to be ordered by a federal court to desegregate. To ensure integration, bus routes were drawn in a horseshoe, looping the city, to pick children up in one neighborhood and deposit them in another. As they later would in Boston and other major cities, white parents vehemently and sometimes violently resisted. Some swore to boycott, others packed up and fled.

Joining the anti-busing protests were many of the city's Chinese families, who asked the courts to pause the desegregation plan.[29] Their children too studied in primarily segregated schools. Decades of restrictive housing laws had had their intended effect, with more than two-thirds of the city's Chinese residents living within Chinatown. But whereas nearly a century earlier Mary Tape had argued that her daughter was so *not*-Chinese that she should be admitted to the white school, now many Chinese parents worried that if their children were distributed throughout the city, their culture, language, and heritage would be lost. The courts were not swayed. On the first days of school in the fall of 1971, nearly half-empty buses circled the city; an estimated 40 percent of students, including many Chinese children, stayed home.[30]

That summer, on a July evening, President Nixon had stunned the nation by announcing he would soon travel to China. Over twenty years earlier the two powers had cut off diplomatic relations. But the following February, Nixon touched down in Beijing. In doing so, he became the first sitting US president ever to visit mainland China. In a minutely choreographed week, Nixon met with Chairman Mao Zedong, toured the Great Wall, wandered the sprawling Forbidden City, and floated along the temple-lined West Lake in Hangzhou. At the concluding banquet Nixon raised his glass to the leaders of Communist China: "This was the week that changed the world."[31]

In San Francisco, Ling-chi Wang breathed a sigh of relief. He had urged Congress to normalize relations with China. But his advocacy branded him an enemy of the Taiwanese-based Chinese government in exile. Nixon's trip, Wang explained to me, was "the lifting of a heavy burden." Realizing "I couldn't have my legs in two different boats," Wang abandoned his plan to complete a PhD in ancient Semitic studies and threw himself fully into the present, as an advocate for immigrants and their education.[32]

When in early 1973 a three-judge panel of the US Court of Appeals for the Ninth Circuit, which covered California, finally ruled on the educational future of Kinney Lau and his peers, its 2–1 decision was callously dismissive. Under *Brown v. Board of Education,* schools were required to furnish the "same facilities, textbooks, teachers and curriculum" to all students. Nothing more. Ironically the court declared, "This is an English-speaking nation" and, in the same breath, absolved schools of any responsibility to teach English to nonnative speakers. California law required that students attend school and required English proficiency to obtain a high school diploma. Yet the court ruled that school supports for learning English were "commendable" but not required. "Every student brings to the starting line of his educational career different advantages and disadvantages caused in part by social, economic and cultural background, created and continued completely apart from any contribution by the school system." As the court concluded, Lau's inability to understand his teachers or his textbooks was "not the result of laws enacted by the State presently or historically, but the result of deficiencies created by the [children] themselves in failing to learn the English language."[33] In short, the court blamed the kids.

Steinman appealed to the Supreme Court. While he waited for the Court to decide whether to hear the case, Shirley Hufstedler, a judge on the Ninth Circuit, requested that the case be reheard *en banc*—that is, by all of the judges on the court. (Hufstedler, who at the time of her appointment to court, in 1968, was the highest-ranking female judge in the federal courts, would later go on to be named the country's first secretary of education.) The court declined to rehear the case, but Hufstedler used the occasion to pen a scathing dissent.

Hufstedler's opinion drew heavily on a powerful amicus brief from Harvard University's Marian Wright Edelman, the first Black woman admitted to the Mississippi Bar who would go on to found the Children's Defense Fund to advocate for the nation's youngest. Hufstedler argued that "access to education offered by the public schools is completely foreclosed to these children who cannot comprehend any of it. They are functionally deaf and mute." Equal access could not be measured purely by offering the same textbooks or the same teachers. As she concluded, "Invidious discrimination is not washed away because the able bodied and the paraplegic are given the same state command to walk."[34]

In the summer of 1973, the US Supreme Court agreed to hear the appeal. Again Edelman filed an amicus brief. Education for San Francisco's non-English-speaking students, her brief declared, amounted to "mere physical presence as audience to a strange play which they do not understand."[35] To underscore the point, this particular sentence carried an unusual footnote: a single untranslated line in Chinese. As Roger Rice, one of the brief's authors, would explain to me, "The idea was to show the Court that equal ain't equal if it is in a language you can't understand."[36] The footnote had its intended effect: As a Court clerk would later confide to Rice, the Court had indeed puzzled over its meaning. It's not known if the justices ever found a translator, but if they had, they would have learned that the line was an apt excerpt from a speech by Chairman Mao Zedong: "When shooting an arrow, one must aim at the target; when playing the lute, one must consider the listener."[37]

———◆———

On a chilly December morning in 1973, now-twenty-nine-year-old Edward Steinman, standing before the country's highest court, argued that public schools were failing EL students. In the seats behind him sat his mother and aunts. As a young Yiddish-speaking immigrant, his mother had dropped out of an American school to support her family, and she now struggled to fathom why her son was bringing this case, but she was supportive. In his argument to the Supreme Court, her son was unequivocal. "The right of students to an educational opportunity is not met merely through the illusion of equal treatment." Students might be given the same textbooks, but for non-English-speaking students "the pages are as if blank." Because, he argued, instruction was "in a tongue unfathomable to these children, the result is not education but at best custodial supervision."[38]

Steinman anchored his argument in Title VI of the 1964 Civil Rights Act and the Equal Protection clause of the Fourteenth Amendment of the US Constitution. Joining him at the Court that day was the US government, which had asked to speak before the Court in support of San Francisco's Chinese-speaking students. The US solicitor general, the conservative Robert Bork—whose roots traced back to Germany and Ireland—had once staunchly opposed the 1964 Civil Rights Act as unconstitutional. But President Nixon, who had keenly courted Latino communities for political victory, had thrown his weight behind educational supports for immigrant-origin children. And so now, at the behest of the president, Bork came to the defense of the nation's youngest newcomers, citing the very same law whose passage he had previously opposed.

The Supreme Court allowed the government to present its views as part of the oral argument in the case. Although Bork had submitted the amicus brief, he did not argue before the justices. Instead, in December 1973, the person who stood in a morning coat at the lectern before the justices was newly appointed Assistant Attorney General for Civil Rights J. Stanley Pottinger, who, as director of the Office for Civil Rights, had written the memorandum issuing guidance for schools with immigrant-origin students.

Steinman's and Pottinger's arguments were supported by an imposing coalition of voices, added by way of amicus briefs. Wang helped to compose the argument for the city's Chinese advocacy organizations. Joining them were leading advocates from the country's Mexican, Puerto Rican, and Jewish communities. A San Francisco lawyers organization invoked Mamie Tape's educational exclusion in detailing over a century of discrimination. And national and state-level teachers associations spoke not just on behalf of Bay Area students but also on behalf of some five million young people across the country, likening the district's conduct to that of an ostrich, its head firmly buried in the sand.

Six weeks later, seventy-five-year-old William O. Douglas, the country's longest serving justice, wrote the decision in *Lau v. Nichols* for a unanimous Court. More than five decades earlier, Douglas had helped pay for college by picking cherries alongside Latino migrant workers and had been inspired to pursue a career in law after he witnessed police brutalize his fellow harvesters. The Court's decision was grounded in the Civil Rights Act and in Pottinger's memorandum. In a way that the lower courts had not, Douglas recognized the arguments made by Wang and Steinman and by Edelman and Hufstedler. For the young Chinese students, Douglas bluntly stated, their schooling was "wholly incomprehensible and in no way meaningful." Regardless of whether the schools intended to discriminate, the effect was what mattered. "Basic English skills are at the very core of what these public schools teach," Douglas noted. "Imposition of a requirement that, before a child can effectively participate in the educational program, he must already have acquired those basic skills, is to make a mockery of public education."[39] For the first time in the nation's history, the Supreme Court found that schools had specific responsibilities to the children of immigrants.

The day after the decision in January of 1974, the *New York Times* devoted to the ruling a single desultory sentence, which managed to misspell Lau as Lad.[40] But in Washington, DC, *Lau v. Nichols* was on the minds of many. The Supreme Court had not specified how schools should support newcomers.[41] So Congress set about codifying schools' obligations. As ESEA came up for reauthorization that year, Ling-chi Wang flew to Washington to testify before the House. By the end of August, as part of the reauthorization, two key provisions were added. The Equal Educational Opportunities Act[42] declared that it was unlawful for schools not to "take appropriate action to overcome language barriers that impede equal participation by its students."[43] In addition, the re-vamped Bilingual Education Act recommended and offered funding for bilingual educational programs throughout the country. And, although bilingual education was squarely seen as a tool to transition students to English, the reauthorization notably acknowledged that children learned best when their language and cultural heritage were viewed as assets. The education law would be one of the very first bills signed by President Gerald Ford, as less than two weeks earlier Richard Nixon had resigned in disgrace.

In the following months, San Francisco public schools, under federal order, set about drafting a six-hundred-page citywide plan to educate non-English-speaking newcomers, Chinese children included. Wang stood at the helm, orchestrating a coalition to draft the proposal. The city's schools would remain for decades under federal supervision, released only in 2019. Wang would go on to advocate for a slew of immersion programs, including helping to open one of the country's first bilingual-bicultural preschools, to which he sent his own children. And in the Capital, Wang was called on to help draft guidance for schools nationwide. In the wake of *Lau v. Nichols*, more than three hundred school districts across the country were found to be in violation. Just as students were set to return to school in 1975, the OCR issued its new guidelines, greatly expanding schools' responsibilities. English as a second language instruction was, in almost all cases, deemed insufficient, and bilingual education with an emphasis on appreciating the cultural diversity of students was all but required. In common parlance, the guidelines would become known as the *Lau* Remedies.

But Kinney Lau himself, now entering sixth grade in a new school, would not benefit from the spate of new programs. In the intervening years, through determination he mastered English. He quietly continued with his education, avoiding the national spotlight. But, in classrooms across the country, compelled by a case that bore his name, educators were rethinking what it meant to teach newcomers.

THE PRESENT: THE INTERNATIONAL SCHOOL AT LANGLEY PARK, MARYLAND

Daniel Sass was dragging his suitcase through a terminal at Dulles International Airport in the fall of 2016 when he got a call from his assistant soccer coach, Sarah Ferrari.

Daniel could tell she was upset: That afternoon their team had played a local rival. Two boys, one from each team, had gotten into a skirmish on the soccer field. Both had been red-carded. The game continued. Their varsity team had gone on to trounce their rival, 6–0. Sarah and the opposing coach believed tempers had cooled, but as Sarah shepherded her players onto their bus, members of the rival team advanced, snarling. "You shouldn't even be allowed to play soccer!" "You all ain't even from this country!" "You f-ing im···igrants ain't even legal!" On the phone with Daniel, Sarah was on the verge of tears. "What do we do?"

Daniel and Sarah worked at an unusual public school in the town of Bladensburg within Prince George's County in Maryland, a mere seven miles from the White House. The International High School at Langley Park (IHSLP) had opened in 2015 with an ambitious mission to create a safe, supportive school for immigrant-origin teenagers.

At the time, 80 percent of the district's high school seniors were graduating, closely tracking the national average. But of the district's English learners, roughly half received a diploma.[44] Countywide one out of every seven students was now an English learner.[45] In 2014, these dismal statistics had driven two organizations, one local, one national to apply for and receive a three-million-dollar grant from the Carnegie Corporation to help fund the creation of two public schools specifically for newcomers. One was IHSLP.

One of the first high schools created solely for immigrant teenagers began in a basement in Queens, New York, in the 1980s. More followed on its success, first within the city and then across the country. In 2004 the schools partnered to create the Internationals Network, to champion and support public schools designed for newcomers. Until 2015, though, there had never been such a program in Maryland.

Daniel first became a high school teacher in 2009 up the coast in Baltimore. While teaching immigrant students, the descendant of Jewish immigrants from Eastern Europe quickly grew appalled by the dearth of school support for newcomers. "I saw students capable of achieving beyond anyone's wildest imagination," he said, but they just needed help to find their footing. Frustrated, he stumbled upon an organization for immigrant students that wove together soccer, tutoring, and community building—Soccer Without Borders (SWB). He threw himself into volunteering—coaching afternoons and weekends, coordinating teams that pulled students from across the city, running an after-practice college application program, helping to manage other volunteers. One afternoon in 2014, while responding to SWB emails, Daniel opened a letter from a man named Carlos Beato. Carlos was starting a school for immigrant students, and he asked if SWB would become a community partner. Daniel grabbed his phone and dialed Carlos: "I'll do you one better," he told his future boss. "Hire me and I'll bring all my training and start a school soccer program." Daniel was one of IHSLP's first hires, as an English teacher and soccer coach. The next year he assumed the role of assistant principal. Because he loved it, Daniel also kept coaching.

On the IHSLP boys' varsity soccer team everyone hailed from elsewhere. The goalkeeper and forwards were Salvadorian, one defender was Ugandan, the midfielders had immigrated from Honduras, Cameroon, and the Ivory Coast. For subs, the team relied on players from Eritrea and Guatemala. The school was equally diverse.

Like educators across the nation, Daniel had watched the presidential campaign apprehensively and saw its xenophobic rhetoric seep into schools. When Sarah called him at the airport it was October 2016, two weeks shy of the presidential election. Teachers from California to Connecticut were reporting an alarming spike in xenophobic bullying. Students marched through hallways chanting "White Power." In classrooms, cafeterias, and playgrounds, students slung insults and threats: "You're going to be deported!" "Go back to Mexico," "Heil Trump," "We can't wait until you and the other brownies are gone." A few weeks before the election, one confident fifth grader told his teacher that he supported Trump because he would "kill all of the Muslims."[46]

The Monday following the match, Daniel and Sarah gathered their team. The boys recounted the altercation. Daniel shared his pride in their maturity for not escalating. Then, quietly, he asked, "How did their comments make you feel?" The team captain, a tall boy born in the United States and raised in the Ivory Coast, shrugged: "Ain't nothing we haven't heard before." Twelve heads nodded. Slurs, the boys told him, were expected in American schools. Daniel knew they were right, but wished desperately they were wrong.

The seed of what grew into IHSLP took root in the Bronx more than two decades earlier in Carlos Beato's own fifth-grade classroom. At the age of five Carlos had moved with his mother from a town in the Dominican Republic to the bustling borough in New York City. He was enrolled in a bilingual classroom. There he stayed until fifth grade, when he was one of the few whose English was deemed strong enough to graduate from the sheltered program. For the first time his classes were conducted solely in English. What Carlos remembers most was how he suddenly "felt like an outsider." No longer was he permitted to speak Spanish, and no longer was he surrounded by his friends. Still, Carlos loved learning. He studied diligently and earned good grades. But one afternoon his teacher walked among her pupils handing out applications to specialized middle school programs. She passed his desk without a glance. Carlos was crushed: "She assumed because I recently exited ELL classes, that I wouldn't get in."

Three years later Carlos graduated as salutatorian of his middle school. Carlos believed high school would cap his formal education—he was undocumented and thus college was an unaffordable dream. Determined to squeeze every ounce out of his final four years, he continued studying. Then, in his senior year, a bulky envelope arrived in the mail. Carlos had been awarded a prestigious Posse Scholarship, enabling him to attend elite Middlebury College at almost no cost to his family. A few months later he graduated high school as salutatorian and soon packed his bags for Vermont. In college too he excelled. When as a sophomore he dreamed of studying abroad, a staff member at the college took it upon herself to look into Carlos's legal status. His family's application for permanent residency had been pending for close to ten years. Within months of Middlebury's advocacy, Carlos received his green card. He celebrated by spending the spring of his junior year studying in Madrid, Spain. The following year he received a college diploma, the first in his family to do so.

Returning to New York City in 2007, Carlos was hired for his dream job as a teacher at a new public school teaching Spanish to mostly Dominican students. A few years later he took a job as a founding college counselor at another school, again working primarily with newcomers. Soon after, he stepped into the role of assistant principal at yet another fledgling school. Then in 2014 a friend sent him an announcement from Prince George's County seeking a leader for a new school for immigrant-origin children. Carlos loathed leaving New York City, but he knew he could not say no. He'd have the chance to design the school he wished he had attended.

At IHSLP, Carlos can rarely be found in his office. At breakfast he sits among students at a blue-topped cafeteria table, biting into a breakfast burrito. After lunch I have spotted him stooping to collect stray wrappers and ketchup packets that invariably scatter the floor like confetti. When the kitchen staff is shorthanded he has been known to don an apron and hairnet to hand out trays. At dismissal he stands out in the rain directing buses. During weekend games, when a coach is unexpectedly out, he assists on the sidelines, retrieving balls and organizing snacks. In the halls, students seek him out to share a joke or to ask a question about a college application. More than once I've watched him stroll with students to class, asking as they walk about a scholarship application that needs submitting or how they are coping: "I know you've been having a hard week." Outside a classroom, Carlos conferred with two boys sent out for being disruptive. What should be their consequence, he asked. "Detention?" one boy offered. Carlos shook his head, "We don't do that here." He gave them an assignment before returning them to class: "Find me tomorrow and tell me what you think the appropriate consequence should be." When teachers text him, he often replies by popping his head into the classroom. He keeps his hair short and his beard thick. He favors beige pullover sweaters when not wearing the blue school fleece. His laugh is high, staccato, warm, and inviting.

Carlos envisioned IHSLP as a school with little resemblance to any program he knew. He wanted a school that did not penalize students for not yet knowing English and that did not put content on hold while students mastered a new language. Curricula would bulge with long-term projects, providing students ample opportunities to practice analyzing data and constructing evidence-backed arguments. His students would be given time and also held to high expectations. And, Carlos was adamant that, by their junior year, every student would be enrolled in advanced placement courses.

Skepticism ran high among district officials. Would the curriculum be academically rigorous? Would EL students truly be capable of succeeding in advanced courses? Students too, Carlos found, were dubious.

With them, Carlos began sharing his own story. Carlos's new students were shocked. How could their principal have been an EL student? How could he have been undocumented? And, if this was true, how had he been awarded a prestigious college scholarship and become so successful?

To succeed, Carlos believes, the school must be a counterpoint to anyone—including students themselves—who expects less of a young person because of where they were born, where they grew up, or what language they speak at home. Before opening day, Carlos defined the school's core values. The first came easy: empowerment. "It's about knowing your worth and being able to project that to the rest of the world without fear," explains Carlos. "It is about allowing kids to be able to find their voice."

The school's first sport was soccer—a shared love of students from Sudan to El Salvador. The fledgling team was dubbed Phoenix United. Like their namesake, the students were remaking themselves, a transformation that would require them to draw on their traditions, their experiences, and each other.

After Phoenix United's game had turned ugly in the fall of 2016, prompting the call from the assistant soccer coach, Sarah Ferrari, assistant principal Daniel had an idea. The following Monday he phoned the rival coach. "What do you think about holding a joint practice?" he asked. The other coach was all in. The following afternoon the two teams met on a stretch of grass near IHSLP. Practice began in a circle, the student captains setting ground rules. Then play began. Each drill had been carefully constructed. "Find a partner from the opposing team who lives with only one parent." To pair up, the kids needed to talk: "My dad's in jail." "My dad's in Guatemala." Dribbling balls across the field, boys swapped stories about growing up without fathers. "When I blow my whistle," Daniel called, "switch balls with someone who speaks the same native language." More conversations. Another whistle: "Pass to someone who has been in the US less than five years." A third whistle: "Find a partner who comes from a different country than you." Two hours filled with boys running, dribbling, passing, playing, laughing. "We were finding common ground," Daniel grinned. "We were talking about what triggers us and what brings us to a soccer field on a Tuesday."

Over the following months friendships bloomed. Squashed into the shell of a former elementary school, IHSLP had no dedicated sports facilities. Their once-rival invited them to use their fields, wrestling room, and tennis courts. In turn, IHSLP welcomed their rivals, who had no indoor winter soccer program, to play on their teams. For home games, their rivals invited Phoenix United to play under the lights on their turf field and came out to cheer them on. When their rivals had nearby games, Phoenix United joined the sidelines to shout encouragement. And mere months later, IHSLP hired the rival coach to be a history teacher and coach.

———•———

The classrooms of IHSLP brim with roughly 350 students from more than 25 countries who speak upwards of 15 languages. Some landed in the country five years ago, others five months ago. A few were born in the United States but left when they were babies, only to return as teenagers. Many have had instruction in English, but the quantity and quality vary. Most attended school regularly, but some have been kept from the classroom by violence or finances. Their skills are uneven. Daniel cited one student who couldn't read *The Cat in the Hat* when he arrived but could passionately analyze the complexities of the Spanish American War.

Where to begin with such a wide array of learners? In the muggy summer months, before school starts, Carlos and his teachers devote hours to interviewing every incoming pupil. What countries have you lived in? What language do you speak at home? When did you come to the United States? What do you miss most about your country? Who do you live with here? What was your favorite school subject? Explain what it means to be a best friend. Describe a typical day in your school. Each student is also evaluated: How advanced is their math, their reading in English, their writing in their first language? Teachers scrutinize the interviews and assessments, and then they set about painstakingly crafting class rosters. Little, they believe, can be left to chance.

No day begins with academics. Students start in advisory classes. They sink into yoga poses, sit silent in meditation, and race to slurp up marshmallows in a class-wide competition. There is time to talk, to laugh, to ask questions. They review grades and set language goals—one girl promises to speak more in class, another hopes to read a more difficult book next month. Relationships deepen over four years. Advisories are carefully constructed communities. A boy whose father is absent is assigned to a math teacher who has connected well with fatherless young men. The two students who miss moms still in their home country are entrusted to Christine Gilliard-Arthur, the health teacher, who has been dubbed by many as Mama Gilliard. A boy who loves basketball is paired with a language teacher who shares that passion.

Academic classes get similar scrutiny. Students spend much of ninth and tenth grade in small mixed cohorts. Classes are balanced: an equal number of boys and girls, a diverse array of countries and languages. Rarely is there a lone Arabic or Nepali or Swahili speaker in a class. A student who is shy is placed, if possible, with another from their country. In each cohort too are students who speak English with confidence and those who speak none at all. This last strategy is common to the roughly thirty schools of the Internationals Network.

Isolation spurred a set of public schools that all work with newcomers to create the Internationals Network in 2004. Each, on its own, had developed academic course offerings, devised school structures, advocated in their districts, and built community partnerships. The network became their way to share best practices among schools and across states. When Carlos opened IHSLP it was with the support of the Internationals Network. The network provided curriculum guides, assessment tools, and technology supports; it sent coaches and mentors, and invited IHSLP teachers to trainings.

Each International School is independently and locally run, from Oakland to Minneapolis, from the Bronx down to Bladensburg. But common to all is an appreciation of their students' strengths, rather than a fixation on their deficits. A newly arrived Honduran student speaks only Spanish, but excels at algebra. A Ugandan boy with limited schooling might struggle to read, but loves leading class discussion on the formation of the US government. Collaboration becomes commonplace. Students teach each other, students learn from each other.

Yet such stark learning disparities pose challenges. Some students speed through assignments on the carbon cycle, others stall—they need more practice, or further explanations, or additional tutoring. In a traditional school, a struggling student would amass low grades, dragging down their GPA. "We've seen the power of what a zero can do to a kid," Daniel reflected. Zeros on an assignment can lead a student to fail courses, which in turn can lead to their dropping out. So Carlos designed a curriculum in which students would be measured on their mastery of content and skills, but not penalized if they needed additional days or even weeks to become proficient. Imagine getting a driver's license, Daniel explained late one afternoon. Everyone might take the same driving course and read the same test booklet, but likely not everyone will pass the road test. Some need to reread the book; others need translated materials. They take the test again. And some still fail. They practice parallel parking or merging onto highways. After the third or maybe the fourth attempt, they succeed. Their new license looks just like that of those who passed on their first try. There are no perks for being first. What matters is that you learned to drive. At IHSLP, classes are organized with a similar philosophy: If a student masters the content, they, like drivers, are not penalized for taking longer. Educators call this competency-based learning—an approach that, while still the exception, is slowly gaining traction in schools across the country. "We go to great lengths to give students opportunities to feel successful," Daniel explained. While it might take longer for some to master the content, "that feeling of success keeps kids coming to school." As Carlos noted, for his students "failure is not an option."

———◆———

The International High School at Langley Park is not actually in Langley Park, Maryland. In 2015 the only available building was in the neighboring city of Bladensburg, five miles away. The inconvenience has advantages. When students board the bus to IHSLP, they leave behind them a neighborhood that for fifteen years has been terrorized by the Mara Salvatrucha gang, more commonly known as MS-13. A search of Langley Park in the *Washington Post*'s online archives turns up story after story about brothels, drug rings, extortion, racketeering, slaughter. Young Central American boys, like many of IHSLP's students, are prime targets for gang recruitment. In late December 2018, in woods near Langley Park, an eighteen-year-old was severely beaten for refusing to join. As a student confided in Carlos, IHSLP "can be a breath of fresh air."

When students return to Langley Park after school, a much-beloved nonprofit that serves the community, CASA, collaborates with IHSLP to keep a watchful eye. CASA helped raise the initial money for the school, and it has remained an essential partner. CASA opens its doors most afternoons to IHSLP students. They offer tutoring, mentoring, and safety. They help families, too, assisting in translating medical documents, filling out tax forms, applying for citizenship, and finding immigration lawyers. CASA is one of many partners Carlos has cultivated—nonprofits and universities that run mentoring programs and photography clubs and that send volunteers to tutor and trainees to support staff. When an organization offers help, Carlos and his team say yes.

Keeping kids in the school building as long as possible, Daniel believes, is crucial, both for their academic success and for their safety. IHSLP hopes to fill their afternoons with programs and surround them with teachers and support. For many the draw is sports—an outlet for frustration or anxiety. For some it provides a community, for others it becomes an alternative to possible gang involvement. More than half of the student body is on a team. Tennis, wrestling, volleyball, softball, basketball, baseball, cross-country, and of course soccer. With few dedicated facilities, the school building becomes a gym after the final bell. Teams run laps along the corridors. They thunder up and down stairs. Wrestlers slap mats in the cafeteria. Nearly half of the school staff doubles as coaches. The AP calculus teacher was an All-American wrestler in college. A counselor who played college volleyball now coaches the sport at IHSLP. An English teacher who serves as head track and field coach had competed in the Olympic trials. (The English teacher, Keishia Thorpe, who immigrated from Jamaica to attend college, would go on to win the 2021 Global Teacher Prize, along with a $1 million award from an international organization, the Varkey Foundation, for her work cofounding a nonprofit to help at-risk students gain college scholarships and support immigrant families, as well as for her teaching at IHSLP.)

But even within the safety of school, troubles and trauma can shadow students. All have left homes thousands of miles away. Many have left mothers and fathers. Some are living with parents they have not seen in years. Others are living alone. Students have suffered violence either at home or here. They have spent months alone in border detention centers. And they have spent years in refugee camps. Success, Carlos recognizes, depends on IHSLP reaching beyond the classroom to offer support.

Carlos has cultivated a support team of counselors and social workers trained to work with newcomers. They meet one-on-one and hold small-group sessions: a group for students coping with grief, a group for young parents, a girls' empowerment group, a group for struggling boys. They train staff about trauma and, when needed, they help in classrooms. Sarah Ferrari—who in 2016, as a program coordinator with Soccer Without Borders, coached soccer with Daniel—is now a licensed social worker. Once a week she meets with five boys in a dimly lit room. "How many people in your life do you trust?" she asked one morning. Heads down, the boys mumble: three, five, zero. In their lives, each has been told they were "bad" and "troublemakers." When the bell rang, a boy in a black hoodie reached out to squeeze Sarah's hand. "Thank you for your honesty," she whispered. He nodded. "I want my kiddos to feel love, support, and safety," Sarah told me later. Without that, it is very hard to learn.

Relationships are nurtured in the classroom and on the field. Teachers are quick to catch the young man who slips in algebra, the young woman who is unusually sullen. Once a week the staff arrives an hour early to discuss how to help struggling students. They strategize: Could an approach that is working in math be used in English class? Could a boy who hopes to be an engineer be connected to others who share the passion? Everyone is watchful. A security guard with a salt-and-pepper beard keeps tabs on older boys who talk of leaving school to take jobs. In the hallways, between classes, he talks them out of it. When a point guard shows up for a basketball game without proper shoes, the front-office secretary unlaces her sneakers and hands them over.

One afternoon, Carlos arrived to a science staff meeting with a black-haired boy in tow. He sat the boy at a desk, his half-completed English paper before him. The boy had been struggling with attendance—and, Carlos suspected, depression. "I am taking him under my wing," he explained quietly. "Helping him get back on track."

●

In the fall of 2017, a year after the incident on the soccer field, IHSLP's boys' varsity soccer team, Phoenix United, trounced their former rival once more—another 6–0 shutout. This time there were no slurs, no tension.

Soccer, for many Phoenix United players, was where they felt most comfortable. It was a reminder of home, an escape from work, a respite from responsibilities, a safe haven from the threat of gangs. It was what they loved. That fall the team won match after match. They practiced ferociously: running drills on their uneven field, running laps through the halls on rainy days. They emerged from the season undefeated and triumphantly headed to the state playoffs. With no regulation-sized field, IHSLP played all its home games on the field of their former rival. Again and again they put the ball in the back of the net—three wins in a row secured them the title of regional champions. They won the quarterfinals next. Match day for the semifinals was bitingly cold and blue. Having driven over an hour, the boys piled out into a gigantic stadium. They could not contain their laughter when the announcer botched each and every one of their names. But the game was a challenge. The opposing team was huge. Not once did they manage to score. Eighty minutes later the game ended in defeat. The bus ride home was subdued. But back at school, as the boys unloaded bags of soccer balls, they began planning. "We need an off-season program," they told Daniel. "We need weights, we need to get better."

Phoenix United reached the semifinals again the next year, and the year after. The boys' soccer team's success was not an anomaly. In 2018 an Eritrean student raised in Sudan was named a regional champion in the 3,200-meter run. In 2019 the girls' varsity soccer team became regional finalists. A Mexican, a Salvadorian, and a Ugandan student excelled in mock trial competitions, a Salvadorian student did the same in a speech competition. The school won awards for its STEM club and its steel pan band. IHSLP students spoke at a New York City gala, a Florida education conference, and Harvard University.

In most schools recently arrived immigrants do not win such honors—they don't captain varsity soccer, chair student government, or fill the seats of AP calculus. In other schools, students may worry about being misunderstood. Seeing few newcomers on teams and in clubs, they may conclude they don't belong. But at IHSLP everyone looks like them, everyone shares a story of migration. "Our kids," Daniel reflected, "have built everything from the ground up, they overcome challenge after challenge. And they have been able to turn those challenges into strengths."

IHSLP's students are crafting a new narrative for young immigrants. A once-shy Salvadorian girl spoke on a university panel about her dreams for her future, a former gang member was accepted and excelled at a New England liberal arts college. The small moments matter, too, like the afternoon when a recently arrived Nepali girl successfully calculated the density of a block of wood. Carlos takes immense pride in the students' success—tweeting when clubs and teams win awards, posting when seniors get accepted to colleges. "Seeing kids be successful when so many people have told them that they can't be," Carlos reflected, "that brings me so much joy." He nodded to himself. "So much joy."

In a large auditorium, in the spring of 2019, IHSLP's first graduating class walked across a stage. Carlos handed each a ribbon-tied diploma. Beside him, ready to shake their hands, stood Daniel, school counselors, teachers, and county officials. Roughly 95 percent of the class graduated that day. With the help of the school's college counselor, most would be heading, come fall, to study at Skidmore, Goucher, Hood, McDaniel, the University of Maryland, and more than thirty-five other colleges. Together they had been offered seven million dollars in aid and scholarships.

I was in Carlos's office one afternoon when a ninth-grade Syrian boy poked his head in. He had a favor to ask. An Afghan friend, he explained, was struggling in a nearby school. Could the boy transfer to IHSLP? He handed over a scrap of paper with a scrawled number. Setting aside his work, Carlos reached for the phone. The Afghan boy answered and anxiously asked if he could attend. Carlos probed, "How are your grades? Why do you want to change schools?" His eyebrows inched up as the boy explained he was failing almost every course and that he had begun cutting classes. But, the boy promised breathlessly, "At your school I will work hard." Carlos sounded skeptical, "How do I know?" He paused, then added, "If you come, I will have you sign a contract that you will be on time, that you will work hard to get your grades up." The boy was jubilant, "Yes, yes, yes, I can do that!" Carlos paused to look up at his Syrian student, "What do you think?" The boy squared his shoulders, bobbed his head. "If he isn't doing good I will try my best to help him." Carlos nodded and told his newest pupil he would see him the following week. Smiling, Carlos put down the phone, "I like him already."

I called Daniel a year later, curious whether the boy from Afghanistan had enrolled. Yes, Daniel reported. He'd arrived the very next Monday and signed Carlos's contract. His attendance ticked up; so too did his grades. And while he had his off days, he had kept his promise—he was trying. And, soon after arriving, he'd joined his new classmates on the soccer field.

THE PERSONAL: CARLA

Carla arrived on the very first day of school in 2016, tiny and boisterous. "What are you doing here?" I asked, laughing.

Carla had been my student the year before, during my first year teaching at Lowell High. She had been one of a motley crew of adolescents who formed my very last class of each long exhausting day. There was the Puerto Rican student so painfully shy that a successful day was when she strung a few words together; the lanky Iraqi teen who was forever dozing off; the Brazilian youth who inked marijuana leaves on his arm and on his assignments. And then there was Carla. She sat front and center in my class, alert, notebook out, pencil sharpened, and almost always with a grin. She loved cartoons—*SpongeBob SquarePants*, *CatDog*, *Teletubbies*. Frequently she dissolved into fits of giggles. But she was also strikingly mature, homework done without fail, always ready to answer a question, and also dependably willing to be partnered with her most disruptive peers, and for that I was profoundly grateful.

Two months earlier I had watched her walk across a stage to accept her diploma in a billowing red robe, ringlets blown straight for the occasion. In just weeks she would be starting at our local community college. But here she was in the doorway. "Can I help in your class this semester?" she asked timidly. Taken aback, I nodded, "Sure."

Every Friday morning after that, Carla met me at my classroom—at an hour at which most college students would prefer to still be asleep. As I rounded a hall corner, keys in hand to unlock my door, she was always there waiting. "What are we teaching today?" was her morning greeting. With no college courses scheduled for Fridays, Carla devoted the hours to my new students. During group work, she wove between desks, pausing to translate a word into Spanish, bending down to help a student parse a speech by President Woodrow Wilson. In the computer lab, she sat side by side with students, sharing tips on how to research labor unions. Many of my students towered over Carla. It wasn't hard: At 4'11" she might easily be mistaken for a high school sophomore. But in our class, within days, no one questioned her authority.

I kept wondering whether a Friday would arrive and I would no longer find Carla. It seemed inevitable that, once she settled into college, coursework and clubs would draw her from our school. But Carla kept returning. Fall slipped into winter. When occasionally she could not come, my students would ask after her: "Where is Carla?" "Will she be here later? "I had something I wanted to ask her."

———•———

Growing up in the second-largest city in the Dominican Republic, Carla had always loved school. A straight-A student in a starched khaki jumper and blue button-down uniform, she never skipped class. Friends were constantly asking to borrow her notes. Three years in a row she was awarded a certificate for academic excellence, one of three students selected in the entire school. "It was a big deal to go to school for us," Carla explained. "If you didn't go to school you were a nobody." Carla steadfastly wanted to be a somebody.

Mornings started in prayer, the girls crowding into the adjacent chapel. Carla's schools always skewed religious. A Seventh-day Adventist school, then an all-girls Catholic colegio. Groggy with sleep, Carla mumbled through the prayers, but by the start of classes she was always wide awake, back straight, ready to learn. Carla gravitated toward teachers who told stories, who made her laugh, who talked about their lives outside of school. Although she was not confident with numbers, math became Carla's favorite subject. "If you have eight *tostones*, but Maria wants an equal number as you," her math teacher would ask, "how many *tostones* will you have remaining on your plate?" Math was filled with laughter, and as Carla recalled, "I always left class hungry."

But what Carla loved most was the community. She played on the school's tennis and basketball teams. For three years she was elected to the student government as class secretary. She joined the school choir and with classmates visited local nursing homes to sing to residents. For Hispanic heritage month each year, she stood before her school and spoke confidently about the history of Colombia, of Uruguay, of Mexico. For an Independence Day play she taped a fake mustache to her upper lip, transforming herself into one of the country's three founding fathers.

School felt like a second home. Even with yard fights that broke out weekly, school felt safe. Outside the high yellow walls were streets that served as the dividing line between two barrios and two rival gangs. Carla's walk might have been short, yet she was always on her guard. Robberies were common; so too were the sound of gunshots. Once, while she was walking to school, a friend passed her on a motorbike. As he turned a corner, shots peppered the air. He thudded to the pavement. Carla, ten at the time, ran. For some time following, she took to carrying a sliver of a razor blade. If she were attacked, she told herself, she would be prepared.

———•———

It was early in the morning, still dark, when Carla's mom roused her from bed. Muggy heat blanketed a sleeping city. Only a few street dogs patrolled the alleyways. Too tired to ask questions, the bleary-eyed fifteen-year-old followed her mother onto a bus and promptly curled up asleep on her mother's lap.

Carla awoke in Santo Domingo, the sun stretching up over the capital. In front of her was a grand beige building, a long line of people already snaking back and forth before it. "Embassy of the United States," read large silver letters. Carla was confused, "What are we doing here?" she asked. "We are filling in the paperwork to move to New York," her mother replied, and left it at that.

Her mother's words refused to register—not in the hours standing in line, not in the small room where a doctor drew her blood, not on the long bus ride back home. Weeks went by. Then one afternoon, Carla was packing away clothes when suddenly she broke into sobs. There would be no more dance troupe, no church choir, no youth group. She would never graduate with her classmates. There would be no more friends, no more tennis, no more milk-drenched coconut cake. She cried and cried, and when her aunt tiptoed in to comfort her, Carla firmly pushed her away.

Carla's family landed in New York City in the midst of a blizzard. Fat flakes, the kind she had seen only in movies, swirled past the windows of the plane. Outside, everything was white and eerie. It was January 1, 2014. A new year, a new life.

———•———

Three years later, almost to the day, I awoke shivering and feverish on the morning that classes were set to resume. I loathed missing school. I rarely took sick days, but that morning my body rebelled. Resigned, I texted Carla. I would be out, so she should stay home. My phone pinged within minutes. "Don't worry, Ms. Lander," she texted back, "I will help today, feel better!" As I shivered under blankets, Carla deftly led my classes. A substitute teacher sat silently in the corner, superfluous. Each hour I received an update: "Period 3: got through everything." "Period 5: doing great." "Everything laid out for tomorrow." Back in August, Carla had asked to volunteer for a single semester. Now in January she made no mention of leaving. With Carla's help I was able to better support more students, I was able to be a better teacher.

The following September, I no longer wondered if Carla would return. She met me on a muggy Monday in August and together we shifted mismatched furniture, unpacked boxes, and filled a wonky cabinet with pencils, pens, and reams of lined paper.

———◆———

Carla enrolled as a sophomore at Lowell High School in the winter of 2014, before I was teaching there. Little about her first day felt auspicious. Her teachers were incomprehensible. Her photo ID was, in her words, "ugly!" She got lost repeatedly, locating the cafeteria just as the bell for the next class blared. That first evening, having trudged home through snow-lined sidewalks, Carla shut herself in her room and wept. "I didn't understand anything. I didn't want to be here. I just wanted to go back to my language, my warm weather. Here everything was freezing." But home was not an option. "We have to make here work," her mother told her, stroking her back.

Carla prided herself on being a straight-A student, but at Lowell, over the coming months, "everything," she recalled, "was frustrating." Reading was challenging, speaking was challenging, writing was challenging. Verb conjugations jumbled on the page, commas confused her. Even mathematics felt foreign, with new methods for multiplying and dividing. Once her favorite, math became her most despised subject. In gym class Carla watched classmates plunge into the pool. Terrified of drowning, she had never learned to swim. Lesson after lesson, she clutched the side of the pool and silently seethed when she received low marks.

Carla cautiously tried to engage in her classes. Back home students often shouted out the answer rather than raise their hands, but when Carla energetically offered an opinion, her new teacher responded curtly: "Here we raise our hands and wait our turn." Carla's face burned with embarrassment. When she asked another teacher to reexplain a problem, the reply was brusque: "I already explained it on the board, go figure it out." When she offered an answer in a third class after raising her hand, the instructor shook their head: "That's wrong, did you not read what I told you to read?" Mortified, Carla looked down. Best not to speak at all, she reasoned. Carla had always had strong connections with her teachers, but now she could barely interpret what they said, and they struggled to understand her. After one failed exchange with a teacher she fled to the bathroom, locked herself in a stall, and let the tears fall until the bell rang.

Each difference—how a teacher taught, explained a topic, organized their classroom, greeted students—Carla held up against her Dominican school and found her new school lacking.

Only peers cheered her up. Classes were brimming with Spanish speakers: Dominican classmates warmly welcomed her, but also students from Colombia, El Salvador, Honduras, Puerto Rico, Mexico, and Guatemala. They sat together in classes, whispering in Spanish. They claimed tables at lunch, spicing their grilled chicken and mashed potatoes with packets of garlicky *sazón*.

But when academic awards were handed out at the end of the year, Carla was not called onstage. It mattered little to her that she had been in the United States for only a semester. "I thought I was good," Carla believed, "but I realized I wasn't good enough." She had always excelled. But without good grades, how, she wondered, would she not be a nobody? "I didn't want to be here. I just wanted to go home."

Six months later Carla got her wish. It was summer break, and she could finally go home. On the plane she was jittery with excitement. She would see her friends, her family, her neighborhood. She would eat heaping plates of French fries, plantains, and fried salami. A crowd would greet her at the airport. There would be balloons, bouquets, and so many hugs. But when she walked into the evening heat, no one was there waiting.

Home in the barrio, Carla found that life had left her behind. Friends had moved away. One was married, another was pregnant. Chubby babies were now crawling. Elderly neighbors struggled to remember the short bubbly girl. Most unsettling was how others spoke to her. "People treated us like we had big money, like I was a gringo." The image they had of Carla's new life bore no resemblance to the cramped apartment, the cold, and the sense of loss that swamped her. "Everyone treated me different," Carla recalled. "But I still felt like the same person."

Confused, Carla flew back to Massachusetts for the start of her junior year. The island no longer felt like home, but neither did the United States. "I felt stuck in the middle." Out of necessity, Carla determined to make Lowell work. Her younger sister had already exited the EL program, which irked her since she was supposed to be the smart student. Stubbornly at night she took to watching back-to-back episodes of *Grey's Anatomy*, the Seattle medical staff serving as surrogate English teachers.

In the following months her coursework slowly grew easier. Carla saw this as a sign. She went to the school office and asked to be switched out of EL classes. But to her shock, her counselor disagreed—she was not ready. What Carla heard was: You are not smart enough. She took to avoiding certain hallways, which she and her friends dubbed "white people places." This was where the AP and high honors classes were taught, and Carla saw few peers who looked like her. Such classes, she convinced herself, must be off-limits to immigrants like her.

On the island, school had been the center of Carla's life. School government, school sports teams, school plays. But in Lowell she was hesitant to join. Again, she saw few faces that resembled hers. She avoided auditioning for school plays or choir; she did not run for school government. She surrounded herself with others who, like her, "spoke crooked English." She briefly considered trying out for sports, but she was too short for basketball and she lacked the money for softball equipment. Instead, Carla worked for hours after school, running a vacuum down the length of office-building hallways alongside her mother. Her wages went to pay for groceries, electricity bills, toiletries.

———•———

I met Carla for the first time at the start of her senior year in 2015, after she flew back to Lowell following yet another summer spent in the Dominican Republic. As a member of my final class of the day, she could always make me smile and often laugh. She was bubbly, boisterous, and ceaselessly curious. Though I did not know it, she still yearned to leave behind classes dedicated to English learners. But at least now, within the shelter of EL courses like mine, she was top of the class once more. When we held a mock debate on the Nineteenth Amendment, Carla skewered the opposition with her questioning. When I created the op-ed project that would become a cornerstone of my class in the coming years, Carla was determined that hers would be selected for publication. She typed head down in the computer lab during class and, when she could, she arrived early to keep editing. When, for the first time, my students' opinions were published in the *Lowell Sun*, Carla's face grinned from the middle of a full-page spread.

But outside of class, Carla remained hesitant. She did not know whom to turn to for help, and so she often asked no one. When seniors began applying to college in the fall, Carla, alone, googled schools, selected two that seemed affordable, and filled out the applications on her own. Both schools rejected her. Carla was crushed. She was supposed to be a somebody, but the schools disagreed. Resigned, she filled in the paperwork for community college.

That spring, one afternoon in a computer lab, Carla beckoned me over. We were in the midst of our semester-long civics project, and Carla's class was designing a schoolwide campaign to tackle Islamophobia. She pointed at an email she was drafting to the head of school. "Ms. Lander, we aren't actually going to send this email. This is pretend, right?" I shook my head. "No, this is a real." Carla's eyebrows ricocheted up. She asked again. Again I gave my answer. Her eyes grew wide. "Oh!" was all she could manage.

She sent the letter, but she remained skeptical that anyone would read it. A month later, in the school's auditorium, she found herself nervously presenting her class's plan to the school's leadership. They had read her letter and shown up to hear her speak.

————•————

The following year, when my students sought to confirm that the letter they were writing to city officials was just a pretend exercise, it was Carla, now a college freshman, who shook her head and explained that no, their letter was real. Some looked taken aback, others nervous. Yet they had come to trust her; as they drafted memos and constructed surveys, they peppered her with questions.

Though in my class she strode between the desks with confidence, in college Carla felt much less at ease. Her new textbooks were crammed with incomprehensible words, her classes larger and intimidating. When a professor asked her to write a ten-page paper, she was flummoxed. Her papers were returned graffitied with red pen. She grew disheartened. "I would put my heart and soul into something. When I got a bad grade I started questioning myself." But instead of staying quiet, this time she reached out for help. As Carla worked with my students, I began to work with her on her college classes. In the quiet moments, before school, during lunch, after the last bell, the two of us began to talk through the structure of essays and map out presentations. On the whiteboard I walked through citation formats and trickier grammatical rules. During course selection, we sifted through possibilities.

When in the spring of 2017 my students traveled down to the Massachusetts State House to present on their semester's civics work, Carla rode with them—corralling, calming, and rehearsing with nervous teens. She herself was not nervous. No longer did she worry that the adults might not listen. Indeed, that morning I stood stunned as she marched up to a state representative and brazenly asked him to support our city safety initiative. To her delight, he said yes.

By her second year in my classroom, word had gotten out. One teacher asked her advice on how to convince a group of freshman Dominican boys to stop cursing under their breath in class. Another sought her help in assisting a new arrival on their first day. Students, too, called on Carla—for relationship advice, for support when friendships grew sour, for help explaining family situations to teachers. With time she grew familiar with a smorgasbord of school resources: counseling services, academic tutoring, and after-school programs. Wistfully she wondered how her own school years might have differed if she had known about such services.

Knowing that Carla had struggled in school, I once asked her what drew her back to the classroom. She considered before answering. "I didn't want other students to feel the way I felt," she replied. Determined, Carla set about filling the holes for my students that had pockmarked her own educational experience. When students sought her help, as increasingly they did, she listened, and she also connected them to counselors, social workers, specific teachers. When new students showed up lost, she walked them to class. When seniors stumbled over college applications, she guided them through the steps and pointed them toward the college counseling office.

That spring, for her work in my class, Carla received an invitation: Would she give a keynote address for an educational nonprofit's gala? In April Carla stood before eight hundred people, sharing the stage with the attorney general of Massachusetts. She needed a step stool to reach the microphone, but her voice could be heard across the room. "Coming back and supporting and teaching younger immigrant students has been so powerful for me," she told the crowd. "I always tell other students that they too can help others find comfort in a new country." There were few dry eyes.

———◆———

By the fall of 2018, Carla was everywhere—confidently redirecting the boy whose eyes wandered during a quiz, fielding questions from two students while I helped a third. When two girls stormed into class upset, she calmly steered them into the hall to mediate. She had no degrees or official training, but Carla had invaluable wisdom drawn from having been an immigrant in our school, and she cared deeply. Every classroom needs a Carla.

That winter I came across a posting for an internship with the Massachusetts attorney general. Together, Carla and I worked through the application after my students—*our* students—had headed home for the day. Fingers crossed, she sent it off.

It was a busy spring. As she had done at our school, Carla had gained a reputation at college. She made friends in the admissions office, the financial aid office, the student engagement office. She volunteered to run student events, she spoke on panels, and she ran for and was elected to student government. When my students filled in forms for community college, I referred them to Carla. She would, I told them, help ensure they were connected and cared for.

For the first time in three years, on the final Fridays of school in 2019, Carla was missing from my classroom. She was in Boston, beginning an internship in the attorney general's office. At the end of her long first day Carla texted me, exhilarated. She had her own desk, she was getting her own official badge, everyone was so friendly. Doubt, she admitted, still lingered. Her fellow interns attended elite institutions. Perhaps she did not deserve to be there. But when she returned the following day, and the day after that, she was treated with the same warmth, held to the same high expectations. No one questioned her presence, and, slowly, Carla stopped questioning it too. When the attorney general arrived at an ice cream social for interns, Carla giddily asked for a photo.

Soon there will come a day where Carla can no longer mentor in my classroom. She has new ambitions, new dreams. But she won't stop speaking up for newcomers. As Carla has told me with confidence, she intends to run for public office. And, I have no doubt she will.

CHAPTER 7

ACCEPTANCE

To make Americans, we must ensure that immigrant-origin students are accepted regardless of their identity or their circumstances. Children may come to the nation's shores without immigration papers or as refugees with limited formal education. Before arriving, they may have been excluded from education because of their gender, sexuality, religion, ethnicity, nationality, legal status, educational experience, abilities, or financial resources. For them, being excluded has often meant living in the shadows. For children to flourish, schools must embrace each student as they come.

This chapter tells three stories. The first is the story of four undocumented families in Texas who risked deportation to advocate for their children's access to education; their fight culminated, in 1982, in a landmark Supreme Court decision that ruled that undocumented children nationwide have the right to public K–12 education and that laid the groundwork for the DREAM Act and Deferred Action for Childhood Arrivals (DACA) program decades later. The second is the story of a school in the suburbs of Atlanta, Georgia, dedicated to teaching refugee girls who, for years, had been denied an education. The third is the story of my own student Diane, who after being born stateless in a Zambian refugee camp and growing up with bounded dreams sought recognition, acceptance, and a new future in America.

THE PAST: *PLYLER V. DOE*

The sun had yet to surface when Lídia and José Lopez gently shook their five children from their slumber, dressed them in their Sunday best, and tucked the family into their white Dodge Monaco. The sedan was piled high with books, clothes, pots, even the family's small TV, but the Lopezes were not embarking on a road trip. Their destination was a mere two blocks away, at the federal district courthouse in Tyler, Texas.

Alfredo, nine and the oldest, remembers little. It was a Friday, the week after the start of school, the year 1977. The little black-haired boy should have been entering second grade, his sister should have been starting first. But just as classes were set to resume, their parents received a letter informing them that tuition was required if they wished their children to study in the public schools. For the Lopez family, the fee was unaffordable.

Just over two years earlier and more than two hundred miles south, in Austin, the legislature had revised the state's education code. But before the final vote was cast, the border city of Brownsville slipped in a provision that, at the time, went largely unnoticed. Going forward, public schools would no longer be obligated to educate their community's undocumented children. And, the state would contribute no funds to support those children's academic futures. Public schools were left with a choice: Cover the cost themselves, charge tuition, or exclude such students altogether.

In the blistering summer heat of 1977, the Tyler School Board, arguing that the city was on the precipice of becoming "a haven" for undocumented families, voted to charge tuition for every student who could not prove legal residence—one thousand dollars per child, roughly one-fourth of most undocumented Texans' annual income.[1]

The city of Tyler, in the eastern corner of Texas, was founded in the mid-1800s, built by enslaved Black Americans, and named for a US president who initiated the annexation of the Lone Star State. Surrounded by vibrant blooms, it was a city that proudly proclaimed itself the "Rose Capital of America." And it was here, in 1969, where José Lopez found work tending rosebuds after crossing the southern border. Within a few years he sent for his wife, and then for his children, who left their home in the small Mexican city of Jalpa and traveled hundreds of miles north to reunite.

On arriving in the United States, Alfredo was enrolled in elementary school and attended dutifully until, in the summer of 1977, the school board changed its policy. Of the city's nearly 16,000 students, less than

60 were undocumented, and they were suddenly ineligible to study in the city's schools.[2]

Growing up in Mexico, neither José nor Lídia Lopez had been able to stay long in school. Their families needed them in the fields. But, for their children they wished for a different future. And so, a week later, a little before 6 a.m., the Lopez family pulled into the parking lot of the federal district courthouse, the sky just beginning to bloom pink. There they met three other undocumented families. Together they had made the perilous choice to sue the city's schools. It was a decision the parents made knowing what might happen. That was why, the night before, Lídia and José Lopez had packed the Dodge Monaco to the brim. As Lídia would recall years later, in walking into the courthouse they were prepared to be immediately arrested and deported. But for their children, it was a risk they chose to take.[3]

———•———

In 1977, on the first day of school in Tyler, Texas, there was chaos. That is what Michael McAndrew, a bilingual social worker at the city's only Catholic church, remembers. McAndrew had arrived in Tyler the previous year, at the invitation of Pastor Milam Joseph, who hoped to better support the growing Latino community within his congregation. Joseph, the son of parents from the mountains of former Syria, now Lebanon, intimately understood the challenges of those seeking belonging. Perhaps this was why in 1976, realizing that the city's famed rose fields were tended primarily by Mexican Americans, he decided his church should conduct a Spanish Mass. The pews quickly filled for the weekly service, four hundred parishioners and more, with a local restaurant manager acting as translator. Wanting to do more, Joseph hired McAndrew to act as a community liaison, to assist congregants with everything from legal aid to educational support. Now, in the fall of 1977, McAndrew set off in search of a lawyer.

When McAndrew walked into a local civil rights law firm, Roberta Rodkin, the young lawyer who greeted him, was incredulous such a law could exist. As she would tell me, "It sounded so ridiculous." Rodkin, whose Jewish ancestors came from Russia and the Austro-Hungarian Empire, was relatively new to Texas.[4] Skeptical, she pulled from the shelf a volume on state law, staring amazed at the fine print when she found it. She knew immediately this was important—important enough to interrupt the firm's partner, Larry Daves, who was away for the week celebrating his birthday. When she got him on the phone, Daves agreed. He told her they needed to call the Mexican American Legal Defense and Educational Fund (MALDEF).

Close to a decade earlier, in 1968, MALDEF had opened in San Antonio. Modeled on the success of the NAACP, MALDEF hoped to use the courts to fight for civil, economic, political, and educational equality for Latino communities nationwide. The civil rights organization had participated in close to one hundred education lawsuits alone. When Rodkin called MALDEF, their response was succinct: "This is the call we have been waiting for."[5]

MALDEF had recently hired a new director for education litigation, Peter Roos. Roos's family had come early to America, Jewish immigrants from Alsace-Lorraine drawn to Nevada during the 1850s silver rush. Just out of law school, Roos had worked for legal assistance offices in Southern California. He had represented Latino families in school desegregation cases and memorably, one weekend, camped out with Cesar Chavez at the Delano headquarters in the midst of the national grape strike. When he later worked in a Harvard University Law School program, his colleagues had composed a series of amicus briefs in education cases, including one with an untranslated Chinese footnote, in support of a young boy from Hong Kong whose mother had sued her city's schools. Within twenty-four hours of Rodkin's call, Roos, now based in MALDEF's San Francisco headquarters, caught a midnight flight bound for Texas.[6]

For nearly a century following the founding of the United States, no one coming into the country was considered undocumented. Only in the late 1800s, most notably with the passage of the Chinese Exclusion Act, did the United States, in the words of historian Erika Lee, reposition itself as a "gatekeeper nation."[7] The laws created new categories of people: those who were welcome and those who were not. To help enforce the new exclusionary laws, an immigration center was opened in 1910 on a heart-shaped island in San Francisco Bay. Angel Island was termed by some "the Ellis Island of the West," but there the resemblance stopped.[8] Whereas the New York immigration halls were for many a place of welcome, from its founding Angel Island was established in large part to detain and to deport.

As the primary port of entry for newcomers from Asia, Angel Island established exhaustive procedures in an attempt to determine which few of thousands would be allowed entry into America. For a Chinese immigrant, one of the only successful ways to enter the country was to be the son or daughter of an American-born person. And soon a vigorous trade in false documents took form. For a fee, Americans of Chinese ancestry would sponsor a cousin, a nephew, or a stranger, claiming them as their child. "Paper sons" and "paper daughters" they were called. The inferno that followed the 1906 San Francisco earthquake was an unforeseen boon. Children, legitimate or not, could claim kinship, blaming an act of nature for the lack of paper proof.

In an attempt to verify lineage, immigration officers interrogated Chinese detainees for days on end, the minutiae of their life in China coming under the microscope. Does your brother's wife have bound feet? Who was your first teacher? Where is the nearest market? How many steps lead up to your house? What material is your living room floor made of? Where do you keep the rice bin? What type of bedding did your father sleep in? How many houses are there in your village? Who lives in the second house in the third row? How many children does that particular family have and what are their names and ages? On and on and on. Reams of typed trivialities that were then cross-referenced with those from sponsors in the United States. A misplaced rice bin, a misremembered age could derail an application. Immigrants at Ellis Island might be held at most two days, but on Angel Island newcomers were detained anywhere from two weeks to two years. Shrouded in harbor fog, on the wooden slats of their prison, Chinese hopefuls carved their anguish into poetry, "America has power, but not justice. In prison, we were victimized as if we were guilty . . . I bow my head in reflection, but there is nothing I can do."[9]

For Central and South American newcomers, for decades America's gates were flung wide in welcome. While the 1924 Johnson-Reed Immigration Act sought to exclude immigrants from much of the world, migration across the Western Hemisphere was largely encouraged. During the height of World War II, with a dearth of men on the home front, the government created a guest worker program to entice Mexican laborers across the border to cultivate US fields. Over the following two decades, more than four million Mexican migrants were welcomed temporarily through the Bracero Program, which was halted in 1964. A year later, with the enactment of the Hart-Celler Immigration Act, for the first time the United States put a cap on immigration from the Western Hemisphere. But by then many US companies, particularly large farms and factories, had come to rely on migrant laborers, whom they could pay little and treat poorly. Companies continued recruiting, and their employees kept coming, but now many were undocumented. They slipped into a country that officially was closing its front door, while simultaneously opening a back door.

Only in the early 1970s, coinciding with an economic recession, did the American public begin fixating on undocumented people. Newspapers and politicians dredged up long-favored metaphors. "Waves" and "floods" of undocumented immigrants were swamping the United States, amounting to, in the words of one Immigration and Naturalization Service (INS) commissioner, "a national crisis."[10] Only a few noted that a decade earlier, many of these same migrants would have been welcomed. Cities stepped up raids targeting Latino communities indiscriminately, an unspoken statement by those in power that if you were Latino, you likely didn't belong. In August of 1977, just two weeks after the Tyler School Board voted to exclude undocumented children, President Jimmy Carter proposed a new national immigration policy. His plan would send more guards to the southern border, harshly penalize businesses for employing undocumented people, and provide for some a one-time path to citizenship. It satisfied few. Some argued it was too lenient, others worried it would open the door to indiscriminate racial profiling and discrimination.

The four families who chose to sue Tyler's school came to East Texas, without papers, in the years following the 1965 Immigration Act. They worked as plumbers, electricians, and carpenters in Tyler's buildings, they tended roses in its fields, and they processed meat in its factories. They rented and bought homes; were taxpayers and community members. They joined the city's Catholic church, headed by an outspoken Lebanese pastor. They raised their families, gave birth to new sons and daughters, and, until the end of August in 1977, they sent their children to school.

Over a sweltering Labor Day weekend, with temperatures refusing to drop below 100, Roberta Rodkin and Peter Roos feverishly built a case in support of Tyler's undocumented children. Rodkin's partner, Larry Daves, returned to Tyler on Labor Day and jumped headfirst into the case. The following morning, less than a week after the start of school, the lawyers filed their lawsuit and went before the federal district judge. Given the undocumented status of their clients, the lawyers asked that the families' names be withheld from the federal government and hearings be conducted in closed session. The judge shook his head—he was not permitted to withhold information from the Department of Justice and the INS. However, to protect the privacy of the families from the public, the judge allowed them to be identified in court documents by pseudonyms: Roe, Boe, Loe, and Doe. And, to sidestep journalists sniffing for a story, the judge proposed an unusual solution. He set the Friday hearing for six o'clock in the morning. No reporter, he reckoned, would show up. His guess proved accurate.

The judge assigned to the case was William Wayne Justice. As the *Washington Post* would write of Justice a decade later, "Justice in Texas is not an abstraction, but flesh and blood and, as only real life can render it, a federal judge."[11] The descendant of Norwegian immigrants and Confederate soldiers, Justice was born in East Texas at the dawn of the Roaring Twenties. He grew up destined for a career in law. His father, a lawyer, left little to chance, designating his son his official legal partner when Justice was just seven years old. A child of the Great Depression, Justice credited his father with teaching him the essence of his name. As Justice would recall, for his father, "A farmer in bib overalls was entitled to no less dignity than the president of a bank in a pinstriped suit."[12]

Decades later, at the urging of Texas senator Ralph Yarborough, President Kennedy appointed Justice as a US attorney, and then President Johnson appointed him a federal district judge. He joined the court two months after Reverend Dr. Martin Luther King Jr. was assassinated in Memphis and arrived in Tyler to a segregated city firmly rooted in the Deep South. Two years into his tenure he definitively ordered the desegregation of Texas schools. When he ordered the city's own Robert E. Lee High School to take down its profusion of Confederate flags, incensed white students took their flags and circled the courthouse shouting epithets. As one student would recall, "Justice was blamed for everything."[13]

Hate mail and death threats flooded the courthouse. Crosses were ignited in the judge's yard. Bumper stickers calling for his impeachment were displayed with pride. Carpenters, upon realizing they were working on Justice's house, walked off the job, and hairdressers refused to style his wife's hair. For decades she drove thirty miles for a trim. As a fellow judge would recall, "When Wayne walked into a restaurant, others would often walk out."[14] Justice never asked for a security detail, though one might have been warranted. Instead he took up tae kwon do, a practice that served, as he would admit, a dual purpose: "It was a great way to take out my frustrations."[15]

In Texas, Justice was hated and revered. A shy, slightly stooped, bookish man, Justice spent a lifetime, as he would share years later, trying to live up to his name.[16]

As a young lawyer in the early 1970s, Larry Daves moved to Tyler with the specific aim of practicing law in Justice's courtroom. Daves grew up, primarily, in the Texas Panhandle and traced his ancestry back to Ireland and Germany, as well as, on his father's side, Indigenous peoples in America. As a law student, Daves had had every intention of moving to Alaska and building a career as an oil and gas attorney. But embarking on his final year of school, he volunteered to collect testimony from children incarcerated in state juvenile detention centers. Over months he recorded a litany of horrific abuse. Guards regularly beat children with their fists, but also with steel rods. Prolonged solitary confinement and sexual abuse were rampant. Children as young as ten were tear-gassed, locked on chain gangs, and, for punishment, made to trudge through pits of sewage. Daves, as he shared with me, was intimately familiar with such abuse: His two younger brothers had been locked away and brutalized in such facilities. At the time they had been just twelve and thirteen years old. The testimonies Daves and others collected were taken at the request of Judge Justice, who would use them as the foundation of a ruling requiring a sweeping overhaul of the state's juvenile justice system. On graduating, Daves knew he could neither live in Alaska nor represent oil. Without pause, he became a civil rights lawyer and moved to East Texas.

In the first week of September 1977, after conferring with Judge Justice, Daves trooped out to the court parking lot to speak with the four undocumented families, with community liaison McAndrew acting as translator. As he did for every client, Daves warned of the personal sacrifices a court case required, risks that were palpably real for the families. "What you are doing today," he told them, "could be very important. Maybe tens of thousands of kids in the state could benefit."[17] But in stepping out of the shadows they risked deportation. The families nodded. They understood. Their courage would stay with Daves for decades. For Rodkin, what struck her most was their "incredible faith in America."[18]

On Friday morning the families filed into Judge Justice's court. They were joined by the state's bleary-eyed assistant attorney general, sporting blue jeans; she had arrived in the wee hours of the morning and the airline, she apologized, had lost her luggage. (As Justice would recall twenty-five years later, "She plainly thought that the whole proceedings were insane, being there early in the morning like that and being confronted with these extraordinary allegations, that the children of illegal aliens would be entitled to a public education. She obviously thought that was such a ridiculous proposition and it really didn't deserve her appearance there.")[19]

As the Tyler parents offered testimony, their children, four-year-olds, six-year-olds, eight-year-olds, watched silently. As Daves recalled, "They were the cutest, quietest, most unbelievably disciplined children I've ever seen. They were probably mystified, but they sat for hours, quiet as mice, watching the proceedings."[20] It would be the last time Daves would see the children at the center of his case. While the full trial would not take place for months, following the Friday hearing, Judge Justice ordered the schools, in the meantime, to readmit their students. The following Monday, Tyler's undocumented children were back behind their desks. They had missed only a week of school.

While the students studied, Roos and Daves set about building their case in earnest, amassing evidence, but also public and private support. Taking a chance, Roos reached out directly to the INS. That spring, President Carter had nominated Leonel Castillo, a Texas native, to be INS commissioner, the first person of Mexican heritage named to the role. Castillo, a Peace Corps alum who had taught in the Philippines, had spent years in Houston consumed by politics, civil rights work, and advocacy for the Latino community. Whereas his predecessor at the INS referred to undocumented people as a "silent invasion,"[21] Castillo saw the nuance. As he would observe years later, the economy of the country's Western states "was built on the assumption and reality of a heavy influx of illegal labor."[22] Under Castillo's leadership, the INS staff was instructed to no longer use the term "illegal aliens," but instead "undocumented workers." As Roos would tell me, he knew Castillo well, as for years Castillo had sat on the MALDEF board. In private, Roos explained the situation and asked that the INS not come to Tyler. Castillo agreed.

Over two days in December, Judge Justice heard arguments in the suit brought by the four undocumented families against Tyler superintendent James Plyler. In court, Daves and Roos were joined by representatives of the US Department of Justice, who came to defend the rights of immigrant children, regardless of their legal status. At the close of trial, Daves was confident. They had justice on their side, figuratively, and, Daves was certain, also literally.[23]

Alfredo Lopez, who had been set to start second grade when he sat in Justice's courtroom, had just begun third grade when Justice handed down his ruling in September 1978. "Already disadvantaged as a result of poverty, lack of English-speaking ability, and undeniable racial prejudices," wrote the judge, "these children, without an education, will become permanently locked into the lowest socio-economic class." As both sides affirmed, "The illegal alien of today may well be the legal alien of tomorrow," acknowledging that many undocumented immigrants might eventually be granted permanent residency. Of the school district's argument that its policy would discourage migration, the judge was dismissive: Such a plan was "ludicrously ineffectual," he wrote. Justice was disdainful too of the district's attempt to slim educational costs by "shav[ing] off a little around the edges." It was a policy, the judge openly suggested, that might have been made because the "children of illegal aliens had never been explicitly afforded any judicial protection, and little political uproar was likely to be raised in their behalf."[24]

In his ruling, for the first time in US legal history, Justice afforded these children explicit protection based on the Fourteenth Amendment of the Constitution. The amendment stated that no state could "deprive any person of life, liberty, or property, without due process of law; nor deny to any person within its jurisdiction the equal protection of the laws." A century earlier, in a San Francisco case involving the discrimination against Chinese business owners, the Supreme Court, pointing to the drafters' choice of the word "person" and not "citizen," ruled that the Due Process Clause applied to everyone. In a case a decade later, the Court found constitutional protection for four undocumented Chinese men. Building on this logic in 1978, Judge Justice ruled that undocumented people were also protected under the Fourteenth Amendment's equal protection clause. As he would describe years later, "I guess I made my own little contribution."[25]

———•———

When Judge Justice ruled that Tyler schools could not bar undocumented children, his decision was bounded by the city limits. The Tyler School District appealed to the Fifth Circuit Court of Appeals, but within four days communities across the Lone Star State, having taken notice of Justice's ruling, started suing their schools. For three years since the state had enacted its exclusionary law, some districts had barred students from classrooms. Educators and community members, unwilling to let little ones languish, crafted makeshift classes. Public school teachers taught free evening sessions, graduate students helped improvise lessons, and when they could, churches offered free tuition to parochial programs for undocumented children. But the solutions were sparse and unsustainable. Justice's decision shifted communities' strategy.

In late 1979, seventeen other lawsuits against school districts were consolidated and presented to Houston's Federal District Judge Woodrow Seals. Like Judge Justice, Seals was appointed by LBJ at the recommendation of Senator Yarborough. His family traced distant roots back to Switzerland and elsewhere. Over an exhaustive trial stretching across six weeks, Judge Seals invited seemingly everyone into his courtroom: historians, professors, immigration experts, state representatives, law enforcement agents, federal census employees, state education officials, superintendents, teachers, clergy. Leonel Castillo, recently retired from the INS, candidly stated that the government's inaction in funding immigration officers amounted to "de facto amnesty." The state's undocumented children, he believed, were here to stay. Experts testified that undocumented families paid the same taxes as their documented neighbors, and the state received federal ESEA funding for those students. Alluding to *Brown v. Board of Education*, one psychologist testified to the intense feeling of inferiority undocumented children internalized when barred from study. And, in the testimony of a little girl, those feelings were given a face. In Tyler, the sixteen children had sat silently in court, but before Judge Seals, at least one child shared her story. She had arrived in the country as a five-month-old and had grown up in New Jersey, Missouri, and now Texas. Here was home. Now, as she described, she watched her younger, American-born, brother head off each morning to school. By chance of birth and documentation, she was forbidden to follow.

While sympathetic, the Texas Education Agency didn't budge. Likening the state to a sinking ship, one official explained, "I am in charge of the life boat and the life boat holds . . . forty people, we already have fifty people." Should he fish more writhing souls from the sea and possibly sink the boat, or "do I allow some of those people out there in the water to drown?" Answering his own question, he reasoned, "You have to determine those that you can save." Undocumented children, by way of his metaphor, must be left to perish. Countering, a Houston bishop spoke of a different calculus. Through exclusion, he argued, "we are manufacturing ignorance." The man of faith looked to the future and the uneducated workforce in the making. "In terms of social cost . . . fifteen years from now, we will pay this bill."[26] But for others, finances factored little. One state official, James Pete Williams, supposedly charged with helping to ensure school desegregation, asserted in a contorted bit of logic that allowing undocumented children to study would make integration "impossible." Moreover, while he had grown up with the message of the Statue of Liberty—which he paraphrased as "send us all, send us everything, the poor, the weak, whatever, we'll take care of it"—he declared definitively in court, "Those days are finished."[27]

Ironically, on the same day that in Houston Williams argued that America's gates were closed, fourteen hundred miles north and east in Washington, DC, President Carter signed the Refugee Act—for the first time in the nation's history committing to annually welcome and support some of the globe's displaced.

In the aftermath of World War II, less than forty years earlier, amid the largest refugee crisis the world had witnessed, the United States formally acknowledged and began explicitly accepting certain refugees. Yet for decades the invitations had been sporadic and specific to particular groups of persecuted peoples: refugees from Poland in the 1940s, Hungary in the 1950s, Cuba in the 1960s, Vietnam in the 1970s. A patchwork of programs. But in the late 1970s the world was faced once again with a staggering refugee crisis. Tens of thousands of Vietnamese refugees were fleeing communism and a country devastated, in significant measure, by US bombs, landmines, and the lingering effects of chemical weapons. They clambered into overcrowded fishing boats and set out into rough waters in search of safety. Starved survivors of Cambodia's brutal Khmer Rouge and Laotian refugees were on the move, too, made homeless by a largely ignored and secret war partially funded by the United States. It would be the magnitude of forced migration, and possibly also guilt, that would compel the US to adopt a new policy.

When Ted Kennedy had stood behind President Johnson as he signed the Hart-Celler Immigration Act in 1965, the young senator was still settling into Congress. In the intervening years he had transformed into a formidable force, and it would be Kennedy who would introduce, champion, and shepherd the new refugee act into being. "By protecting refugees from persecution, we honor our nation's finest traditions," Kennedy wrote years later. "A mark of a great nation is how fairly it treats the most vulnerable."[28] The new law committed the country to welcoming 50,000 refugees annually, from any country, not just some; providing aid in resettling and rebuilding a life; and creating a process for responding to emerging global crises. In addition, the law created a new classification, asylum seeker: someone who could seek sanctuary on US shores.

The new law was barely a month old when it was put to the test. Tens of thousands of Cuban refugees packed like sardines in boats began washing into Miami waters. President Jimmy Carter greeted the new arrivals with "an open heart and open arms." As he reminded the nation, "Ours is a country of refugees. . . . Those of us who have been here for a generation or six or eight generations ought to have just as open a heart to receive the new refugees as our ancestors were received in the past."[29] Cuban nationals kept coming. Within months more than a hundred thousand had landed. Public opinion did a sharp about-face. The refugees were no longer officially refugees. They were "status pending." Some called them economic immigrants, others asylum seekers, and by still more, they were labeled undocumented. The Cuban boat crisis foreshadowed a government practice in years to come of selectively identifying who among the world's persecuted would be considered refugees, and who would not.

In the midst of the refugee crisis in July 1980, Judge Seals delivered a ruling that stretched across more than eighty pages. Like Judge Justice, Seals thought little of the state's cost-saving efforts. More important to the judge was the role of schools in shaping new Americans, regardless of their legal status. As both sides acknowledged, most children would remain. But barred from school, one sociologist testified, children would fail to learn "the laws, the customs, the procedures, [and] the organization" of the country. Consequently, "[These children] would probably be unable . . . to integrate themselves . . . as productive members of society."[30] School, Judge Seals wrote, helped "perpetuate our culture" and "provide a moral compass for our children." Turning philosophical, he concluded, "As residents of a country which is re-examining its history and future as a home for persons of all nationalities and cultures, we cannot forget the role that the public schools have played providing unity to our community of immigrants."[31] The exclusion of children prevented them from learning how to become upstanding Americans; without that education, Seals worried that the country would fracture. Schools across the state were ordered to allow their undocumented students back into the classroom.

Three months later in New Orleans, the Fifth Circuit Court of Appeals issued its ruling on the Tyler school district's appeal in *Plyler v. Doe*. Earlier that year, when Roos and Daves had arrived for oral argument, they had been surprised to see a judge not originally slated to hear their case. Frank Johnson Jr. was relatively new to the court of appeals, but he had long been accustomed to national attention. As a federal judge in Alabama, it was Johnson who had struck down the segregation of buses, after Rosa Parks refused to give up her seat. In the years following, he ordered the desegregation of bus depots after the vicious attack on John Lewis and other Freedom Riders, the integration of libraries, and the integration of schools statewide. After police brutalized marchers in Selma, and Governor Wallace then refused to allow the march to resume, it was Judge Johnson who overturned the governor's order, clearing the roads to Montgomery. In *Plyler*, Johnson would write the unanimous decision in support of Tyler's undocumented children. Tyler schools, joined by the state of Texas, had offered a range of reasons that sought to justify their right to charge for tuition: Undocumented children financially burdened schools, they were more likely to carry communicable diseases, and many new parents would be drawn across the border by the promise of free education. They also argued that educating undocumented children was a waste, asserting that the more educated the children were, the more likely they would be targeted for deportation: Why bother teaching them at all? Johnson was not swayed. As he wrote for the court, "Denying a person a basic education is tantamount to ensuring that the person remains at the lowest socio-economic level of modern society." Johnson was unequivocal. "We think that aliens illegally within this country are clearly persons within the jurisdiction of the state . . . and thus fall under the simple language of the Fourteenth Amendment."[32] The state promptly appealed. Six months later, the Supreme Court agreed to weigh in, consolidating *Plyler v. Doe* with the case involving additional school districts, argued before Judge Seals.

On the first morning of December 1981, the oral argument at the Supreme Court was particularly animated. The hottest moment came from the questioning by Justice Thurgood Marshall. "Could Texas deny [undocumented people] fire protection?" Marshall asked Tyler's attorney. John Hardy, with a thick twang, appeared confused. "Deny them fire protection?" "Yes sir," Marshall replied. "F-i-r-e." Hardy floundered, "If—a—their home is—on fire, their home is going to be protected with the local fire services just . . ." Marshall pounced. "But could Texas pass a law and say they cannot be protected?" Hardy struggled to reply, "Because—I am going to take the position that—that is an entitlement of the—Justice Marshall, let me think a second. You—that is—I don't know. That is a tough question." Marshall was incredulous. "Somebody's house is more important than his child?"[33] Hardy could think of no adequate reply.

But the real challenge came after the oral argument, as the justices drafted their opinions and debated the extent to which education was a fundamental right under the Constitution.

It was the second time in less than a decade that the Court had considered the question. In 1973, the Court had decided *San Antonio Independent School District v. Rodriguez*, a case in which parents in a low-income, largely Latino neighborhood in San Antonio, Texas, argued that the policy of financing public schools through local property taxes violated the Equal Protection Clause of the Fourteenth Amendment.

While the low-income district taxed residents at significantly higher rates than wealthy neighboring districts, it raised far less money for its schools because of much lower property values.

In a contentious 5–4 decision, the Court ruled that inequalities in public school funding based on wealth did not violate the Equal Protection Clause of the Fourteenth Amendment. The majority held that education, while important, was not a fundamental protected right that was "explicitly or implicitly guaranteed by the Constitution." Because education was not a "fundamental" right, Texas was free to choose any policy for financing its public schools, provided it served a "legitimate state interest." The Court judged that having each community decide the level of financial support for education served the state's interest in allowing "local control" of schools.[34]

Justice Marshall, who less than two decades earlier, had stood before the Court as a lawyer arguing in *Brown v. Board of Education of Topeka*, penned a blistering dissent in *Rodriguez*. "The majority's holding can only be seen as a retreat from our historic commitment to equality of educational opportunity and as unsupportable acquiescence in a system which deprives children in their earliest years of the chance to reach their full potential as citizens."[35] Marshall argued that, in *Brown*, the Court had already acknowledged the fundamental importance of education. A system that inherently resulted in unequal school funding based on the wealth of a community's residents, he contended, was blatantly discriminatory.

While ruling in favor of Texas, the Court majority noted that it might be unconstitutional for the state to adopt a funding system that resulted in "an absolute denial of educational opportunities to any of its children."[36] Nearly a decade later, in *Plyler v. Doe*, it was this small opening that the lawyers for the undocumented families in Tyler, Texas, had bet on.

In the Court's chambers the discussions about *Plyler v. Doe* grew heated. Justice William Brennan, the son of Irish immigrants who had arrived before most newcomers were considered documented or undocumented, argued strongly that undocumented children had a right to education. When Justice William Rehnquist referred to the children as "wetbacks," Justice Marshall erupted in anger. Unapologetic, Rehnquist justified the slur, saying it was still in use in his home state. Marshall slung back that others used the same rationale to call him the N-word.[37]

In the end, it would be Justice Lewis Powell, a former chair of a Virginia school board and the author of the majority opinion in *Rodriguez* in 1973, who provided the decisive fifth vote in favor of the undocumented students. And it would be the impassioned Brennan who would write for the Court. Affirming Judge Justice's logic, his majority opinion confirmed that "an alien is surely a 'person' in any ordinary sense of that term" and thus was protected under the Fourteenth Amendment. Texas's law was troubling, he wrote, because it created a permanent "underclass" entirely inconsistent with the ideals of the nation and punished "innocent" children living in the country. To be consistent with its ruling in *Rodriguez*, the opinion held that, while education was not a protected right, "neither is it merely some governmental 'benefit.'" Schooling existed in some in-between space. "Education has a fundamental role in maintaining the fabric of our society." Schools ensured the continuation of the country's "political and cultural heritage." The Texas law "imposes a lifetime hardship" on certain children; barred from school, "we deny them the ability to live within the structure of our civic institutions, and foreclose any realistic possibility that they will contribute in even the smallest way to the progress of our Nation."[38] No matter their legal status, the Court ruled, children were entitled to study in American public schools.

In court, both sides in *Plyler v. Doe* had agreed that the children were likely here to stay. Four years later, in 1986, that prediction proved accurate. Congress passed and Ronald Reagan signed the Immigration Reform and Control Act, a revised version of President Carter's proposal nearly a decade earlier. In essence the law was a trade, offering a one-time path to citizenship for some in exchange for increased border security and penalties for businesses that hired undocumented employees. Included in the nearly three million granted amnesty were the sixteen children in Tyler and their parents who had risked deportation in the pursuit of education. In the years to come most of the children would remain in Tyler. They graduated high school, fell in love, got married, bought homes, and raised their own children. Many became citizens. For years, their connection to the landmark court case remained concealed. Indeed, many of the children themselves for years were unaware of the case's outcome. Judge Justice had sent them back to school within a week, and as Alfredo Lopez shared with me, "for us, that was the end of it."[39] It would be decades before they realized the gravity of what their parents had accomplished. Laura Alvarez, who was ten when she sat silently in Justice's courtroom, for years worked for the school district that had tried to exclude her, employed as a teacher's aide supporting Spanish-speaking students. "Without an education," she reflected, "I don't know where I'd be right now."[40]

But while granting amnesty for some, the 1986 law also began a process of militarizing the southern border and did little to incentivize businesses not to entice or hire undocumented people. Many in power had little wish to dismantle a system reliant on exploitation. Where once men had crisscrossed the border as seasonal labors, the heightened security made the repeated passage too dangerous. So, many brought their families and settled into the shadows of the nation. Their children grew up and, because of the courage of Tyler's parents, went to school. In their classrooms many came to see themselves as American. But that belonging was bounded. With no path to legalized status, as Harvard professor Roberto Gonzales has written, "for undocumented youth, the transition to adulthood is accompanied by a transition to illegality. . . . Youthful feelings of belonging give way to new understandings of the ways that they are excluded from possibilities they believed were theirs."[41]

And so new families took up the mantle. They marched, testified, organized. They advocated for everyone in the shadows. In 2001 Texas became the first state to allow undocumented teenagers access to in-state tuition for college, making higher education suddenly financially possible for some. The state's Republican governor declared, "We must say to every Texas child learning in a Texas classroom, 'we don't care where you come from, but where you are going, and we are going to do everything we can to help you get there.'"[42] Undocumented students today, he proclaimed, were some of tomorrow's leaders.

Two months later, Republican senator Orrin Hatch and Democratic senator Richard Durbin introduced what became known as the federal DREAM Act, a bill that would create for undocumented children a path to citizenship. It was a dream that would be deferred—again and again. A decade later, after the bill died in Congress, President Barack Obama devised a temporary solution for children who had grown up believing they belonged. He announced his program, the Deferred Action for

Childhood Arrivals (DACA) on the thirtieth anniversary of the Supreme Court's decision in *Plyler v. Doe.*

One DACA recipient, Jin K. Park, first traveled as a seven-year-old from Seoul, South Korea, to New York City's Flushing neighborhood. Like Alfredo Lopez, Park was promptly enrolled in second grade. He grew up in American schools. As a high school student, within months of Obama's announcement, as he told me, Park applied for DACA. In 2020, now as a Harvard medical student, activist, and the first undocumented Rhodes Scholar, Park would write in the *Atlantic*, "We still don't know if we can count on staying for good, but we have always known that we are Americans, and that our advocacy for our place here is an essentially American endeavor."[43] His was a sentiment Alfredo Lopez shared. As Lopez told me, "I feel just as American as my wife who was born here."[44]

In the living room of his parents' home hangs a framed copy of the Supreme Court's synopsis of its decision in *Plyler v. Doe*. Lídia and José Lopez have lived in the same house for more than forty years. It is the same house where, before sunrise one morning in 1977, they woke their children and bundled them into their packed Dodge Monaco to drive two blocks to the federal district courthouse.

Near the end of his life, looking back over nearly four decades as a federal district judge, Judge William Wayne Justice singled out one case out of hundreds he had decided: *Plyler v. Doe*. "I feel that's the most important case that I've ever had."[45] Justice wasn't sure how many children had been able to study because of the decision; he reckoned a hundred thousand at least. In actuality, the count is more than a million. Of his career, he had one wish: "I hope people remember me for someone trying to do justice. That's what I've tried to do."[46]

THE PRESENT: THE GLOBAL VILLAGE PROJECT, GEORGIA

The streets of Clarkston, Georgia, were dark and almost entirely empty as we bounced along back roads in a small school bus early one morning. In the driver's seat sat Crispin Ilombe Wilondja, the school support specialist for the Global Village Project (GVP), which is the only school in the United States dedicated to teaching refugee girls.

We pulled up alongside an apartment complex and out of the darkness two girls, one Syrian and one Congolese, emerged and quietly boarded. A third was missing. Crispin picked up his phone: "*Salaam alaikum!*" On the other end of the line, the girl's father explained she was late, but he would drive her. We continued on. At the next stop, three girls bounded onto the bus. "You're late, Mr. Crispin!" they accused in mock indignation. Crispin chuckled. "Good morning! I think I'm exactly one minute late." The girls laughed as they took their seats.

For many of the students at GVP, Crispin is more than a bus driver, or a math teacher, one of his other roles at the school. He is like a family member. He knows the girls' birthdays, their favorite school subjects, the songs they like to sing. He has sat in their living rooms, and their families' numbers are logged in his phone. For fifteen young women, a third of the GVP school, he was their case manager when they were resettled in the United States. As girls board the bus, he can tell me the exact date and time each landed in America. He knows because he was there to greet them at the Hartsfield-Jackson Atlanta International Airport.

As they buckled up, Crispin took out his phone to call two Congolese sisters. "*Hu Jambo!*" His Swahili is warm and expressive. "Are you ready for school? Have you eaten enough *ugali?*" The sisters, Naomi and Casifa, had joined the school a month ago after arriving in the country two months earlier. When, in their first few days at GVP, they failed to meet the bus, Crispin went to their apartment to collect them. On the fourth morning, he suggested they set an alarm. Naomi didn't know how, so he taught her. He promised, too, to call every morning.

Never before had either sister attended school—not here, not in a Uganda refugee camp, not in the Democratic Republic of the Congo. But soon after the girls arrived in the United States, public school officials placed seventeen-year-old Naomi in eleventh grade. Understanding little and unable to communicate with either her peers or her teachers, she decided to drop out. Her mother needed help; her younger siblings needed food, clothing, and money for school supplies. She planned to get a job in the nearby chicken factories. That was when Crispin learned of the new family. He went to meet them, and soon after he introduced the two oldest sisters to GVP. Although dubious about American schools, Naomi decided to enroll.

Naomi and her sister were waiting for us when we pulled up to a row of brick apartments. Two Burmese sisters and another Congolese student scampered on just behind them. As the sky ripened to peach, we headed back across town lines to Decatur, a wealthier suburb of Atlanta.

Two of the girls were blasting Bollywood on their headphones, singing along in Hindi. "See, Mr. Crispin, we are learning a new language!" Crispin laughed, a rumbling chuckle. When we reached school, the girls piled out singing. The side of the bus was painted in bold purple letters: "The Global Village Project: One Girl at a Time."

———•———

The Global Village Project, located on the second floor of a church on the outskirts of Atlanta, teaches roughly forty young women, all born into conflict. They come from Cameroon, Colombia, and Chad, from Syria, Myanmar, Rwanda, Afghanistan, Pakistan, Eritrea, and the Democratic Republic of the Congo. They have spent years living in refugee camps in Uganda, Malaysia, Tanzania. Collectively they have lived in more than seventeen countries and speak at least as many languages, from Turkish to Tigrinya to Thai. The girls range in age from eleven to eighteen and on average have missed three years of formal education. Some, like Naomi, have never attended school in their life.

Their story is shared by roughly 130 million girls worldwide who, according to UNESCO, are not able to study—a class size so large that it equals roughly the entire population of Mexico.[47] Of those, approximately one in nine will likely never enter a classroom. The reasons are varied. The journey to school is unsafe. School uniforms and supplies are too expensive. Some girls remain home because they lack feminine hygiene products; others must care for younger siblings or work. In some communities their brothers' education takes priority or parents expect daughters to marry young. When families are displaced, the challenges for girls are compounded. Classrooms in refugee camps are invariably overcrowded, up to one hundred children to a class. School days are truncated, sometimes just two hours long. School resources are scarce and teachers are overworked and underpaid. Refugee girls attend primary school at lower rates than refugee boys. By the time they reach secondary school they are less likely to remain enrolled.[48]

These global statistics were deeply personal for Afghan families who began arriving in Clarkston, Georgia, in the early 2000s. For some of them, their daughters' formal education had ended when the Taliban had forced schools for girls to shut. Those Afghan girls, many now teenagers, were enrolling in middle and high school. But as many had been out of school for years, unsurprisingly, they understood little of what they were taught. Some began attending a local tutoring program. It was there that they met two professors retired from the University of Hawaii who themselves had recently come to the South. Suzie and Ricky Jacobs, hoping to grow connections in their new community, had begun volunteering to help children with their homework after school. When they met the teenage Afghan girls they were dumbfounded. Where did one begin in attempting to reclaim years of lost learning? Schools were ill equipped to meet their varied needs. The pressure to work or to marry weighed heavily. How, the couple wondered, could they help prevent the girls from dropping out? As Suzie, now in her eighties with sparkling blue eyes, remembered, "We thought, if only for those girls, could we do something?"

Suzie and Ricky began meeting with other wealthy, retired professionals in the community. Within months they had opened a free two-hour weekend program for high school refugee and immigrant students. They planned to offer academic tutoring. On the program's first Saturday, dozens of residents arrived—not just teenage girls, but also their grandmothers and their baby brothers, their fathers and mothers, their aunts, cousins, and friends. Some sought tutoring, others came with questions about job applications, or with the hope of practicing English.

The seed of an idea grew in the hours of the Saturday tutoring program—an experiment that could form a bridge between global conflict and American high schools. Suzie, Ricky, and a handful of other volunteers began writing grants and raising money. In downtown Decatur, a church offered up its second-floor classrooms. In the fall of 2009 GVP opened, a private middle school with thirty girls drawn from across the world. By then a few of the Afghan girls had, with support, successfully graduated high school or aged out of the system. But Suzie and the others knew that there were many more who shared their story.

Sun was one of those young women. Before being resettled in Clarkston at the age of twelve, Sun, a Burmese girl of the persecuted Karen people, had lived all her life in a Thai refugee camp. On arrival in America, Sun spoke no English and had only ever attended the camp's small, ill-staffed schools. She was assigned to fifth grade and hated it. "No one wanted to be my friend or even sit on the bus with me." In class she comprehended little. She had been in the country a little over a year when a woman approached her family. A new school had recently opened, one for girls like her. Hesitantly, Sun enrolled.

In the small classrooms above the church she was shocked by what she found. Her new classmates might come from all around the world, might be all different ages, might speak an array of languages, but their stories were surprisingly similar. And at GVP, everyone was curious about her and about her heritage. Her teachers showed up at the local Karen new year celebration; in the classroom girls swapped food from home.

Feeling accepted, Sun finally had space to study. She graduated from GVP and enrolled in high school. In 2016, as a high school senior, she received a thick packet in the mail. In it, she found a remarkable letter. The young Karen woman had been selected as one of just one thousand high school students nationwide to receive a Millennium Gates Scholarship. The scholarship would fully fund her undergraduate education, as well as graduate studies after college.[49] As Sun told me in 2019, she dreamed of one day becoming a teacher.

———•———

In a classroom, the principal of GVP, Dr. Amy Pelissero, held aloft a potted fern in front of a group of mesmerized young women. Her actions had been spurred by a question asked by a girl wearing a black hijab: "What does it mean to be 'uprooted'?"

We were in the midst of a reading class. Seven girls had books spread across two tables. Behind black-rimmed glasses, Amy considered her students. Together they sat about dissecting the word. A Congolese girl supplied a definition of roots. "They keep trees standing straight and give them food and water." An Afghan student in a teal headscarf exuberantly spotted the connection between flora and fauna. "If you are from the United States, you belong in this country. Rooted means you belong!" A Pakistani student almost leapt from her seat. "So, uprooted means you move from a country!"

That was when Amy spotted the fern and took it down from the windowsill. "Is it easy," she asked, "to uproot and replant this fern?" "No!" the girls chorused. Nodding, Amy took hold of the thin stems and yanked. The girls gasped. Exposed roots dangle, shedding dirt. "You are right, uprooting is more than just moving from one place to another. It can be hard. When you find a new place you also have to find soft ground to grow new roots." The Pakistani girl's eyes lit up. "Like us! It's like how we move from one place to another and find a better place to live." Amy smiled. "Yes, sometimes you might find a better place, or even just a different place. But you too might have to have some soft ground to grow in." Around the classroom, everyone nodded.

What does it mean to belong? For nearly 26 million refugees across the globe, roughly 50 million people internally displaced because of conflict, and millions more internally displaced because of natural disasters, exclusion is a daily, lived experience.[50] As Harvard professor Sarah Dryden-Peterson describes, for refugees, "the foundation of many conflicts is built on a lack of belonging." Dr. Dryden-Peterson has devoted her career to working with refugees and those who support displaced people around the world. She is particularly concerned about the future of young people caught up in an eddy of conflicts, epidemics, and natural disasters. How do the world's 13 million refugee children imagine a future when there is a very real worry that tomorrow they will no longer be welcome?[51] As Dr. Dryden-Peterson puts it, "Your sense of belonging is always tattered at the edges, because you don't know when someone else is going to make a decision that means you can't stay."

The vast majority of the globe's displaced children will grow up with this uncertainty. According to the United Nations High Commissioner for Refugees (UNHCR), each year less than 1 percent of the world's refugees are granted permanent residence in another country—providing them the chance to feel they belong to both a community and a country once more.[52] Schools, Dr. Dryden-Peterson believes, have an essential role to play in welcoming and grounding displaced students. But it is not enough that schools deliver academic content. For a refugee child, Dr. Dryden-Peterson explains, "If they don't have the sense of 'I am comfortable here, I can imagine myself here, I feel safe here,' then very little learning can happen."

At GVP, Amy knows her most important goal is to ensure her students understand they belong. Amy has been at the school since close to its founding, first as a teacher and then as its head. For nearly a decade she has been grappling with how her school can best support students like Sun and Naomi. For children who have long been denied access to school, where does one begin? Academically a girl might enter GVP clutching a first-grade education. But for years she might have been forced to assume the role and responsibilities of adults—working, negotiating government systems, surviving. Curriculums must honor both realities.

The task for Amy and her teachers is herculean: in two to three years, to have the girls master as much as possible of an accelerated pre-K–eighth-grade curriculum so they can have a fighting chance at high school. While officially a middle school, GVP has no grade levels. Where to place a fifteen-year-old Burmese student? Age would put her in tenth grade, academic tests might suggest second grade. The disparities can be confusing, or embarrassing. Instead, GVP has three levels that loosely correlate with a collection of grades. Flexibility is essential. Instruction, by necessity, must be tailored, allowing each girl the best chance at jump-starting her education.

Growing up as a Somali refugee in Djibouti, Nasteho recalls her father telling her from the time she was little, "I never want you to depend on a man. I want you to be educated." But for a displaced person in a sprawling refugee camp, schooling was scarce. In 2014, when her family secured resettlement in Georgia, Nasteho was fourteen yet had managed to cobble together only a handful of school semesters. Based on her age, she was placed in sixth grade. Her new school was huge. She was ignored by teachers, bullied by students. A month after arriving, she heard of a special school designed for refugee girls. Nasteho, who favors black hijabs, grins in remembering her arrival at GVP. The small school felt like home. Every one of the many adults knew her by name; they also knew her parents, her sister, her cousins. School was a family affair.

Volunteers conceived of GVP, and to this day volunteers remain the backbone of the program. More than a hundred mostly older white women and men commit an hour, sometimes more each week. Mindful of the potential pitfalls in pairing well-meaning white volunteers with largely nonwhite students, Amy and the GVP staff hold mandatory evening trainings for volunteers to examine and discuss power and privilege. It is essential, challenging, and ongoing work that Amy thinks about often. During the school day, volunteers sit one-on-one with students, providing the individual attention most teachers can only dream of. Together they read books, review math problems, discuss historical movements. One afternoon an older British woman sat side by side with a seventeen-year-old Eritrean student. Together they contemplated a story of giraffe conservation. The girl, her finger following the text, began to read, word by slow word.

For a refugee child seeking to belong, learning the language of their new country is one of their first hurdles. It is a messy, painstaking process. Mistakes are a must, but few teenagers will willingly make mistakes in the presence of peers. I vividly remember my own high school Spanish class. My rehearsed words always tangled in my mouth, my cheeks flamed, my heart raced. I hated the class for how it made me feel. My newcomer students can relate. GVP's volunteers provide an elegant solution. Women, many the age of grandmothers, are far less intimidating than teenagers. The volunteers give the girls a chance to sound out imperfect sentences and struggle through conversations with native speakers without the pressure of trying to impress. This is how Nasteho, years ago, learned to read, with one of GVP's founders sitting next to her.

Nasteho was in her second year at GVP in 2015 when Crispin, then still a refugee resettlement case manager, first learned of the school. Crispin's calling defies definitions. He has been a secondary school principal, a university professor, and a pastor in his home country of the Democratic Republic of the Congo (DRC). He has worked as a hospital chaplain in Nigeria and Benin. He holds master's degrees in philosophy, theology, and biology. He wrote his master's thesis on HIV/AIDS prevention while studying in California. But Crispin never intended to make the United States his home. His work and life were in Kinshasa, the capital of the DRC, and it was there that he began speaking out in sermons and on the streets in defense of the poor and against a corrupt Congolese government. For his activism he was arrested repeatedly. When Crispin heard whispers that he was to be assassinated, he fled into the jungle. There he hid for a year until friends smuggled him out to the United States in 2011. Degrees and professional experience notwithstanding, when Crispin was first granted political asylum, the only place that would hire him was Goodwill. He cleaned floors for $7.25 an hour. It would take four years before Lutheran Services hired him as a case manager to help refugees restart their lives.

One afternoon in 2016 he was asked to bring a newly arrived girl to tour an unusual school. The girl, like Naomi, had never attended formal school, could not even scratch out the letters of her name. Crispin, who accompanied her on the tour of GVP, was mesmerized. From that day on, every time he believed a girl on his caseload might be eligible, he brought her family to tour the school. If he heard of other girls in the Clarkston refugee community, he invited them too. When, a year later, the school had an opening for a bus driver, Crispin did not hesitate to apply. For him GVP worked miracles. "I see a girl who does not know how to write her name and then three years later she is reading and speaking confidently." He sighed deeply in satisfaction. Every adult in the school—teachers, volunteers, support staff—holds a common belief: that these young women belong in school; that they belong here. It is a belief they are not shy about reminding their students. "Education is the best gift we can offer these girls," Crispin told me. A pastor at heart, he often speaks in sermons. "I tell them the future of your family depends on you. Your parents are struggling. They hold night jobs and have low wages. You have these opportunities. You have to break the cycle of poverty. My dream is to see you one day become doctors and lawyers. And you can do it. You will do it. That is what I tell them."

When Nasteho, the young Somali student, graduated from the Global Village Project in 2016, she left with more than a diploma; she took with her a whole community. Her family had known no one when they landed in Georgia. The multigenerational community that once anchored their daily life in Djibouti was dispersed. In the United States much had to be relearned: new language, new government systems, new schools—all made more challenging without support. Over two years in the suburbs of Atlanta, Nasteho's family had rebuilt a community. GVP had been the connector—not just for her and her sister, but for her parents as well.

Yet GVP's principal, Amy Pelissero, and her teachers knew that two or three years would never be sufficient time to fully rebuild a community that would support their students through high school. So the school decided to extend their support long past graduation. GVP assembled a bevy of volunteers, mostly older women, to act as mentors.

Nasteho was paired with such a mentor, a local professional who had sent her own three children through the school system. Nasteho's parents were unfamiliar with American report cards, high school course tracks, and extracurricular offerings, but Nasteho's mentor could explain them.

When her parents could not attend school functions and teacher conferences, Nasteho's mentor, with their permission, went in their stead. When Nasteho wanted to learn to drive, her mentor's husband patiently taught her.

All GVP graduates, if they wish, are paired with mentors—adults who edit their job applications, review scholarship opportunities, make sense of report cards, and recommend school clubs. GVP's mentoring program was created to last through a graduate's freshman year of high school, smoothing the transition between schools. But for many pairings the relationships last far longer. Eight years after graduating from GVP, Sun still meets weekly with her mentor. As a high school senior, Nasteho does the same. "My parents work a lot," Nasteho explained. "They would love to help, but they don't know how, so my mentor steps in."

Often mentors meet to swap suggestions: who is the high school's best math teacher, what English teacher should be avoided. Many have already navigated these secondary school systems for their own children. This mentoring is a role I know well. I too call financial aid offices, help decode tax forms, assist as students fill in internship applications. I've looked over apartment contracts and medical bills. They are tasks my parents, American-born, did for me. But for many families new to the country, language barriers, long work schedules, and opaque school bureaucracies can make it hard for them to always be effective advocates for their children. High schools, too, are not always welcoming to refugee families. Sometimes GVP mentors—often privileged by skin color, English fluency, and relative wealth—step in to advocate, because schools are often more likely to listen to them.

Young women like Nasteho are themselves learning to become advocates for their parents. "You become the eyes to the world for your parents," Nasteho reflected. She and her peers decipher bills and official paperwork for their families and their neighbors. With burgeoning skills and confidence, the young women have begun speaking up for their community.

Sometimes, however, these young women's newly acquired authority is greeted with ambivalence by their families. Society's expectations and refugee experiences can limit what girls and their families imagine for their futures. "These girls accomplish so much," Amy reflected one afternoon. "But ultimately, because they are women there are still so many forces exerted upon them and not enough freedom to choose." As they reclaim years of lost education, sometimes students find they need help convincing their families of their new goals.

"These girls have dreams, and sometimes their family is not ready to help them," Crispin explained. Crispin, though, is undeterred. He is an indispensable link between the communities of Decatur and Clarkston. When Crispin visits families, he is a preacher, a teacher, and a case manager rolled into one. "I use everything from psychology to philosophy." Speaking close to a dozen languages, he is able to talk with many in their home tongue. When he cannot, as for a recently arrived Afghan family, he enlists the help of school families. This way, he noted, conversations "are often more open." For Crispin, his students' challenges are personal. His own mother attended school only until the second grade. She married at thirteen, gave birth to his brother at fourteen. "If my mother had been educated," Crispin mused, "our lives could have been different."

The students at the Global Village Project exist within two neighboring communities on the edge of Atlanta—cosmopolitan Clarkston, where they live, and whiter and wealthier Decatur, where they study. The two cities were not always so dissimilar. Clarkston was once a small, sleepy suburb, majority white, and heavily conservative. Southeast Asian refugees were resettled there soon after President Carter signed the Refugee Act of 1980. More followed. In Clarkston, the newcomers found affordable houses recently vacated by white families fleeing an influx of Black families, and they traveled to downtown jobs on newly built public transportation lines. Today, Clarkston is dubbed by many "the most diverse square mile in America"—home to families from close to sixty nations. Decatur, though, never underwent this transformation.

Amy worries about the gap between the communities. She understands that tension can arise between recently arrived refugee families and longtime residents. Across the globe, displaced newcomers are not always welcomed. Refugees often eat different food, wear different clothes, believe in different faiths, practice different customs. Some are seen as a threat or as a burden. Others are accused of taking jobs, of monopolizing resources, of being extremists in disguise. Three days before I first rode the bus with Crispin in the winter of 2020, the US government announced an extension of its policy excluding most immigrants from several countries, a policy referred to by many as a "Muslim ban." The list originally included Iraq, Somalia, and Syria; now added to the ban were Sudan, Nigeria, Tanzania, Eritrea, Myanmar, and Kyrgyzstan. For some of the girls at GVP, these countries were once home. What, Amy wondered, will residents of Decatur think of her students? And what can the school do to help connect the two communities?

For this reason, on four Fridays throughout the year, the school opens its doors to the city for "Authors' Teas." In a large hall in the church's basement, students recite original poems, perform short skits, and give presentations on what they have recently studied. Families, mentors, GVP alumni, and many curious community members act as audience. I sat amid such a crowd in the fall of 2019, watching a willowy woman, Elise Witt, conduct the school's choir: "The moon's the only face I know / In this new land I roam / But where I see a friendly face / I can make a home."[53] Now-graduated GVP girls composed the song years ago with a visiting artist. Perhaps it was her family history that first drew Elise, the school's artist in residence and director of musical programs, to GVP close to a decade ago. Her mother had fled Nazi Germany. Born in Switzerland after the war, Elise immigrated with her family to upstate New York at the age of four. For her first six months in school she did not speak at all.

For refugee children to believe they belong, they must feel welcomed and accepted—not just by peers, but by neighbors. And for this, Dr. Dryden-Peterson notes, long-established residents must believe that arriving refugees will enrich their community and that supporting newcomers will not come at the expense of those already there.

Amy and teachers like Elise increasingly seek out opportunities for their students to interact with Decatur residents and the greater Atlanta community. The girls perform frequently at local colleges, museums, libraries, film festivals, and art centers. I sat in on rehearsal one afternoon. An exuberant Congolese student clapped her hands, calling her peers to order. "Attention please, USA people!" That day they are practicing for yet another upcoming public performance. "If I drop my bags will you take my hand? / Will you take a while with me in this new land?"[54]

As the final notes floated in the air, an Afghan girl wearing a navy blue headscarf nodded in appreciation. "We sound like professionals."

Still, Amy worries whether wealthier, established residents will patronize or pity her pupils. How can she ensure they recognize the girls' strengths and come to see them as part of their community? In 2013 the school devised an unusual idea. On a crisp fall morning, seventy-five mothers and daughters—those newly arrived and those who had been there for generations, GVP families and community neighbors—walked the five miles from Clarkston to Decatur. Every year since, the walk has been repeated. In 2019 more than three hundred set off together from Clarkston, along busy streets and under bypasses, past parks and through quiet neighborhoods. Some brought their dogs, others pushed strollers. Many linked arms. Passing cars slowed and honked. "It was a sight to behold," Amy recalled.

Some in the Decatur community, she had learned, were unaware of the large neighboring resettlement community. Others, as she had witnessed, were openly prejudiced. But many, Amy acknowledged, simply "never had an opportunity to speak with or know our refugee brothers and sisters." On the morning of the walk, Amy watched families walking hand in hand. "These are folks that might not have otherwise ever known or met each other—walking together for education, for equity, for dreams. It is a beautiful thing." The walk's finish line is the lawn outside GVP. There, the school hosts a party: dancing, face painting, hula hooping. In 2019 Nasteho stood before a jubilant crowd. "Global Village is a family to me," she proclaimed proudly. "If you're lucky enough to enter into this community, you get a lifelong community and lifelong support."

———◆———

Late one evening in December of 2019, Amy saw her phone light up with a text. "Ms. Amy, this is Nasteho. I have really good news!" Nasteho had spent the fall semester applying to colleges. With her mentor's help she had written, edited, and revised essays, and at her mentor's urging she had applied for scholarships. Out of more than 15,000 nominations, Nasteho, a young Somali refugee who had spent years out of school, was awarded a prestigious Posse Scholarship, which would fully cover tuition at George Washington University. Amy still recalls the day Nasteho arrived at GVP five years earlier, new to the country. "Sometimes you are blown away when you meet a person. I remember thinking Nasteho was going to rock the world."

I spoke with Nasteho early in 2020. "I can now see," she told me, "what my father imagined for me." The young woman, who has always loved math and science, plans to build a career in public health. But she wants to do even more: "As a refugee, you need that sense of community. Once you get that, you thrive." One day she hopes to return the favor to others who will follow.

One afternoon I accompanied Crispin on the school bus once more. There was none of the sleepiness of the morning ride. A Congolese student braided the hair of her Burmese classmate, a Syrian girl hummed a song. One student pretended to deliver a fiery speech, to the amusement of her seatmates. Mostly there was laughter.

The hours and days I spent at GVP were filled with laughter—more laughter than I have ever heard in a middle or high school. Girls broke out into chuckles on successfully completing a multiplication table; they were prone to giggle while constructing a timeline of ancient civilizations. Laughter bounced off the walls between classes. School felt like classrooms full of cousins. The girls laughed at themselves, at each other, with each other. Here, learning was loved.

Riding on the bus that afternoon I joined in the laughter. Slowly the bus emptied. The girls trooped down the steps, waving good-bye, disappearing again into apartment complexes. Our last stop was at the home of Naomi and Casifa, the school's newest students—the girls who only a month ago had begun attending school for the first time. The girls' younger siblings raced out of the house to hug Crispin. They climbed onto the bus. "We want to come to school too," they told him.

On the drive back, Crispin was thoughtful. "It is a joy to see them so happy. War is dehumanizing." But, he explained, "Education is a restorative process." In his life Crispin has had many professions, but now he cannot imagine more meaningful work. "My joy is to witness the progress of our girls. My joy is to see those girls becoming leaders in their families. My joy is to see the girls who have graduated now doing great in high school." And, he added quietly, "If I can contribute in any way, that will be my joy."

THE PERSONAL: DIANE

"Miss?!" Nineteen-year-old Diane called out in exasperation from across the room. "There is no way for me to answer this question!" It was mid-October 2018, and ten of my seniors were busy in an after-school session, filling in the college Common Application. For more than two hours I had been bouncing between computers answering questions.

As I sat down next to Diane, she jabbed her finger at a question on the screen: "List the countries you are a citizen of," the application requested. "What do I put?" she asked, perplexed. "I'm a citizen of nowhere."

Diane came into the world in the spring of 1999, in a grass-thatched hut in a sprawling refugee camp near the northern border of Zambia. Barely thirty miles away, her parents' home country, the Democratic Republic of the Congo (DRC), was embroiled in the second of two brutal wars.

Her parents were newlyweds when the first Congolese War erupted in their eastern province four years earlier. Diane's family had been well off—her mother an accountant who loved numbers, her father a successful businessman. Yet as bloodshed engulfed their homeland, few were safe. In the spring of 1997, the couple fled south with Diane's older sister, then two years old, and pregnant with Diane's older brother. Her mother gave birth barely a week after the dictator Mobutu Sese Seko fled into exile. Peace was declared, but home was no longer home, and so the small family continued, mostly on foot, traveling more than five hundred miles, until they staggered across the Zambian border. A small mud hut in a burgeoning border refugee camp became home, and that is where their third child, Diane, was born.

Diane grew up believing she was Zambian. Her family cooked Zambian dishes, they worshiped in a Zambian church, they spoke the Zambian language Nyanja. Her parents rarely talked of the DRC, and Diane chose not to ask. Dwelling on the Congo only conjured impossible futures. What if there had been no war? What if her parents had not lost their jobs? What if they could afford to go to a good school? "If I was there," she wondered, "would I have to suffer as much?" It was less painful to not ask.

Her neighbors in the camp hailed from Rwanda, Burundi, Angola, and the DRC, but in school she and her classmates dutifully read in their textbooks that Zambians were people born in Zambia, and so they believed that this is what they were. As Diane reflected, "I took the meaning I wanted."

But officially Diane was not Zambian. Nor was she officially Congolese. Diane is one of a handful of my students who is stateless, one of more than four million such people globally, according to the UNHCR.[55] Throughout her life, no country has ever claimed her as theirs. Nowhere does she legally belong.

Now in 2018, sitting in the computer lab on that crisp fall afternoon, we realized that even the Common Application would not acknowledge Diane's existence.

———◆———

Diane first walked into my classroom a year earlier, in 2017. She was a boisterous member of my first-period US history class, sitting side by side with Safiya and two seats down from Robert. By her own admission, she was decidedly not a morning person, but Diane was surprisingly bubbly in class—chatting with classmates from the Ivory Coast, Spain, Japan, and the Dominican Republic. Like in the camp, her new peers came from many countries. A global classroom, to her, felt like home.

Once the bell rang, Diane was a reliable leader of group discussions. While many of my students, still mastering English, often grew shy when asked to participate, Diane was categorically confident. During our debate on women's suffrage she argued ferociously. When we studied chemical weapons used in World War I, she asked sharp questions. Never was she timid about speaking her mind, and often her insights and her conviction made me smile in admiration.

But for Diane, as I would learn many months later, school had not always been a place where she felt at home. It was in a Zambian classroom that Diane was first told she didn't belong. In 2012, at the age of thirteen, Diane moved with her family to the town of Solwezi, a few bumpy hours' drive from the refugee camp. Her father had secured a small shop, filling the shelves with kitchen and cleaning supplies. As long as they returned monthly to check in, the family was granted permission to live outside the camp's perimeters. Diane was in her new school less than a week when a classmate pointed at her during the lunch break lull. "*Caburunda!*" she accused.

The slur, technically denoting a person from Burundi, was a common catchall for any refugee. As Diane explained, "They didn't even bother to ask where you came from, it just meant you didn't belong here." Never before had anyone called her *caburunda*. Diane was furious, but also confused. She was confidently and proudly Zambian. But when she marched home, incensed, to tell her father, she was shocked by his resignation. "That's what they call us," he told his daughter.

Doubt sprouted, first small, but it grew steadily, watered daily by peers who called her *caburunda, caburunda, caburunda.* If parents saw their children playing with Diane, they too hurled the epithet. Friends took to hiding if they saw their parents coming—they feared being seen publicly with a refugee. "I started thinking, who am I?" Diane would write in my class years later. "Where do I belong if not in Zambia? I realized that if Zambia didn't recognize me as its citizen, then I had no country to call my own." Some days at school the otherness became too much. Diane would hide her head in her arms, weeping silently onto her desk.

In 2013 Diane, now in seventh grade, had lived in the town of Solwezi for a year when one night a pounding thrust her from sleep. With a bang the family's front door slapped open. Burly policemen barged inside. Diane's father was thrown to the floor. There were screams and shouts and then silence. Her parents, older sister, and brother were arrested and taken into the night. Fourteen-year-old Diane stood wide-eyed in the living room, her five younger siblings, the littlest only four, clutching at her hands.

Terrifying questions ricocheted through her mind: What if her family was deported? What if they never returned? In the inky hours of early morning, Diane realized that she was now her family's protector. "I had to grow up that night," she told me years later. As light broke over the horizon, none of the children changed into school uniforms. Diane locked the doors and kept her family inside. Scrolling through her mother's phone, Diane dialed a pastor in the refugee camp. Within hours his wife arrived bearing food. Diane busied herself with cooking. "Mom and Dad will return tomorrow," she promised her siblings. Day became night and they did not return. A second day and still no news. When anxiety swamped her, Diane slipped into her room to cry, reemerging face dry and composed. She had to be tough.

Close to twilight on the third day, her family returned. They smelled of sweat and urine. But they were home. Later, Diane learned it had been a policeman who frequented her parents' shop who had reported her family, angered when Diane's mom had finally requested that he pay for what he took.

Never again did Diane believe herself to be a Zambian. But she watched her classmates with envy. Zambians, Diane explained, "move like free people. They can be wherever they want, they can speak however they want, they can do whatever they want." For Diane every step, every word was carefully calculated. "We lived like in a little cage."

Three years later, and more than sixteen years after her parents first applied for refugee resettlement, Diane's family learned that the United States would welcome them. It was still dark the morning the family quietly slipped out of their apartment. Hardly anyone knew of their departure. Diane had never made close friends. As a result, leaving was easier; there were no painful good-byes. Through the final interviews and immunizations Diane silently fretted that at any moment they would be sent back, told to start over, told to wait another seventeen years. But their luck held, and in late August 2016 her family landed in Massachusetts.

———◆———

Although Diane had arrived in the United States on the very first day of a new school year, it would take nearly two months until she stepped foot into a classroom. At first she did not mind the delay. Everything was new, beautiful, beckoning to be explored—the arching tree-lined streets, the elegant brick buildings, the grassy lawns. There were early lessons in American living to take in. No, milk did not flow from the taps, despite what a cousin had reported. And no, you should not place hot pans on the floor. Frying fish one day, Diane had moved a pot of oil to cool on the floor only to find it had melted a ghastly black ring into the plastic flooring—back home the floor was earth.

But within weeks after the family had settled into a new home, one by one they began leaving for classes, many of her siblings to school and her parents to language classes at a local nonprofit. But seventeen-year-old Diane was left waiting. Stuck at home, she began to worry. What if they didn't let her attend school? To still her mind, she cleaned every inch of the apartment. She cooked Zambian stews and mashed fufu. And then one day, as the autumn air grew crisp, she finally heard the words she had been waiting for: She could go to school.

Nervously, Diane stepped into her first class in an American high school: biology. She should have been entering eleventh grade, but due to missing paperwork she was enrolled in ninth alongside her sister. "You must be Diane," a young woman greeted her, "Welcome." Diane stopped short, shocked. In Zambia she had always been one among a crowded sea of faces. "Hey you" or "you there" was how teachers referred to her, if they singled her out at all. But here, a teacher was calling her by her name. "She knows me!" Diane thought excitedly. "It felt good," she remembered years later. "I felt acknowledged." The feeling was unfamiliar.

Biology quickly grew to become her favorite class at Lowell, closely followed by math. Unlike some students, Diane's transition was relatively smooth. For years her Zambian instructors had lectured in English. Studying came easily, too; memorization was an essential skill in her Zambian classes that relied heavily on taking copious notes. But in Lowell, lessons were rarely limited to the blackboard. Instead of attempting to imagine cells and molecules, in biology class they watched videos, handled models, created replicas. Learning became physical, and to Diane much more real.

Growing up in the refugee camp, Diane had not attended school to learn. She attended to eat. Often she arrived hungry and, as she would write years later in my class, "My only option was to make friends who had food. So my mission at school wasn't to learn, but to get on these students' good side in order to eat." Classes burst with students squished into desks. Latecomers were relegated to squatting on the floor. Diane was often late. Unable to read, she and some other girls took to tearing out pages of their textbook, sheet by sheet, to fashion paper dolls. Then one day in third grade, her dad saw her abysmal grades and asked to see her books. Two lonely pages remained. Sternly he asked his daughter to read a sentence. Diane could not formulate words out of letters. Chagrined, Diane started studying. By eighth grade she began showing up extra early, ensuring that she secured a seat at a desk.

But even as Diane began to excel, learning could not always be a priority. After her family moved from the refugee camp to the city, they were still required most months to check in with the camp, a round trip that often translated into days of missed school. "We have to visit our grandmother," Diane would lie to her teachers. "We have to visit our aunt," she would offer up the next month. Each trip necessitated a new fictitious relative. School could never know where they were really going.

In the United States however, learning, perhaps for the first time, took priority. And Diane thrived. She read her first novel, led her first group presentation. Now, with ready access to Wi-Fi, if a topic was confusing—meiosis or verb conjugations—she could simply look it up and study it. Here her math teacher didn't yell at her, her science teacher didn't strike her with a cane. If she needed extra help, there were tutors in the sprawling library. Unlike before, she made friends with ease, including with other girls from across Africa—new arrivals from Sierra Leone, Liberia, the Ivory Coast. At the end of her first year in the United States, Diane not only passed all her classes—she made honor roll.

Some learning was harder. Barely two months into school, Diane read for the first time of the brutality of American slavery. She had never liked history: Her family's past was too painful, and her Zambian classes taught a history that could never be hers. Safest to distance herself. But in a crowded second-floor New England classroom Diane could not stop herself from caring. At lunch, she and the other girls from across sub-Saharan Africa conferred. How could slavery have happened? It seemed too abhorrent to contemplate. In class Diane read about the Middle Passage, the slave auctions, the cotton fields. The history was too much. She could not stop her eyes from filling. Wanting no one to see, she hid her head in her hands and feigned fatigue.

Despite her grades and English fluency, Diane was not sure where she fit in. Her new classmates were of every shade, representing so many ethnicities, so many countries. She learned quickly never to assume but to ask which peers were Chinese, which Cambodian, which Japanese. Yet what was she? "I can't call myself African American because I wasn't born here," Diane reasoned. She was African, but from where? The DRC had never been home, Zambia had never recognized her. When others asked, she told them Zambia, and did not elaborate.

Only a few months after arriving in Lowell, her father came home one evening with a pronouncement. "From now on," he told his family, "we will no longer speak Nyanja. I only want to hear English, nothing else." His children peered at him skeptically; his wife smiled. Sure, they nodded. But within a week they were all speaking Nyanja once more.

When Diane joined my US history class as a sophomore, in 2017, she was only starting her second year in the United States. I already knew her younger sister, who had been a quiet member of my freshman world history class the year before. But Diane, eighteen, and slowly feeling more comfortable in the halls of our school, never seemed shy.

When in October we embarked on writing a class cookbook, she wrote about Zambian samosas, a family favorite that her mom had prepared when Diane was nervous on her very first day of school. A good meal, her mother had promised, would help calm her down. To celebrate our recipes, each student brought in their family dishes and shared them with the class. Diane piled her plate high with her friends' offerings— silky *chawanmushi*, pillowy *pão de queijo*, crispy *kubba*.

In school she was no longer anxious. She knew her way around the warren of halls, felt confident asking for help if she needed it. She found herself with friends—not just Africans, but many others pulled from across the globe. In January she teamed up with two classmates to write an op-ed that was published two months later in the local newspaper. In March she joined forces with her classmate Safiya to take the lead in organizing our class's civic advocacy. She was beginning to realize that others cared less about where she came from and more about what she contributed.

That summer, soon after school let out, Diane came home one afternoon to find a jumble of large priority-mail envelopes. Home alone, Diane excitedly sat down to open them. Out of the first fell her sister's US green card. Diane's eyes bulged. For months she had pestered her mother each morning: When might the cards arrive? Now, here they were. She ripped open the next: her brother's green card. Envelope after envelope. Her dad's card, her mother's card, her other siblings' cards. Then there were no more envelopes left to open. Yet her card was nowhere to be found.

Hurriedly Diane pawed through the mail again. Perhaps she had missed it. But she had not. Fear filled her body. "Did I do anything wrong?" she panicked. "Are they going to ship me back?"

That night her siblings celebrated. Diane plastered on a smile. She wanted to share in their joy, but dread clogged her throat. The green card "shows that I'm identified," Diane explained, "that the country knows me, that I live here, that I belong here." Like in Zambia, without identification Diane believed that her security remained in jeopardy, and so too her future.

Each day following, Diane returned home and went directly to the mail, pushing through the envelopes, searching in vain. And then, a number of days later, one more priority envelope finally arrived. Ripping it open, Diane held in front of her a green card with her name printed in small black type. She shouted and jumped and danced across the living room. For the first time in her life, Diane felt recognized.

Diane returned to school in the fall of 2018 as a green card holder and as a high school senior. Near the end of the previous academic year, the school system had credited Diane for courses she had taken in Zambia. For this reason, she entered her third year not as a junior, but as a senior. With the switch, Diane found herself scrambling to select and apply to colleges, to plan for the future.

Diane was ten years old when she realized she must become a doctor. Still living in the refugee camp, she had slipped out of school early one morning, not to play hooky, but to go to the camp's hospital with her friend who was shivering, likely with malaria. Diane had always avoided the hospital; many did, if they could. No yearly checkup, no visits when she occasionally fell sick. Like many of her neighbors, her family bought medicine in the market and self-medicated at home. But that morning the two girls found a space in a crowded dirty hallway and waited to be seen. Mothers soothed wailing infants on their hips, elderly men dozed against a grimy wall. Noxious disinfectant that permeated the air made Diane lightheaded. Hours trudged by, yet few were called. Diane grew incensed. Why were sick people left waiting? Why were the halls so filthy? Why were the nurses so curt? As morning slid into afternoon, the girls, resigned, sighed, stretched, shook out stiff limbs, and walked home. After some time her friend recovered. Diane never returned to the hospital, and she vowed to study medicine.

That conviction drove her slow and steady improvement in classes. Year after year her grades crept upward. She fell in love with biology, took a liking to numbers. But when she entered high school in Solwezi, she watched her older brother and sister graduate and find themselves unemployable. Diane realized that without legal status her future was bounded. Lack of citizenship trumped diplomas. Without papers, she had no hope of becoming a doctor, no chance of legally getting a job. What, Diane wondered, was the point of going to college? What was the point of dreaming of a future that was unattainable?

Hers is a question shared by many displaced young people worldwide. In a majority of the countries boasting large refugee camps, occupants are rarely allowed to work outside the camp's perimeter. Governments understandably worry first about employment opportunities for their own citizens. But as only a tiny fraction of the world's refugees are ever resettled, displaced children are left to grow up knowing that, for them, most careers are unattainable. One needs tremendous motivation to keep studying, to keep dreaming, to hope that one day laws will change, wars will end, or countries will welcome you. In the United States, undocumented children face a similar struggle. When they realize that legal work is foreclosed to them, it can take enormous will to keep working to succeed in school, when they know that effort likely will not be acknowledged.

For Diane, the United States gave her back a future—the chance to dream, and to plan, and to study. In the fall of 2018 Diane became a reliable member of my cohort of students meeting weekly after school in the computer lab to look up colleges and edit personal statements. It was on one such afternoon we stumbled upon the Common Application's demand: "List the countries you are a citizen of." After much deliberation, and rabbit holes of research, we put Zambia—it was not correct, but no option was.

———•———

That fall Diane had joined my upper-level seminar, a course exploring America's diversity and history of social justice movements. I explained to my students I wanted them to also study their personal histories, as they would help us create a better understanding of the United States. In late October I asked my class to construct a family tree. They did not need to limit themselves to biological relatives, I told them. They could choose who counted as their family. Tell us about each person you include, I asked, perhaps where they live, or what language they speak, or what they love. Students spread out across the room; some pulled out phones and called up mothers, uncles, grandmothers. Diane sat quietly near a window, unsure. "I never wanted to think about back home . . . it was just too much." Even in the United States, her family continued to speak little of the past, and Diane continued not to ask. "I preferred to just move on. I didn't want to look back. It would get me thinking about what happened and I didn't want to think. I just wanted to move forward, to live life thinking about tomorrow."

But as her classmates began mapping connections, Diane hesitantly put pencil to paper. In vibrant colors she shaded in a wide-trunked, branching tree. She started with her siblings: the sister who loved reading, the brother who loved cars. And then, at home, she tentatively began to ask questions. To the upper branches she added others, grandmothers and grandfathers who lived in a country her parents had fled before she was born.

As the days grew shorter, students began selecting stories—one story each to include in a book we were writing about what it meant to be American. Already they had begun to share with each other small moments of their lives. For Diane, those snippets were a revelation. "Sometimes you feel like you go through things by yourself," Diane remembers thinking. But in class, she described, "I realized that others had gone through their own struggles, it was not just me alone." Diane decided that she was ready to look back.

Occasionally, back in Zambia, Diane would sit alone and write and write and write, pouring her worries, her anguish, her anger out onto lined paper. No sooner did she finish than she shredded her words into nothing. But now, for the first time, the sentences remained intact. She unburied memories—writing, and editing, and rewriting for weeks. She wrote about the refugee camp, about school, about being called *caburunda*, about not belonging. Once she started, she found she couldn't stop. "It felt like I was letting go."

In the last week of the semester I gathered my students in a circle on the floor. Quietly I passed out their stories, making sure everyone got someone else's to read. For the next forty-five minutes they sat and read, passing the stories around the circle. Occasionally a smile flitted across a student's face, another might gasp. But mostly it was silent. Only the piercing school bell broke their concentration.

We gathered once more on the last morning of the semester for a final group reflection. Diane drew a breath to speak. She told them of how she had never looked back, never shared. Only now did she realize how much she had lived through, and, she added quietly, how strong she was. Around the room her classmates nodded. Her story was now public. Diane felt an odd sense of peace. "It's not stuck inside of me. I got it out. I can move on."

Over the months, our class had debated what it meant to be American. Unlike in Zambia, Diane reflected, here she could be different without being an outsider. Here, she explained, everyone was different. They brought their language, their food, their traditions, their religion. In the United States, Diane believed, "whatever you bring to the table they take. They don't tell you to be one kind of person. I can be my own person. Here I am a free person."

So is she an American?" I asked her. "Not yet," she replied. Life has taught her to be cautious. To never again assume she belongs. Her green card was a first step, but it does not guarantee her acceptance. And, as Diane has come to learn, what she may or may not feel doesn't matter to governments. Diane is still waiting for a country to recognize her, to claim her as theirs. "As soon as I receive my US citizenship, that is when I will become an American," she explained. "As soon as I raise my hand to take the oath, then nobody can take that away from me."

CHAPTER 8

VOICE

To make Americans, it is essential that young people have the chance to develop their voice—to master a new language, continue to nurture their mother tongue, and learn to express their own ideas clearly and powerfully. Schools and communities should be ready to listen and learn from students when they lift their voices.

This chapter tells two stories. The first story is about a fifty-year-long debate about bilingual education. A 1970s law in Massachusetts established a blueprint for bilingual instruction across the nation, before the pendulum swung hard in the opposite direction, with local and state referendums requiring English-only education for newcomers. In recent years, though, a new understanding of immigrant education has emerged, along with more nuanced laws. The story brings the past up to the present. The second story is about what I hope might become possible for immigrant education in the years ahead. I distill what I have learned from my travels across the country to visit innovative schools, and I offer advice for educators, community members, and policy makers. I also discuss the need to connect educators into a vibrant nationwide community dedicated to reimagining education for newcomer children.

THE PAST: BILINGUAL EDUCATION

Over the first fifteen years of this century, the number of English-learner children in Massachusetts schools increased by nearly 70 percent.[1] Yet many were not receiving a strong education. The 2015 National Assessment of Educational Progress found that the proportion of the state's

English learners deemed at or above proficiency in reading was only one in eight among fourth graders and only one in sixteen among eighth graders. They were also dropping out of school at an alarming rate: three times higher than for other students in the state. While roughly one in nine students statewide failed to graduate high school within four years, the rate for English learners was more than one in three.[2]

It was in the fall of 2015 that I arrived at Lowell High School in Lowell, Massachusetts, to teach recently arrived immigrant children from more than thirty countries. As I set up my classroom, crafted lessons, and got to know students from Cambodia to Colombia, unbeknownst to me a coalition of educators, activists, and policy makers across the state was busily reimagining a key aspect of immigrant education.

The coalition was propelling a national conversation that had begun nearly fifty years earlier, in Massachusetts. In the 1970s the state had pioneered legislation to support the instruction of EL students by implementing bilingual education, the approach of teaching in both a student's primary language and English. The approach was rapidly replicated across the country and helped transform how schools taught immigrant-origin students.

These efforts across the nation were spurred in part by the Supreme Court's decision in *Lau v. Nichols,* which held that schools had a responsibility to support EL students, but prescribed no specific approach. Bilingual education came to be seen, by many, as the best solution. But the movement also triggered a powerful nationwide backlash. Over the next half-century, educators, policy makers, and others grappled with what it meant for schools to make Americans.

Much of the debate centered on the teaching of language—specifically, the benefits or disadvantages of bilingual education. Some saw such programs as a crucial remedy for schools' historic neglect of non-English-speaking students. Some saw it as a means of maintaining heritage. Others believed it to be an impediment to assimilation—or even a threat to national unity. The motivation of opponents ranged widely, from those who hoped to promote newcomers' success to those bent on excluding immigrants. The debate about language was, at its heart, a debate about American identity.

Now, in 2015, the Massachusetts coalition had come together to petition the state legislature to reimagine immigrant education again—to replace failed approaches with research-backed strategies, and to embrace the inherent strengths of immigrant-origin children. If the bill passed, the coalition hoped, Massachusetts might once more spark a national movement.

———•———

Nearly half a century earlier, in 1968, Sister Francis Georgia Vicente was troubled. An outspoken bilingual nun and the daughter of Spanish immigrants, she had taught for a time in Puerto Rico and elsewhere in the United States. Now, Sister Francis Georgia was working in the Boston mayor's office, assigned to gather demographic information about the city's growing Puerto Rican community. She went door to door, speaking often with newly arrived mothers. Again and again, she spotted school-age children at home. Why were they not in school, she asked? The reasons mothers gave varied. Some, who spoke only Spanish, could not navigate the school registration process. Some had been told their children were too old, and too behind academically, to attend. Some had children who attended school, but sat in classes conducted solely in English, which they found entirely incomprehensible. In all cases, the children's lack of English barred them from attending or from comprehending the state's supposedly universal public education.

Appalled, Sister Francis Georgia began documenting the exclusion of newcomer children. And she began to demand that school officials take action. Her work caught the attention of Hubert Jones, a Black social worker and civic activist. Jones had just been appointed executive director of the Roxbury Multi-Service Center, a community hub in a Boston neighborhood built in the spirit of Jane Addams's Hull House and the Settlement House Movement. He, too, had begun noticing the striking number of children missing school.

Building on Sister Francis Georgia's work, Jones spurred the creation of a task force, which he led, to investigate the problem. In the fall of 1970 its findings were published in a scathing report, "The Way We Go to School: The Exclusion of Children in Boston." The conclusion: Upwards of ten thousand city children were being denied an education. Those most affected were immigrants and Spanish-speaking Puerto Rican children. Boston, the report concluded, had woefully few programs to support newcomers. Across the country in San Francisco, activists had come to a similar conclusion with respect to Chinese-speaking newcomers and only months earlier had filed a case in federal district court, *Lau v. Nichols.*

In Boston, the task force report had an almost immediate effect. Barely four months after its release, in 1971, the Massachusetts legislature passed a bilingual education law, the first of its kind in the nation. It required that every district with twenty or more pupils speaking the same non-English language must create a program that gradually transitioned from bilingual to English-only learning.

The Massachusetts law became a blueprint for the nation. From Alaska to Maine, California to Louisiana, more than twenty states soon adopted similar laws. They were spurred by grassroots organizing and by national policy. The Massachusetts law followed on the heels of the federal 1968 Bilingual Education Act. It was soon bolstered by the Equal Educational Opportunities Act in 1974. In the same year, the US Supreme Court issued its unanimous ruling in *Lau v. Nichols,* which led to the Office for Civil Rights (OCR) releasing, the next year, the so-called *Lau* Remedies, which all but required schools to implement bilingual education.

Sister Francis Georgia testified before Congress in 1974, speaking alongside activist and scholar Ling-chi Wang, who had helped to propel the *Lau* case. "What is it to be an American?" she asked, reminding her audience that nearly all had ancestors who were once new to US shores. For too long, she argued, the country had disregarded the strength found in the rich diversity of those who came to this country and now call it home. "As a bilingual-bicultural person of another era who refused to get into the melting pot," she concluded, "I find this a glorious time to be alive and a part of this great movement to open our hearts, to loosen our tongues, and to tune our ears to the new sounds of many peoples sharing and united. *Muchas gracias.*"[3]

Across the country, districts scrambled to hire bilingual teachers and create programs for current EL students, some faster and more competently than others. At the same time, the number of newcomers arriving in the United States was growing. When, in 1965, LBJ successfully helped persuade Congress to dismantle the immigration quotas imposed in 1924, it dramatically changed who was allowed to come to America. In the twenty-year span beginning in 1970, the number of immigrants living in the United States roughly doubled—from about ten million to twenty million. More and more of the newcomers were arriving from Latin America and Asia, and fewer arrived from Europe.

These trends troubled many Americans, who fixated on what they perceived to be a growing problem: that the newcomers didn't speak English. They viewed bilingual education with suspicion. What, they asked, was the purpose of such programs? Was the goal purely to ease children's transition to English? Or, as some educators and activists proposed, was it also to maintain and nurture the home languages of newcomers? Federal laws and regulations were ambiguous.

An increasing number of politicians and others believed bilingual education should be strictly remedial, a rapid stepping-stone to English fluency. Bilingual education that nurtured other languages, they believed, could be an impediment to assimilation. "The American taxpayer, while recognizing the existence of cultural diversity, still wants the schools to be the basis of an American melting pot," wrote Albert Shanker, who had started school in New York speaking only Yiddish and had risen to become president of the American Federation of Teachers.[4]

In the 1920s the loyalty of Americans who maintained their German language and culture had been questioned. Now, the speed with which newcomers embraced English was again becoming a litmus test of allegiance. Perhaps the trend was not surprising. US policies and practices had long equated language with identity. From the mid-1800s to the mid-1900s, hundreds of thousands of Indigenous children had been compelled to attend schools that sought to "civilize" them, sometimes by kidnapping them from their families. "Kill the Indian, save the man," asserted the first superintendent of Pennsylvania's Carlisle Indian School. A key strategy of assimilation was to force children to abandon their cultures, communities, and their native languages.[5]

When Ronald Reagan took office in 1981, bilingual education found itself on the chopping block. A growing number of reports documented how immigrant-origin children were failing to learn English and had high dropout rates. "It is absolutely wrong and against American concepts to have a bilingual education program that is now openly, admittedly dedicated to preserving their native language," Reagan declared, "and never getting them adequate in English."[6] Under the new administration, the *Lau* Remedies were rapidly retracted.

In the spring of 1981, California senator S. I. Hayakawa, a Canadian immigrant and son of Japanese immigrants, took aim at bilingualism and bilingual education. "Language is a powerful tool. A common language can unify; separate languages can fracture and fragment a society," he wrote.[7] English, he argued, had been the key ingredient that made the American melting pot a success. Policies that nurtured other languages were deluding immigrants about what was necessary to become successful Americans. He proposed an amendment to the US Constitution declaring English the country's official language.

Hayakawa's proposal never made it out of committee, but it caught the attention of a small-town Michigan ophthalmologist, environmentalist, and beekeeping enthusiast named John Tanton. Not long after, Tanton reached out to Hayakawa with a question: Would he cofound an organization dedicated to advocating "English-only" policies? Hayakawa agreed, and the organization U.S. English was born. The organization, Tanton believed, would help the United States become clear-eyed about what he saw as a growing threat: rising immigration.

For years Tanton had been active in the environmental movement as a member of the National Audubon Society and founder of a local Sierra Club chapter. Population growth, he came to believe, endangered his beloved outdoors. To protect it, he reasoned, the United States must limit new arrivals. In 1979 Tanton had founded the Federation for American Immigration Reform (FAIR), an advocacy group that aimed to restrict immigration. Over the next two decades, Tanton would found or help establish a plethora of like-minded and interconnected organizations: the foundation U.S. Inc.; the think tank Center for Immigration Studies (CIS); the Social Contract Press; and the advocacy organization NumbersUSA.

Early on, Tanton had discovered that one of the most unsettling aspects of immigration was, for many people, the profusion of languages spoken by newcomers. Tanton's U.S. English embarked on campaigns across the country to halt the "erosion of the English language."[8] It took aim at bilingual ballots, bilingual 911 emergency operators, and bilingual yellow pages. One zealous local coordinator directed her energies toward halting the printing of bilingual menus at McDonald's.

A primary target of U.S. English was bilingual education in public schools. "Government should not stand idly by and let the core culture, the shared culture formed by generations of earlier immigrants, slip away," argued the organization's executive director, who was a Holocaust survivor, who had herself learned English in US schools. Bilingualism caused longtime "citizens to feel like strangers in their own land," she believed. "If anyone has to feel strange, it's got to be the immigrant, until he learns the language." Bilingual education, the organization believed, posed a growing threat to national unity and security. To see the danger, it claimed, one only had to look at violent separatist and secessionist movements drawn along linguistic lines in Sri Lanka, Belgium, and Canada. "Prolonged bilingual education in public schools," Hayakawa cautioned in a fundraising letter for U.S. English, "threatens to divide us along language lines."[9]

The English-only movement arrived in Lowell, Massachusetts, in the spring of 1987. Once a center of America's industrial revolution, the city had long ago slipped into decay. Only in the last decade had it emerged, phoenix-like, with the help of federal aid, political allies, and the entrepreneurial efforts of Chinese immigrant, computer engineer, and inventor An Wang, who had founded the highly successful Wang Laboratories. Lowell was touted as a paragon of the "Massachusetts Miracle." At the same time, the city was undergoing a demographic metamorphosis. In 1980, roughly six hundred residents of Asian descent lived in Lowell. Within a decade the number was more than ten thousand. Many were Cambodian survivors of the Khmer Rouge genocide. With them came Laotian and Vietnamese immigrants. An increasing number of Dominican and Puerto Rican newcomers also called Lowell home. Whereas in 1975 fewer than 5 percent of the city's students were children of color, by 1987 they accounted for 40 percent. Required by law to implement bilingual education in multiple languages, the school district was overwhelmed and ill prepared. Six-year-olds studied next to eleven-year-olds in overcrowded classes. Partitions jigsawed school cafeterias into makeshift classrooms for Khmer-, Laotian-, and Spanish-speaking children. Auditoriums, hallways, and boiler rooms were hastily converted to accommodate the influx of newcomers. At one middle school, recent arrivals studied in a former bathroom alongside a urinal.[10]

In that spring of 1987, a hundred angry Southeast Asian and Latino parents arrived at a local school committee meeting to speak on behalf of their children. When the parents asked to use interpreters, a long-standing school committee member grew incensed and stormed out. "This is an English-only school committee in an English-only America," he later declared.[11] The son of Greek immigrants, he himself had once learned English in a US school. The angry parents refused to be silenced and went on to sue the school district on behalf of their children.

Soon after students returned to school in the fall, the city was shocked by an attack on an immigrant child. An eleven-year-old white boy accosted a thirteen-year-old Cambodian survivor of the Khmer Rouge on a street in Lowell. Vandy Phorng's attacker punched him, slung racial slurs, dragged him down a set of stairs, and flung him into the Merrimack River. Although rescued, the boy died a day later. The attacker's father was a vocal English-only advocate. Animosities grew. Two years later, city voters approved a nonbinding resolution declaring that English was the official language of Lowell.

Lowell was not an anomaly. Across the country, cities and states passed similar referendums and legislation, many spurred and backed by Tanton's organization, U.S. English. By the early 1990s more than ten states had adopted such measures; more would join in the coming years. U.S. English had swelled into a multimillion-dollar-a-year operation. Tanton had found deep-pocketed allies, including the Pioneer Fund, a eugenicist organization founded to pursue "race betterment." A founding member of the Pioneer Fund had been the eugenicist Harry Laughlin, whose research and testimony had underpinned the 1924 immigration quotas, and one of its directors had been John Trevor Jr., who had testified against the 1965 Immigration Act that ended the quota system. In the fall of 1988 a two-year-old internal memo, in which Tanton decried the influx of nonwhite immigrants, was leaked. "Will there be strength in this diversity? Or will this prove a social and political San Andreas Fault?" Tanton wrote. He warned ominously of an impending "Latin onslaught." Latin American immigrants, he declared, had larger families and were less moral, less educated, and less eager to assimilate. "As Whites see their power and control over their lives declining," Tanton asked, "will they simply go quietly into the night? Or will there be an explosion?"[12]

A few years later, in the summer of 1993, California governor Pete Wilson had a problem. Running for reelection the next year, he was trailing his likely Democratic opponent dismally in the polls. The state was in crisis, facing a five-year drought, an economic recession, high unemployment, the aftermath of the brutal police beating of Rodney King and the sweeping riots that followed the officers' acquittal, and a budget deficit of more than twelve billion dollars. Hoping to retain power, Wilson sought a scapegoat.

He found his answer in a ballot initiative codrafted by a former commissioner of the US Immigration and Naturalization Services (INS) and former lobbyist for Tanton's FAIR. The sweeping proposal would bar undocumented immigrants from accessing all nonemergency health care, social services, and, in direct violation of the Supreme Court's decision in *Plyler v. Doe*, public schools. In addition, teachers, doctors, nurses, and social service workers would be required to report on the undocumented status of those they served. The initiative was christened "Save Our State."

Wilson threw his support behind the initiative. The academic future of undocumented children was not California's responsibility, he declared. If California excluded them, Wilson promised the state could provide personal computers at school to all other fourth graders.[13] One of the initiative's organizers was more explicit: "You get illegal alien children, Third World children, out of our schools, and you will reduce the violence. . . . You're not dealing with a lot of shiny face, little kiddies. . . . You're dealing with Third World cultures who come in, they shoot, they beat, they stab and they spread their drugs around in our school system."[14]

Coming to the defense of the state's undocumented communities was an unusual ally—Ron Unz, a thirty-two-year-old conservative Republican and Silicon Valley software entrepreneur, who entered the governor's race, self-financing his million-dollar bid. Immigrants, he argued, bolstered the economy, bringing their talents to low-skilled and high-tech companies. His campaign, he later explained, was galvanized by Wilson's "immigrant bashing."[15] The ballot initiative, Unz felt, would coerce "small children to inform on the status of their parents," a practice he found reminiscent of Soviet Russia.[16]

Unz had grown up in the home of his grandparents, Ukrainian Jewish immigrants. His mother was a schoolteacher who had moved back in with her parents and onto welfare to raise her boy. Unz proved to be a talented student. In high school he won the prestigious Westinghouse Science Talent Search competition.[17] He went on to study ancient history and theoretical physics at Harvard, Cambridge, and Stanford, before working as a software developer and then starting his own software company that served Wall Street analysts. According to articles about Unz, his résumé claimed he had an IQ of 214, roughly double the level regarded as average intelligence.[18]

Unz lost in the 1994 primary, and Wilson went on to win reelection. And the Save Our State initiative, commonly known as Proposition 187, passed handily (although it would eventually be overturned in part because it violated constitutional protections articulated in *Plyler v. Doe*).

Three years later, however, in the summer of 1997, Unz reappeared in the political spotlight—this time with a ballot initiative of his own. "The English language is the national public language . . . the leading world language for science, technology, and international business," read the opening of Unz's Proposition 227. Immigrant parents wanted their children to learn English, it stated, "allowing them to fully participate in the American Dream." Yet the state, it argued, was failing to teach them English. At the time, one in every four students statewide was considered an English learner. Unz believed that bilingual education was to blame. Fifty years earlier, Gonzalo and Felícitas Mendez, alongside other Latino parents, had sued five Orange County school districts for segregating their children. Now, Unz's advocacy campaign asserted, bilingual education was failing EL students by "segregating them into an educational dead-end." His proposal: Replace most bilingual education programs statewide with a one-year crash course in English. "A young child can learn English in months," Unz asserted, "a year max. And to deny them that is the worst kind of paternalism." He called his initiative and the associated organization English for the Children.[19]

To the untrained observer, there was an alluring appeal to the claim that immigrant children could master a new language within a year. There was just one problem: The claim, researchers explained, was flawed. While children might be able to learn relatively quickly to communicate in spoken English, researchers agreed that children require five to seven years of deliberate study to acquire true proficiency in academic reading, writing, and speaking.[20] And it was this proficiency that would have a profound effect on success after school.

Unz had no children, was not a K–12 educator, and by his own admission, had never stepped foot in a bilingual classroom. He dismissed academic research of educational experts as biased. His conviction was based on anecdotes and popular articles. "I just asked friends how long it took them to learn English," he explained. Why see a classroom, he asked, when "it would have reinforced what I read and saw on TV. But I've talked with parents and teachers."[21] His own mother had spoken Yiddish when she entered school, and he touted that she had picked up English just fine. "Bilingual education," he confidently declared, "is utter lunacy."[22]

Unz said his interest was prompted by the activism of Latino parents in Los Angeles who, in the winter of 1996, pulled more than eighty children out of a public elementary school for over a week to protest the school's bilingual education program, which, they argued, failed to teach children English. In fact, Unz's interest in the issue seems to have begun much earlier. In immigrant families he saw an opportunity, and in bilingual education a threat. Writing in *Policy Review* in the fall of 1994, Unz had argued that Republicans, rather than demonizing immigrants, should embrace them because "immigration could serve as the issue that breaks the Democratic Party and forges a new and dominant conservative/Republican governing coalition."[23] To do so, the party would need to find common ground between multigenerational Americans and recent arrivals. A solution, he believed, was to look back one hundred years to the emergence of the Americanization movement, which had sought to rapidly assimilate newcomer children. "Millions of impoverished, poorly educated Jews, Slavs, and Italians became proud and productive Americans through a public school system that emphasized English language skills and American culture," Unz wrote. The country must return to this approach and "eliminate the native-language instruction and divisive multiculturalism programs that could fragment our society."[24]

In 1997, aiming to court immigrants, Unz selected his spokespeople for English for the Children with precision. They included a long-established first-grade teacher and daughter of Mexican migrants who until recently had served on the board of directors of Tanton's U.S. English and a Bolivian immigrant math teacher—Jaime Escalante, the hero of the movie *Stand and Deliver* and arguably the most famous school-teacher in America at the time. In championing Unz's Prop 227, Escalante offered a simple calculus: "If you immigrate to this country, you are part of the system. You have to integrate yourself into the system. And the integration path is the language."[25]

Unz and his organization kept up a drumbeat of claims. Although only one in three English learners in California studied in bilingual programs, he argued that bilingual education was responsible for immigrant children's inability to speak English, and his initiative cited it as a cause of the high dropout rates among Latino students.[26] California reported that 5 percent of the state's English learners achieved proficiency each year. Unz argued that these data meant the state must be failing 95 percent of the students.[27] Opponents explained that that conclusion was based on the incorrect assumption that students—regardless of their age, educational background, or length of time in the country—should be able to achieve academic mastery in a single year.[28]

Californians went to the polls in June of 1998 to vote on, among other things, Prop 227: English for the Children. It passed handily. But Unz was not one to rest. The California win, he hoped, would trigger a domino effect, causing other states to follow California's lead. "I think the rest of the nation will just crumble like the Berlin Wall," he mused.[29] Leaving little to chance, he took to the road, helping to introduce, fund, and organize a nearly identical initiative in Arizona two years later, which also proved successful.[30]

As Unz would write, it was time to return to the American melting pot. "Our public schools . . . must be restored as the engines of assimilation they once were," he wrote. One hundred years ago, amid the Americanization movement, schools had "turned Italian or Polish children into good Americans." Bilingual education kept immigrant children from doing the same, he argued.[31]

In the summer of 2001, Unz set his sights on Massachusetts. It was here that the modern bilingual education movement had been born nearly three decades earlier. And it was here, he hoped, that it would die. If his campaign could win in Massachusetts, a long-standing hub of "intellectual and media influence . . . similar measures would win anywhere and everywhere else," Unz boasted.[32]

Less than two months later, two Boeing 767s took off from Boston's Logan Airport bound for Los Angeles. Within the hour the world would watch in horror as they slammed into New York City's Twin Towers.

Following the horrors of 9/11, Americans set about attacking Americans. Men, women, and children around the country were threatened and beaten because of the color of their skin and the clothes they wore. Their homes, shops, and places of worship were vandalized, ransacked, and firebombed. In schools, Muslim children were harassed and bullied by peers. A week after the attack, President George W. Bush, speaking from a Washington, DC, mosque, condemned the growing violence: "That's not the America I know. That's not the America I value."[33]

Four months later, in January of 2002, President Bush spoke again to the nation—specifically to the nation's children—promising to root out terrorism. In his next breath he made another commitment: to ensure that each child would receive a "first-class" education. That morning the president signed the reauthorization of the 1965 Elementary and Secondary School Education Act (ESEA), a sweeping reimagining of the law aimed at closing the achievement gap by holding schools and states accountable for their students' academic success. In particular, the law focused on students who had historically been poorly served by the education system, including immigrant-origin students still mastering English. No child, Bush said, would be left behind. The pledge became the law's name.[34]

NCLB renamed, reorganized, and rethought much in ESEA. In the shuffle Title VII, the 1968 Bilingual Education Act, disappeared altogether. In fact, practically every mention of bilingual education was scrubbed from the law. The Department of Education's Office of Bilingual Education and Minority Languages Affairs was reborn as the Office of English Language Acquisition, Language Enhancement, and Academic Achievement for Limited English Proficient Students. Going forward, the law seemed to imply, children would be identified by their lack of English—that is, by their deficits. The law prioritized rapid English fluency. Children in high-quality bilingual programs tended to show substantial academic benefit after a few years of sustained study, but NCLB required almost immediate progress. As a consequence, bilingual programs nationwide began shutting down.

Less than a year earlier, the Supreme Court had undermined the foundation of *Lau v. Nichols*. It ruled that families no longer had the right to sue schools to provide language supports for their children. It left open the possibility that federal agencies might bring such cases, although some legal scholars believed it would require showing not just that schools were failing non-English-speaking students but that the discrimination was intentional.

But in Massachusetts, in the winter of 2002, a coalition of teachers, parents, lawyers, lobbyists, and organizers was fighting to save bilingual education. It was a fight Roger Rice, executive director of Multicultural Education, Training & Advocacy, Inc. (META), had known for years was coming to the Commonwealth.

The grandson of Eastern European Jews, Rice had moved to Boston in the 1970s to work for Marian Wright Edelman at Harvard's Center for Law and Education. In 1973 he found himself helping to write an amicus brief for a case then before the Supreme Court, brought by a San Francisco lawyer on behalf of Chinese students. In it he and his colleagues had added the deliberately untranslated footnote in Chinese characters.[35]

But Rice's primary task at the center was to help enforce the state's then-new bilingual education law. He visited classrooms, attended school committee meetings, organized with parents, and met with school administrators. In the 1980s he founded META to broaden his advocacy for immigrant children. It was META that collaborated with the families in Lowell to sue their school district for failing to provide adequate education to non-English-speaking students. And it was META's San Francisco office's codirector who had, with colleagues, successfully won the *Plyler* decision on behalf of the four undocumented families in Tyler, Texas, and unsuccessfully sued to block implementation of Unz's California initiative. For years Rice had helped stave off attempts to end bilingual education in Massachusetts. But Unz's ballot initiative, Rice knew, had a lot of money and momentum behind it.

Unz had brought with him to Massachusetts his successful strategies from California and Arizona, as well as his personal financial backing. He'd also helped assemble a local team of advocates, including a Cuban-born former high school principal and an Italian-born former bilingual teacher. But Unz's most important and unexpected support came from a man of English, Scottish, and German descent who was running for governor and enthusiastically endorsed the initiative. "I'd end the failed idea of bilingual education and teach every child English instead,"[36] declared Mitt Romney in campaign ads on television.

Hoping to get ahead of Unz, Rice and a coalition of organizations collaborated with two state representatives—Antonio Cabral, a former high school bilingual education teacher who decades earlier had started school in the United States after immigrating from the Azores, and Jarrett Barrios, the son of Cuban immigrants. Together the legislators introduced a bill, intended as an alternative to Unz's initiative, that would reform the 1971 Massachusetts bilingual education law to create more flexibility for schools educating EL students, including allowing but not requiring bilingual education. In August 2002, the bill became law. It was set to go into effect in the next year—if not superseded by Unz's initiative. Groups rallied against the Unz initiative—they funded TV ads, composed jingles, wrote op-eds, testified at hearings, organized rallies, hosted community meetings, and gathered testimonials of teachers, parents, and students.[37]

But, as Rice and others feared, the Unz initiative, Question 2 on the ballot, carried in the November election.[38] With wins in California, Arizona, and Massachusetts, Unz had affected the education of roughly 40 percent of all English learners in the country.[39]

Even as he anticipated defeat at the polls, Rice spent Election Day driving to polling locations across central Massachusetts to lay the groundwork for continuing the fight. In California, Unz's English for the Children organization had asserted that Latino communities supported ending bilingual education.[40] Skeptical about that claim, Rice and others fanned out into Latino neighborhoods to hear directly from voters. Their goal, Rice told me, was "building the legacy." From polling place to polling place, Rice dropped off and collected interview forms. The survey found that more than 90 percent of Latino voters polled had voted no.

———•———

Fifteen years would pass before Massachusetts would reverse course and reimagine the education of EL students. Bringing about this change would take a combination of advocacy, evidence, and research.

It would take the persistence of state legislators. The same evening Question 2 passed, Jeffrey Sánchez, a self-described "Nuyorican" (born in New York of native Puerto Rican parents) was elected to the state's house of representatives. In his first year in office he took up the fight for bilingual education, filing a version of the reform law that had been championed by Antonio Cabral but nullified by the passage of Question 2. His bill was not voted on, but Sánchez was undeterred. Over the next decade he filed versions of the bill again, and again, and again. "I kept filing it," he told me, "to keep it alive."[41]

It would take accumulating evidence of the damage done to a generation of EL children. Cuban-born Boston bilingual teacher Berta Rosa Berriz still remembers the weeks after Question 2 passed. Hallways began to fill with discarded bilingual textbooks. She and her elementary school students surreptitiously ferried boxes of the suddenly unwanted books to the sanctuary of her classroom. She remembers too the quiet, confused, and fearful questions her students asked her, "*Maestra?* Why do they hate us because we speak Spanish?"[42] For years, Berriz kept teaching EL students, though now teaching only in English. Each year her students sat for a panoply of state tests, an exercise in futility not lost on her pupils. As one child asked her, "*¿Cuántas veces les tengo que comprobar a esta gente que no sé leer ni escribir en ingles?*" "How many times do I have to prove to these people that I cannot read or write in English?"[43]

Across the state, a decade after the Unz initiative, English learners continued to trail their peers in testing and academic success. As the Commonwealth struggled, the number of EL students continued to tick upwards. By 2015 nearly one in every ten students in Massachusetts public schools was an English learner.[44]

It would take a growing body of research indicating possible cognitive benefits of multilingualism. Some studies found benefits for the brain's executive functions—including increased ability to focus, multitask, and solve problems—in bilingual and multilingual individuals, compared to their monolingual peers. Other studies suggested benefits for elderly bilingual individuals in staving off Alzheimer's disease. And, of greatest relevance, studies showed that English learners studying in dual-language programs had better academic outcomes than those instructed only in English.[45]

It would take new ideas and approaches to educating immigrants pioneered elsewhere. In 2011 California became the first state in the nation to create a special recognition for graduating seniors who were multilingual. The following spring more than ten thousand California seniors graduated with a "Seal of Biliteracy" on their diploma. By 2015, fifteen states had followed suit.[46] In the two decades since the passage of California's Prop 187, aimed at undocumented peoples, millions of Latino residents had been galvanized to register to vote and become politically active. In 2016 California voters overwhelmingly voted to overturn Unz's Prop 227.

And it would take a coalition of activists. In 2014 four Massachusetts organizations, some created in the wake of the 1971 bilingual education act to support bilingual education and EL students, came together to form the Language Opportunity Coalition.[47] Together they built alliances with lawyers, lobbyists, educators, and community members; they met again, and again, and again with state legislators. They imagined a law that might not only restore the opportunity to teach bilingual education but would also recognize and nurture the languages and other strengths brought by newcomer children.

By 2017, nearly fifteen years after being elected, Jeffrey Sánchez had risen to become the chair of the influential House Ways and Means Committee. The newest version of the language bill was now supported by a cadre of influential legislators. That summer the Language Opportunity for Our Kids (LOOK) bill ran the gauntlet of the house and senate. The bill reimagined education for English learners in Massachusetts. It would provide educators the flexibility to use research-proven practices to teach EL children, including bilingual education. It would require the state's department of education to invest in training teachers and supporting schools to ensure the success of EL students. It would establish councils of parents of EL students to act as advisers. And it would create a "seal of biliteracy" to recognize students' linguistic strengths.

In the end, of the nearly two hundred members of the state legislature, only one voted in opposition. On the eve of Thanksgiving 2017, Republican governor Charlie Baker signed the LOOK Act into law.

In the spring of 2019, my own students read through the LOOK Act with excitement. We were embarking on our semester-long civics project, and one of my classes, noting that the LOOK Act had yet to be implemented in many cities, decided it was time to put the promise of the law into action. They surveyed students, crafted memos, drafted letters to parents, and met with citywide school officials. Together they formulated recommendations, learning how to express their ideas clearly and persuasively. That spring a delegation of my students headed to the Massachusetts State House to proudly present their advocacy. "We come from eleven countries and speak eight languages. We want opportunities to succeed in the US, our new country," they wrote. There they spoke with local and national civic leaders and with journalists, sharing their opinions and convictions. "We have a lot of strengths and skills to share. But we feel that our many strengths are not always recognized," they explained. "We want immigrant students to believe in their strengths, and have a better opportunity to succeed in high school . . . in college and life."

A month later my students walked across the graduation stage at our high school. Soon after, I set forth from my classroom to begin work on this book—visiting innovative schools working to support immigrant-origin students, delving into the history of our country's approaches to immigrant education, and learning from my own students.

I believed that, to reimagine how our country could educate newcomer children, we would need to understand our past, explore present innovations, and listen to the personal stories of young people themselves.

THE POSSIBLE: REIMAGINING IMMIGRANT EDUCATION

Two years after I set out to research this book, I returned to my classroom in Lowell, in August of 2021.

For the 2019–20 school year, I had taken a leave of absence from the classroom—flying to Texas, California, North Carolina, Georgia, Illinois, and elsewhere to visit classrooms and speak with teachers, principals, researchers, and policy makers. When not traveling, I spent hours with my former students learning about their immigration and education experiences. When the COVID-19 pandemic grounded me, I dove into historical research, no airplane tickets required. At the start of the next school year, I'd returned to teaching amid the pandemic. My students logged on from their kitchens, living rooms, bedrooms, and basements. I worked from home, teaching by day and continuing my research and writing by night. As the school year came to a close, so did my research.

With the summer before me, I turned to extracting lessons from the past, the present, and the personal. I thought too about how to bring what I had learned to my own classroom.

On a muggy morning in August 2021, I drove to Lowell High. There I met some of my former students—Carla, Safiya, Julian, and Srey Neth included. Together we unpacked boxes and reconfigured desks. We then began to transform the classroom based on the creativity and expertise of the educators I had visited across the nation. We tucked a small herbaceous garden near the window for students who were feeling anxious, sad, or upset, modeled on what I had found at Houston's Las Americas. We posted a huge collage of photos of my students presenting at the State House, speaking with community leaders, beaming at graduation—akin to what I saw in Leah Juelke's class in North Dakota. We lined the room with the flags of my students' home countries and covered the door with greetings in all the languages they spoke—drawing inspiration from Georgia's Global Village Project. I set about devising plans to deepen my engagement with families and communities in light of what I'd learned from ENLACE in Massachusetts and the Aurora ACTION Zone in Colorado. I began rewriting lessons to support students' exploration of complex texts and rethinking projects to elevate student collaboration, as I'd witnessed in Guilford, North Carolina, and at IHSLP in Maryland. I looked critically too at my curriculum, noticing the glaring gaps where stories, policies, and court cases that underlie the country's immigration history were missing. It was history I had never learned in school. My students, I resolved, would grapple with it.

Just as I was eager to integrate these new ideas, I found that many of the educators at the innovative schools I'd visited were excited to learn from each other. Connections began organically. Hearing about challenges at one school, I mentioned approaches I'd seen at another. I was struck by how educators at innovative school programs were isolated from each other.

I began more actively connecting these educators—sharing emails and making introductions. Daniel Sass, the assistant principal at Maryland's

IHSLP, made plans to travel north to Lawrence, Massachusetts, to witness ENLACE's family engagement work in action. Teachers at Georgia's GVP were eager to know more about the trauma-therapy approach embedded in Houston's Las Americas. The superintendent of Aurora's ACTION Zone spoke of sending a team to Guilford County, North Carolina, to observe their approach to teaching rich academic tests at scale. Together, we were excited to see if solutions forged at one school could be applied successfully to another.

But what about the tens of thousands of schools throughout the country? Today, almost every school and every community is home to newcomers. Roughly one in every four students under the age of seventeen is an immigrant or the child of immigrants. What are the practices and approaches that schools and communities can implement to best nurture immigrant-origin students?

I set about distilling principles from what I had learned from educators, organizers, activists, and young people. After considering the stories, strategies, and experiences, I have concluded that eight elements are essential for supporting immigrant-origin young people. These are the elements I shared in the introduction, and I list them again below, now in a slightly different order. Each is distinct, but they are closely interconnected.

The elements are:

- opportunities for *new beginnings*
- *chances to dream*
- assurance of *security*
- *acceptance* for who students are and where they come from
- supportive *communities*
- committed *advocates*
- recognition of students' *strengths* and assets
- opportunities for students to develop their *voice*—and valuing those voices

For each of these eight elements, I have tried to extract specific practices and policy suggestions for achieving them. My goal is to create a guide to help teachers, schools, districts, communities, local organizations, and city and state officials interested in transforming their approach to supporting immigrant-origin students. I have labeled the guide "version 1.0" because I know it will grow and change with the added expertise of educators across the country.

ADVICE FOR EDUCATORS, COMMUNITIES, AND POLICY MAKERS ON SUPPORTING NEWCOMER STUDENTS (VERSION 1.0)

For more than a century, legislators, communities, schools, and educators have sought to turn immigrant students into Americans, guided by their own views, philosophies, prejudices, and power. However, the most important message of this book is that each young newcomer is the rightful author of their own American identity. The primary role and responsibility of educators and others is to support them. Below are ideas for how to do so.

New Beginnings

For newcomers to succeed, it is essential they have the chance to begin again. Many have come here for opportunities they cannot attain elsewhere. I think of my student Diane, who, having grown up stateless in Zambia, hoped for a country to finally accept her as theirs. And I think of my own family, who more than a century ago fled persecution and traveled across a continent and an ocean to seek a better future for their children, grandchildren, and great-grandchildren.

But starting over in a strange land is immensely challenging. Students new to the country often endure frustrations, humiliations, and loneliness—teachers they can't understand, unfamiliar school expectations, classmates who are not yet friends. What can we do to ensure newcomers can have the chance to begin again?

We can learn from strategies used at Las Americas in Texas, the International High School at Langley Park in Maryland, and Georgia's Global Village Project.

- School enrollment procedures should be straightforward and supported by staff who can help translate into newcomers' languages. Families should be surveyed to elicit students' educational history and identify possible academic gaps. After enrollment, schools should have a mentorship program to connect each new student with current students who can introduce them to classmates, teachers, and programs, and who can answer questions and create connections.

- Districts should provide educators and school staff with information about the countries and context from which their students are coming and about the approaches to education they would have experienced abroad. A few nonprofit organizations could create such materials and make them available to schools across the country. Such knowledge will help teachers to better understand and support students adjusting to the structure and expectations of a new educational system.

- Mindful that immigrant families may be in the process of putting down roots and navigating new government systems, schools and districts could create events and programs and hire staff to help connect families to the community and to resources.

- Communities with many new arrivals should consider creating a newcomer center, like Las Americas in Houston, the Doris Henderson Newcomers School in Guilford County, North Carolina, or dozens of others across the country. These one-year programs would help orient newcomers to the US education system, provide intensive English-language classes, and connect families with wraparound social services and support. Communities with many students who have had limited or interrupted formal education (SLIFE students) should look to create specific programs, like those at the Global Village Project, that teach academic fundamentals in a manner that acknowledges and respects the age and maturity of older students.

- Because immigrant-origin children will likely be part of almost every community, state policy makers should pass legislation requiring all educators, no matter what subject they teach, to have basic training in how to teach English learners and a basic understanding of students' countries and cultures.

- State and national assessments should be rethought to accurately assess EL students' learning. For students still mastering English, many standardized exams intended to measure students' academic knowledge may instead primarily measure their English proficiency. The resulting low test scores discourage students and penalize schools.

Chances to Dream

Perhaps more than for any other country, dreams draw people to the United States. It is important that schools support newcomer families and their children in pursuing their dreams. I am reminded of the courage of the four undocumented families in Tyler, Texas, whose dreams for their children led them to risk deportation. I think of my student Srey Neth, who grew up in Cambodia dreaming of coming to the United States and attending college.

While dreams propel immigrants across oceans and deserts, once here they often face hurdles that can seem insurmountable. They encounter xenophobia, prejudice, and low expectations; language barriers can make it hard to communicate both in and out of school; newcomers may find it challenging to know what classes they should take to prepare for college and career; and family responsibilities can keep students from participating in after-school activities.

To remove barriers and help newcomers pursue their dreams, we can learn from the Guilford School District in North Carolina and the International School at Langley Park in Maryland.

- Schools should apply effective strategies for teaching language to EL students that help them learn grade-level language in the context of grade-level content; the more time EL students spend studying language that is oversimplified or separated from content, the farther they will fall behind their peers.
- For students with strong academic knowledge, but comparatively lower English proficiency, schools and districts should invest in approaches that enable students to access grade-level content with home-language supports.
- At the high school level, schools should invest in college and career counselors with in-depth knowledge about how to support immigrant students, recognizing that many families will be unfamiliar with US college and job application processes.
- Colleges and universities should rethink their admissions processes to value a fuller range of applicants' experiences. These institutions often favor applicants who have taken AP courses, have high standardized test scores, and have participated in exceptional summer internships and volunteer experiences—criteria that favor students from advantaged backgrounds. Institutions should broaden their criteria for identifying promising students. An initiative at Harvard's

Making Caring Common project has been working with institutions to create applications that value students' contributions to supporting their family, holding down jobs, and watching over siblings.

Security

Without security, it is nearly impossible for young people to succeed. For immigrant-origin students, there are two key facets of security to consider. First is the trauma they may carry with them. Some have survived war, violence, natural disasters, or crippling poverty in the years before they arrived. Some have experienced violence or traumatic ordeals in their journey here. Some children have left behind families and are living with relatives they hardly know. Second is the hostility and xenophobia they may face in their new communities. Many are bullied, harassed, and even attacked for the language they speak, the clothes they wear, the way they look, or the religion they practice. I think of my student Choori and how tense and on edge he was in the halls and classrooms of our school; I think of Leah Juelke's students who felt targeted by North Dakota's proposed anti-refugee law.

To ensure newcomers have security, there is much we can learn from Las Americas in Texas and from Leah Juelke's classroom in North Dakota.

- Teachers in their classrooms and schools in their buildings can create calm and quiet safe spaces where students who feel overwhelmed or upset can come to refocus and to recenter themselves.
- Schools should train all staff to understand and identify possible signs of trauma. When a child lashes out, seems excessively tired, or shuts down quickly, these might be scars of trauma.
- Schools should invest in hiring—or perhaps partnering with local universities and nonprofits to provide—mental health professionals, social workers, and counselors who can meet one-on-one with students when they are in crisis, as well as meet regularly to develop strategies for managing trauma. Schools should also invest in developing teachers' abilities to support students' social and emotional well-being and growth.
- Schools and districts should examine their procedures to see if they may trigger trauma. Seemingly small choices can make a big difference: The pitch of a bell signaling the end of a class or inconsistency between classroom setups or expectations might heighten anxiety, stress, or fear for some students.

- Schools should seek to employ a restorative approach to discipline, focusing not on one-size-fits-all punishments but on approaches that seek to understand and address the underlying causes of why a student acts out.
- Teachers and school leaders need to actively confront bullying—addressing incidents in the moment and the larger issue through class curricula.
- Teachers should teach about the United States' complicated history toward immigrants, to help students understand the historical roots of xenophobia today.
- Policy makers should work to prevent or dismantle policies that aim to exclude and target immigrant-origin peoples based on where they come from or the languages they speak.

Acceptance

Many children feel out of place when they first enroll in US schools. The language they speak, the clothes they wear, and their legal status in the country can stand as barriers between them and their new peers. Some students arrive having been explicitly excluded from education or prevented from enrolling in school because of poverty, violence, gender, race, ethnicity, sexuality, or religion. The United States itself has a long history of refusing to accept certain young people in school. I am reminded of seven-year-old Sylvia Mendez in Southern California and nine-year-old Alfredo Lopez in East Texas, who were barred from schools because of the color of their skin or their legal status. While the country has overturned such laws, many students still wonder if schools will accept them. I think of some of my own students who have been bullied by classmates for wearing the hijab. I think of today's undocumented students who are sometimes fearful to attend school, and of some of the young women at Georgia's Global Village Project who worry that there is no place for them in schools because they have missed too many years of education before arriving in the United States.

To help ensure newcomers are accepted in their new communities, we can learn from the strategies used in Leah Juelke's classroom in North Dakota and at the Global Village Project in Georgia.

- Teachers and schools should actively celebrate traditions, cultures, and histories of all their students. This could be done through hall decorations for holidays, expanding the languages used for school signage and communication, and class projects that encourage students to learn from, explore, and possibly share about their history, country, and culture.

- Schools and districts must ensure undocumented students feel welcome and safe in school. To better support these students, educators should be familiar with the historical underpinnings and legal rights of undocumented students and with the research and writings by and about the experience of being undocumented. School counselors can compile and offer targeted resources, specifically those regarding college scholarships and programs.
- Some schools and districts have been known to discourage or prevent students with limited or interrupted formal education (SLIFE) from enrolling. Students have a right to attend school and should be welcomed. Recognizing that SLIFE students will have academic gaps, schools and districts should set up systems to identify students' gaps and should offer academic support both during and after school.
- State-level departments of education should track the academic progress of SLIFE students. Without data, it is difficult to identify successful school practices. Policy makers should also rethink models of accountability that don't penalize schools for enrolling SLIFE students.

Community

Newly arrived families have often left behind vibrant communities—extended family who helped raise children as well as friends who stepped in during hard times. Children have lost their cousins, classmates, best friends, teammates, and mentors. Families must set about creating new networks of support and friendship. I think of my student Safiya, whose family, after fleeing Iraq, was scattered across the globe, and my student Julian, who created his own community on the school crew team.

To help foster community, we can learn a lot from the approaches used at ENLACE in Massachusetts and in the Aurora ACTION Zone in Colorado.

- Schools should begin by investing in building partnerships with families. They will need to train staff on how to build trusting relationships. They will also need to designate time in the school week, or provide compensation for after-school work, so that teachers can build those relationships.
- Teachers can embed the teaching of migration history into their curriculum to help all students, not just newcomers, trace and claim their personal migration stories. This can help build empathy and

connections by breaking down barriers that can arise between students whose families have been here for generations and those who have recently arrived.

- Schools should examine what clubs and sports teams newcomers do and do not join, seeking to understand and actively address barriers to participation.
- Schools could invest in staff who are specifically responsible for building relationships with community partners, rather than relying on individual teachers to build connections in an ad hoc manner. These partnerships could help connect students to learning opportunities, internships, and after-school activities as well as to social services and health services.
- Districts should consider transforming schools into full-fledged community hubs, opening buildings after hours and inviting community partners, families, and members to use the space for meetings, classes, clubs, and events.

Advocates

To advance education for immigrant-origin students, America needs fierce, dedicated advocates.

People from all walks of life have played important roles as advocates: teachers and lawyers; community activists, nuns, and politicians; judges and students; parents and presidents. They include the coalition of educators and activists who worked with policy makers in Massachusetts to pass recent legislation that changed how EL children are taught; the lawyers and organizers who teamed up on behalf of San Francisco's Chinese-speaking students in the 1970s; families, including the Mendezes, who helped to end school segregation in California; Jane Addams, who cofounded Hull House in Chicago and traveled the country promoting policy reforms; and President Lyndon Johnson, whose experiences as a teacher and principal in a segregated Mexican school contributed to his fight to transform federal education policy.

We still need such advocates, from the local community to the national level. It is important to nurture and support them.

- Teachers of newcomers are often powerful personal advocates for their students—helping them navigate new classes and cultures, connecting families with resources, providing job references, writing college recommendations, and nominating students for awards and recognitions. Schools should recognize teachers for this work and allow them to take time for it during the school day, and they should help connect educators with community resources.

- Teachers also have a powerful role to play in influencing systemic change at levels ranging from individual schools to the state and federal governments. Nonprofit organizations should take up the cause of mentoring teachers to be effective policy advocates, helping them to translate their classroom expertise into programmatic and policy recommendations. Teachers' unions and teacher preparation programs can also help to train and support teachers in helping to create system-level change.

- Schools and districts should actively work to hire and retain more multilingual and immigrant-origin teachers who speak the languages and are a part of the cultures of a community's young people. Overcoming teacher shortages will likely require communities to think creatively about recruiting new teachers, both young and old, to the profession.

- Schools must recognize and build collaborative partnerships with families—who are children's first advocates in life. Historically, the advocacy of immigrant families has been central in landmark court cases and transforming education policy. In addition to training staff about family engagement, schools must commit to creating policies and practices that seek and welcome families' collaboration and that recognize families as equal partners.

- Community nonprofits, businesses, and faith-based organizations that support and advocate for newcomer children and families often work in isolation from each other. To magnify their impact, organizations could partner with each other—meeting regularly to strategize about shared challenges, augmenting each other's programs, and collaborating to create umbrella initiatives that make it easier for newcomers to access resources and supports.

- Policy makers should actively seek out educators, other community advocates, and young newcomers to serve as ongoing advisers to help craft education policy and legislation. And, they and others should provide support to help them learn how to be effective advisers.

Assets

Immigrant-origin students are often defined by what they can't do—namely, speak fluent English. But there is so much they *can* do. Newcomers arrive with tremendous strengths.

In journeying to this country newcomers have often become masters at negotiation, problem solving, and teamwork. In the United States they develop powerful skills as linguistic and cultural translators for their families. They bring to school a maturity acquired by serving as caregivers for younger siblings or taking jobs to contribute financially to their families. They carry to class a breadth of knowledge and perspectives about the world gained from having experienced different governments and cultures. They have perseverance and grit, honed by learning to live in a new land.

I think of my student Robert for whom English is not a second language, but his *tenth*. I think of my students who accompany their parents to doctors' visits to translate or are asked to read government forms for their families.

To better recognize and draw on the many assets of immigrant-origin students, we can learn a lot from the International High School at Langley Park (IHSLP) in Maryland and in the Aurora ACTION Zone in Colorado.

- To help ensure that students' limited fluency in English doesn't delay their opportunity to grapple with rigorous academic content, teachers can make use of long-term projects, which allow students opportunities to master more complex material in parallel to developing language skills. Long-term projects often have advantages for *all* students.
- To tap into students' skills of grit, perseverance, and problem solving, schools can adopt mastery-based approaches to learning, like that embraced at Maryland's IHSLP. Rather than testing whether students learn a specific set of skills or body of knowledge in a defined period of time (and, if not, giving them a failing grade or making them repeat the course), mastery-based approaches focus on students cumulatively achieving proficiency—even if it takes longer to do so. Such approaches could likely benefit *all* students.
- Schools should set high expectations for what immigrant-origin students can achieve, to best prepare them for college, careers, and life. Schools should adopt approaches, such as those described above, that enable students to master grade-level content while mastering a new language—and should provide rigorous training to educators about how to do so.
- Schools should actively recognize and celebrate the strengths that immigrant-origin students bring with them, just as they often highlight students who have high grades, succeed in athletics, or perform on the stage.

- Immigrant young people, both recent high school and college graduates, can be powerful mentors, teachers, and role models for younger immigrant students. Schools should create opportunities to foster such regular ongoing mentorship both in academic classrooms and outside.
- Schools and districts can recognize the value of multilingual students—and encourage native English speakers to invest in language learning—by adopting the Seal of Biliteracy. Policy makers in states that have not yet adopted the Seal of Biliteracy should advocate to do so.

Voice

It is essential that our schools and communities help immigrant-origin students develop their voices. First, we must honor their mother tongues, recognizing their languages as strengths that connect them—and the United States—to global communities. Second, we must support them in mastering a new language. Third, we must help each student find their own individual voice—gaining the skills and confidence to express their ideas—and make their own American identity; this requires making space for them to express opinions and to learn to do so in a clear and compelling way. I think of my own extraordinary students—Carla, Choori, Diane, Julian, Robert, Safiya, and Srey Neth who developed powerful voices, in part by working to strengthen and support their communities. There are thousands of students like them across the nation with ideas, drive, and expertise that enrich our country.

To help immigrant-origin students develop their voices, we can learn from ENLACE in Massachusetts, from public schools in Guilford County, North Carolina, and from Leah Juelke's classroom in North Dakota.

- Schools and districts should tailor their approach for teaching the fundamentals of language to the specific community they support. This could include adopting bilingual programs in specific languages when there are a large number of children speaking the same language or implementing programs designed specifically for SLIFE students. All schools should consider teaching rich, grammatically complex language through approaches like those used in Guilford County, North Carolina. Policy makers should pass legislation that encourages communities to implement the best research-based approaches for their specific student populations, rather than requiring schools to adopt a single approach. Recent legislation passed in California and Massachusetts can be used as a model.

• To preserve and nurture students' connections to families, traditions, and history abroad, teachers should create opportunities in the curriculum to allow students to share, if they wish, their stories and cultures. This approach also provides powerful opportunities for children's classmates and community members to learn from them.

• Schools should create civics classes in which students can work with their communities to learn how to have an impact on causes they care about. Policy makers should pass civics education laws that provide training for educators and support for schools in this work. Such courses can be highly motivating for students and can teach them how to develop their voice as contributors to our nation. They are valuable not just for newcomers, but for all students.

Beyond Immigrant Education

Although this guide was derived from observations about immigrant education, many of the elements and practices may also apply to supporting students whose families have lived here for generations.

In particular, the lessons may be relevant to educating children who come from communities that have historically been marginalized—and, in many cases, are still marginalized—because of the color of their skin, their ethnicity, their gender, their sexuality, their abilities, their socioeconomic status, or their faith.

Like newcomers, these children need security and acceptance both inside and outside of school. They need supportive communities and passionate advocates. Too often, their assets are not recognized, and their voices are not honored.

Applying the ideas outlined here to children from marginalized communities—and perhaps, in some cases, to all students—is worth exploring. Their utility will need to be carefully considered by educators and others who are experts in the relevant communities and settings, and it will necessarily vary by context. But the prospect of communities collaborating and learning from each other could be powerful.

The guide above offers concrete actions that individual teachers, schools, districts, community members, and policy makers can take now to support the education of newcomers. But to truly transform immigrant education, we will need a whole community of educators across the country working together.

As I traveled throughout the United States, I was struck by how isolated remarkable teachers and innovative programs were from one another. Compared to many other professions in the country, teachers are too often disconnected—with few opportunities and little time to learn from colleagues in their communities, let alone from those in other states.

To overcome this barrier, I think we will need new kinds of programs and organizations that bring together the energy, expertise, and wisdom of educators from across the country interested in exploring, creating, and sharing strategies for classrooms, schools, districts, and states.

Such organizations could facilitate regular, ongoing collaboration between educators. As is evident from our response to the COVID-19 pandemic, such collaboration is no longer limited by geography.

They could support educators in creating materials that distill best practices in instruction, in school design, and in supporting specific groups of newcomers. And they could assist in disseminating those materials widely.

They could, with the support of funders, arrange for schools to send teams of teachers and administrators to visit innovative and successful classrooms and schools across the country, enabling educators to learn firsthand from other educators.

They could develop and fund mentorship programs that pair schools struggling to support newcomers with schools that have been successful, which can serve as sounding boards, offer support, and share effective strategies. They could also advise teacher preparation programs.

These organizations could help bridge the gap between policy experts, policy makers, and teachers. Fostering such collaboration would enable educators to have a seat at the table in crafting new policies and laws to support immigrant students and replicating successful examples from other states.

Finally, they could connect exceptional teachers and schools with universities, to ensure that innovative practices are studied through longitudinal research so that their impact is better understood.

I am confident that a vibrant community of educators working collaboratively can create ideas, practices, and policies that our students, schools, and country need.

My hope is that this book can help serve as a call to action and as a catalyst.

———◆———

At the end of August 2021, after hanging the walls with flags and maps, planting a corner garden filled with herbs, rethinking and rewriting lesson plans, I welcomed into our classroom more than one hundred young people from roughly two dozen countries across the globe.

The pandemic had kept most of my students away from our school buildings and from each other for more than eighteen months. For many of them, the months had been filled with severe hardship. Like teenagers across the country and the world, many had made the difficult but necessary choice to devote many hours to jobs to help support their families, logging into online classes from work. Many had juggled responsibilities at home, caring for siblings or elderly family members. Most struggled with shaky, unreliable internet and with loneliness. Some grappled with depression. As my students now returned to school, many were shy and unsure.

I hoped that in our classroom and in our school they would find support to help them study and a nurturing community to help them grow.

In looking to the school year ahead, I reflected on the eight elements that are essential for helping newcomer students succeed—on what is possible when young people have chances for new beginnings and opportunities to dream, when they have community, security, acceptance, and advocates, when their strengths are recognized and their voices valued.

Together these elements make possible for my students something that is fundamental: a sense of belonging.

Belonging is at the heart of what my students, what all of us, are seeking. And a sense of belonging should be at the core of what it means *to be* an American.

Unlike in most countries, no single ethnicity, religion, culture, heritage, or history connects all the peoples of the United States. Rather, the country's strength is rooted in the premise that anyone from anywhere can belong here. It is a commitment that the country has often failed to keep. But the country's success depends on fulfilling that promise.

My students have taught me the most about the fundamental importance and transformative power of belonging.

At the beginning of the school year in 2021, my students' discussions were halting. They were reserved with me and with each other. It took time to tease from their tongues ideas and opinions.

But as weeks slipped into months, we slowly grew to know one another. In our classroom I watched a transformation as these young people grew more comfortable, more confident, more courageous.

Sudanese and Dominican students studied side by side. A girl from Brazil teamed up to work with a boy from India. I watched friendships bloom between young Congolese and Cambodian teenagers. Class conversations grew boisterous. Students began stopping by before school, after school—often just to say hi.

And at lunch, students began arriving, to eat and to talk. At first they knocked timidly on the classroom door, but soon they were strolling in to turn desks into lunch tables. They came with questions about their studies and about the future, they came with stories about their families back home in countries far away, and they came with ideas for projects and programs they hoped to advocate for or create.

Together, they were well on their way to creating a place where they felt they belonged. And with that sense of belonging came the freedom to stretch, to grow, to connect, to dream, and to act.

That sense of belonging is something every child, every person craves. We all have roles to play in guaranteeing that young newcomers come to believe they belong here. It is what every educator, every school, and every community should fight for and should ensure for every single student.

For, when we do, when young people grow up knowing they belong—in a classroom, in a school, in a community, and in a country—they will make a home here and they will go out into the world and do remarkable things.

BELONGING

The final story returns to my student Robert, whose journey spans this book. Born and raised in the Democratic Republic of the Congo, Robert fled as a child to neighboring Uganda after his family was murdered. As an orphaned teenager, Robert began attending formal school, reunited with extended family in a refugee camp, and, having been offered a new home in the United States, landed in the country on the morning after the 2016 presidential election. The book concludes with Robert's journey after he arrived in the United States, where he built a new community in school and out, shaped a future for himself in this country, began to see himself as an American—and found, as he shared with me, a sense of belonging.

THE PERSONAL: ROBERT, PART 3

Robert, dapper in a navy blue suit and red-checkered tie, stood transfixed by the ochre marble and the historical murals blanketing the grand rotunda of the Massachusetts State House. It was May 2018. For months Robert, now a high school junior, had been learning the tools of active civic engagement. Robert and his classmates collaborated to do extensive research, draft proposals, write letters to state senators, conduct surveys, and make presentations. Now, representatives of the class had traveled to the State House to present their work publicly alongside students from schools across the state.

My students were jittery, nervous, and openly doubting that they belonged in such a majestic and important building. In just a few moments they would spread out into the high-ceilinged halls to speak about their semester's work with community members—lawyers, entrepreneurs, and doctors—acting as judges at a showcase for youth civic engagement. But for a moment more, it was just us.

I gathered my students close. "Your hard work brought you here," I said. As we had studied in class, I reminded them, this building was the people's building: It was their building.

In the hours that followed, Robert and his teammates would go on to win a statewide award for their civic engagement work on community safety. Before a crowd he would stand, slightly dazed but grinning broadly, alongside his classmates, including Safiya and Diane, to accept a plaque declaring them changemakers.

Years later, Robert would remind me of how we stood in a circle at the center of the rotunda that early morning. "I never thought that, as a refugee, that I could be in a position to make change. I thought I was limited." That day, he shared, "changed my perspective." He had not been born in the United States, but he was helping to make a difference here. "I realized that no matter how I saw myself before, I could be an American. I could do great things."

———— • ————

Robert's first American friend was a Dominican immigrant, a twenty-six-year-old named Vladimir Saldaña who worked at a community development organization. In late January 2017, Vladimir's mentor and friend Luis Pedroso had received a call from the resettlement organization assisting Robert's family: A Congolese family had recently arrived; could Luis help welcome the newcomers? Luis, who himself had immigrated from the Azores as a child, agreed and immediately reached out to Vladimir to ask if he would join him.

Vladimir had also come to the United States as a child. He knew from experience that one of the most difficult hurdles for newcomers was finding a sense of belonging. Without hesitation he promised to welcome the new arrivals.

Vladimir and Luis met Robert and his family at a local steakhouse. The family was shy, reserved—all but Robert, who could not stop talking about everything he saw that was new and fascinating: the profusion of brick buildings, the snow flurries, the towering grocery store aisles stacked with food. Over the following months Vladimir invited Robert and his high school–age uncles out into the community. Robert said yes every time. He joined Vladimir and his friends for games of pickup soccer, football, and volleyball. "There was something about Robert," Vladimir recalled. "He seized opportunities. I wanted to make sure that he felt he had somebody he could rely on."

In those early months, when everything felt foreign, Vladimir became a reliable constant. At school Robert spoke little, but with Vladimir he opened up. "It's always been easier to connect with people who are older," Robert admitted. With Vladimir, almost ten years his senior and more mature, almost fatherly, Robert grew in confidence. He became a regular at Vladimir's family home. Vladimir's mother relished cooking Dominican classics for the appreciative Congolese boy. Oxtail soup became his favorite. "We make this too in my country!" he exclaimed the first time he tasted the broth. When Robert caught his first winter cold, Vladimir's mother brewed him cup after cup of herbal tea. When Robert's aunt, who served as his guardian, felt too intimidated to speak with teachers and administrators about her nephew's progress, Vladimir went in her stead. When Robert needed help on an assignment, it was Vladimir he would turn to. And when after only a few months, Robert—still a sophomore—realized he needed to find a job, he reached out to Vladimir and Luis.

Within weeks, Luis had secured interviews for Robert and his young uncles at a sprawling Catholic nursing home in Lowell. On the day of the interview the boys set off on foot. They passed the high school and crossed the churning Merrimack River. In his hand Robert held his new phone, attempting to use Google Maps for the first time. Robert had never navigated by GPS and, after an hour of walking, he realized they were lost. Sheepishly he dialed the nursing home. A kindly voice offered instructions. Confidently the boys set out again, but after another thirty minutes they realized they were once again turned around. Embarrassed, they called again for help. It would take nearly two hours before they located the center's long driveway.

Despite the mishaps, Robert and an uncle were hired to work in one of the kitchens of the nursing home campus. They composed trays of food for wrinkled, white-haired residents, many hunched over in wheelchairs. Robert grew to know residents first by what they did and did not eat. This resident gets puréed potatoes, that one gets potatoes and gravy. What was gravy? Robert wondered.

In the kitchen, the boys kept to themselves, talking quietly in Kihema as they worked. Robert overheard other staff complaining, "Why are they always talking in another language?" "They didn't realize that we were trying to learn," he recalled thinking. Speaking in Kihema was one small comfort, one way to feel less lost. But Robert kept his thoughts to himself. When he made mistakes—forgot a side dish, switched two residents' trays—the chef barked reprimands. Robert considered quitting, but the pay was decent, the work steady. His family needed the money.

For weeks Robert and his uncle walked each afternoon the more than three miles from school to the nursing home, and then from work to home. But that spring Luis purchased bikes for the boys. Robert was fond of bikes. He had learned to ride as a little boy, pedaling past scrub brush and tall grass in the plains of the Democratic Republic of the Congo, waking up early to sell his mother's cows and goats at market. Once more, wheels carried him to work. Although now, he kept watch for swerving cars in the road, rather than for lions. At the start of summer break Robert took on more shifts, often double shifts on the weekends.

———◆———

On the last day of August 2017, Robert returned to school as a junior and for his first full year in an American high school. His very first class that morning was my US history course. It was on that morning, amid the swirl of new students, that I first met Robert. He selected a seat near the wall. In a crowded and boisterous room of twenty-eight teenagers, Robert was quiet and disciplined.

We opened our study of US history with an exploration of immigration, specifically the stories of immigrants from more than a century ago. We reflected on Emma Lazarus's poem at the base of the Statue of Liberty, and we dissected the Chinese Exclusion Act. We examined the photographs of immigrant families in tenements and immigrant children in factories. And we studied the rise of the labor movement and unions, often filled with and sometimes led by immigrants, or the children of immigrants, standing up for safer or equal working conditions.

When I'd set about constructing my lesson plans, I was struck by all the activities and lesson plans I found online that started with some version of, "Imagine you had to leave your home . . ."; "Imagine you were coming to a new country . . ." My students didn't have to imagine. My students were experts.

Drawing on inspiration from a former elementary school teacher of mine, I composed a culminating project to bridge the past and the present: I asked my students to share a slice of their own migration story, told through a favorite family recipe. Over weeks, each student selected and translated a recipe and wrote about what it meant to them. After much consideration, Robert chose *mwana mbonka*, a beef and cabbage stew that was a staple of his family's Christmas celebrations.

He had yet to find a place in the United States, in school or out, that acknowledged the traditions, language, or heritage of his people. Maybe in America, he wondered, "there's no space for it." The project, Robert shared years later, provided him an opportunity to be seen. It felt good to share about his culture, to have others want to learn more. "It makes you feel like your culture contributes to a larger community."

I began to know Robert from class discussions, but also from informal conversations. Often Robert came early or stayed late. Our conversations ranged from the political to the historical to the everyday.

In the depths of February, I announced our multimonth civics project aimed at tackling a community challenge. Robert sat near Diane and Safiya, and together, on the heels of the shooting at Marjory Stoneman Douglas High School in Parkland, Florida, their class voted to tackle gun violence. Our civics work required intense collaboration. No individual assignments. For many students, the project is one of the first times they have to work together on an extended academic project.

For the boy who had struggled to connect, Robert's work that spring marked a turning point. "We had to work together. We had to disagree. We had to agree. We developed so many relationships in that class." Slowly Robert began to grow comfortable in school. In a corner of a computer lab, he gathered peers around him; five heads huddled around an old Dell monitor with Robert at the center, methodically typing out a memo, letter by letter, about proposed state legislation. One afternoon he drove with his classmates to visit, nervously, the office of a state representative to advocate in support of the legislation.

In May, his peers voted for him to serve as one of the class's representatives to travel with me down to the State House to present their work.

That morning in the rotunda we formed our circle, sharing the moment. And it was there, at the end of the day, that a handful of students asked me to take a picture before we headed back to Lowell. Smiling, I snapped a photo of five grinning young men, faces aglow and arms slung across each other's shoulders: two Dominicans, an Iraqi, a Venezuelan, and Robert—a boy born in the Democratic Republic of the Congo.

———•———

During the spring of Robert's junior year, a collection of nurses who every day wheeled and walked residents into the dining hall of the nursing home approached Robert with an idea. It had been almost a year since he had begun work there, and many on staff had come to care for Robert—impressed by the staggering number of shifts he took, touched by how kind he was to residents, and grateful for how efficient he was in helping ensure meals ran smoothly. They thought he should apply to become a certified nursing assistant (CNA)—and even printed out an application for him.

A school counselor located a local certification program and, for a time, Robert's world became a revolving door of classes and kitchens. Months later, he arrived at work bearing his CNA certificate; the nurses cheered. The once-skeptical head chef beamed with pride.

Stepping out of the kitchen, Robert took responsibility for a slate of residents, helping them bathe and dress and eat. He quickly became a favorite on the halls. There was the woman who crooned when she saw Robert, "Here comes my boyfriend." Another proudly introduced him to her extended family.

And then there was Larry, a blind cab dispatcher with a thick local accent. Larry loved to talk. "The prince is here!" he'd proclaim upon recognizing Robert's voice. Over long afternoons Robert and Larry talked sports, about which Robert had been reading up—the two trading thoughts on baseball games and heavyweight matches. With equal interest, Larry followed Robert's academic progress, asking about his grades and his classes week after week. But most often they passed the time joking. "Are we going to the gym today?" Robert might ask. "You won't be able to keep up," Larry would chuckle. "I'm benching 700, with one arm. I don't want to put you to shame."

After tucking Larry into bed, Robert would himself head to the gym to work out. Heading into his senior year, Robert maintained a grueling schedule: up before dawn to complete homework, six hours of school, eight hours at the nursing home, an hour of reps, free weights, and bench presses, and then, finally, sleep. He filled his weekends with double shifts, spending time not with high school friends but with wrinkled men and women in their seventies, eighties, and nineties.

———————◆———————

On the first day of his senior year in 2018, Robert bounded into my room. He was not on my rosters for the fall, but he wanted to say hi nonetheless. I would teach him again, he reminded me, in the spring, as he was enrolled in my seminar class. The classroom filled that morning with a gaggle of newly anointed seniors—Safiya, Srey Neth, Choori, Julian, Diane, and so many others. They traded handshakes, hugs, slaps on the back. They shared stories of the summer and compared course schedules. Later Robert texted me, "It's nice to see u again miss. praise be to the Lord for keeping us alive amidst this uncertain times and in this troubled world. I am looking forward to learning more and seeking more academic and life advice from you."

That fall, Robert dove voraciously into his studies. He quickly fell in love with his course on American literature. There he came upon classics—*The Great Gatsby, The Crucible,* and others—that were like forgotten friends, stories he'd first deciphered in a Ugandan border town and in a refugee camp.

But the course that most captivated him was one devoted to the literature of the Holocaust. There he lost himself in the stark black-and-white images of the graphic novel *Maus,* the story of a son processing his parents' violent experience in Nazi Europe and their survival in the Auschwitz concentration camp. In class he learned about the devastating impact of *bystanders*, who chose inaction, and the essential role of *upstanders*, who risked their lives to save others. He became captivated by an online TED Talk in which a former neo-Nazi described his own radicalization as a teenager and how as an older man he extracted himself from the group and founded an organization dedicated to helping others escape extremism, violence, and hate.

Although he did not share the resemblance aloud, in the photographs, documentaries, and stories of the Third Reich, Robert saw the faces of the Lendu people, who had, nearly a decade earlier, murdered his family.

Thousands of miles from home, Robert was finding the words and the space to begin to process his past. "I had faced terrible experiences of losing people, of oppression, of terror," he told me later. "But in studying other people who had been through such terrible things, I realized that these things didn't only happen to me." On quiet afternoons, Robert, knowing I was Jewish, sought me out to share what he was learning in the class. When at work he overheard an antisemitic slur, he arrived the next day upset. "How do people learn to hate so much?" he asked me.

One Saturday that fall, a middle-aged white man stormed the Tree of Life Synagogue in Pittsburgh, Pennsylvania, gunning down worshippers in the midst of Saturday morning services—murdering eleven congregants and injuring six more. While I was scrolling through the news reports, horrified, Robert texted me. Of everyone I knew in the world, he was the first to reach out: "Ms. I'm so sorry about the shooting. It's so disgusting how people hurt others who have never hurt them."

———◆———

Although I was not Robert's teacher that fall, I saw him many afternoons after the final bell. He and others gathered in a computer lab to begin applying to college. Robert was initially reluctant. He loved learning, but college seemed too expensive to consider. Nevertheless, he agreed to rearrange his work schedule—with no computer at home, Robert relied on school computers to type out his applications. He came in early and stayed late, his typing faster and more fluid than when he had searched for lions in the months after arriving in America.

Poring over his list of possible colleges, I suggested one addition: Brandeis University, an elite New England institution founded by the American Jewish community in the wake of the Holocaust. When Robert researched the tuition, he stared aghast at the price tag: roughly $70,000 per year. But we had learned that the university had a scholarship program for twenty young people each year who had "demonstrated academic promise, leadership potential, and resilience in their life experiences" but who had, like Robert, been unable to take AP courses or fill their afternoons with extracurricular activities. It was a long shot. But just maybe Robert could be one of the next year's twenty.

Yet to apply to any institution, Robert needed to write the dreaded college essay, that 650-word story meant to set his application apart from those of his peers. Robert was stumped. What could he say? He was not on any sports teams, nor had he mastered an instrument. He partook in no clubs. No summer internships adorned his résumé. His work at the nursing home had, by necessity, consumed most afternoons and evenings.

One essay prompt suggested he describe his background and his identity. Rarely before had Robert shared either. He had come to believe that being a refugee was a liability. Refugees, he thought, were more likely to drop out of school, less likely to succeed. Yet looking to the future, Robert chose to begin writing about his past. "I am a Ugandan Congolese . . . I am a refugee twice over."

That fall, Robert began to share his story with colleges, and that spring he began to open up to classmates.

On the first day of Robert's final semester of high school, he sat once more in my classroom, one of twenty-eight students joining my upper-level seminar. "What does it mean to be American?" I asked the class. As I explained on that chilly February morning, each student would be tasked with answering that question in the form of a personal story to be included in a book we would write together.

After the bell, Robert hung back to confer. As a child growing up in the Democratic Republic of the Congo, Robert had avidly followed President Obama's election; as a young teenager in a Ugandan refugee camp he had devoured American history; as a young man he had presented about legislation at the Massachusetts State House. Robert had, in recent years, begun to see himself as an American. But, he worried that others would not agree.

That afternoon, he decided, hesitantly, to continue what he had begun with his college essay. "Only write what you feel ready to share," I cautioned. By then, Robert was twenty, give or take. It had been eight years, likely to the month, since he had fled across the Semliki River. To survive, to move forward, he had refused to dwell on the past. As he explained, "I always wanted to keep away from the grief." When friends had fashioned alternate identities for him, ones filled with loving, living parents, he did not correct them. College applications were read by strangers, but this story he knew would be read by friends.

In the coming weeks Robert wrote and wrote and wrote.

He wrote about gardening at sunrise with his mother and the advice she would share, "Good things come to those who get out and make them happen"; about his childhood home, a mud-thatched house with a door so low one had to duck to enter; about the deadly Lendu attack and his panicked dash to Uganda; about the lonely years herding cows in Ntoroko. Remembering set him on edge. He snapped at friends, was curt at work. His temper, usually nonexistent, sizzled. It took him weeks to recognize the cause. In writing, he had begun reliving moments of his childhood. "I realized how sad I was going into these moments."

But still Robert wrote. He wrote about the unexpected jubilation of finding family in a refugee camp; about the tent they lived in and the lack of food and water; about going to school in the camp. "My mother used to tell me education was the best thing I could have, and that education could never be taken away. And so I looked to school as my hope for a better life."

And he wrote about his journey to the United States. "I couldn't imagine how life would be, but I hoped it would be better. I got the chance to attend Lowell High School, which changed my life completely. Here, I have met tremendous people who have recognized, accepted, and supported me spiritually, academically, and emotionally. I now understand my mother's answer to my questions all those years ago. I have learned that our parents' words can guide us even in their absences. Everywhere I have gone her lessons have been the key to opening doors in my life."

That spring, Robert's class published their book of personal stories. In class they sat in a circle to read about each other's lives, passing around the pages of their book, so captivated that for forty-five minutes not a word was spoken. After school, Robert brought a copy to the nursing home. Three nurses sought him out soon afterward—gripped his arm, his hand. "We are so sorry." "We never knew." "We are so proud of you." "You are inspiring." His boss printed copies and passed them around. She found him later: "Will you speak to the residents? They have so much to learn from you." Robert was flabbergasted. "I was just a refugee," he thought. "Many people have the same sad story." Larry, being blind, could not read Robert's story, but another resident sat by his wheelchair and read Robert's words out loud. When Robert came later to check on him, Larry was unusually serious. He gripped the young man's hand. "You are really great," he said.

For Robert, the attention was unexpected, yet surprisingly comforting. "I felt like I was not alone," Robert remembers. "Yes, sad, terrible things happened, but that shouldn't define me. . . . It was only a part of me." All the friends, the colleagues, the teachers reaching out reminded Robert of the community surrounding him, the community "helping me to keep moving forward."

———•———

That spring, as college decisions began trickling in, Robert and his classmates were thinking more and more about what the future might hold. Robert received his first college acceptance, then his second, then his third. Invitations piled up, and he marveled at the choices. Offers in hand, we set about creating a spreadsheet to compare financial aid packages. Robert, just shy of his twenty-first birthday, was a breadwinner for his family. Selecting a college would be determined not by offered courses or clubs, but by cost.

Then, late one Tuesday, Robert texted me, stunned. He had just been accepted as one of twenty students to Brandeis University's Myra Kraft Transitional Year Program. As a recipient, he was offered a five-year, nearly fully paid scholarship.

Over spring break I met Robert at Brandeis to tour the campus. The sky was cloudless, the temperature unusually balmy. We ambled across the sloping lawns and wandered through corridors, poking our heads into empty science labs. Robert told me about a friend in Uganda who loved science and how he wished he could study here. At Robert's insistence we trekked up to a dorm resembling a castle. Looking up at the turrets, he shook his head. "This place is in another world."

In early June 2019, Robert strode across a graduation stage. Tears rolled continuously down my cheeks much of the evening. After the ceremony, as graduates streamed out into the night, Vladimir stopped Robert and his family, who were about to head home. "You can't just go home! We are going to celebrate." Smiling, they traipsed after him.

The following September I met Robert once more at Brandeis. He was no longer a visitor, but a proud college freshman. Confidently he guided me along the paths, gushing about his classes, the soccer team he'd joined, the fraternity he was considering rushing. But what made me smile most was that, as we walked, every few minutes it seemed, someone stopped Robert to say hi. Amused, I pointed out how popular he had become. Robert grinned, "I thought it would always be hard for me to make connections with Americans, but here they want to know you, they care about you, they think you are great, and that empowers me."

Every few weeks over the coming months, Robert would text me with updates: His introduction to law class was fascinating; a computer science assignment was particularly confusing. He told me about chapatis he cooked for his hallmates and about the foot-long beard he wore to a college costume party.

One Saturday in February 2020, Robert invited me to visit the nursing home where he had worked, excitedly introducing me to nurses and residents. Less than a month later the COVID-19 pandemic swamped the United States. Robert was sent home from university, forced to Zoom into classes with a flickering internet connection. Although nursing homes across the country were quickly becoming deadly epicenters of the outbreak, Robert needed to help pay for rent and support the family. So once more he began picking up shifts. Even so, in June, Robert's transcript bloomed with A's.

Semester slipped into semester. Robert wrote about reforestation efforts in the United States and in East African countries for one class, presented on a Supreme Court case addressing immigration in another. Every few months we would meet, walking along a river or around a pond, and he would regale me with stories of his courses. Once we passed by a used bookshop with a display of one-dollar books. Drawn by the worn spines, Robert gently picked up one volume, then another. As he read, I was reminded of the library he had once amassed as a child at the Ugandan border and of the two books he had chosen to carry with him on his journey: *Jane Eyre* and *Best Poems of 1998*. Forty minutes later we left the shop, Robert cradling a bag twenty titles heavy. He was, he told me, in the midst of compiling a new library here.

That spring Robert was named to the university's dean's list in recognition of his academic achievements. School had barely let out when he packed his bags and boarded a plane, the first since he had arrived in the United States five years earlier on the morning after the 2016 presidential election. He had enlisted in the National Guard and would spend the following months in training, returning just days before the start of school.

Robert returned to campus as a junior, majoring in environmental studies and minoring in legal studies. Although his scholarship provided him the opportunity to complete a bachelor's degree in five years, he was on track to finish in four. But he hoped to stay a while longer at school. Looking toward his senior year, he was already planning to apply to one of the university's master's programs. As Robert shared with me, he hoped to pursue a degree in conflict resolution and coexistence.

ACKNOWLEDGMENTS

In the spring of 2015 Robert DeLossa and Stephen Gervais, two department chairs at Lowell High School, met me early on a Saturday morning. They'd driven south and I north to meet in the middle at a cafe along a railroad track. Over tea, they told me about the school and community where they taught. That morning they encouraged me to join their team, to teach history to immigrant-origin students. It was a conversation that altered the course of my life.

As semester slipped into semester, I realized how much my extraordinary students, newly arrived from around the world, were teaching me about life. They taught me about perseverance, strength, and determination. They taught me about curiosity, creativity, courage, and compassion. And, over the years, together we took our learning into the world—with my students publishing articles, writing books, advocating for laws, working with local officials and others to create community change.

In Lowell I found the work I hope will fill my lifetime. I began seeking out ways to advocate for and with my students outside the classroom—writing newspaper op-eds and magazine articles, working with policy makers, training teachers. In quiet moments, the idea for this book took root. It germinated among lessons, was nurtured by conversations with my students, and was sustained by our community work. Robert and Stephen encouraged me and helped make it possible for me to take a one-year leave. I sought out, too, the advice of my students—they were unequivocal in their support. And so, with their blessing, I set forth to learn and to write.

In writing about education, I've been privileged to learn from so many people, across the country and across my life, who generously become my teachers.

MY STUDENTS. Carla, Choori, Diane, Julian, Robert, Safiya, and Srey Neth inspire me every day. It has been an enormous honor to teach them and learn from them. Over years I have watched them grow, met their families, offered support in hard times, celebrated their successes, and collaborated with them on local and national projects. It is a tremendous privilege to now tell some of their stories. They have courageously and compassionately shared their experiences so educators and others may learn from them. I'm so honored by their and their families' trust. These seven young people are the heart of the book and a light to the world. They fill me with hope.

INNOVATIVE IMMIGRANT-EDUCATION PROGRAMS. I set out from my classroom to learn in the classrooms of others. As a teacher, I know the trust and time it takes to let an outsider observe, discuss, and profile one's educational practices. I am grateful for the generosity of the leaders, educators, and support staff—those mentioned by name and many more who are not—at the programs profiled: Las Americas, Aurora ACTION Zone; Fargo South High, ENLACE, Guilford County School District, International High School at Langley Park; and Global Village Project. These educators welcomed me into their communities. They set aside work to teach me about their programs; shared documents and lessons; arranged for me to talk with many in their communities; answered dozens of emails filled with questions; let me shadow them in classrooms, school hallways, and meetings; and invited me to lunches and dinners to continue our conversations. And, they shared with me their own ideas, struggles, stories, and goals.

I was also honored to visit and learn from many other exceptional educators and their colleagues, including Luma Mufleh, founder of Fugees Academy; Kari Croft, founder of Da Vinci RISE High; Emma Vogel at Teen Response; Angela Sisi and Mario Perez at The Newcomer Center; Ashley Simpson Baird and Lauren Stoltzfus at Briya Public Charter School; Monico Rivas, principal at Liberty High School; Maria Tukeva, principal at Columbia Heights Educational Campus; Lauren Markham at Oakland International High School; and Ben Gucciardi and Mary Connor, cofounders of Soccer Without Borders; members of the Council of the Great City Schools; as well as educators at the Social Justice Humanities Academy, Thomas Jefferson International Newcomers Academy, and Boston International Newcomers Academy.

In understanding current innovation and challenges in immigrant education, I learned from many educators, scholars, policy makers, organizers, and others who shared their experiences, teaching practices, wisdom, and research, in particular Sarah Bernadette Ottow, Gabriela Bobadilla, Verónica Boix-Mansilla, David Cutler, Romy Drucker, Arne Duncan, Anpao Duta Flying Earth, Jana Echevarria, Karla Estrada, Larry Ferlazzo, David Flink, Astrid Emily Francis, Amaya Garcia, Sheldon Horowitz, Myrna Jacobs, Patrick Kearns, David Lai, Vanessa Luna, Mandy Manning, Eva Millona, Sarahí Monterrey, Linda Nathan, Ariadne Paredes, Margaret Proffitt, Anthony Rebora, Claudia Rinaldi, Carol Salva, Steve Sofronas, Sonia W. Soltero, Molly Hegwood, Carola Suárez-Orozco, Alhassan Susso, the late Ruby Takanishi, Natalie Tamburello, Margalit Tepper, Megan Trcka, Gabriela Uro, and Conor P. Williams.

HISTORY OF IMMIGRANT EDUCATION. I am a history teacher, but in writing this book I've been privileged to become a history student myself. I'm grateful to the authors of the dozens of books and hundreds of articles I read in the course of this work. It has been a special honor to learn directly from those whose lives are intimately intertwined with the historical struggles chronicled in the book. They generously answered my letters; shared the extraordinary stories of how their families shaped history; and reviewed the text for accuracy. I am grateful to so many people. With respect to *Meyer v. Nebraska*: Luree Wiese, Raymond Parpart's daughter, and David Feddern, current pastor of the Zion Lutheran Church where Robert Meyer taught. With respect to *Mendez v. Westminster*: Sylvia Mendez, whose parents along with others sued California school districts; Akiko Munemitsu, whose parents leased their farm to the Mendez family, and her niece Janice Munemitsu; Maria Lane, whose father David Marcus represented the families in court; and Robert DeLapp, Marcus's grandson, and his wife Lori DeLapp. With respect to *Lau v. Nichols*: Lucinda Lee Katz, Kinney Lau's teacher; Edward Steinman, the lawyer who sued the San Francisco School District; Ling-chi Wang, the community leader who advocated on behalf of San Francisco's Chinese community; Stanley Pottinger, who wrote the memorandum that helped shape the Supreme Court's decision; Roger Rice, who coauthored the amicus brief with the single untranslated footnote in Chinese; and Larry Katz, friend of Lucinda Lee Katz and a legal intern with San Francisco Neighborhood Legal Assistance. With respect to *Plyler v. Doe:* Alfredo Lopez, whose parents risked deportation to sue the Tyler school district, and his wife Angie Lopez; Michael McAndrew, the social worker who advocated for Tyler's undocumented families; Bobbi Thami (then Roberta Rodkin), Larry Daves, and Peter Roos, who represented the families, and Martha McCabe, who worked with them; Pastor Milam Joseph who, in the 1970s, led a Catholic congregation in Tyler; Ruth Epstein, Judge Justice's law clerk when the case was filed; Jan Westwater, a relative of Judge Justice; Joan Marie Wicker, a relative of Judge Seals; and Jin K. Park, who, in 2020, wrote in the *Atlantic* about his experience as an undocumented young person. With respect to the history of bilingual education: Roger Rice, executive director of Multicultural Education, Training & Advocacy, Inc.; Tom Louie, director of the Massachusetts English Plus Coalition; Charles Glick, who consulted on the campaign against Question 2 in Massachusetts; Berta Rosa Berriz, who taught immigrant-origin students in Boston before and after passage of Question 2; Representatives Antonio Cabral and Jeffrey Sánchez, who advocated for legislation to support EL students; Helen Solórzano, current executive director of the Massachusetts Association of Teachers of Speakers of Other Languages (MATSOL); Paula Merchant, former executive director of MATSOL; and Phyllis Hardy, executive director of Multistate Association for Bilingual Education, Northeast. In addition, I thank those who connected me with some of the individuals above and provided other invaluable assistance with my research, including Judge Rachel Daugherty, Wendy Dethlefs, Jan Dick, Roberto G. Gonzales, Bridget Grumet, Jeff Hittenberger, Ross Stanton Jordan, Fernanda Marinho Kray, Cynthia Levinson, Tom Mela, Sister Nora M. Nash, Russell Nauman, Vincent Pan, Antonio Ramirez, Katherine Toy, Barry Vogel, Alice Wolf, and Christina Wong.

As I sought to understand the complex history of immigrant education and to make it leap from the page, many librarians and archivists kindly agreed to become my teachers. I particularly thank Jennifer Cuddeback, Jill Duffy, Kate Hallgren, Violet Hurst, Frances Kaplan, Sister Helen Jacobson, Thomas Lester, Carla M Lillvik, Pastor David Palomaki, Meghan Pipp, Liza Talbot, and Annie Tang.

THOUGHT PARTNERS. Great teachers see and cultivate students' potential. Emerson Collective did this for me. Years ago the Emerson Collective team saw in my work things that I had yet to see. They generously provided me with a remarkable yearlong fellowship, supporting me to travel and learn from teachers across the country and giving me the time and resources to research and write this book. Beth Schmidt, Daimen Sagastume, Patrick D'Arcy, and Amy Low became indispensable thought partners and enthusiastic cheerleaders. And, I want to express my deepest gratitude to Laurene Powell Jobs, founder and president of Emerson Collective, for her vision, compassion, and generosity, and for her dedication to helping to heal the world.

I'm deeply grateful to the Re-Imagining Migration community for being essential thought partners and to Adam Strom, cofounder and director, who invited me to be a fellow of this organization devoted to rethinking education for immigrant-origin young people and working to create schools that nurture inclusive communities.

PRODUCING THIS BOOK. From our very first conversation Rachael Marks, senior editor at Beacon Press, believed in me and in this book. She has been a steadfast partner and cheerleader. I am grateful for her enthusiasm, caring, and dedication. I thank the entire team at Beacon Press, who shared their creativity and compassion and became my collaborators in bringing this book into the world. I so admire the mission and values that are the heart of Beacon Press. I'm grateful to Paul Golob whose honest and supportive feedback led me to completely restructure the book. I am indebted to my fact-checker Hilary McClellen, for her enthusiasm for historical sleuthing and fastidious attention to detail; to Gabriela Rivero for her precision and positive energy in tackling citations; and to Laura Kenney for her keen eye in copyediting.

My thinking was enriched and the book strengthened by the wisdom and critiques of many colleagues and friends who devoted time from their busy lives to read chapters, discuss ideas, and share advice. I particularly want to thank Kendra Bauer, Lois Bridges, Tony Clark, Thalia Yarina Carroll-Cachimuel, Linda Chin, Ellen Clegg, Robert De-Lossa, Sarah Dryden-Peterson, Niko Emack, Charles FitzGibbon, Carra Fraker, Stephen Gervais, Sarah Ladipo Manyika, Martha Minow, Anupama Pattabiraman, Adam Strom, Ellie Wisbach Sánchez, Daniel Sass, Carolyn Smith-Lin, Priya Tahiliani, Bina Venkataraman, Bari Walsh,

Lauren Whitehead, and Ellen Zucker. And, to my fellow educator and good friend Sara R. Shaw: I am forever grateful to her for allowing my work to monopolize many evenings and mornings as she read every paragraph, every word, for wide-ranging connections and microscopic detail. I'm thankful too for many friends who, over recent months and years, provided tremendous support and at times tore me away from writing and other work for adventures and rejuvenation.

MY TEACHERS. As a teacher writing about teaching, I am reminded of my own teachers who nurtured my love of learning, challenged me, and inspired me to contribute to my communities. I'm grateful to elementary school teachers who helped me—a young girl with dyslexia struggling to read, spell, and speak clearly—to fall in love with learning, to follow my curiosity, and to be an upstander in the face of injustice, including Connie Biewald, Grace Harriman, Jenn K. Goodman, and Lucy Wittenberg. In high school I was introduced to creative nonfiction writing and learned to develop my voice; I particularly thank Cammie Thomas, Sandy Stott, and Andrea Yañes-Taylor. At university, I had the honor of studying the art of writing with John McPhee and constitutional law with Christopher Eisgruber. I'm grateful to many faculty members in graduate school who pushed me to grapple with education policies and practices, and to look honestly and critically at myself and my work, including Sarah Dryden-Peterson, Tom Hehir, Karen Mapp, Pasi Sahlberg, and Dean James Ryan. I've also been privileged to learn from powerful mentors outside of school who, time and again, have been there for me—sharing wisdom, championing my work, offering counsel in rough times, and celebrating with me in joyous moments. I am forever grateful to Ellen Clegg, Adam Strom, and Bari Walsh.

EDUCATIONAL COMMUNITIES. My teaching practice has been shaped by educators and students at many schools and programs at which I have been privileged to work, including Princeton in Asia, Chiang Mai University, Citizen Schools, Clarence R. Edwards Middle School, the Harpswell Foundation, The Possible Project, and the Cambridge Community Learning Center. I have also been nurtured, challenged, and renewed by educators, policymakers, and others at many organizations, including Generation Citizen, Facing History and Ourselves, the Massachusetts Council for the Social Studies, MATSOL, Teach Plus, and the Massachusetts Department of Elementary and Secondary Education.

Mostly recently, I have been privileged to be part of a remarkable community of global teachers honored by the Varkey Foundation.

LOWELL HIGH. I am grateful beyond words to the many people in Lowell who support our young people, including Superintendent Joel Boyd, the Lowell School Committee, Phala Chea, Latifah Phillips, head of LHS Michael Fiato, former head Brian Martin, the LHS leadership team, and my dean Deidre Haley. I'm grateful to all of my colleagues at Lowell High School for their collaboration, and I'm forever indebted to Robert and Stephen for welcoming me to LHS, championing our work, and always being there to offer advice and support. And, to all of my extraordinary LHS students, past and present, and to their families: I am honored to know you and to learn from you.

MY FAMILY. This book came into being through the steadfast support, wisdom, and love of my family. Our dog, Mochi, was my companion on many meandering walks as I stitched sentences and wove ideas in my mind. My brothers, Daniel and David, read chapters, opined on words, and offered advice again and again. My deepest gratitude is to my parents—to my mom, Lori, whose compassion and generosity are my mainstay, and to my dad, Eric, my stalwart mentor, editor, and travel companion through the words and pages of these stories. Together, my parents are my greatest teachers, and together they taught me how to be and live in this world. To my entire family: I love you with all my heart and more.

NOTES

INTRODUCTION

1. "Children in immigrant families in the United States," Kids Count Data Center, Dec. 2020; "Immigrant Children," Child Trends, Dec. 28, 2018.

2. Jeffrey S. Passel and D'Vera Cohn, "U.S. Population Projections: 2005-2050," Pew Research Center, February 11, 2008.

CHAPTER 1: NEW BEGINNINGS

1. National Educational Association, *Journal of Proceedings and Addresses of the Forty-Fourth Annual Meeting* (Winona, MN: The Association, 1905), 113.

2. The Educational Alliance, Sixth Annual Report, 1898.

3. Selma C. Berrol, "In Their Image: German Jews and the Americanization of the Ost Juden in New York City," *New York History* 63, no. 4 (1982): 424.

4. Selma C. Berrol, "When Uptown Met Downtown: Julia Richman's Work in the Jewish Community of New York, 1880–1912," *American Jewish History* 70, no. 1 (1980): 44.

5. Richman, "The Immigrant Child," 107.

6. Berrol, "When Uptown Met Downtown," 35.

7. William H. Maxwell, *Education of the Immigrant* (Washington, DC: United States Bureau of Education, 1913), 18.

8. *Documents of the Assembly of the State of New York, One Hundredth and Thirty-Sixth Session* (Albany, NY: Lyon, 1913), 61.

9. Israel Zangwill, *The Melting Pot* (New York: Macmillan, 1909), Act I.

10. Recent research has suggested that Bellamy may have taken much of the language for the pledge from a 13-year-old boy's submission to a children's contest. Sam Roberts, "We Know the Pledge. Its Author, Maybe Not," *New York Times*, April 2, 2022.

11. *The Illustrated American*, vol. 22 (New York: Illustrated American Publishing Co., 1897), 258.

12. Christopher Petrella, "The Ugly History of the Pledge of Allegiance—and Why It Matters," *Washington Post*, November 3, 2017.

13. National Educational Association, *Journal of Proceedings and Addresses: Session of the Year 1894 Held at Asbury Park, New Jersey* (St. Paul, MN: National Education Association, 1895), 257.

14. Ellwood P. Cubberley, *Changing Conceptions of Education*, ed. Henry Suzzallo (New York: Houghton Mifflin, 1909), 15.

15. Calvin N. Kendall, "Plain Talk about Schools," *Journal of Education* 90, no. 12 (1919): 311.

16. Leonard H. Covello and Guido D'Agostino, *The Heart Is the Teacher* (New York: McGraw-Hill, 1958), 43–44.

17. Eugene Lyons, *Assignment in Utopia* (New Brunswick, NJ: Transaction Publishers, 1991), 4–5.

18. Leonard H. Covello, *The Social Background of the Italo-American School Child: A Study of the Southern Italian Family Mores and Their Effect on the School Situation in Italy and America,* ed. Francesco Cordasco (Leiden, Netherlands: E.J. Brill, 1967), 411.

19. I have chosen to use the Gregorian calendar here; however, some historical sources will place these events about thirteen days earlier, as the Russian Empire used the Julian calendar until 1918.

20. Anna Maggin, shared with granddaughter, 1974.

21. The proportion of the Khmer residents cited is taken from the 2010 census (Virak Chan, "The Linguistic Landscape of a Cambodia Town in Lowell, Massachusetts," *Journal of Southeast Asian American Education and Advancement* 13, no. 1 [2018]). Some community leaders believe the census undercounts the proportion.

22. Carola Suárez-Orozco, Mona M. Abo-Zena, and Amy K. Marks (eds.), *Transitions: The Development of Children of Immigrants* (New York: New York University Press, 2015), 32–44.

CHAPTER 2: COMMUNITY

1. Gioia Diliberto, *A Useful Woman: The Early Life of Jane Addams* (New York: Scribner, 1999), 261.

2. Victor Weybright, "Jane Addams, the Tireless, at Seventy," *New York Times,* August 31, 1930.

3. Legislative Committee of the Peoples' Freedom Union, "The Lusk Committee: A Report on the Activities of the Committee to Investigate Seditious Activities in the State of New York" (New York, 1920).

4. Halvdan Koht, "The Nobel Peace Prize 1931 Presentation Speech" (Nobel Committee, Oslo, December 10, 1931).

5. Jacob Riis, letter to Jane Addams, March 9, 1901, digital.janeaddams.ramapo.edu/items/show/113.

6. Jacob Riis, *The Battle with the Slum* (New York: Macmillan, 1902), 395.

7. Mary Rozet Smith, letter to Jane Addams, October 22, 1901, digital.jane addams.ramapo.edu/items/show/1152.

8. Jane Addams, *Twenty Years at Hull House* (Seattle: Pacific Publishing Studio, 2011), 33.

9. Leonard H. Covello and Guido D'Agostino, *The Heart Is the Teacher* (New York: McGraw-Hill, 1958), 43–44.

10. National Education Association, *Journal of Proceedings and Addresses of the Forty-Sixth Annual Meeting Held at Cleveland, Ohio, June 29–July 3, 1908* (Chicago: University of Chicago Press, 1908).

11. Jean Bethke Elshtain, *The Jane Addams Reader* (New York: Basic Books, 2002), 236.

12. Addams, *Twenty Years at Hull House*, 87.

13. Sarah Ruffing Robbins, "Collaborative Writing as Jane Addams's Hull-House Legacy," in *Learning Legacies: Archive to Action through Women's Cross-Cultural Teaching* (Ann Arbor: University of Michigan Press, 2017), 85.

14. Elshtain, *The Jane Addams Reader*, 236.

15. Addams, *Twenty Years at Hull House*, 73.

16. Addams, *Twenty Years at Hull House*, 72.

17. Jane Addams, "Remarks on Immigrant Children and Public School Teachers, March 1906," *American Education* (1906), digital.janeaddams.ramapo.edu /items/show/4230.

18. Elshtain, *The Jane Addams Reader*, 238.

19. Elshtain, *The Jane Addams Reader*, 238.

20. Grace Abbott, *The Immigrant and the Community* (New York: Century Co., 1917), 228.

21. Francis A. Walker, "Restriction of Immigration," *Atlantic*, June 1896.

22. National Conference of Social Work, *Proceedings of the National Conference of Social Work, Formerly, National Conference of Charities and Correction, at the Forty-Seventh Annual Session Held in New Orleans, Louisiana, April 14–21, 1920* (Chicago: University of Chicago Press, 1920), 62.

23. City of Aurora, "Who Is Aurora? 2016 Demographic Report" (Aurora, CO: Planning and Development Services, 2016), 13.

CHAPTER 3: SECURITY

1. Because accounts have been inconsistent as to which passage Raymond was reading, I reviewed the 1920 district court trial transcript. The confusion, I believe, stems from the fact that Raymond, at the time eleven years old, referred in his testimony to the passage in German as *Die Himmelsleiter* (which biblically refers to Jacob's ladder), but in English as "Joseph's ladder"). Some accounts have also listed Raymond's age at the time as ten. However, he was born in January 1909, according to both his daughter and public records, and thus would have been eleven.

2. Pastor David Feddern (pastor of Zion Lutheran Church in Hampton, Nebraska), phone interview with the author, May 18, 2020.

3. Benjamin Franklin, letter to Peter Collinson, May 9, 1753, founders.archives .gov/documents/Franklin/01-04-02-0173.

4. Roger Daniels, *Coming to America: A History of Immigration and Ethnicity in American Life* (New York: Harper Perennial, 2019), 146.

5. Philip Davis, ed., *Immigration and Americanization: Selected Readings* (Boston: Ginn and Company, 1920), 649.

6. "Explains Our Voting Power in the League," *New York Times*, September 27, 1919.

7. William W. Guth, "The Teaching of German," *New York Times*, June 24, 1918.

8. Lafayette Young, "German in the West," *New York Times*, August 11, 1918.

9. "Colonel for 'Knockout,'" *New York Times*, May 28, 1918.

10. Jack W. Rodgers, "The Foreign Language Issue in Nebraska, 1918–1923," *Nebraska History* 39 (1958): 13.

11. Arthur F. Mullen, *Western Democrat* (Whitefish, MT: Kessinger Publishing, 2010), 218.

12. Kelly J. Baker, "Make America White Again?," *Atlantic*, March 12, 2016.

13. Kylie Kinley, "When Nebraskans Celebrated July 4th with KKK Cross Burning," *History Nebraska* (blog), n.d.

14. "Good for Judge Jeffers," *Aurora Sun*, July 22, 1920.

15. United States Congress, House Committee on Immigration and Naturalization, "Biological Aspects of Immigration," *Hearings Before the Committee on Immigration and Naturalization, Sixty-Sixth Congress, Second Session*, April 16–17, 1920 (Washington, DC: Government Printing Office, 1920), 13.

16. United States Senate, "Emergency Immigration Legislation," *Hearings Before the Committee on Immigration, Sixty-Sixth Congress, Third Session* (Washington, DC: Government Printing Office, 1921), 13.

17. House of Representatives, "Temporary Suspension of Immigration," *Sixty-Sixth Congress, Third Session, Report 1109*, December 6, 1920 (Washington, DC: Government Printing Office, 1920), 182.

18. *Congressional Record: Proceedings and Debates of the Third Session of the Sixty-Sixth Congress of the United States of America* (Washington, DC: Government Printing Office, 1921), 227.

19. Daniel Okrent, *The Guarded Gate: Bigotry, Eugenics, and the Law That Kept Two Generations of Jews, Italians, and Other European Immigrants Out of America* (New York: Scribner, 2019), 288.

20. *Meyer v. State*, 107 Neb. 657 (1922).

21. Ernest Knaebel, *United States Reports, Volume 262: Cases Adjudged in the Supreme Court at October Term, 1922, from April 10, 1923, to and Including June 11, 1923* (Washington, DC: Government Printing Office, 1923), 394.

22. Knaebel, *United States Reports, Volume 262*, 394.

23. Elizabeth Dorsey Hatle and Nancy M. Vaillancourt, "Minnesota's Ku Klux Klan in the 1920s," *Minnesota History Magazine*, Winter 2009, 365.

24. William Guthrie, brief for *Meyer v. Nebraska* as amici curiae supporting respondents, 3, *Meyer v. Nebraska*, 262 U.S. 390 (1923).

25. Mullen, *Western Democrat*, 224–25.

26. "Judiciary: Alone," *Time*, December 4, 1939.

27. *Meyer v. Nebraska*, 262 U.S. 390 (1923).

28. *Meyer v. Nebraska*.

29. "Ends 21 States' Ban on Foreign Tongues," *New York Times*, June 5, 1923.

30. *School and Society*, vol. 8, ed. J. McKeen Cattell (New York: Science Press, 1918), 26.

31. *Congressional Record*, 88th Congress, 1st session, vol. 109, part 12, August 23, 1963 (Washington, DC: Government Printing Office, 1963).

32. *Congressional Record*, 68th Congress, 1st session, vol. 65, part 6, April 5, 1924 (Washington, DC: Government Printing Office, 1924).

33. *Congressional Record*, 68th Congress, 1st session, vol. 65, part 6, April 9, 1924.

34. *Congressional Record*, 68th Congress, 1st session, vol. 65, part 6, April 8, 1924.

35. Emanuel Celler, "No Choice in Immigrants," *New York Times*, July 6, 1923.

36. "Calls Quota Law Cruel," *New York Times*, January 27, 1924.

37. David A. Reed, "America of the Melting Pot Comes to End," *New York Times*, April 27, 1924.

38. Calvin Coolidge, "Whose Country Is This?" *Good Housekeeping*, February 1921.

39. Albert Johnson, foreword to Roy L. Garis, *Immigration Restriction: A Study of the Opposition to and Regulation of Immigration into the United States* (New York: Macmillan, 1927), viii.

40. Okrent, *The Guarded Gate*, 344.

41. Pastor David Feddern, phone interview with the author, May 18, 2020.

42. Luree Wise (daughter of Raymond Parpart), phone interview with the author, May 20, 2020.

43. It is important to acknowledge the devastating impact European settlers had on Indigenous communities and the genocide they committed against Indigenous peoples. In recent decades, Indigenous communities and others have gathered annually at Plymouth to mourn and to remember, as part of the National Day of Mourning, founded and organized by the United American Indians of New England.

44. "When Fargo Is Far from Home," *Fund for Teachers* (blog), May 15, 2018.

45. The Global Teacher Prize is awarded annually by the Varkey Foundation, an international organization.

CHAPTER 4: OPPORTUNITIES TO DREAM

1. Theodore Henry Hittell, *The General Laws of the State of California, from 1850 to 1864, Inclusive* (San Francisco: H.H. Bancroft, 1870), 998.

2. Charles Wollenberg, "Mendez v. Westminster: Race, Nationality, and Segregation in California Schools," *California Historical Quarterly* 53, no. 4 (1974): 318.

3. David Torres-Rouff, "Becoming Mexican: Segregated Schools and Social Scientists in Southern California, 1913–1946," *Southern California Quarterly* 94, no. 1 (2012): 117.

4. Annie Reynolds, *The Education of Spanish-Speaking Children in Five Southwestern States*, bulletin 1933, no. 11 (Washington, DC: Government Printing Office, 1933), 53.

5. Vicki L. Ruiz, "South by Southwest: Mexican Americans and Segregated Schooling, 1900–1950," *OAH Magazine of History* 15, no. 2 (Winter 2001): 24.

6. Ronald Takaki, "'Occupied' Mexico," in *The Latino/a Condition: A Critical Reader*, ed. Richard Delgado and Jean Stefancic (New York: New York University Press, 2011), 136–41.

7. Janice Munemitsu (daughter of Seiko Munemitsu), in conversation with the author, June 10, 2020.

8. Akiko Nakauchi, in conversation with the author, June 26, 2020.

9. House of Representatives, "A Proclamation—No. 2525," *Seventy-Seventh Congress, Second Session, Report No. 2100, May 7, 1942* (Washington, DC: US Government Printing Office, 1942), 296; "Executive Order 9066," National Archives, February 19, 1942.

10. *Mendez v. Westminster*, No. 4292-M-Civil (S.D. Cal), trial transcript, July 10, 1945.

11. Gilbert G. Gonzalez, *Chicano Education in the Era of Segregation* (Denton: University of North Texas Press, 1990), 118.

12. Herbert Hoover, "Second State of the Union Address," December 2, 1930, Miller Center of Public Affairs, University of Virginia.

13. Diane Bernard, "The Time a President Deported 1 Million Mexican Americans for Supposedly Stealing U.S. Jobs," *Washington Post*, August 13, 2018.

14. Rodolfo Acuña, *Anything but Mexican: Chicanos in Contemporary Los Angeles* (New York: Verso, 1995), 112.

15. Gardner Jackson, "Doak the Deportation Chief," *Nation*, March 1931, 295–96.

16. Alex Wagner, "America's Forgotten History of Illegal Deportations," *Atlantic*, March 6, 2017.

17. Petition 4292-M, March 2, 1945.

18. *Mendez v. Westminster*, No. 4292-M-Civil (S.D. Cal), trial transcript, July 5, 1945.

19. *School and Society*, vol. 19, ed. J. McKeen Cattell (New York: Science Press, 1924), 142.

20. T. R. Garth, "The Intelligence of Mexican School Children," *School & Society* 27 (1928): 7–9, psycnet.apa.org/record/1928-03235-001.

21. *Mendez v. Westminster*, No. 4292-M-Civil (S.D. Cal), pre-trial transcript, June 26, 1945.

22. *Mendez v. Westminster*, No. 4292-M-Civil (S.D. Cal), trial transcript, July 9, 1945.

23. Sylvia Mendez, in conversation with the author, June 29, 2020.

24. *Mendez v. Westminster*, No. 4292-M-Civil (S.D. Cal), trial transcript, July 11, 1945.

25. *Mendez v. Westminster*, No. 4292-M-Civil (S.D. Cal), trial transcript, July 11, 1945.

26. *Mendez v. Westminster School District of Orange County*, No. 4292-M-Civil (S.D. Cal.1946).

27. Gonzalez, *Chicano Education in the Era of Segregation*, 21.

28. Wollenberg, "Mendez v. Westminster, 327.

29. Carey McWilliams, "Is Your Name Gonzales?," *Nation*, March 1947, 302.

30. *Brown v. Board of Education of Topeka*, 347 U.S. 483 (1954).

31. Akiko Nakauchi, in conversation with the author, June 26, 2020.

32. For more information about the impact of family engagement, see Karen L. Mapp, Ilene Carver, and Jessica Lander, *Powerful Partnerships: A Teacher's Guide to Engaging Families for Student Success* (New York: Scholastic, 2017); and Anne T. Henderson, Karen L. Mapp, Vivian R. Johnson, and Don Davies, *Beyond the Bake Sale: The Essential Guide to Family-School Partnerships* (New York: New Press, 2007).

33. Jay Atkinson, "Lawrence, MA: City of the Damned," *Boston Magazine*, February 2012.

34. Dave Copeland, "Listen to Fire Fighters as Explosions Started: 'This Is Crazy,'" Patch, September 17, 2018.

35. Aviva Luttrell, "'It Just Looked Like an Absolute War Zone': Andover Crews Respond to 38 Fires after Suspected Gas Main Explosion," *MassLive*, January 29, 2019.

36. Gwen Aviles, "Latino Immigrant Students Harness Tragedy to Create Scientific Innovation," *NBC News* (online), March 29, 2019.

37. Thalia Varelas, "Escuela secundaria de lawrence gana concurso estatal!" *Noticias Ya Univisión*, January 4, 2019, video, 2:29, youtube.com/watch?v=c4Ptx6VnMmc.

38. Lawrence Public Schools, "ENLACE Samsung Project," YouTube, March 27, 2019, video, 4:37, youtube.com/watch?v=4i9z_sTh9JQ.

39. UNHCR report, "Four Million Refugee Children Go without Schooling," UNHCR, August 29, 2018.

40. Jonathan Clayton, "Over One Million Sea Arrivals Reach Europe in 2015," UNHCR, December 30, 2015.

CHAPTER 5: ADVOCATES

1. Robert Caro, *The Path to Power: The Years of Lyndon Johnson* (New York: Vintage Books, 1990), 166–73; Texas State University, "Teaching in Cotulla," University Archives, exhibits.library.txstate.edu/univarchives/exhibits/show/lyndon-b-johnson/school-days/cotulla.

2. Lyndon Baines Johnson, letter to Mrs. S. E. Johnson (mother), October 17, 1928.

3. Caro, *The Path to Power*, 166–67.

4. Daniel Garcia, interview by Ted Gittinger, December 17, 1985, interview 1, oral history transcript, LBJ Library Oral Histories, LBJ Presidential Library.

5. Lyndon Baines Johnson, phone call with Reverend Dr. Martin Luther King Jr., November 25, 1963, Miller Center of Public Affairs, University of Virginia.

6. Lyndon B. Johnson, "Address to Joint Session of Congress," November 27, 1963, House Chamber, Washington, DC, 24:30, Miller Center of Public Affairs, University of Virginia.

7. Lyndon B. Johnson, "State of the Union," January 8, 1964, House Chamber, Washington, DC, 40:33, Miller Center of Public Affairs, University of Virginia.

8. David A. Gamson, Kathryn A. McDermott, and Douglas S. Reed, "The Elementary and Secondary Education Act at Fifty: Aspirations, Effects, and Limitations," *Russell Sage Foundation Journal of the Social Sciences* 1, no. 3 (2015): 11.

9. George C. Wallace, "The Inaugural Address of Governor George C. Wallace," January 14, 1963, Capitol in Montgomery, Alabama.

10. President Lyndon Baines Johnson, "Annual Message to Congress on the State of the Union," United States House of Representatives, January 4, 1965.

11. "Conversation with Martin Luther King and Office Secretary," January 15, 1965, Secret White House Tapes, 13:43, Miller Center of Public Affairs, University of Virginia.

12. Francis Keppel, "Federal Aid: The Head of the Class," *Time*, October 15, 1965.

13. Jim Killacky and Mary Catherine Conroy, "ESEA Twenty Years Later: A Talk with Francis C. Keppel and Harold Howe," *College Board Review* 138, no. 1 (1985): 5.

14. Francis Keppel, "In the Battle for Desegregation, What Are the Flanking Skirmishes? What Is the Fundamental Struggle?," *Phi Delta Kappan* 46, no. 1 (1964): 3.

15. Lyndon Baines Johnson, "President Johnson's Special Message to Congress: The American Promise," March 15, 1965, 48:53, video and transcript, LBJ Presidential Library.

16. Lyndon Baines Johnson, "Johnson's Remarks on Signing the Elementary and Secondary Education Act," April 11, 1965, Johnson City, Texas, transcript, LBJ Presidential Library.

17. Julia Hanna, "The Elementary and Secondary Education Act: 40 Years Later," *Harvard Graduate School of Education*, August 18, 2005.

18. John F. Kennedy, *A Nation of Immigrants* (New York: Harper Perennial, 2008), 50–51.

19. "U.S. Policy During WWII: The Wagner-Rogers Bill (1939)," *Jewish Virtual Library*, American-Israeli Cooperative Enterprise, copyright 2020.

20. United States Senate, *Congressional Record,* March 2, 1953 (Washington, DC: Government Printing Office, 1953), 1518.

21. Tom Gjelten, *A Nation of Nations: A Great Immigration Story* (New York: Simon & Schuster, 2015), 114.

22. Lyndon B. Johnson, "State of the Union," January 8, 1964.

23. United States Congress Committee on the Judiciary, Subcommittee on Immigration and Naturalization, *Immigration: Hearings Before the Subcommittee on Immigration and Naturalization of the Committee on the Judiciary, United States Senate, Eighty-Ninth Congress, First Session, on S. 500 to Amend the Immigration and Nationality Act, and for Other Purposes,* Part 1 (Washington, DC: Government Printing Office, 1965), 837.

24. Erika Lee, *America for Americans: A History of Xenophobia in the United States* (New York: Basic Books, 2019), 236–37.

25. "Immigration: Hearings Before the Subcommittee No. 1 of the Committee on the Judiciary," House of Representatives, 89th Congress, 1st session, May 20, 1965, 241.

26. United States Congress Committee on the Judiciary, Subcommittee on Immigration and Naturalization, "Immigration," 63.

27. Lyndon Baines Johnson, "LBJ on Immigration: President Lyndon B. Johnson's Remarks at the Signing of the Immigration Bill," October 3, 1965, Liberty Island, New York, transcript, LBJ Presidential Library.

28. Lyndon Baines Johnson, "Remarks at the Welhausen Elementary School, Cotulla, Texas," November 7, 1966, transcript, The American Presidency Project, UC Santa Barbara.

29. Johnson, "Remarks at the Welhausen Elementary School."

30. "Crisis in Education," *Life*, March 1958.

31. Richard Pearson, "Ralph W. Yarborough Dies," *Washington Post*, January 28, 1996.

32. National Education Association Department of Rural Education, *The Invisible Minority: Report of the NEA-Tucson Survey on the Teaching of Spanish to the Spanish-Speaking* (Washington, DC: National Education Association of the United States, 1966), iv, 5, 10, 11.

33. Emily Langer, "Franklin McCain, Who Helped Inspire Sit-ins for Civil Rights as Part of Greensboro Four, Dies," *Washington Post*, January 13, 2014.

CHAPTER 6: SEEING STRENGTHS

1. Lucinda Lee Katz, interview with the author, July 10, 2020. *Note:* Some previous accounts say Kinney arrived in 1969. To confirm I reviewed Kinney's petition for naturalization.

2. Katz, interview with the author, July 10, 2020.

3. Brief by Chinese Consolidated Benevolent Association for *Lau. v. Nichols*, as Amici Curiae Supporting Petitioners, 414 U.S. 563 (1973) (no. 72-6520), 7; *Lau v. Nichols*, 483 F.2d 791, no. 26155 (United States Court of Appeals, 9th Circuit), 1973.

4. "Success Story of One Minority Group in U.S.," *U.S. News & World Report*, December 26, 1966.

5. Tom Wolfe, "The New Yellow Peril," *Esquire*, December 1969, 109.

6. I have not been able to confirm precisely how or why Kam Wai Lau went to the Legal Aid Office. Lucinda Lee remembers telling her about the office. Edward Steinman remembers her being involved in another case being handled by the office.

7. "What a Chinese Girl Did: An Expert Photographer and Telegrapher," *Morning Call*, November 23, 1892, published in "Mary Tape, An Outspoken Woman," *OAH Magazine of History* 15, no. 2 (2001): 18–19.

8. In 1886, in the landmark case *Yick Wo v. Hopkins*, the Supreme Court struck down as unconstitutional an 1880 San Francisco ordinance that made it illegal to operate a laundry in a wooden building without a permit, given at the discretion of the board of supervisors. Although the majority of city laundries were operated by Chinese Americans and two hundred Chinese Americans applied for permits, only one permit was granted. In contrast, almost all applications by non-Chinese Americans were granted. The Supreme Court ruled that a law whose text was "race-neutral" but administered in a prejudicial manner violated the Equal Protection Clause of the Fourteenth Amendment.

9. Yucheng Qin, *The Cultural Clash: Chinese Traditional Native-Place Sentiment and the Anti-Chinese Movement* (Lanham, MD: University Press of America, 2016), 200.

10. United States Congress, *Congressional Record: Containing the Proceedings and Debates of the Forty-Fourth Congress, First Session; Also Special Session of the Senate*, vol. 4 (Washington, DC: Government Printing Office, 1876), 2853.

11. Lee, *America for Americans*, 80.

12. "What a Chinese Girl Did," 18–19.

13. Lee, *America for Americans*, 106; Barbara Perry, *In the Name of Hate: Understanding Hate Crimes* (New York: Routledge, 2001), 200.

14. Joyce J. Kuo, "Excluded, Segregated, and Forgotten: A Historical View of the Discrimination of Chinese Americans in Public Schools," *Asian Law Journal* 5, no. 181 (1998): 197.

15. Charles Wollenberg, "Mendez v. Westminster: Race, Nationality, and Segregation in California Schools," *California Historical Quarterly* 53, no. 4 (1974): 318.

16. "The Chinese School Problem," *Daily Alta California*, March 5, 1885.

17. "Mary Tape, an Outspoken Woman," *OAH Magazine of History* 15, no. 2 (2001): 17. Grammar and spelling errors are as they appear in the original document.

18. John Arthur, "Document 28: Letter from John Arthur to Watson Squire, Washington Territorial Governor, November 4, 1885," 1885, in *Report of the Governor of Washington Territory to the Secretary of the Interior 1886* (Washington, DC: Government Printing Office, 1886), 875, Special Collections, University of Washington Libraries.

19. "The Statue Unveiled," *New York Times*, October 29, 1886.

20. L. Ling Chi Wang, "Lau v. Nichols: History of a Struggle for Equal and Quality Education," *Asian American Bilingual Center Newsletter* 1, no. 1, supplementary excerpt (1975).

21. Edward Steinman, interview with the author, July 2, 2020.

22. Appendix for *Kinney Kinmon Lau et al. v. Alan H. Nichols et al.*, 414 U.S. 563 (1973) (no. 72-6520). Martha Minow, professor and former dean of the Harvard Law School, noted to me certain similarities and differences between the legal strategies in *Lau v. Nichols* and *Brown v. Board of Education*. In both cases the plaintiffs showed that schools had deprived students of an education. But, whereas the deprivation in *Brown* stemmed from Black students being treated differently than white students, the deprivation in *Lau* was caused by students being treated in the same way—namely, by all students being taught in English, regardless of the fact that some did not understand the language.

23. Edward Steinman, interview with the author, July 2, 2020.

24. Stanley Pottinger, interview with the author, July 16, 2020.

25. Department of Health, Education and Welfare, Office of the Secretary, "DHEW Memo Regarding Language Minority Children" (memorandum, Washington, DC, 1970).

26. Department of Health, Education and Welfare, Office of the Secretary, "DHEW Memo Regarding Language Minority Children."

27. United States Congress, House Committee on the Judiciary, *Hearings Before the Civil Rights Oversight Committee (Subcommittee No. 4) of the Committee on the Judiciary, House of Representatives, Ninety-Second Congress, Second Session on Reports of the U.S. Commission on Civil Rights on the Education of the Spanish Speaking*, June 8 and 14, 1972, Serial No. 35 (Washington, DC: Government Printing Office, 1972), 40.

28. Steinman noted to me that his primary argument *in Lau v. Nichols* was that the San Francisco School District had violated Chinese-speaking students' rights under the Fourteenth Amendment rights. However, he decided also to include a claim under Title VI of the Civil Rights Act. It was for this reason he delayed submitting the "draft opinion" to Judge Burke until after Pottinger released his memo on Title VI.

29. While the legal standard in the desegregation cases in San Francisco required plaintiffs to show that racial discrimination was intentional, the *Lau v. Nichols* case only required showing that the defendant's actions had the effect of causing racial discrimination, regardless of intention.

30. Karen D. Thompson, "Is Separate Always Unequal? A Philosophical Examination of Ideas of Equality in Key Cases Regarding Racial and Linguistic Minorities in Education," *American Educational Research Journal* 50, no. 6 (2013): 1257.

31. Richard Nixon, "Toasts of the President and Chairman Chang Ch'un-ch'iao at a Banquet in Shanghai" (speech, Shanghai, February 27, 1972), The American Presidency Project, UC Santa Barbara.

32. Ling-chi Wang, interview with the author, July 27, 2020.

33. *Lau v. Nichols*, 483 F.2d 791 (9th Cir. 1973).

34. *Lau v. Nichols*, 483 F.2d 791 (9th Cir. 1973).

35. Brief by the Center for Law and Education, Harvard University, for *Kinney Kinmon Lau. et al. v. Alan H. Nichols et al.* as Amici Curiae Supporting Petitioners, 414 U.S. 563 (1973) (no. 72-6520).

36. Roger Rice, interview with the author, August 3, 2020.

37. Mao Tse-tung, "Oppose Stereotyped Party Writing," February 8, 1942, Yenan, China, transcript, marxists.org/reference/archive/mao/selected-works /volume-3/mswv3_07.htm.

38. Brief by Edward H. Steinman, Clarence Moy, and Kenneth Hecht for *Kinney Kinmon Lau et al. v. Alan H. Nichols et al.* as Amici Curiae Supporting Petitioners, 414 U.S. 563 (1973) (no. 72-6520).

39. *Lau v. Nichols*, 414 U.S. 563 (1974).

40. "Summary of Actions Taken by the Supreme Court," *New York Times*, January 22, 1974, which read: "Reversed a decision that it was not unconstitutional to deny English language instruction to Chinese-speaking pupils in the San Francisco Public school system (No. 72-6520, Lad v. Nichols)."

41. The Supreme Court decision had not specified how the schools should support newcomers, because the plaintiffs had not asked for any specific remedy, but rather only to establish their right.

42. Steinman noted to me that the 1974 Equal Educational Opportunity Act was particularly important in codifying the impact of the *Lau* decision. While Title VI of the 1964 Civil Rights Act applied only to state and local governments that received federal education funding, the 1974 Equal Educational Opportunity Act applied to all state and local governments.

43. Equal Education Opportunities Act of 1974, Pub. L. 93-380 (1974).

44. Amaya Garcia, "International High School at Key Largo Aims to Boost Graduation Rates of EL Students," *New America*, Feb. 24, 2016.

45. Kayla M. Good, "Policy Brief: The State of Education for Students Learning English in Maryland and Prince George's County Public Schools," Maryland Equity Project, June 2019, 4, Figure 3.

46. Maureen S. Costello, "The Trump Effect: After Election Day" (Montgomery: Southern Poverty Law Center, 2016); Maureen S. Costello, "The Trump Effect" (Montgomery: Southern Poverty Law Center, n.d.); Hannah Natanson, John Woodrow Cox, and Perry Stein, "Trump's words, bullied kids, scarred schools," *Washington Post*, Feb. 13, 2020; Lindsey Bever, "Video shows Pennsylvania teenagers celebrating, shouting 'white power' after Trump win," *Washington Post*, November 11, 2016.

CHAPTER 7: ACCEPTANCE

1. Paul Feldman, "Texas Case Looms Over Prop. 187's Legal Future," *Los Angeles Times*, October 23, 1994.

2. *Plyler v. Doe*, No. 80-1538 (Supreme Court of the United States), appendix.

3. Paul Feldman, "Texas Case Looms Over Prop. 187's Legal Future: Justice: U.S. High Court Voided That State's '75 Law on Illegal Immigrants. But Panel Has Since Shifted to Right," *Los Angeles Times*, October 23, 1994.

4. Roberta Thami [formerly Rodkin], interview with the author, August 6, 2020.

5. Thami [formerly Rodkin], interview with the author, August 6, 2020.

6. Peter Roos, interview with the author, July 30, 2020.

7. Lee, *America for Americans*, 93.

8. Erika Lee and Judy Yung, *Angel Island: Immigrant Gateway to America* (New York: Oxford University Press, 2010), 8.

9. Him Mark Lai, *Island: Poetry and History of Chinese Immigrants on Angel Island, 1910–1940*, edited by Genny Lim and Judy Yung (Seattle: University of Washington Press, 2014), Poem 33, 72.

10. M. A. Farber, "Battle Expected on Tighter Laws to Curb Illegal Aliens," *New York Times*, December 31, 1974.

11. David Maranis, "Justice, Texas Style," *Washington Post*, February 28, 1987.

12. Judge William Wayne Justice, "A Life in the Law," *San Antonio Lawyer*, September–October 2001, 7.

13. Maranis, "Justice, Texas Style."

14. Judge Keith Ellison, "William Wayne Justice 1920–2009," eulogy, Austin, TX, October 19, 2009, law.utexas.edu/wp-content/uploads/sites/32/2016/08/KEllison_Eulogy.pdf.

15. Stuart Taylor Jr., "U.S. Judge in Texas Draws Widespread Hostility with Liberal Rulings," *New York Times*, November 21, 1982.

16. Francisco Vara-Orta, "'Activist' Judge Still Battling Injustice," *Austin American Statesman*, August 12, 2006.

17. Larry Daves, interview with the author, August 4, 2020.

18. Roberta Thami [formerly Rodkin], interview with the author, August 6, 2020.

19. Judge William Wayne Justice, interview by David Weiser, January 3–4, 2002, oral history transcript, Fifth Circuit Court of Appeals Library, New Orleans, LA.

20. Larry Daves, interview with the author, August 4, 2020.

21. James Reston, "'The Silent Invasion,'" *New York Times*, May 4, 1977.

22. Louis Hyman, "The Undocumented Workers Who Built Silicon Valley," *Washington Post*, August 30, 2018.

23. Larry Daves, interview with the author, August 4, 2020.

24. *Doe v. Plyler*, 458 F. Supp. 569 (United States District Court, E.D. Texas, Tyler Division), 1978.

25. Linda P. Campbell, "In the Name of Justice," *Fort Worth Star-Telegram*, July 12, 1998.

26. *In re Alien Children Ed. Litigation*, 501 F. Supp. 544, MDL No. 398 (United States District Court, S.D. Texas), 1980.

27. *Plyler v. Doe*, No. 80-1538 (Supreme Court of the United States), appendix.

28. Senator Edward Kennedy, foreword to Andrew I. Schoenholtz, Jaya Ramji-Nogales, and Philip G. Schrag, *Refugee Roulette: Disparities in Asylum Adjudication and Proposals for Reform* (New York: New York University Press, 2009), xv.

29. Jimmy Carter, "League of Women Voters Remarks and a Question-and-Answer Session at the League's Biennial National Convention," May 5, 1980, Sheraton Washington Hotel, transcript, The American Presidency Project, UC Santa Barbara.

30. *In re Alien Children Ed. Litigation*, 501 F. Supp. 544, MDL No. 398 (United States District Court, S.D. Texas), 1980.

31. *In re Alien Children Ed. Litigation*.

32. *Doe v. Plyler*, 628 F. 2d. 448 (United States Court of Appeals, 5th Circuit), 1980.

33. "Plyler v. Doe, Oral Argument—December 1, 1981," 1:29:40, audio recording and transcript, apps.oyez.org/player/#/burger8/oral_argument_audio/17970.

34. *San Antonio Independent School District v. Rodriguez*, 411 U.S. 1 (1973).

35. *San Antonio Independent School District v. Rodriguez*.

36. *San Antonio Independent School District v. Rodriguez*.

37. Jim Newton, "Brennan Dishes on His Colleagues," *Slate*, January 11, 2007.

38. *Plyler v. Doe*, 457 U.S. 202, 1982.

39. Alfredo and Angie Lopez, interview with the author, August 13, 2020.

40. Feldman, "Texas Case Looms Over Prop. 187's Legal Future."

41. Roberto Gonzales, *Lives in Limbo: Undocumented and Coming of Age in America* (Oakland: University of California Press, 2016), 11–12.

42. Governor Rick Perry, "Gov. Rick Perry's Remarks to the Border Summit" (speech, Edinburg, August 22, 2001).

43. Jin K. Park, "DACA Isn't What Made Me an American: Being a Dreamer Is," *Atlantic*, June 23, 2020.

44. Alfredo and Angie Lopez, interview with the author, August 13, 2020.

45. Judge William Wayne Justice, interview by David Weiser, January 3–4, 2002, oral history transcript, Fifth Circuit Court of Appeals Library, New Orleans, LA.

46. Francisco Vara-Orta, "'Activist' Judge Still Battling Injustice," *Austin American Statesman*, August 12, 2006.

47. "Girls' Education," World Bank, October 26, 2021, worldbank.org/en/topic /girlseducation#1.

48. Filippo Grandi, "Her Turn," UNHCR, n.d., unhcr.org/herturn/.

49. Gates Millennium Scholars 2022, Gates Millennium Scholars Program, gmsp.org/a-gates-millennium-scholars-program/#1521250133122-b46231c7-9dd7.

50. "Figures at a Glance," UNHCR, 2021, unhcr.org/en-us/figures-at-a-glance .html.

51. "Four Million Refugee Children Go without Schooling: UNHCR Report," UNHCR USA, August 29, 2018.

52. "Resettlement," UNHCR USA, 2022, unhcr.org/en-us/resettlement.html.

53. Elliot Ray and Global Village Project students, lyrics to "I Can Make a Home."

54. Elliot Ray and students, lyrics to "I Can Make a Home."

55. The United Nations High Commissioner for Refugees notes that it is difficult to determine the number of stateless people in the world, and that the number is likely much higher. "Figures at a Glance," UNHCR, 2021.

CHAPTER 8: VOICE

1. National Center for Education Statistics, "English Language Learner (ELL) Students Enrolled in Public Elementary and Secondary Schools, by State: Selected Years, Fall 2000 through Fall 2015," Table 204.20.

2. The Massachusetts Department of Elementary and Secondary Education, "Cohort 2015 Four-Year Graduation Rates—State Results."

3. House of Representatives, "Bilingual Education Act," *Hearings Before the General Subcommittee on Education of the Committee on Education and Labor, Ninety-Third Congress* (Washington, DC: Government Printing Office, 1974), 140.

4. Albert Shanker, "Bilingual Education: Not 'Why' But 'How,' *New York Times Magazine*, November 3, 1974, 233.

5. Captain R.H. Pratt, "The Advantages of Mingling Indians with Whites," *Proceedings of the National Conference of Charities and Correction at the Nineteenth Annual Session held in Denver, Colorado, June 23-29, 1892*, 46. I encourage readers to learn more about the history and devastating impact of the boarding school movement that targeted Indigenous children in the United States. A good resource: boardingschoolhealing.org/education/resources/book-list-for-indigenous-peoples-day-2020/.

6. Lou Cannon, "Reagan Warns Foes of Economic Plan," *Washington Post*, March 3, 1981.

7. *The English Language Amendment: Hearing Before the Subcommittee on the Constitution of the Committee on the Judiciary, United States Senate, Ninety-Eighth Congress, Second Session, on S.J. Res. 167, June 12, 1984* (Washington, DC: Government Printing Office, 1985), 131.

8. Matt Schudel, "John Tanton, Architect of Anti-Immigration and English-Only Efforts, Dies at 85," *Washington Post*, July 21, 2019.

9. James Crawford, "Conservative Groups Take Aim at Federal Bilingual Programs," *Education Week*, March 19, 1986.

10. Peter N. Kiang, email message to the author, July 2021; and Peter N. Kiang, "Education and Community Development Among Nineteenth-Century Irish and Contemporary Cambodians in Lowell, Massachusetts," *New England Journal of Public Policy* 9, no. 1(6) (1993): 56.

11. Kiang, email message to the author, July 2021; and Peter N. Kiang, *Southeast Asian Parent Empowerment: The Challenge of Changing Demographics in Lowell, Massachusetts* (Jamaica Plain: Massachusetts Association for Bilingual Education, 1990), 10.

12. "'Witan Memo' III," *Southern Poverty Law Center*, n.d., splcenter.org/fighting-hate/intelligence-report/2015/witan-memo-iii.

13. Governor Pete Wilson and Treasurer Kathleen Brown, "California Gubernatorial Debate" (televised debate, Sacramento, October 14, 1994).

14. Kevin R. Johnson, "Proposition 187 and Its Political Aftermath: Lessons for U.S. Immigration Politics after Trump," *UC Davis Law Review* 53 (2020): 1859.

15. Phil Garcia, "Unz Keeps Focus on Bilingual Issue," *Sacramento Bee*, January 19, 1998.

16. Ron K. Unz and Mark Fiore, "Perspective on Immigration: Scaling the Heights of Irrationality, A Vote to Jail People for Working and Sending Their Children to School Is a Vote for Fiscal and Moral Bankruptcy," from the series "Prop. 187: Measure Would Deny Public Health, Education, and Welfare Benefits to Illegal Immigrants," *Los Angeles Times*, October 3, 1994.

17. Douglas Foster, "Being Ron Unz," *LA Weekly*, November 24, 1999.

18. Frank Bruni, "The California Entrepreneur Who Beat Bilingual Teaching," *New York Times*, June 14, 1998; Amy Wallace, "Unlikely Path Led to Wilson Foe's Far-Right Challenge," *Los Angeles Times*, May 8, 1994.

19. William Booth, "A Plan to Write Off Bilingual Education," *Washington Post*, February 28, 1998.

20. Laurie Olsen, "The Role of Advocacy in Shaping Immigrant Education: A California Case Study," *Teachers College Record* 111, no. 3 (March 2009): 817–50; James Crawford, "Bilingual Education," *Issues in U.S. Language Policy,* 1998, languagepolicy.net/archives/biling.htm.

21. Tia O'Brien, "The English Man," *San Jose Mercury News West Magazine,* January 11, 1998.

22. Olsen, "Role of Advocacy," 831.

23. Ron K. Unz, "Immigration or the Welfare State?," *Policy Review* (1994).

24. Unz, "Immigration or the Welfare State?"

25. Wayne Hanson and Bob Graves, "Jaime Escalante: Excellence Means 'Do It Right the First Time,'" *Government Technology,* July 27, 2010. Originally published in *Visions Magazine* (December 1998).

26. David Hill, "English Spoken Here," *Education Week,* January 14, 1998; Ron K. Unz, "The Right Way for Republicans to Handle Ethnicity in Politics," *American Enterprise,* April 1, 2000, retrieved from English for the Children, onenation.org/opinion/the-right-way-for-republicans-to-handle-ethnicity-in-politics/; Unz, "Bilingual Is a Damaging Myth," *Los Angeles Times,* October 19, 1997; "Proposition 227—Full Text of the Proposed Law," California Secretary of State, n.d., vigarchive.sos.ca.gov/1998/primary/propositions/227text.htm.

27. Unz, "Bilingual Is a Damaging Myth."

28. Olsen, "The Role of Advocacy."

29. O'Brien, "The English Man."

30. In 2002, an Unz-sponsored ballot initiative lost in Colorado.

31. Unz, "Right Way for Republicans."

32. Ron K. Unz, "English in Boston!," *Unz Review,* August 2, 2001.

33. George W. Bush, "Islam Is Peace," Islamic Center of Washington, DC, September 17, 2001, George W. Bush White House (archived website).

34. Office of the Press Secretary, "President Signs Landmark No Child Left Behind Education Bill," January 8, 2002, George W. Bush White House (archived website).

35. Roger Rice, interview with the author, August 3, 2020.

36. "Massachusetts Campaign Commercials," C-Span, October 4, 2002.

37. In addition to Roger Rice, I spoke extensively with two other advocates who played central roles in the events: Charles Glick, who consulted on the anti-Question 2 campaign, and Tom Louie, who was director of the Massachusetts English Plus Coalition. I am deeply grateful for their generosity in sharing the history.

38. In addition to ending bilingual programs for newcomers, the Massachusetts initiative also ended all dual-language programs, in which students—both native English speakers and newcomers—study in two languages at the same time. In the years immediately following, language advocates successfully advocated to pass legislation allowing for dual-language programs again.

39. National Center for Education Statistics, "Number and Percentage of Public School Students Participating in Programs for English Language Learners, by State: Selected Years, 2002–03 through 2011–12, Table 204.20."

40. "The 1998 California 'English for the Children' Initiative," English for the Children, 1997, onenation.org/.

41. Former Massachusetts Representative Jeffrey Sánchez, in conversation with the author, July 22, 2021.

42. Berta Rosa Berriz, in conversation with the author, July 13, 2021.

43. Berta Rosa Berriz, "Unz Got Your Tongue: What Have We Lost with the English-Only Mandates?" *The Radical Teacher*, no. 75 (2006): 14.

44. The Massachusetts Department of Elementary and Secondary Education, "Enrollment Data, School Year 2015–2016."

45. There is a growing body of research indicating possible cognitive benefits of multilingualism. A few articles describing this research include Neel Burton, "Beyond Words: The Benefit of Being Bilingual," *Psychology Today*, July 28, 2018; Ingrid T. Colón, "New Research Examines the Economic Benefits of Bilingualism," *New America*, April 25, 2019; and Blanka Klimova et al., "Bilingualism as a Strategy to Delay the Onset of Alzheimer's Disease," *Clinical Interventions in Aging* 12 (October 19, 2017): 1731–37.

46. By 2020, the Seal of Biliteracy program had been adopted in forty US states and in Washington, DC.

47. The four founding members of the Language Opportunity Coalition were Massachusetts Association for Bilingual Education (MABE), Massachusetts Foreign Language Association (MaFLA), Massachusetts Educators of English Language Learners (MATSOL), and Massachusetts Immigrant and Refugee Advocacy Coalition (MIRA Coalition). I am grateful to Helen Solórzano, executive director of MATSOL, and Phyllis Hardy, executive director of MABE, for teaching me about the formation and advocacy of the coalition.

INDEX

Vargas, Shaddai, 143, 147, 149
Varkey Foundation, 226
Vicente, Francis Georgia, 285, 286
Vidaurri, Soledad, 120, 124
Voting Rights Act of 1965, 170

Walker, Francis, 61
Wallace, George, 166, 253
Wang, An, 289
Wang, Ling-chi, 203–04, 209, 212, 213, 215, 216, 217, 286
War Relocation Authority, 134
Warren, Earl, 135–36

Washington, Booker T., 56
Wiles, Susan, 189
Williams, James Pete, 251
Wilondja, Crispin Ilombe, 258–60, 265–66, 268, 271
Wilson, Pete, 291–92
Wilson, Woodrow, 85, 230
Witt, Elise, 269
WWI (Great War), 61–62, 85–87

Yarborough, Ralph, 174–76, 246
Youth's Companion magazine, 25

Zangwill, Israel, 25